THE FOUNTAINHEAD SERIES

TO BE
Identity in Literature
REALITY IN CONFLICT
Literature of Values in Opposition
THE HUMAN CONDITION
Literature Written in the English Language
OF TIME AND PLACE
Comparative World Literature in Translation

LITERATURE OF THE EASTERN WORLD
I/YOU—WE/THEY
Literature By and About Ethnic Groups
COMMENT
An Anthology in Prose
TRAITS & TOPICS
An Anthology of Short Stories
UPSTAGE/DOWNSTAGE
A Theater Festival
SCIENCE FACT/FICTION
FANTASY
Shapes of Things Unknown
MYTH, MIND, AND MOMENT
AMERICAN MODELS
A Collection of Modern Stories
BRITISH MOTIFS
A Collection of Modern Stories
MARQUEE
Ten Plays by American and British Playwrights
THE LYRIC POTENTIAL
Arrangements and Techniques in Poetry
PERSON, PLACE, AND POINT OF VIEW
Factual Prose for Interpretation and Extension
LITERATURE FROM GREEK AND ROMAN ANTIQUITY
RUSSIAN AND EASTERN EUROPEAN LITERATURE
TRANSLATIONS FROM THE FRENCH
ITALIAN LITERATURE IN TRANSLATION
BLACK AFRICAN VOICES
FROM SPAIN AND THE AMERICAS
Literature in Translation
TEUTONIC LITERATURE
In English Translation

LITERATURE OF THE EASTERN WORLD

JAMES E. MILLER, JR.

Professor of English, University of Chicago.
Awarded Fulbright to Italy, lectured at
Oriental Institute, Naples, and the University
of Rome, 1958–1959. Fulbright lecturer in
American Literature at University of Kyoto
and Doshisha University, Kyoto, Japan, 1968.
President of the National Council of Teachers
of English, 1970. Author of *F. Scott Fitzgerald:
His Art and His Techniques* and *Quests Surd and
Absurd: Essays in American Literature*.

ROBERT O'NEAL

Humanities Coordinator for the Indiana Humanities
Project. Former Professor and Chairman of the
English Department, San Antonio College. Author
of *Teachers' Guide to World Literature for the High
School* and co-author and photographer of *English
for You*.

HELEN M. McDONNELL

Chairman, English Department, Ocean Township
High School, Oakhurst, New Jersey. Chairman of
the Committee on Comparative and World Literature,
National Council of Teachers of English. Contributor
of articles to *Scholastic Teacher*, *New Educational
Materials*, and other professional magazines.

INTRODUCTION BY LING CHUNG

Scott, Foresman and Company

Editorial Direction / LEO B. KNEER

Development / MARGARET RAUSCH

WITH GHIA BRENNER, DOROTHY KOEBER,
EDUARDO SCHOUA, AND SUSAN BERGER

Design / ROBERT AMFT

The authors and editors of *Literature of the
Eastern World* wish to express their appreciation
to the following teachers. Acting as reader-consultants,
they chose from the many selections submitted to
them those that they believed were most relevant
to the interests and needs of today's youth. They tested
their opinions against classroom use and contributed
ideas that evolved during the give-and-take of
class discussion.

SISTER EUGENE FOX, S.C.
Denver, Colorado

MR. RONALD MIDKIFF
Rome, Georgia

MR. THOMAS GAGE
Concord, California

MR. ELMER E. MOORE, JR.
Dobbs Ferry, New York

MRS. JEANNE LUCKETT
Jackson, Mississippi

MR. ROBERT ROMANO
Wilmington, Massachusetts

MRS. ELIZABETH DRUM MCDOWELL
Nashville, Tennessee

ISBN: 0–673–10232–7

CONTENTS

12 A HUMANIZED WORLD: AN APPRECIATION OF CHINESE LYRICS
by Ling Chung

1 CHINESE LITERATURE

Poetry

Anonymous
17 WOMAN

Fu Hsüan
18 WOMAN

Anonymous
19 SOUTH OF THE GREAT SEA

General Su Wu
20 TO HIS WIFE

Yüan Chi
21 REGRET

Anonymous
22 PLUCKING THE RUSHES

Li Po
from *The Jade Mountain*
23 A BITTER LOVE
23 A SIGH FROM A STAIRCASE OF JADE
24 ON HEARING CHÜN THE BUDDHIST MONK FROM
SHU PLAY HIS LUTE
24 A SONG OF CH'ANG-KAN
25 PARTING AT A WINE-SHOP IN NAN-KING

Tu Fu
from *The Jade Mountain*
26 ON MEETING LI KUÊI-NIEN DOWN THE RIVER
26 REMEMBERING MY BROTHERS ON A MOONLIGHT NIGHT
27 A NIGHT ABROAD
27 ON THE GATE-TOWER AT YO-CHOU
28 A HEARTY WELCOME
28 TO MY RETIRED FRIEND WÊI
29 NIGHT IN THE WATCH-TOWER
30 A DRAWING OF A HORSE BY GENERAL TS'AO AT SECRETARY WÊI FÊNG'S HOUSE
31 A SONG OF WAR-CHARIOTS

Po Chü-i
33 GOLDEN BELLS
33 REMEMBERING GOLDEN BELLS
34 CHU-CH'ÊN VILLAGE
36 THE PHILOSOPHERS
36 THE RED COCKATOO

Wang Chien
37 HEARING THAT HIS FRIEND WAS COMING BACK FROM THE WAR

Su Tung-p'o
38 ON THE BIRTH OF HIS SON

Han-shan
39 THE COLD MOUNTAIN POEMS OF HAN-SHAN

Prose

Anonymous
50 THE LADY WHO WAS A BEGGAR (*Ming Tale*)

Lao Shê
65 THE LAST TRAIN (*short story*)

Lusin
77 THE WIDOW (*short story*)

Mao Tun
90 SPRING SILKWORMS (*short story*)

Tuan-mu Hung-liang
103 THE SORROWS OF THE LAKE OF EGRETS (*short story*)

2 BABYLONIAN LITERATURE

Anonymous
111   THE ADVENTURES OF GILGAMESH (*epic*)

3 HEBREW LITERATURE

from *The Bible* (King James Version)
125   THE STORY OF SAMSON (Judges 13–16)
132   PSALM 8
133   PSALM 19
133   PSALM 23
134   PSALM 45
135   PSALM 95
135   PSALM 98
136   ECCLESIASTES 3

Aharon Amir
138   NOTHINGNESS (*poem*)

David Avidan
139   PRELIMINARY CHALLENGE (*poem*)

Avraham Ben-Itzhak
141   BLESSING (*poem*)
142   AVENUE IN ELLUL (*poem*)

Ory Bernstein
143   BIRDS HAVE THOUGHTS (*poem*)

Hayyim Nahman Bialik
144   SUMMER IS DYING (*poem*)
145   ON MY RETURN (*poem*)

Maxim Ghilan
146   ARS PO (*poem*)

Ka-Tzetnik 135633
147   from THE CLOCK OVERHEAD (*poem*)

Yehudah Karni
157   EVENING IN JERUSALEM (*poem*)

Aharon Megged
158 THE NAME (*short story*)

Dan Paggis
170 EPILOGUE TO ROBINSON CRUSOE (*poem*)

Shin Shalom
171 THE DANCE OF THE TORCHES (*poem*)
173 THE CAT (*poem*)

Yaakov Shteinberg
174 THE BLIND GIRL (*short story*)

4 HINDUSTANI LITERATURE

Mulk Raj Anand
181 THE GOLD WATCH (*short story*)

Anonymous
from the *Mahabharata*
189 SAVITRI'S LOVE / Sanskrit (*short story*)

Chauras
194 from BLACK MARIGOLDS / Sanskrit (*poem*)

Dhumketu
201 THE LETTER / Gujerati (*short story*)

Achintya Kumar Sen Gupta
207 THE BAMBOO TRICK / Bengali (*short story*)

Bhatta Somadeva
213 THE CONFIDENCE MEN / Sanskrit (*short story*)

Rabindranath Tagore
218 MY LORD, THE BABY / Bengali (*short story*)

5 BURMESE LITERATURE

U Win Pe
224 PRELUDE TO GLORY (*short story*)

6 ISLAMIC LITERATURE

from *The Koran* / Arabic
236 THE OVERTHROWING
237 THE CLEAVING
238 THE UNITY

Abul-'Ala al-Ma'arri
239 from THE MEDITATIONS / Arabic (*poetry*)

Hafiz
241 from THE DIVAN / Persian (*poetry*)

Tawfiq al-Hakim
245 THE RIVER OF MADNESS / Arabic (*drama*)

Al-Jahiz
from *The Book of Animals*
253 FLIES AND MOSQUITOES / Arabic (*essay*)

Jibran Khalil Jibran
255 SONG OF MAN / Arabic (*poem*)

Omar Khayyám
257 from THE RUBÁIYÁT OF OMAR KHAYYÁM / Persian (*poem*)

Khalil Matran
262 CHILDHOOD IN ZAHLA / Arabic (*poem*)

Mikha'il Nu'ayma
263 O BROTHER / Arabic (*poem*)

Rumi
265 REMEMBERED MUSIC / Persian (*poem*)
266 THE TRUTH WITHIN US / Persian (*poem*)
266 THE EVIL IN OURSELVES / Persian (*poem*)
267 THE SOUL OF GOODNESS IN THINGS EVIL / Persian (*poem*)
268 THE PROGRESS OF MAN / Persian (*poem*)

Jamil Sidqi al-Zahawi
269 TO MY WIFE / Arabic (*poem*)

Poetry / Tanka

Akahito
271 V

Hitómaro
272 XVII
272 XXI
272 XXII
272 XXIII

Lady Horikawa
273 XXX

Narihira
273 LVI

Tsurayuki
274 LXXXV

Yakamochi
274 LXXXIX

Poetry / Naga Uta

Hitómaro
275 CIV
277 CV

Poetry / Haiku

Matsuo Bashō
278 PERSISTENCE
278 CLOUDS
279 IN A WIDE WASTELAND
279 THE POOR MAN'S SON
279 THE SUN PATH
279 SUMMER VOICES
279 LIGHTNING AT NIGHT

Taniguchi Buson
280 THE SOUND
280 SYMPHONY IN WHITE
280 SPRING BREEZE
280 SUMMER GARMENTS

Issa
281 CONTENTMENT IN POVERTY
281 THE GREAT BUDDHA AT NARA
281 CONSCIENCE
281 A WISH

Masaoka Shiki
282 THE APPRENTICE PRIESTLING
282 THE NEW AND THE OLD
282 TREASURE TROVE
282 IN THE MOONLIGHT

The Nō Play

Seami
284 THE DAMASK DRUM (old drama)

Yukio Mishima
290 THE DAMASK DRUM (new drama)

Prose

Akutagawa Ryūnosuke
307 HELL SCREEN (short story)

Anonymous
328 THE BAMBOO CUTTER AND THE MOON CHILD (tale)
340 HŌICHI THE EARLESS (tale)

Ibusé Masuji
347 THE CHARCOAL BUS (short story)

Kikuchi Kan
354 THE MADMAN ON THE ROOF (drama)

Shiga Naoya
363 SEIBEI'S GOURDS (short story)

Junichiro Tanizaki
367 THE THIEF (short story)

Tayama Katai
376 ONE SOLDIER (short story)

389 Asian Languages
391 Discussion Questions
408 Biographies of Authors
417 Pronunciation Key
418 Index of Authors and Titles
420 Index of Translators

A HUMANIZED WORLD:

An Appreciation of Chinese Lyrics

BY LING CHUNG

> *"Fair, fair," cry the ospreys*
> *On the island in the river.*
> *Lovely is this noble lady,*
> *Fit bride for our lord.*
>
> —from "Kwan Chu," translated by Arthur Waley,
> *The Book of Songs* [*Shih Ching*].

The most famous collection of Chinese poetry, *Shih Ching*, which is supposed to have been compiled by Confucius in the early fifth century B.C., starts with a wedding song, "Kwan Chu." This poem begins with the echoing of the birds on an island to celebrate a happy marital union in the human world. This poem anticipates a dominant thematic aspect of the Chinese lyric tradition for more than two thousand years thereafter: the harmonious relationship between man and nature, and among men.

The relation between man and nature in Chinese poetry has often been misinterpreted by the Western world. There are no figures equivalent to Odysseus, Coleridge's Ancient Mariner, or Byron's Childe Harold. When these Western heroes find themselves in lofty mountains or on the vast sea, they are exiled into a hostile and challenging world. When a Chinese hermit-poet finds himself alone in nature, however, he is utterly at peace with his environment because he believes that man and nature are one. This difference in the relationship between man and nature in the cultures of China and of the Western world is often the cause of misinterpretation in translation. Gary Snyder, for example, is an excellent translator, with his knowledge of Chinese language and literature, his enthusiasm for the Oriental style of life, and his poetic rendering of Chinese poetry into English; yet he like other Western translators has distorted the Chinese concept of nature in his translation of a poem by Han-shan. In No. 9 of his translation of *The Cold Mountain Poems* [1] Snyder translates the Chinese

---

Miss Chung, a native of China, studied at the University of Wisconsin. She is editor of a bilingual journal, The Constellation Poetry Quarterly, *and has published poetry, short stories, and essays in numerous journals. A collection of her essays written in Chinese,* Barefoot on the Meadow, *has recently been published.*

From THE BOOK OF SONGS, translated by Arthur Waley. Reprinted by permission of Grove Press, Inc., and George Allen & Unwin Ltd.

1. See page 45.

word for *deep* as "rough" to describe the mountain trail, *round stone* as "sharp cobble," *cold* as "icy," *lone* as "bleak," an onomatopoeia of the light, cool wind as "whip, whip," *blows* as "slaps" to describe the wind, and *descending thickly* as "whirled and tumbled" to describe the snow. These deliberate, crucial changes of natural images result in a different picture of nature. In Snyder's version nature is aggressive: it whips man, slaps his face, and tends to bury him with snow. The original poem, however, presents the traditional poetic image of a hermit sitting in the snow, appreciating in tranquility the natural beauty that surrounds him.

W. B. Yeats in his poem "Lapis Lazuli" describes a Chinese mountain scene, carved on lapis lazuli, which depicts two hermits, a servant carrying a musical instrument, and a bird. Yeats imagines the hermits looking down on a tragic scene below them. One asks the other to play a mournful melody, and refreshed by the music they are gay.

Actually, in Chinese poetry and art rarely is a mountain hermit such a heroic figure that he can completely transcend the tragedy of mankind and achieve an immovable gayety. Even a Chinese Buddhist monk, supposed to have achieved the state of Nirvana, or eternal bliss, will not stare at the wretched world with gayety, but more likely, with compassion. These heroic hermits of Yeats are distorted pictures, because Yeats has imposed his own notions about life and nature on his interpretation of the Chinese mind. A genuine picture of Chinese hermits and their relation with nature can be found in Li Po's "On Hearing Chün the Buddhist Monk from Shu Play His Lute."[2] In this poem the music, man's mind, and nature are blended into one. In the second couplet, a figure of speech has brought the artificial music and the natural music, the song of the pines, together. In the third couplet man's music and that of nature become fused in even more poetic images. This couplet, amplified by the classical allusions, can be paraphrased as follows:

> *The melody like the tone Flowing Stream played by the great*
> *ancient musician Po-ya, cleanses the heart of a traveller;*
> *its final notes fade into the sound of temple bells which is*
> *vibrated by the fallen frost.*

The music played by man is likened to that of a mountain stream; and the bell's song, caused by the fallen frost, merges with the music of man. When the music ceases in the last couplet, the perspective is shifted to a panorama of a serene, autumnal landscape:

> *And I feel no change though the mountain darkens*
> *And cloudy autumn heaps the sky.*

---

2. See page 24.

This device of shifting the perspective fuses man's consciousness and the man-made music into a timeless universe.

A great portion of Chinese lyrics are songs written on simple, personal themes. They are songs expressing love for natural beauty and peaceful rural life, and expressing warm thoughts for the members in the family, for the homeland and the country. The tone may be intensified when the poet is agitated because of suffering brought on by wars, famines, and corrupted bureaucracy, or because of the inevitable tragic transiency of human life. There is also a certain degree of artifice and sophistication in some of the narrative poetry and love lyrics.

In ancient China, the Confucian gentry would require a poet to go through a pattern of life: that is, to take the imperial examinations, become an officer to serve the emperor and the people, succeed in a career and acquire fame. At the same time, the Taoist-Buddhist's belief always urges the poet to enjoy a tranquil and leisurely life in the mountains and countryside. The majority of Chinese poets incline to the latter, because they regard it either as a Utopian form of life worth pursuing or an escape from the tumult of political intrigue. Yüan Chi's "Regret," [3] Po Chü-i's "Chu-ch'ên Village," [4] and the poetry of the greatest Chinese poet of nature, T'ao Ch'ien, manifest this inclination. Tu Fu in his "A Hearty Welcome" [5] depicts how a scholar-farmer-poet would enjoy an impractical, yet aesthetic, life: watching the flying gulls, drinking wine with friends, and writing poetry. Furthermore, in a society generally dominated by Confucianism, certain human relations are emphasized, especially those between emperor and subject, father and son, husband and wife, between friends, and between brothers. Chinese poetry of all ages has devoted considerable attention to short lyrics expressing the sorrow caused by separation from the beloved one. Li Po's poems for departure, Su Wu's "To His Wife," [6] Tu Fu's "Remembering My Brothers on a Moonlight Night," [7] and Su Tung-po's tz'u poems written for his brother Tze-Yuo and for his deceased wife, are among the most famous.

In Chinese poetry great generals and warriors are praised because of their valour and military strategy, but war itself is not glorified. On the contrary, it is frequently condemned. In Shih Ching [The Book of Songs] there are many anti-war folk songs written by anonymous poets. Tu Fu, the greatest humanist among Chinese poets, and also one of the greatest humanists who ever lived, witnessed the climactic blooming of the T'ang Dynasty as well as its decline in the eighth century. The ceaseless disasters, the wars, deaths, famines, and plagues, that befell him, his family, and the Chinese people, inspired him out of his compassion to sing in a tone of suppressed anger against evil and corruption. In "A Song of War-

---

3. See page 21.   4. See page 34.   5. See page 28.   6. See page 20.   7. See page 26.

Chariots"[8] he first gives a very vivid picture of new recruits marching out of a city, and of families running with the army, crying and tugging at the sleeves of the drafted young men. Then his vision shifts to the vast land of China, barren because of the war and taxation. The poem ends with a striking and pathetic scene—ghosts of the old dead and the new dead mingling in the remote border land. Witter Bynner's translation is certainly touching, but the sound effect of an onomatopoeia is missed in the translation: "Ch'iu Ch'iu" in the last line, a mixture of the sound of rain and the ghosts, intensifies the protest of the dead and of a furious universe.

The degree of sophistication is slight in the love songs among the traditional folk lyrics. Love songs from *Shih Ching*, the anonymous songs "South of the Great Sea" and "Plucking the Rushes,"[9] are still naive, straightforward, and autobiographical. Gradually in about the second century the image of a lovelorn woman is isolated and becomes a popular topic. The poet will assume a situation for such a lovelorn woman— either her husband has gone away to war, to trade, or to another woman. The psychology of this woman will be carefully described either in a direct dramatic monologue or in detailed elaboration of the background scenery as a foil for the interior movement in the woman's psychology. Li Po, the greatest romantic genius in Chinese poetry, not only writes on weighty subjects such as the grandeur of nature and the tragic passing of human life in the stream of time but also excels in assuming the pose and psychology of a woman. In "A Song of Ch'ang-kan"[10] he has successfully recreated the tone of a girl naive and deeply in love. His "A Sigh from a Staircase of Jade"[11] is a highly sophisticated poem. The original merely presents an artistic, objective picture, while Witter Bynner in his translation has put down all the implicit meanings which are only suggested in the original such as "cold," "she lingered," "behind her closed casement, why is she still waiting." This type of sophisticated artistry, which flourishes in the *tz'u* and *ch'u* poetry from the tenth century on, is an important formalistic aspect of Chinese poetry.

---

8. See page 31.   9. See pages 19 and 22.   10. See page 24.   11. See page 23.

A SELECTED BIBLIOGRAPHY
FOR THE STUDY
OF ORIENTAL POETRY

Chinese Poetry

Anonymous. *The Jade Mountain, or Three Hundred Poems of the T'ang Dynasty.* tr. by Kiang Kang-hu and Witter Bynner. Garden City, Doubleday, 1964.

Ayling, Alan, and Duncan Mac Kintosh, trs., *A Collection of Chinese Lyrics.* Nashville, Vanderbilt University Press, 1967.

Birch, Cyril, and Donald Keene, eds., *Anthology of Chinese Literature.* New York, Grove Press, 1965.

Hung, William. *Tu Fu, China's Greatest Poet.* Cambridge, Harvard University Press, 1952.

Liu, James L. *The Art of Chinese Poetry.* Chicago, The University of Chicago Press, 1962.

Waley, Arthur. *The Book of Songs.* New York, Grove Press, 1960.

Watson, Burton. *Early Chinese Literature.* New York, Columbia University Press, 1962.

Indian Poetry

Bhartrihari. *Bhartrihari: Poems.* Barbara Stoler Miller, tr., New York, Columbia University Press, 1967.

Brough, John, tr., *Poems from the Sanskrit.* Baltimore, Penguin Books, 1968.

Dimock, Edward C., and Denise Levertov. *In Praise of Krishna: Songs from the Bengali.* Garden City, Doubleday, 1967.

Tagore, Rabindranath. *A Tagore Reader.* Chakravarty, Amiya, ed., Boston, Beacon Press, 1966.

Yohannan, John. *A Treasury of Asian Literature.* New York, Mentor, 1959.

Japanese Poetry

Brower, Robert H., and Earl Miner. *Japanese Court Poetry.* Stanford University Press, 1961. For a more concise study, see Earl Miner's *An Introduction to Japanese Court Poetry* (Stanford, 1968).

Henderson, Harold G. *An Introduction to Haiku.* Garden City, Doubleday, 1958.

Keene, Donald, ed., *Anthology of Japanese Literature: Earliest Era to Mid-Nineteenth Century.* New York, Grove Press, 1956.

Keene, Donald, ed., *Japanese Literature: An Introduction for Western Readers.* New York, Grove Press, 1955.

Rexroth, Kenneth, tr., *One Hundred Poems from the Japanese.* New York, New Directions, 1955.

1 CHINESE LITERATURE

Poetry

In naming the authors of these selections, the Chinese practice of placing the surname before the first name has been observed.

Anonymous (500 B.C.)

Woman

Translated from the Chinese by

H. A. Giles

A clever man builds a city,
A clever woman lays one low;
With all her qualifications, that clever woman
Is but an ill-omened bird.
A woman with a long tongue   5
Is a flight of steps leading to calamity;
For disorder does not come from heaven,
But is brought about by women.
Among those who cannot be trained or taught
Are women and eunuchs.   10

"Woman" from SHI KING, BOOK OF ODES, translated by H. A. Giles.

Fu Hsüan [1] (d.287 A.D.)

Woman

Translated from the Chinese by

Arthur Waley

How sad it is to be a woman!
Nothing on earth is held so cheap.
Boys stand leaning at the door
Like Gods fallen out of Heaven.
Their hearts brave the Four Oceans,   5
The wind and dust of a thousand miles.
No one is glad when a girl is born:
By *her* the family sets no store.
When she grows up, she hides in her room
Afraid to look a man in the face.   10
No one cries when she leaves her home—
Sudden as clouds when the rain stops.
She bows her head and composes her face,
Her teeth are pressed on her red lips:
She bows and kneels countless times.   15
She must humble herself even to the servants.
His love is distant as the stars in Heaven,
Yet the sunflower bends toward the sun.
Their hearts more sundered than water and fire—
A hundred evils are heaped upon her.   20

Her face will follow the years' changes:
Her lord will find new pleasures.
They that were once like substance and shadow
Are now as far as Hu from Ch'in.[2]
Yet Hu and Ch'in shall sooner meet   25
Than they whose parting is like Ts'an and Ch'ên.[3]

From TRANSLATIONS FROM THE CHINESE (170 CHINESE POEMS), translated by
Arthur Waley. Copyright 1919, 1941 by Alfred A. Knopf, Inc. and renewed 1947 by
Arthur Waley. Reprinted by permission of Alfred A. Knopf, Inc., and Constable Publishers.
1. *Fu Hsüan* (fù shγən'). 2. *Hu from Ch'in*, two states which existed prior to the
unification of China. 3. *Ts'an and Ch'ên*, two stars.

Anonymous

South of the Great Sea

Translated from the Chinese by
Arthur Waley

My love is living
To the south of the Great Sea,
What shall I send to greet him?
Two pearls and a comb of tortoise-shell;
I'll send them to him packed in a box of jade.   5
They tell me he is not true:
They tell me he dashed my box to the ground,
Dashed it to the ground and burnt it
And scattered its ashes to the wind.
From this day to the ends of time   10
I must never think of him,
Never again think of him.
The cocks are crowing,
And the dogs are barking—
My brother and his wife will soon know.[1]   15
The autumn wind is blowing;
The morning wind is sighing.
In a moment the sun will rise in the east
And then *it* too will know.

From TRANSLATIONS FROM THE CHINESE (170 CHINESE POEMS), translated by
Arthur Waley. Copyright 1919, 1941 by Alfred A. Knopf, Inc. and renewed 1947 by
Arthur Waley. Reprinted by permission of Alfred A. Knopf, Inc., and Constable Publishers.
1. *My brother . . . know.* They will soon know that the narrator has been abandoned by
her love.

General Su Wu? (c.100 B.C.)

To His Wife

Translated from the Chinese by
Arthur Waley

Since our hair was plaited and we became man and wife
The love between us was never broken by doubt.
So let us be merry this night together,
Feasting and playing while the good time lasts.

I suddenly remember the distance that I must travel;   5
I spring from bed and look out to see the time.
The stars and planets are all grown dim in the sky;
Long, long is the road; I cannot stay.
I am going on service, away to the battle-ground,
And I do not know when I shall come back.   10
I hold your hand with only a deep sigh;
Afterwards, tears—in the days when we are parted.
With all your might enjoy the spring flowers,
But do not forget the time of our love and pride.
Know that if I live, I will come back again,   15
And if I die, we will go on thinking of each other.

From TRANSLATIONS FROM THE CHINESE (170 CHINESE POEMS), translated by Arthur Waley. Copyright 1919, 1941 by Alfred A. Knopf, Inc. and renewed 1947 by Arthur Waley. Reprinted by permission of Alfred A. Knopf, Inc., and Constable Publishers.

Yüan Chi[1] (210–263)

Regret

Translated from the Chinese by
Arthur Waley

When I was young I learnt fencing
And was better at it than Crooked Castle.[2]
My spirit was high as the rolling clouds
And my fame resounded beyond the World.
I took my sword to the desert sands,   5
I watered my horse at the Nine Moors.
My flags and banners flapped in the wind,
And nothing was heard but the song of my drums.

War and its travels have made me sad,
And a fierce anger burns within me: 10
It's thinking of how I've wasted my time
That makes this fury tear my heart.

From TRANSLATIONS FROM THE CHINESE (170 CHINESE POEMS), translated by Arthur Waley. Copyright 1919, 1941 by Alfred A. Knopf, Inc. and renewed 1947 by Arthur Waley. Reprinted by permission of Alfred A. Knopf, Inc., and Constable Publishers.
1. *Yüan Chi* (yʏ än chē). **2.** *Crooked Castle,* a famous general.

Anonymous (4th century A.D.)

Plucking the Rushes[1]

Translated from the Chinese by
Arthur Waley

Green rushes with red shoots,
Long leaves bending to the wind—
You and I in the same boat
Plucking rushes at the Five Lakes.
We started at dawn from the orchid-island: 5
We rested under the elms till noon.
You and I plucking rushes
Had not plucked a handful when night came!

From TRANSLATIONS FROM THE CHINESE (170 CHINESE POEMS), translated by Arthur Waley. Copyright 1919, 1941 by Alfred A. Knopf, Inc. and renewed 1947 by Arthur Waley. Reprinted by permission of Alfred A. Knopf, Inc., and Constable Publishers.
1. *Plucking the Rushes.* A boy (the poem's narrator) and a girl have been sent to gather rushes for thatching.

from *The Jade Mountain*

Li Po (c.701–c.762)

Translated from the Chinese by
Kiang Kang-hu and Witter Bynner

A Bitter Love

How beautiful she looks, opening the pearly casement,
And how quiet she leans, and how troubled her brow is!
You may see the tears now, bright on her cheek,
But not the man she so bitterly loves.

A Sigh from a Staircase of Jade

Her jade-white staircase is cold with dew;
Her silk soles are wet, she lingered there so long . . .
Behind her closed casement, why is she still waiting,
Watching through its crystal pane the glow of the autumn moon?

On Hearing Chün the Buddhist Monk from Shu Play His Lute

The monk from Shu with his green silk lute-case,
Walking west down O-mêi Mountain,[1]
Has brought me by one touch of the strings
The breath of pines in a thousand valleys.
I hear him in the cleansing brook,   5
I hear him in the icy bells;
And I feel no change though the mountain darkens
And cloudy autumn heaps the sky.

A Song of Ch'ang-kan[1]

My hair had hardly covered my forehead.
I was picking flowers, playing by my door,
When you, my lover, on a bamboo horse,
Came trotting in circles and throwing green plums.
We lived near together on a lane in Ch'ang-kan,   5
Both of us young and happy-hearted.
. . . At fourteen I became your wife,
So bashful that I dared not smile,
And I lowered my head toward a dark corner
And would not turn to your thousand calls;   10
But at fifteen I straightened my brows and laughed,
Learning that no dust could ever seal our love,
That even unto death I would await you by my post
And would never lose heart in the tower of silent watching.

From THE JADE MOUNTAIN: A CHINESE ANTHOLOGY, translated by Witter Bynner. Copyright 1929 and renewed 1957 by Alfred A. Knopf, Inc. Reprinted by permission of the publisher.
ON HEARING CHÜN: 1. *O-mêi Mountain*, a mountain situated in the province of Szechwan, in southern China.
A SONG OF CH'ANG-KAN: 1. *Ch'ang-kan*, a city in the province of Kwantung, in southern China.

. . . Then when I was sixteen, you left on a long journey   15
Through the Gorges of Ch'ü-t'ang,[2] of rock and whirling water.
And then came the Fifth-month, more than I could bear,
And I tried to hear the monkeys in your lofty far-off sky.
Your footprints by our door, where I had watched you go,
Were hidden, every one of them, under green moss,   20
Hidden under moss too deep to sweep away.
And the first autumn wind added fallen leaves.
And now, in the Eighth-month, yellowing butterflies
Hover, two by two, in our west-garden grasses. . . .
And, because of all this, my heart is breaking   25
And I fear for my bright cheeks, lest they fade.
. . . Oh, at last, when you return through the three Pa districts,
Send me a message home ahead!
And I will come and meet you and will never mind the distance,
All the way to Chang-fêng Sha.   30

Parting at a Wine-Shop in Nan-king

A wind, bringing willow-cotton, sweetens the shop,
And a girl from Wu, pouring wine, urges me to share it
With my comrades of the city who are here to see me off;
And as each of them drains his cup, I say to him in parting,
Oh, go and ask this river running to the east   5
If it can travel farther than a friend's love!

From THE JADE MOUNTAIN: A CHINESE ANTHOLOGY, translated by Witter Bynner. Copyright 1929 and renewed 1957 by Alfred A. Knopf, Inc. Reprinted by permission of the publisher.
A SONG OF CH'ANG-KAN: **2.** *Gorges of Ch'ü-t'ang*, gorges in Tibet, a province of southwest China.

Tu Fu (712–770)

Translated from the Chinese by
Kiang Kang-hu and Witter Bynner

On Meeting Li Kuêi-nien[1] down the River

I met you often when you were visiting princes
And when you were playing in noblemen's halls.
. . . Spring passes. . . . Far down the river now,
I find you alone under falling petals.

Remembering My Brothers on a Moonlight Night

A wanderer hears drums portending battle.
By the first call of autumn from a wildgoose at the border,
He knows that the dews tonight will be frost.
. . . How much brighter the moonlight is at home!
O my brothers, lost and scattered,   5
What is life to me without you?
Yet if missives in time of peace go wrong—
What can I hope for during war?

From THE JADE MOUNTAIN: A CHINESE ANTHOLOGY, translated by Witter
Bynner. Copyright 1929 and renewed 1957 by Alfred A. Knopf, Inc. Reprinted by per-
mission of the publisher.
ON MEETING LI KUÊI-NIEN: 1. *Li Kuêi-nien* (lĕ kwä nyan).

A Night Abroad

A light wind is rippling at the grassy shore. . . .
Through the night, to my motionless tall mast,
The stars lean down from open space,
And the moon comes running up the river.

. . . If only my art might bring me fame
And free my sick old age from office!—
Flitting, flitting, what am I like
But a sand-snipe in the wide, wide world!

On the Gate-Tower at Yo-chou[1]

I had always heard of Lake Tung-t'ing—
And now at last I have climbed to this tower.
With Wu country to the east of me and Ch'u[2] to the south,
I can see heaven and earth endlessly floating.
. . . But no word has reached me from kin or friends.
I am old and sick and alone with my boat.
North of this wall there are wars and mountains—
And here by the rail how can I help crying?

.

From THE JADE MOUNTAIN: A CHINESE ANTHOLOGY, translated by Witter
Bynner. Copyright 1929 and renewed 1957 by Alfred A. Knopf, Inc. Reprinted by per-
mission of the publisher.
ON THE GATE-TOWER: 1. *Yo-chou,* a city situated on Lake Tung-t'ing in the province of
Hunan, in southern China. 2. *Wu . . . Ch'u,* formerly, two powerful states in China.

A Hearty Welcome

TO VICE-PREFECT TS'UÊI

North of me, south of me, spring is in flood,
Day after day I have seen only gulls . . .
My path is full of petals—I have swept it for no others.
My thatch gate has been closed—but opens now for you.
It's a long way to the market, I can offer you little—   5
Yet here in my cottage there is old wine for our cups.
Shall we summon my elderly neighbour to join us,
Call him through the fence, and pour the jar dry?

To My Retired Friend Wêi[1]

It is almost as hard for friends to meet
As for the morning and evening stars.
Tonight then is a rare event,
Joining, in the candlelight,
Two men who were young not long ago   5
But now are turning grey at the temples.
. . . To find that half our friends are dead
Shocks us, burns our hearts with grief.
We little guessed it would be twenty years
Before I could visit you again.   10
When I went away, you were still unmarried;
But now these boys and girls in a row
Are very kind to their father's old friend.
They ask me where I have been on my journey;

From THE JADE MOUNTAIN: A CHINESE ANTHOLOGY, translated by Witter
Bynner. Copyright 1929 and renewed 1957 by Alfred A. Knopf, Inc. Reprinted by permission of the publisher.
TO MY RETIRED FRIEND WÊI: 1. *Wêi* (wā).

And then, when we have talked awhile,   15
They bring and show me wines and dishes,
Spring chives cut in the night-rain
And brown rice cooked freshly a special way.
. . . My host proclaims it a festival,
He urges me to drink ten cups—   20
But what ten cups could make me as drunk
As I always am with your love in my heart?
. . . Tomorrow the mountains will separate us;
After tomorrow—who can say?

Night in the Watch-Tower

While winter daylight shortens in the elemental scale
And snow and frost whiten the cold-circling night,
Stark sounds the fifth-watch with a challenge of drum and bugle.
. . . The stars and the River of Heaven pulse over the three moun-
        tains;
I hear women in the distance, wailing after the battle;   5
I see barbarian fishermen and woodcutters in the dawn.
. . . Sleeping-Dragon, Plunging-Horse, are no generals now, they are
        dust—
Hush for a moment, O tumult of the world.

A Drawing of a
Horse by General Ts'ao[1] at
Secretary Wêi Fêng's House

Throughout this dynasty no one had painted horses
Like the master-spirit, Prince Chiang-tu—
And then to General Ts'ao through his thirty years of fame
The world's gaze turned, for royal steeds.
He painted the late Emperor's luminous white horse.   5
For ten days the thunder flew over Dragon Lake,
And a pink-agate plate was sent him from the palace—
The talk of the court-ladies, the marvel of all eyes.
The General danced, receiving it in his honoured home. . . .
After this rare gift, followed rapidly fine silks   10
From many of the nobles, requesting that his art
Lend a new lustre to their screens.
. . . First came the curly-maned horse of Emperor T'ai-tsung,[2]
Then, for the Kuos, a lion-spotted horse . . .
But now in this painting I see two horses,   15
A sobering sight for whosoever knew them.
They are war-horses. Either could face ten thousand.
They make the white silk stretch away into a vast desert.
And the seven others with them are almost as noble. . . .
Mist and snow are moving across a cold sky,   20
And hoofs are cleaving snow-drifts under great trees—
With here a group of officers and there a group of servants.
See how these nine horses all vie with one another—
The high clear glance, the deep firm breath.
. . . Who understands distinction? Who really cares for art?   25
You, Wêi Fêng, have followed Ts'ao; Chih Tun preceded him.
. . . I remember when the late Emperor came toward his Summer
          Palace,

From THE JADE MOUNTAIN: A CHINESE ANTHOLOGY, translated by Witter Bynner. Copyright 1929 and renewed 1957 by Alfred A. Knopf, Inc. Reprinted by permission of the publisher.
1. *Ts'ao* (tsou). 2. *Emperor T'ai-tsung* (tī tsŭng), one of China's outstanding emperors (597–649), who defeated her enemies and instituted domestic reforms.

The procession, in green-feathered rows, swept from the eastern
      sky—
Thirty thousand horses, prancing, galloping,
Fashioned, every one of them, like the horses in this picture. . . .   **30**
But now the Imperial Ghost receives secret jade from the River-
      God,[3]
For the Emperor hunts crocodiles no longer by the streams.
Where you see his Great Gold Tomb, you may hear among the
      pines
A bird grieving in the wind that the Emperor's horses are gone.

A Song of War-Chariots

The war-chariots rattle,
The war-horses whinny,
Each man of you has a bow and a quiver at his belt.
Father, mother, son, wife, stare at you going,
Till dust shall have buried the bridge beyond Ch'ang-an.[1]   **5**
They run with you, crying, they tug at your sleeves,
And the sound of their sorrow goes up to the clouds;
And every time a bystander asks you a question,
You can only say to him that you have to go.
 . . . We remember others at fifteen sent north to guard the river   **10**
And at forty sent west to cultivate the camp-farms.

From THE JADE MOUNTAIN: A CHINESE ANTHOLOGY, translated by Witter
Bynner. Copyright 1929 and renewed 1957 by Alfred A. Knopf, Inc. Reprinted by per-
mission of the publisher.
A DRAWING OF A HORSE: 3. *Imperial Ghost . . . River-God.* Since early times, the Chi-
nese have considered jade the most valuable stone. It was used as a sacred symbol and,
according to mythology, was given by the gods to their lords as a symbol of recognition.
A SONG OF WAR-CHARIOTS: 1. *Ch'ang-an,* a city in the province of Shensi, in southern
China.

The mayor wound their turbans for them when they started out.
With their turbaned hair white now, they are still at the border,
At the border where the blood of men spills like the sea—
And still the heart of Emperor Wu is beating for war.   15
. . . Do you know that, east of China's mountains, in two hun-
      dred districts
And in thousands of villages, nothing grows but weeds,
And though strong women have bent to the ploughing,
East and west the furrows all are broken down?
. . . Men of China are able to face the stiffest battle,   20
But their officers drive them like chickens and dogs.
Whatever is asked of them,
Dare they complain?
For example, this winter
Held west of the gate,   25
Challenged for taxes,
How could they pay?
. . . We have learned that to have a son is bad luck—
It is very much better to have a daughter
Who can marry and live in the house of a neighbour,   80
While under the sod we bury our boys.
. . . Go to the Blue Sea, look along the shore
At all the old white bones forsaken—
New ghosts are wailing there now with the old,
Loudest in the dark sky of a stormy day.   85

Po Chü-i (772–846)

Translated from the Chinese by
Arthur Waley

Golden Bells

When I was almost forty
I had a daughter whose name was Golden Bells.
Now it is just a year since she was born;
She is learning to sit and cannot yet talk.
Ashamed,—to find that I have not a sage's heart: 5
I cannot resist vulgar thoughts and feelings.
Henceforward I am tied to things outside myself:
My only reward,—the pleasure I am getting now.
If I am spared the grief of her dying young,
Then I shall have the trouble of getting her married.   10
My plan for retiring and going back to the hills
Must now be postponed for fifteen years!

Remembering Golden Bells

Ruined and ill,—a man of two score;
    Pretty and guileless,—a girl of three.
Not a boy,—but still better than nothing [1]:
To soothe one's feeling,—from time to time a kiss!
There came a day,—they suddenly took her from me;   5
Her soul's shadow wandered I know not where.
And when I remember how just at the time she died
She lisped strange sounds, beginning to learn to talk,
Then I know that the ties of flesh and blood
Only bind us to a load of grief and sorrow.   10

From TRANSLATIONS FROM THE CHINESE (170 CHINESE POEMS), translated by
Arthur Waley. Copyright 1919, 1941 by Alfred A. Knopf, Inc. and renewed 1947 by
Arthur Waley. Reprinted by permission of Alfred A. Knopf, Inc., and Constable Publishers.
REMEMBERING GOLDEN BELLS: 1. *Not a boy . . . nothing.* In China women were con-
sidered, in all respects, inferior to men. See Fu Hsüan's poem "Woman" on page 18.

At last, by thinking of the time before she was born,
By thought and reason I drove the pain away.
Since my heart forgot her, many days have passed
And three times winter has changed to spring.
This morning, for a little, the old grief came back,   15
Because, in the road, I met her foster-nurse.

Chu-ch'ēn Village

In Hsü-chou,[1] in the District of Ku-fēng
There lies a village whose name is Chu-ch'ēn—
A hundred miles away from the county-town,
Amid fields of hemp and green of mulberry-trees.
Click, click goes the sound of the spinning-wheel;   5
Mules and oxen pack the village-streets.
The girls go drawing the water from the brook;
The men go gathering firewood on the hill.
So far from the town Government affairs are few;
So deep in the hills, man's ways are simple.   10
Though they have wealth, they do not traffic with it;
Though they reach the age, they do not enter the Army.
Each family keeps to its village trade;
Grey-headed, they have never left the gates.

Alive, they are the people of Ch'ēn Village;   15
Dead, they become the dust of Ch'ēn Village.
Out in the fields old men and young
Gaze gladly, each in the other's face.
In the whole village there are only two clans;
Age after age Chus have married Ch'ēns.   20
Near or distant, they have kinsmen in every house;
Young or old, they have friends wherever they go.
On white wine and roasted fowl they fare
At joyful meetings more than "once a week."
While they are alive, they have no distant partings;   25

From TRANSLATIONS FROM THE CHINESE (170 CHINESE POEMS), translated by
Arthur Waley. Copyright 1919, 1941 by Alfred A. Knopf, Inc. and renewed 1947 by
Arthur Waley. Reprinted by permission of Alfred A. Knopf, Inc., and Constable Publishers.
CHU-CH'ĒN VILLAGE: 1. Hsü-chou (shᵧ jō).

To choose a wife they go to a neighbour's house.
When they are dead,—no distant burial;
Round the village graves lie thick.
They are not troubled either about life or death;
They have no anguish either of body or soul.   80
And so it happens that they live to a ripe age
And great-great-grandsons are often seen.

I was born in the Realms of Etiquette;
In early years, unprotected and poor.
Alone, I learnt to distinguish between Evil and Good;   85
Untutored, I toiled at bitter tasks.
The World's Law honours Learning and Fame;
Scholars prize marriages and Caps.
With these fetters I gyved my own hands;
Truly I became a much-deceived man.   40
At ten years old I learnt to read books;
At fifteen, I knew how to write prose.
At twenty I was made a Bachelor of Arts;
At thirty I became a Censor at the Court.
Above, the duty I owe to Prince and parents;   45
Below, the ties that bind me to wife and child.
The support of my family, the service of my country—
For these tasks my nature is not apt.
I reckon the time that I first left my home;
From then till now,—fifteen Springs!   50
My lonely boat has thrice sailed to Ch'u;
Four times through Ch'in my lean horse has passed.
I have walked in the morning with hunger in my face;
I have lain at night with a soul that could not rest.
East and West I have wandered without pause,   55
Hither and thither like a cloud astray in the sky.
In the civil-war my old home was destroyed;
Of my flesh and blood many are scattered and lost.
    North of the River, and South of the River—
In both lands are the friends of all my life;   60
Life-friends whom I never see at all,—
Whose deaths I hear of only after the lapse of years.
Sad at morning, I lie on my bed till dusk;
Weeping at night, I sit and wait for dawn.
The fire of sorrow has burnt my heart's core;   65
The frost of trouble has seized my hair's roots.
In such anguish has my whole life passed;
Long I have envied the people of Ch'ēn Village.

The Philosophers[1] (Lao-tzu[2])

"Those who speak know nothing;
Those who know are silent."
These words, as I am told,
Were spoken by Lao-tzŭ.
If we are to believe that Lao-tzŭ   5
   Was himself *one who knew*,
How comes it that he wrote a book
   Of five thousand words?

The Red Cockatoo

Sent as a present from Annam—[1]
A red cockatoo.
Coloured like the peach-tree blossom,
Speaking with the speech of men.
And they did to it what is always done   5
To the learned and eloquent.
They took a cage with stout bars
And shut it up inside.

From TRANSLATIONS FROM THE CHINESE (170 CHINESE POEMS), translated by
Arthur Waley. Copyright 1919, 1941 by Alfred A. Knopf, Inc. and renewed 1947 by
Arthur Waley. Reprinted by permission of Alfred A. Knopf, Inc., and Constable Publishers.
THE PHILOSOPHERS: 1. *The philosophers*. The title is in the plural as the original poem
contains a second verse about another philosopher. 2. *Lao-tzŭ* (lou tsə), Chinese philosopher (c. 604? B.C.), the reputed founder of Taoism, one of the principal Chinese religions
or philosophies. It teaches that man can acquire happiness by leading a life of absolute
simplicity and renouncing material desires.
THE RED COCKATOO: 1. *Annam*, a region in Southeast Asia, now part of Vietnam.

Wang Chien (c. 830 A.D.)

Hearing That His Friend Was Coming Back From the War

Translated from the Chinese by
Arthur Waley

In old days those who went to fight
In three years had one year's leave.
But in *this* war the soldiers are never changed;
They must go on fighting till they die on the battle-field.
I thought of you, so weak and indolent,   5
Hopelessly trying to learn to march and drill.
That a young man should ever come home again
Seemed about as likely as that the sky should fall.
Since I got the news that you were coming back,
Twice I have mounted to the high hall of your home.   10
I found your brother mending your horse's stall;
I found your mother sewing your new clothes.
I am half afraid; perhaps it is not true;
Yet I never weary of watching for you on the road.
Each day I go out at the City Gate   15
With a flask of wine, lest you should come thirsty.
Oh that I could shrink the surface of the World,
So that suddenly I might find you standing at my side.

From TRANSLATIONS FROM THE CHINESE (170 CHINESE POEMS), translated by
Arthur Waley. Copyright 1919, 1941 by Alfred A. Knopf, Inc. and renewed 1947 by
Arthur Waley. Reprinted by permission of Alfred A. Knopf, Inc., and Constable Publishers.

Su Tung-p'o (1036–1101)

On the Birth of His Son

Translated from the Chinese by
Arthur Waley

Families, when a child is born
Want it to be intelligent.
I, through intelligence,
Having wrecked my whole life,
Only hope the baby will prove   5
Ignorant and stupid.
Then he will crown a tranquil life
By becoming a Cabinet Minister.

From TRANSLATIONS FROM THE CHINESE (170 CHINESE POEMS), translated by
Arthur Waley. Copyright 1919, 1941 by Alfred A. Knopf, Inc. and renewed 1947 by
Arthur Waley. Reprinted by permission of Alfred A. Knopf, Inc., and Constable Publishers.

Han-shan (7th or 8th century)

THE COLD MOUNTAIN POEMS OF HAN-SHAN

Translated from the Chinese by

Gary Snyder

In the Japanese art exhibit that came to America in 1953 was a small sumi sketch [1] *of a robe-tattered wind-swept long-haired laughing man holding a scroll, standing on a cliff in the mountains. This was Kan-zan, or Han-shan, "Cold Mountain"—his name taken from where he lived. He is a mountain madman in an old Chinese line of ragged hermits. When he talks about Cold Mountain he means himself, his home, his state of mind. He lived in the T'ang dynasty—traditionally* A.D. *627–650, although Hu Shih dates him 700–780. This makes him roughly contemporary with Tu Fu, Li Po, Wang Wêi, and Po Chü-i. His poems, of which three hundred survive, are written in T'ang colloquial: rough and fresh. The ideas are Taoist, Buddhist, Zen.* [2] *He and his sidekick Shih-te (Jittoku in Japanese) became great favorites with Zen painters of later days—the scroll, the broom, the wild hair and laughter. They became Immortals and you sometimes run onto them today in the skid-rows, orchards, hobo jungles, and logging camps of America.—*G.S.

---

1. *sumi sketch,* a sketch drawn in a black ink made from plant soot and glue and much used by calligraphers and artists. 2. *Taoist, Buddhist, Zen.* A *Taoist* is a believer in the religious doctrine of Taoism, one of the principal Chinese religions, founded by Lao-tzŭ (c. 604? B.C.). It teaches man to acquire happiness by leading a life of absolute simplicity and renouncing material desires. A *Buddhist* is a believer in the religious doctrine of Buddhism, founded by Buddha who lived in India (563?–483? B.C.). Buddhism teaches that man can attain enlightenment by freeing himself from suffering through following "the noble eightfold path": right belief, right resolve, right speech, right action, right conduct, right effort, right thought, and right meditation. *Zen* is a form of meditative Buddhism which originated in China around 500 A.D. Its adherents believe that true insight into reality can be found by inward looking into one's heart, rather than in good deeds and rituals.

Preface to the Poems of Han-shan
by Lu Ch'iu-yin, Governor of T'ai Prefecture

No ONE KNOWS just what sort of man Han-shan was. There are old people who knew him: they say he was a poor man, a crazy character. He lived alone seventy li [3] west of the T'ang-hsing district of T'ien-t'ai at a place called Cold Mountain. He often went down to the Kuo-ch'ing Temple. At the temple lived Shih-te, who ran the dining hall. He sometimes saved leftovers for Han-shan, hiding them in a bamboo tube. Han-shan would come and carry it away; walking the long veranda, calling and shouting happily, talking and laughing to himself. Once the monks followed him, caught him, and made fun of him. He stopped, clapped his hands, and laughed greatly—Ha Ha!—for a spell, then left.

He looked like a tramp. His body and face were old and beat. Yet in every word he breathed was a meaning in line with the subtle principles of things, if only you thought of it deeply. Everything he said had a feeling of the Tao in it, profound and arcane secrets. His hat was made of birch bark, his clothes were ragged and worn out, and his shoes were wood. Thus men who have made it hide their tracks: unifying categories and interpenetrating things. On that long veranda calling and singing, in his words of reply Ha Ha!—the three worlds revolve. Sometimes at the villages and farms he laughed and sang with cowherds. Sometimes intractable, sometimes agreeable, his nature was happy of itself. But how could a person without wisdom recognize him?

I once received a position as a petty official at Tan-ch'iu. The day I was to depart, I had a bad headache. I called a doctor, but he couldn't cure me and it turned worse. Then I met a Buddhist Master named Feng-kan, who said he came from the Kuo-ch'ing Temple of T'ien-t'ai especially to visit me. I asked him to rescue me from my illness. He smiled and said, "The four realms are within the body; sickness comes from illusion. If you want to do away with it, you need pure water." Someone brought water to the Master, who spat it on me. In a moment the disease was rooted out. He then said, "There are miasmas in T'ai prefecture, when you get there take care of yourself." I asked him, "Are there any wise men in your area I could look on as Master?" He replied, "When you see him you don't recognize him, when you recognize him you don't see him. If you want to see him, you can't rely on appearances. Then you can see him. Han-shan is

---

3. *seventy li* (lē), about twenty-three miles. A li is approximately one third of a mile.

a Manjusri hiding at Kuo-ch'ing. Shih-te is a Samantabhadra.[4] They look like poor fellows and act like madmen. Sometimes they go and sometimes they come. They work in the kitchen of the Kuo-ch'ing dining hall, tending the fire." When he was done talking he left.

I proceeded on my journey to my job at T'ai-chou, not forgetting this affair. I arrived three days later, immediately went to a temple, and questioned an old monk. It seemed the Master had been truthful, so I gave orders to see if T'ang-hsing really contained a Han-shan and Shih-te. The District Magistrate reported to me: "In this district, seventy li west, is a mountain. People used to see a poor man heading from the cliffs to stay awhile at Kuo-ch'ing. At the temple dining hall is a similar man named Shih-te." I made a bow, and went to Kuo-ch'ing. I asked some people around the temple, "There used to be a Master named Feng-kan here. Where is his place? And where can Han-shan and Shih-te be seen?" A monk named Tao-ch'iao spoke up: "Feng-kan the Master lived in back of the library. Nowadays nobody lives there; a tiger often comes and roars. Han-shan and Shih-te are in the kitchen." The monk led me to Feng-kan's yard. Then he opened the gate: all we saw was tiger tracks. I asked the monks Tao-ch'iao and Pao-te, "When Feng-kan was here, what was his job?" The monks said, "He pounded and hulled rice. At night he sang songs to amuse himself." Then we went to the kitchen, before the stoves. Two men were facing the fire, laughing loudly. I made a bow. The two shouted HO! at me. They struck their hands together—Ha Ha!—great laughter. They shouted. Then they said, "Feng-kan—loose-tongued, loose-tongued. You don't recognize Amitabha,[5] why be courteous to us?" The monks gathered round, surprise going through them. "Why has a big official bowed to a pair of clowns?" The two men grabbed hands and ran out of the temple. I cried, "Catch them"—but they quickly ran away. Han-shan returned to Cold Mountain. I asked the monks, "Would those two men be willing to settle down at this temple?" I ordered them to find a house, and to ask Han-shan and Shih-te to return and live at the temple.

I returned to my district and had two sets of clean clothes made, got some incense and such, and sent it to the temple—but the two men didn't return. So I had it carried up to Cold Mountain. The packer saw Han-shan, who called in a loud voice, "Thief! Thief!" and retreated into a mountain cave. He shouted, "I tell you man, strive hard!"—entered the cave and was gone. The cave closed of itself and they weren't able to follow. Shih-te's tracks disappeared completely.

I ordered Tao-ch'iao and the other monks to find out how they had lived, to hunt up the poems written on bamboo, wood, stones, and cliffs—and also

---

4. *Manjusri . . . Samantabhadra. Manjusri* is the Bodhisattva (one who has attained enlightenment and, in a future incarnation, will become a Buddha) of wisdom. *Samantabhadra* is the Bodhisattva of love. 5. *Amitabha*, the Bodhisattva of mercy.

to collect those written on the walls of people's houses. There were more than three hundred. On the wall of the Earth-shrine Shih-te had written some *gatha*.[6] It was all brought together and made into a book.

I hold to the principle of the Buddha-mind. It is fortunate to meet with men of Tao, so I have made this eulogy.

TWENTY-FOUR POEMS BY HAN-SHAN

1

The path to Han-shan's place is laughable,
A path, but no sign of cart or horse.
Converging gorges—hard to trace their twists
Jumbled cliffs—unbelievably rugged.
A thousand grasses bend with dew,   5
A hill of pines hums in the wind.
And now I've lost the shortcut home,
Body asking shadow, how do you keep up?

2

In a tangle of cliffs I chose a place—
Bird-paths, but no trails for men.
What's beyond the yard?
White clouds clinging to vague rocks.
Now I've lived here—how many years—   5
Again and again, spring and winter pass.
Go tell families with silverware and cars
"What's the use of all that noise and money?"

PREFACE: **6.** *gatha.* A *gatha* is a Buddhist verse or song.

3

In the mountains it's cold,
Always been cold, not just this year.
Jagged scarps forever snowed in
Woods in the dark ravines spitting mist.
Grass is still sprouting at the end of June,   5
Leaves begin to fall in early August.
And here am I, high on mountains,
Peering and peering, but I can't even see the sky.

4

I spur my horse through the wrecked town,
The wrecked town sinks my spirit.
High, low, old parapet-walls
Big, small, the aging tombs.
I waggle my shadow, all alone;   5
Not even the crack of a shrinking coffin is heard.
I pity all these ordinary bones,
In the books of the Immortals they are nameless.

5

I wanted a good place to settle:
Cold Mountain would be safe.
Light wind in a hidden pine—
Listen close—the sound gets better.
Under it a gray-haired man   5
Mumbles along reading Huang and Lao.[1]
For ten years I haven't gone back home
I've even forgotten the way by which I came.

---

1. *Huang and Lao*, Huang Ti, the Yellow Emperor, was the legendary first emperor of China, Lao-tzŭ, the founder of Taoism, was the author of *Tao Te Ching*, a philosophical work written in verse. See "The Philosophers" on page 36.

6

Men ask the way to Cold Mountain
Cold Mountain: there's no through trail.
In summer, ice doesn't melt
The rising sun blurs in swirling fog.
How did I make it?   5
My heart's not the same as yours.
If your heart was like mine
You'd get it and be right here.

7

I settled at Cold Mountain long ago,
Already it seems like years and years.
Freely drifting, I prowl the woods and streams
And linger watching things themselves.
Men don't get this far into the mountains,   5
White clouds gather and billow.
Thin grass does for a mattress,
The blue sky makes a good quilt.
Happy with a stone underhead
Let heaven and earth go about their changes.   10

8

Clambering up the Cold Mountain path,
The Cold Mountain trail goes on and on:
The long gorge choked with scree [2] and boulders,
The wide creek, the mist-blurred grass.
The moss is slippery, though there's been no rain   5
The pine sings, but there's no wind.
Who can leap the world's ties
And sit with me among the white clouds?

---

2. *scree*, a heap of stones or rocks.

Rough and dark—the Cold Mountain trail,
Sharp cobbles—the icy creek bank.
Yammering, chirping—always birds
Bleak, alone, not even a lone hiker.
Whip, whip—the wind slaps my face   5
Whirled and tumbled—snow piles on my back.
Morning after morning I don't see the sun
Year after year, not a sign of spring.

10

I have lived at Cold Mountain
These thirty long years.
Yesterday I called on friends and family:
More than half had gone to the Yellow Springs.
Slowly consumed, like fire down a candle;   5
Forever flowing, like a passing river.
Now, morning, I face my lone shadow:
Suddenly my eyes are bleared with tears.

11

Spring-water in the green creek is clear
Moonlight on Cold Mountain is white
Silent knowledge—the spirit is enlightened of itself
Contemplate the void: this world exceeds stillness.

12

In my first thirty years of life
I roamed hundreds and thousands of miles.
Walked by rivers through deep green grass
Entered cities of boiling red dust.
Tried drugs, but couldn't make Immortal;   5
Read books and wrote poems on history.
Today I'm back at Cold Mountain:
I'll sleep by the creek and purify my ears.

13

I can't stand these bird-songs
Now I'll go rest in my straw shack.
The cherry flowers out scarlet
The willow shoots up feathery.
Morning sun drives over blue peaks
Bright clouds wash green ponds.
Who knows that I'm out of the dusty world
Climbing the southern slope of Cold Mountain?

14

Cold Mountain has many hidden wonders,
People who climb here are always getting scared.
When the moon shines, water sparkles clear
When wind blows, grass swishes and rattles.
On the bare plum, flowers of snow
On the dead stump, leaves of mist.
At the touch of rain it all turns fresh and live
At the wrong season you can't ford the creeks.

15

There's a naked bug at Cold Mountain
With a white body and a black head.
His hand holds two book-scrolls,
One the Way and one its Power.[3]
His shack's got no pots or oven,
He goes for a walk with his shirt and pants askew.
But he always carries the sword of wisdom:
He means to cut down senseless craving.

---

3. *the Way . . . Power*, a reference to Lao-tzŭ's work, the *Tao Te Ching*.

Cold Mountain is a house
Without beams or walls.
The six doors left and right are open
The hall is blue sky.
The rooms all vacant and vague   5
The east wall beats on the west wall
At the center nothing.

Borrowers don't bother me
In the cold I build a little fire
When I'm hungry I boil up some greens.   10
I've got no use for the kulak [4]
With his big barn and pasture—
He just sets up a prison for himself.
Once in he can't get out.
Think it over—   15
You know it might happen to you.

If I hide out at Cold Mountain
Living off mountain plants and berries—
All my lifetime, why worry?
One follows his karma [5] through.
Days and months slip by like water,   5
Time is like sparks knocked off flint.
Go ahead and let the world change—
I'm happy to sit among these cliffs.

Most T'ien-t'ai men [6]
Don't know Han-shan
Don't know his real thought
& call it silly talk.

---

4. kulak, a wealthy peasant. [Russian] 5. karma, in Buddhism a person's actions in one stage of his existence that determine his fate in the next. 6. T'ien-t'ai men, townsmen of T'ien-t'ai, a town in the highlands of Chekiang Province in southwest China.

19

Once at Cold Mountain, troubles cease—
No more tangled, hung-up mind.
I idly scribble poems on the rock cliff,
Taking whatever comes, like a drifting boat.

20

Some critic tried to put me down—
"Your poems lack the Basic Truth of Tao"
And I recall the old-timers
Who were poor and didn't care.
I have to laugh at him,   5
He misses the point entirely,
Men like that
Ought to stick to making money.

21

I've lived at Cold Mountain—how many autumns.
Alone, I hum a song—utterly without regret.
Hungry, I eat one grain of Immortal-medicine
Mind solid and sharp; leaning on a stone.

22

On top of Cold Mountain the lone round moon [7]
Lights the whole clear cloudless sky.
Honor this priceless natural treasure
Concealed in five shadows, sunk deep in the flesh.

---

7. *lone round moon.* In Buddhism it is believed that certain objects, in this case the full moon, symbolize the Buddha nature (the seed of perfection) existing in all beings.

23

My home was at Cold Mountain from the start,
Rambling among the hills, far from trouble.

Gone, and a million things leave no trace
Loosed, and it flows through the galaxies
A fountain of light, into the very mind—   5
Not a thing, and yet it appears before me:
Now I know the pearl [8] of the Buddha-nature
Know its use: a boundless perfect sphere.

24

When men see Han-shan
They all say he's crazy
And not much to look at—
Dressed in rags and hides.
They don't get what I say   5
& I don't talk their language.
All I can say to those I meet:
"Try and make it to Cold Mountain."

---

8. *the pearl,* another symbol of the Buddha nature existing in all beings.

Prose

Anonymous (17th century)

THE LADY WHO WAS A BEGGAR

Translated from the Chinese by
Cyril Birch

> *That side the wall, the branches—this side, the broken blossoms,*
> *Fallen to earth, the playthings of every passing breeze.*
> *The branches may be bare, but they will put out more flowers—*
> *The flowers, once adrift, may never regain the trees.*

THIS IS THE "SONG OF THE REJECTED WIFE," by a poet of former times. It likens the position of a wife to that of the blossom on the branch: the branch may be stripped of its blossom, but it will bloom again in the spring; the flowers, once they have left the branch, can never hope to return. Ladies, if you will listen to me, then serve your husband to the extent of your powers, share with him joy and sorrow, and follow one to the end. Unless you wish to lay up repentance in store, do not scorn poverty and covet riches, do not let your affections wander.

Let me tell you now of a famous statesman of the Han dynasty [1] whose wife, in the days before he had made his name, left him because "though she had eyes, she did not recognize Mount T'ai." [2] In vain did she repent in later years. Who was this man, you ask, and where did he come from?

From STORIES FROM A MING COLLECTION, THE ART OF THE CHINESE STORY-TELLER translated by Cyril Birch. Copyright © 1958 by Cyril Birch. Reprinted by permission of Indiana University Press and The Bodley Head.
1. *Han dynasty* (206 B.C.–220 A.D.). 2. *Mount T'ai.* In Chinese mythology the mountain known as Mount T'ai was believed to be the source of life and consequently was considered to be the ruler of fate and destiny. The author is saying that the wife failed to recognize her husband's potential.

Well, his name was Chu Mai-ch'en, he was styled Weng-tzu, and he came from the region of Hui-chi in the south-east. Of poor family, he had as yet found no opening, but lived, just himself and his wife, in a tumbledown cottage in a mean alley. Every day he would go into the hills and cut firewood to sell in the market place for the few cash he needed to carry on existence. But he was addicted to study, and a book never left his hand. Though his back was bowed down under a weight of faggots, grasped in his hand would be a book. This he would read aloud, rolling the phrases round his mouth, chanting as he walked along.

The townspeople were used to him, they knew Mai-ch'en was here with his firewood as soon as they heard the sound of intoning. They all bought from him out of sympathy for a poor Confucian; moreover, he never haggled but simply took whatever you wanted to give him, so that he never found his firewood difficult to sell. But there were always gangs of idlers and street urchins ready to make fun of him as he came along, intoning the classics with a load of faggots on his shoulders.

Mai-ch'en never noticed them. But one day when his wife went out of doors to draw water, she felt humiliated by the sight of these children making fun of Mai-ch'en with his burden. When he came home with his earnings she began to upbraid him: "If you want to study, then leave off selling firewood, and if you want to sell firewood then leave studying to others. When a man gets to your age, and in his right senses, that he should act like that and let children make fun of him! It's a wonder you don't die of shame."

"I sell firewood to save us from penury," replied Mai-ch'en, "and I study to win wealth and esteem. There is no contradiction there. Let them laugh!"

But his wife laughed at this. "If it's wealth and esteem you're after, then don't sell any more firewood. Who ever heard of a woodcutter becoming a mandarin? And yet you talk all this nonsense."

"Wealth and poverty, fame and obscurity, each has its time," said Mai-ch'en. "A fortune-teller told me my rise would begin when I had passed fifty. They say you can't measure out the ocean with a gallon can—don't you try to measure my mind for me."

"Fortune-teller indeed!" said his wife. "He could see you were simple and deliberately made fun of you. You should pay no heed to him. By the time you're fifty you'll be past even carrying firewood. Death from starvation, that's what's in store for you, and then you talk about becoming a mandarin! Unless, of course, the King of Hades wants another judge in his court and is keeping the job vacant for you!"

"Chiang T'ai-kung was still a fisherman on the River Wei at the age of eighty," replied Mai-ch'en, "but when King Wen of Chou found him he took him into his chariot and honoured him as counsellor. Kung-sun Hung, a Chief Minister of the present dynasty, was still herding swine by the

Eastern Ocean at the age of fifty-nine. He was turned sixty when fate presented him to the present Emperor, who made him a general and a marquis. If I begin when I am fifty I shall be some way behind Kan Lo,[3] but in front of the two I have just mentioned. You must be patient and wait a while."

"There's no need to ransack all the histories," said his wife. "Your fisherman and swineherd were full of talent and learning. But you, with these useless books of yours, you'll still be the same at a hundred. What is there to hope for? I was unlucky enough to marry you, and now, what with the children following you about and poking fun at you, you've taken my good name away too. If you don't do as I say and throw those books away, I'm determined I won't stay with you. We'll each lead our own life, and then we shan't get in each other's way."

"I am forty-three this year," said Mai-ch'en. "In seven years' time I shall be fifty. The long wait is behind us, you have only to be patient for a little longer. If you desert me now in such a callous fashion you will surely regret it in years to come."

"The world's not short of woodcutters," his wife rejoined. "What shall I have to regret? If I remain with you another seven years it will be my corpse as well as yours that is found starved by the roadside. It will count as a good deed if you release me now, for you will have saved my life."

Mai-ch'en realized that his wife had set her heart on leaving him and wouldn't be gainsaid. So he said, with a sigh, "Very well, then. I only hope that your next husband will be a better man than Chu Mai-ch'en."

"Whatever he's like he could hardly be worse," returned his wife, whereupon she made two obeisances and went joyfully out of the house and away without so much as looking back.

To relieve his distress, Chu Mai-ch'en inscribed four lines of verse on the wall of his cottage:

> *Marry a dog, follow a dog,*
> *Marry a cock, follow a cock.*
> *It was my wife deserted me,*
> *Not I rejected her.*

By the time Chu Mai-ch'en reached his fiftieth birthday the Han Emperor Wu-ti had issued his edict summoning men of worth to serve their country. Mai-ch'en went to the Western Capital, submitted his name and took his place among those awaiting appointment. Meanwhile his abilities were brought to the notice of the Emperor by a fellow-townsman, Yen Chu. Reflecting that Chu Mai-ch'en must have intimate knowledge of the

---

3. *Kan Lo*, a hero who at the age of eleven, during the Warring States period (fifth century B.C.), was honored for public services.

people of his native place and of their condition, the Emperor appointed him Prefect of Hui-chi, and he rode off to take up his appointment.

Learning of the impending arrival of the new Prefect, the officials of Hui-chi mobilized great numbers of men to put the roads in order. Among these coolies was Chu Mai-ch'en's marital successor; and at this man's side, attending to his food, was Mai-ch'en's ex-wife, barefoot and with matted hair. When the woman heard the din of the approach of the new Prefect and his suite, she tried to get a glimpse of him—and saw her former husband, Chu Mai-ch'en. Mai-ch'en also, from his carriage, caught sight of her and recognized his ex-wife. He summoned her and seated her in one of the carriages of his suite.

At the official residence, the woman did not know where to put herself for shame. She kotowed and poured out a confession of her faults. Mai-ch'en ordered her second husband to be summoned to his presence, and it did not take them long to bring him in. He grovelled on the floor, not daring to raise his eyes. Mai-ch'en burst out laughing: "A man like this—I don't see that he is much of an improvement on Chu Mai-ch'en?"

His ex-wife went on kotowing and confessing. She had eyes but no pupils and had not recognized his worth; she would wish to return as humble slave or concubine; as such she would serve him to the end of her days. Chu Mai-ch'en ordered a bucket of water to be brought and splashed on the floor. Then he told his wife: "If this spilt water can go back into the bucket, then you can come back to me. But in memory of our childhood betrothal, I grant you waste land from my demesne sufficient to support yourself and your husband."

When the woman left the residence with her second husband the passers-by pointed her out to each other: "That's the wife of the new Prefect!" Humiliated beyond measure, when she reached her piece of land she jumped in the nearby river and drowned herself.

There is a verse in evidence of all this:

The general Han Hsin, starving, was looked after by a washerwoman,
But this poor scholar is deserted by his own good wife.
Well aware that spilt water cannot be recovered
She repents that in time past she would not let him study.

A second poem maintains that to despise poverty and esteem only wealth is a commonplace in this world, and not limited to such a woman as the wife of Chu Mai-ch'en:

Using success or failure as the sole gauge of merit
Who can discern the dragon lying hidden in the mud?
Do not blame this woman for her lack of perception,
More than one wife in this world has kicked over the traces.

After this story of a wife rejecting her husband, let me tell one now about a husband rejecting his wife. It was equally a case of scorning the poor and adulating the rich, at the expense of justice and mercy alike, so that all that was gained in the end was a name among all and sundry for meanness and lack of feeling.

It is told that in the Shao-hsing reign-period of the Sung dynasty (1131–1163), although Lin-an had been made the capital city and was a wealthy and populous district, still the great number of beggars had not diminished. Among them was one who acted as their head. He was called the "tramp-major," and looked after all the beggars. Whenever they managed to beg something, the tramp-major would demand a fee for the day. Then when it was raining or snow lay on the ground, and there was nowhere to go to beg, the tramp-major would boil up a drop of thin gruel and feed the whole beggar band. Their tattered robes and jackets were also in his care. The result was that the whole crowd of the beggars were careful to obey him, with bated breath like a lot of slaves, and none of them dared offend him.

The tramp-major was thus provided with a regular income, and as a rule he would lend out sums of money among the beggars and extort a tidy interest. In this way, if he neither gambled nor went carousing, he could build up a going concern out of it. He depended on this for his livelihood, and never for a moment thought of changing his profession. There was only one drawback: a tramp-major did not have a very good name. Though he acquired land by his efforts, and his family had prospered for generations, still he was a boss of the beggars and not to be compared with ordinary respectable people. No one would salute him with respect if he showed himself out of doors, and so the only thing for him to do was to shut his doors and play the great man in his own home.

And yet, distinguishing the worthy from the base, we count among the latter only prostitutes, actors, yamen-runners [4] and soldiers: we certainly do not include beggars. For what is wrong with beggars is not that they are covered in sores, but simply that they have no money. There have been men like the minister Wu Tzu-hsü, of Ch'un-ch'iu times, who as a fugitive from oppression played his pipes and begged his food in the market place of Wu; or Cheng Yüan-ho of T'ang times who sang the beggar's song of "Lien-hua lo," but later rose to wealth and eminence and covered his bed with brocade. These were great men, though beggars: clearly, we may hold beggars in contempt, but we should not compare them with the prostitutes and actors, the runners and soldiery.

Let us digress no longer, but tell now how in the city of Hangchow there was once a tramp-major by the name of Chin Lao-ta. In the course of seven generations his ancestors had developed the profession into a perfect family

4. *yamen-runners*, agents or collectors for a public official.

business, so that Chin Lao-ta ate well and dressed well, lived in a fine house and cultivated good land. His barns were well-stocked with grain and his purse with money, he made loans and kept servants; if not quite the wealthiest, he was certainly one of the rich. Being a man of social aspirations, he decided to relinquish this post of tramp-major into the hands of a relative, "Scabby" Chin, while he himself took his ease with what he had and mingled no more with the beggar band. But unfortunately, the neighbours were used to speaking of "the tramp-major's family," and the name persisted in spite of his efforts.

Chin Lao-ta was over fifty. He had lost his wife and had no son, but only a daughter whose name was Jade Slave. Jade Slave was beautiful, as we are told by a verse about her:

> Pure to compare with jade,
> Gracious to shame the flowers,
> Given the adornments of the court
> Here would be another Chang Li-hua.[5]

Chin Lao-ta prized his daughter as a jewel, and taught her from an early age to read and write. By the age of fifteen she was adept in prose and verse, composing as fast as her hand could write. She was equally proficient in the womanly crafts, and in performing on the harp or flute: everything she did proclaimed her skill. Her beauty and talent inspired Chin Lao-ta to seek a husband for her among the scholar class. But the fact was that among families of name and rank it would be difficult to find anyone anxious to marry the girl—no one wanted a tramp-major's daughter. On the other hand, Lao-ta had no desire to cultivate a liaison with humble and unaspiring tradespeople. Thus, while her father hovered between high and low, the girl reached the age of seventeen without betrothal.

And then one day an old man of the neighbourhood came along with news of a student by the name of Mo Chi who lived below the T'ai-ping Bridge. This was an able youth of nineteen, full of learning, who remained unmarried only because he was an orphan and had no money. But he had graduated recently, and was hoping to marry some girl in whose family he could find a home.

"This youth would be just right for your daughter," said the neighbour. "Why not take him as your son-in-law?"

"Then do me the favour of acting as go-between," said Chin Lao-ta; and off went the old man on his errand, straight to the T'ai-ping Bridge.

There he sought out the graduate Mo Chi, to whom he said, "There is one thing I am obliged to tell you: the ancestors of Chin Lao-ta followed

5. *Chang Li-hua*, a concubine famous for her beauty and wisdom.

the profession of tramp-major. But this was long ago: and think, what a fine girl she is, this daughter of his—and what's more, what a prosperous and flourishing family! If it is not against the young gentleman's wishes, I will take it upon myself to arrange the whole thing at once."

Before giving his reply, Mo Chi turned the matter over in his mind: "I am not very well-off for food and clothes just now, and I am certainly not in a position to take a wife in the usual way. Why not make the best of it and marry into this family? It would be killing two birds with one stone; and I needn't take any notice of ridicule." Turning to the old man, he said, "Uncle, what you propose seems an admirable plan. But I am too poor to buy the usual presents. What do you suggest?"

"Provided only that you accept this match," replied the old man, "you will not even be called on to supply so much as the paper for the exchange of horoscopes. You may leave everything to me." With this he returned to report to Chin Lao-ta. They selected an auspicious day, and the Chin family even provided clothes for Mo Chi to wear at the wedding.

When Mo Chi had entered the family and the ceremony was over, he found that Jade Slave's beauty and talents exceeded his wildest hopes. And this perfect wife was his without the outlay of a single copper! He had food and clothes in abundance, and indeed everything he could wish. Even the ridicule he had feared from his friends was withheld, for all were willing to make allowances for Mo Chi's penniless condition.

When their marriage had lasted a month Chin Lao-ta prepared a generous banquet at which his son-in-law could feast his graduate friends and thus enhance the dignity of the house. The drinking went on for a week: but what was not foreseen was the offence which all this gave to the kinsman "Scabby" Chin. Nor was Scabby without justification.

"You're a tramp-major just as much as I am," said he in his heart, "the only thing is that you've been one for a few generations longer and have got some money in your pocket. But if it comes to ancestors, aren't yours the very same as mine? When my niece Jade Slave gets married I expect to be invited to drink a toast—here's a load of guests drinking for a week on end to celebrate the first month, but not so much as a one-inch by three-inch invitation-card do I receive. What is this son-in-law of yours—he's a graduate, I know, but is he a President of a Board or a Prime Minister as well? Aren't I the girl's own uncle, and entitled to a stool at your party? Very well," he concluded, "if they're so ready to ignore my existence, I'll go and stir them up a bit and see how that pleases them."

Thereupon he called together fifty or sixty of his beggars, and took the lot of them along to Chin Lao-ta's house. What a sight—

Hats bursting into flower, shirts tied up in knots,
A rag of old matting or a strip of worn rug, a bamboo stick and a
  rough chipped bowl.

Shouting "Father!" shouting "Mother!" shouting "Benefactor!" what
  a commotion before the gate!
Writhing snakes, yapping dogs, chattering apes and monkeys, what
  sly cunning they all display!
Beating clappers, singing "Yang Hua," [6] *the clamour deafens the ear;*
Clattering tiles, faces white with chalk, [7] *the sight offends the eye.*
A troop of rowdies banded together, not Chung K'uei [8] *himself could*
  contain them.

When Chin Lao-ta heard the noise they made he opened the gate to look out, whereupon the whole crowd of beggars, with Scabby at their head, surged inside and threw the house into commotion. Scabby himself hurried to a seat, snatched the choicest of the meats and wines and began to stuff himself, calling meanwhile for the happy couple to come and make their obeisances before their uncle.

So terrified were the assembled graduates that they gave up at once and fled the scene, Mo Chi joining in their retreat. Chin Lao-ta was at his wits' end, and pleaded repeatedly, "My son-in-law is the host today, this is no affair of mine. Come another day when I will buy in some wine specially for you and we will have a chat together." He distributed money among the beggar band, and brought out two jars of fine wine and some live chickens and geese, inviting the beggars to have a banquet of their own over at Scabby's house; but it was late at night before they ceased their rioting and took their leave, and Jade Slave wept in her room from shame and rage.

That night Mo Chi stayed at the house of a friend, returning only when morning came. At the sight of his son-in-law, Chin Lao-ta felt keenly the disgrace of what had happened, and his face filled with shame. Naturally enough, Mo Chi on his part was strongly displeased; but no one was anxious to say a word. Truly,

> *When a mute tastes the bitterness of cork-tree wood*
> *He must swallow his disgust with his medicine.*

Let us rather tell how Jade Slave, conscious of her family's disrepute and anxious that her husband should make his own name for himself, exhorted him to labour at his books. She grudged neither the cost of the works, classical and recent, which she bought for his use, nor the expense of engaging tutors for learned discussion with him. She provided funds also for the entertaining that would widen her husband's circle of acquaintances. As a result, Mo Chi's learning and reputation made daily advances.

He gained his master's degree at the age of twenty-two, and ultimately

---

6. *"Yang Hua,"* a song sung by beggars in ancient China. 7. *faces . . . chalk,* a ruse for feigning poverty and hunger. 8. *Chung K'uei,* in Chinese mythology a slayer of demons whose image was displayed to repel evil spirits.

his doctorate, and at last the day came when he left the great reception for successful candidates and, black hat, doctor's robes and all, rode back to his father-in-law's house. But as he entered his own ward of the city a crowd of urchins pressed about him, pointing and calling—"Look at the tramp-major's son-in-law! He's an official now!"

From his elevated position Mo Chi heard them, but it was beneath his dignity to do anything about it. He simply had to put up with it; but his correct observance of etiquette on greeting his father-in-law concealed a burning indignation. "I always knew that I should attain these honours," he said to himself, "yet I feared that no noble or distinguished family would take me in as a son-in-law, and so I married the daughter of a tramp-major. Without question, it is a lifelong stain. My sons and daughters will still have a tramp-major for their grandfather, and I shall be passed from one man to the next as a laughing stock! But the thing is done now. What is more, my wife is wise and virtuous, it would be impossible for me to divorce her on any of the seven counts.[9] Marry in haste, repent at leisure—it's a true saying after all!"

His mind seethed with such thoughts, and he was miserable all day long. Jade Slave often questioned him, but received no reply and remained in ignorance of the cause of his displeasure. But what an absurd figure, this Mo Chi! Conscious only of his present eminence, he has forgotten the days of his poverty. His wife's assistance in money and effort are one with the snows of yesteryear, so crooked are the workings of his mind.

Before long, Mo Chi presented himself for appointment and received the post of Census Officer at Wu-wei-chün. His father-in-law provided wine to feast his departure, and this time awe of the new official deterred the beggar band from breaking up the party.

It so happened that the whole journey from Hangchow to Wu-wei-chün was by water, and Mo Chi took his wife with him, boarded a junk and proceeded to his post. After several days their voyage brought them to the eddies and whirlpools below the Coloured Stone Cliff,[10] and they tied up to the northern bank. That night the moon shone bright as day. Mo Chi, unable to sleep, rose and dressed and sat in the prow enjoying the moonlight. There was no one about; and as he sat there brooding on his relationship with a tramp-major an evil notion came into his head. The only way for him to be rid of life-long disgrace was for his wife to die and a new one to take her place. A plan formed in his mind. He entered the cabin and inveigled Jade Slave into getting up to see the moon in its glory.

---

9. *seven counts.* In ancient China a husband could divorce his wife for one of the following seven counts: adultery, failure to bear a son, disobedience to her in-laws, nagging, stealing, jealousy, or contracting a contagious disease. 10. *Coloured Stone Cliff.* According to legend the poet Li Po (page 23) was drowned here when he plunged into the water to embrace the reflection of the moon.

Jade Slave was already asleep, but Mo Chi repeatedly urged her to get up, and she did not like to contravene his wishes. She put on her gown and crossed over to the doorway, where she raised her head to look at the moon. Standing thus, she was taken unawares by Mo Chi, who dragged her out on to the prow and pushed her into the river.

Softly he then woke the boatmen and ordered them to get under way at once—extra speed would be handsomely rewarded. The boatmen, puzzled but ignorant, seized pole and flourished oar. Mo Chi waited until the junk had covered three good miles before he moored again and told them that his wife had fallen in the river while gazing at the moon, and that no effort would have availed to save her. With this, he rewarded the boatmen with three ounces of silver to buy wine. The boatmen caught his meaning, but none dared open his mouth. The silly maidservants who had accompanied Jade Slave on board accepted that their mistress had really fallen in the river. They wept for a little while and then left off, and we will say no more of them. There is a verse in evidence of all this:

> *The name of tramp-major pleases him ill;*
> *Hardened by pride he casts off his mate.*
> *The ties of Heaven are not easily broken;*
> *All he gains is an evil name.*

But don't you agree that "there is such a thing as coincidence"? It so happened that the newly-appointed Transport Commissioner for Western Huai, Hsü Te-hou, was also on his way to his post; and his junk moored across from the Coloured Stone Cliff just when Mo Chi's boat had disappeared from view. It was the very spot where Mo Chi had pushed his wife into the water. Hsü Te-hou and his lady had opened their window to enjoy the moonlight, and had not yet retired but were taking their ease over a cup of wine. Suddenly they became aware of someone sobbing on the river bank. It was a woman, from the sound, and her distress could not be ignored.

At once Hsü ordered his boatmen to investigate. It proved indeed to be a woman, alone, sitting on the bank. Hsü made them summon her aboard, and questioned her about herself. The woman was none other than Jade Slave, Madam Chin, the wife of the Census Officer at Wu-wei-chün. What had happened was that when she found herself in the water her wits all but left her, and she gave herself up for dead. But suddenly she felt something in the river which held up her feet, while the waves washed her close to the bank. Jade Slave struggled ashore; but when she opened her eyes, there was only the empty expanse of the river, and no sign of the Census Officer's junk. It was then that she realized what had happened: "My husband, grown rich, has forgotten his days of hardship. It was his deliberate plan to drown his true wife to pave the way for a more advantageous marriage. And now, though I have my life, where am I to turn for support?"

Bitter reflections of this kind brought forth piteous weeping, and confronted by Hsü's questioning she could hold nothing back, but told the whole story from beginning to end. When she had finished she wept without ceasing. Hsü and his wife in their turn were moved to tears, and Hsü Te-hou tried to comfort her: "You must not grieve so; but if you will agree to become my adopted daughter, we will see what provision can be made."

Hsü had his wife produce a complete change of clothing for the girl and settle her down to rest in the stern cabin. He told his servants to treat her with the respect due to his daughter, and prohibited the boatmen from disclosing anything of the affair. Before long he reached his place of office in Western Huai. Now it so happened that among the places under his jurisdiction was Wu-wei-chün. He was therefore the superior officer of Mo Chi, who duly appeared with his fellows to greet the new Commissioner. Observing the Census Officer, Hsü sighed that so promising a youth should be capable of so callous an action.

Hsü Te-hou allowed several months to pass, and then he addressed the following words to his staff: "I have a daughter of marriageable age, and possessing both talent and beauty. I am seeking a man fit to be her husband, whom I could take into my family. Does any of you know of such a man?"

All his staff had heard of Mo Chi's bereavement early in life, and all hastened to commend his outstanding ability and to profess his suitability as a son-in-law for the Commissioner. Hsü agreed: "I myself have had this man in mind for some time. But one who has graduated at such a youthful age must cherish high ambitions: I am not at all sure that he would be prepared to enter my family."

"He is of humble origin," the others replied. "It would be the happiest of fates for him to secure your interest, to 'cling as the creeper to the tree of jade'—there can be no doubt of his willingness."

"Since you consider it practicable," said Hsü, "I should like you to approach the Census Officer. But to discover how he reacts, say that this plan is of your own making: it might hinder matters if you disclose my interest."

They accepted the commission and made their approach to Mo Chi, requesting that they should act as go-betweens. Now to rise in society was precisely Mo Chi's intention; moreover, a matrimonial alliance with one's superior officer was not a thing to be had for the asking. Delighted, he replied, "I must rely entirely on you to accomplish this; nor shall I be slow in the material expression of my gratitude."

"You may leave it to us," they said; and thereupon they reported back to Hsü.

But Hsü demurred: "The Census Officer may be willing to marry her," said he, "but the fact is that my wife and I have doted on our daughter and have brought her up to expect the tenderest consideration. It is for this reason that we wish her to remain in her own home after marriage. But I suspect that the Census Officer, in the impatience of youth, might prove insufficiently tolerant; and if the slightest discord should arise it would be most painful to my wife and myself. He must be prepared to be patient in all things, before I can accept him into my family."

They bore these words to Mo Chi, who accepted every condition.

The Census Officer's present circumstances were very different from those of his student days. He signified acceptance of the betrothal by sending fine silks and gold ornaments on the most ample scale. An auspicious date was selected, and Mo Chi itched in his very bones as he awaited the day when he should become the son-in-law of the Transport Commissioner.

But let us rather tell how Hsü Te-hou gave his wife instructions to prepare Jade Slave for her marriage. "Your step-father," Mrs. Hsü said to her, "moved by pity for you in your widowhood, wishes to invite a young man who has gained his doctorate to become your husband and enter our family. You must not refuse him."

But Jade Slave replied, "Though of humble family, I am aware of the rules of conduct. When Mo Chi became my husband I vowed to remain faithful to him all my life. However cruel and lawless he may have been, however shamefully he may have rejected the companion of his poverty, I shall fulfil my obligations. On no account will I forsake the true virtue of womanhood by remarrying."

With these words her tears fell like rain. Mrs. Hsü, convinced of her sincerity, decided to tell her the truth, and said, "The young graduate of whom my husband spoke is none other than Mo Chi himself. Appalled by his mean action, and anxious to see you reunited with him, my husband passed you off as his own daughter, and told the members of his staff that he was seeking a son-in-law who would enter our family. He made them approach Mo Chi, who was delighted by the proposal. He is to come to us this very night; but when he enters your room, this is what you must do to get your own back. . . ."

As she disclosed her plan, Jade Slave dried her tears. She remade her face and changed her costume, and made preparations for the coming ceremony.

With evening there duly appeared the Census Officer Mo Chi, all complete with mandarin's hat and girdle: he was dressed in red brocade and had gold ornaments in his cap, under him was a fine steed with decorated saddle and before him marched two bands of drummers and musicians. His colleagues were there in force to see him married, and the whole procession was cheered the length of the route. Indeed,

To the roll and clang of music the white steed advances,
But what a curious person, this fine upstanding groom:
Delighted with his change of families, beggar for man of rank,
For memories of the Coloured Stone Cliff his glad heart has no room.

That night the official residence of the Transport Commissioner was festooned with flowers and carpeted, and to the playing of pipe and drum all awaited the arrival of the bridegroom. As the Census Officer rode up to the gate and dismounted, Hsü Te-hou came out to receive him, and then the accompanying junior officers took their leave. Mo Chi walked straight through to the private apartments, where the bride was brought out to him, veiled in red and supported by a maidservant on either side. From beyond the threshold the master of ceremonies took them through the ritual. The happy pair made obeisances to heaven and earth and to the parents of the bride; and when the ceremonial observances were over, they were escorted into the nuptial chamber for the wedding feast. By this time Mo Chi was in a state of indescribable bliss, his soul somewhere above the clouds. Head erect, triumphant, he entered the nuptial chamber.

But no sooner had he passed the doorway than from positions of conceal-ment on either side there suddenly emerged seven or eight young maids and old nannies, each one armed with a light or heavy bamboo. Mercilessly they began to beat him. Off came his silk hat; blows fell like rain on his shoulders; he yelled perpetually, but try as he might he could not get out of the way.

Under the beating the Census Officer collapsed, to lie in a terrified heap on the floor, calling on his parents-in-law to save him. Then he heard, from within the room itself, a gentle command issued in the softest of voices: "Beat him no more, our hard-hearted young gentleman, but bring him before me."

At last the beating stopped, and the maids and nannies, tugging at his ears and dragging at his arms like the six senses [11] tormenting Amida Buddha [12] in the parable, hauled him, his feet barely touching the ground, before the presence of the bride. "What is the nature of my offence?" the Census Officer was mumbling; but when he opened his eyes, there above him, correct and upright in the brilliance of the candlelight, was seated the bride—who was none other than his former wife, Jade Slave, Madam Chin.

Now Mo Chi's mind reeled, and he bawled, "It's a ghost! It's a ghost!" All began to laugh, until Hsü Te-hou came in from outside and addressed

11. *six senses,* literally, "six robbers": sight, hearing, smell, taste, touch, and thought.
12. *Amida Buddha,* the great protector of mankind; a Buddha of the Mahayana sect, a later form of Buddhism developed in India in the second century A.D. and surviving in China and Japan.

him: "Do not be alarmed, my boy: this is no ghost, but my adopted daughter, who came to me below the Coloured Stone Cliff."

Mo Chi's heart ceased its pounding. He fell to his knees and folded his hands in supplication. "I, Mo Chi, confess my crime," he said. "I only beg your forgiveness."

"This is no affair of mine," replied Hsü, "unless my daughter has something to say. . . ."

Jade Slave spat in Mo Chi's face and cursed him: "Cruel wretch! Did you never think of the words of Sung Hung? 'Do not exclude from your mind the friends of your poverty, nor from your house the wife of your youth.' It was empty-handed that you first came into my family, and thanks to our money that you were able to study and enter society, to make your name and enjoy your present good fortune. For my part, I looked forward to the day when I should share in your glory. But you—forgetful of the favours you had received, oblivious of our early love, you repaid good with evil and threw me into the river to drown. Heaven took pity on me and sent me a saviour, whose adopted daughter I became. But if I had ended my days on the river-bed, and you had taken a new wife—how could your heart have been so callous? And now, how can I so demean myself as to rejoin you?"

Her speech ended in tears and loud wails, and "Cruel, cruel!" she continued to cry. Mo Chi's whole face expressed his shame. He could find no words, but pleaded for forgiveness by kotowing before her. Hsü Te-hou, satisfied with her demonstration of anger, raised Mo Chi to his feet and admonished Jade Slave in the following words: "Calm your anger, my child. Your husband has now repented his crime, and we may be sure that he will never again treat you ill. Although in fact your marriage took place some years ago, so far as my family is concerned you are newly-wed; in all things, therefore, show consideration to me, and let an end be made here and now to recriminations." Turning to Mo Chi, he said, "My son, your crime is upon your own head, lay no blame on others. Tonight I ask you only to show tolerance. I will send your mother-in-law to make peace between you."

He left the room, and shortly his wife came in to them. Much mediation was required from her before the two were finally brought into accord.

On the following day Hsü Te-hou gave a banquet for his new son-in-law, during which he returned all the betrothal gifts, the fine silks and gold ornaments, saying to Mo Chi, "One bride may not receive two sets of presents. You took such things as these to the Chin family on the previous occasion, I cannot accept them all over again now." Mo Chi lowered his head and said nothing, and Hsü went on: "I believe it was your dislike of the lowly status of your father-in-law which put an end to your love and almost to your marriage. What do you think now of my own position? I am only afraid that the rank I hold may still be too low for your aspirations."

Mo Chi's face flushed crimson, and he was obliged to retire a few steps and acknowledge his errors. There is a verse to bear witness:

> *Full of fond hopes of bettering himself by marriage,*
> *Amazed to discover his bride to be his wife;*
> *A beating, a cursing, an overwhelming shame:*
> *Was it really worth it for a change of in-laws?*

From this time on, Mo Chi and Jade Slave lived together twice as amicably as before. Hsü Te-hou and his wife treated Jade Slave as their own daughter and Mo Chi as their proper son-in-law, and Jade Slave behaved towards them exactly as though they were her own parents. Even the heart of Mo Chi was touched, so that he received Chin Lao-ta, the tramp-major, into his official residence and cared for him to the end of his days. And when in the fullness of time Hsü Te-hou and his wife died, Jade Slave, Madam Chin, wore the heaviest mourning of coarse linen for each of them in recompense for their kindness to her; and generations of descendants of Mo and of Hsü regarded each other as cousins and never failed in friendship. A verse concludes:

> *Sung Hung remained faithful and was praised for his virtue;* [13]
> *Huang Yün divorced his wife and was reviled for lack of feeling.* [14]
> *Observe the case of Mo Chi, remarrying his wife:*
> *A marriage is predestined: no objection can prevail.* ✳

---

13. *Sung Hung . . . virtue.* In 26 A.D. Sung Hung was made a marquis by Emperor Kwang Wu. He nobly rejected the royal command to abandon his wife, who was a commoner, and marry a princess. 14. *Huang Yün . . . feeling.* During the Later Han dynasty (25–220), Huang Yün, a man famous for his genius, divorced his wife to marry the niece of a man of high station. His wife, in return, destroyed his career by giving a party at which she recounted his infamy.

Lao Shê [1] (1899–1966)

THE LAST TRAIN

Edited and translated from the Chinese by
Yuan Chia-hua and Robert Payne

THE TRAIN STARTED a long while ago, and now the wheels rumbled mournfully along the rails, the passengers sighed and counted the hours: seven o'clock, eight, nine, ten—by ten o'clock the train would arrive, and they would be home around midnight. It might not be too late, for the children might already be put to bed. It was New Year's Day, and they were all in a hurry to get home. They looked at the cans, the fruit and the toys heaped up on the shelves, and already they could hear the children crying "Papa, papa!" and thinking of all this, they lost themselves in their thoughts; but there were others who were well aware that they would not be home before daybreak. They studied their fellow passengers, and to their consternation they discovered that there was not a single soul with whom they could claim the faintest acquaintance. When they reached home it would already be the New Year! And there were others who cursed the train, because it was moving only at a snail's pace, and though they remained physically in the carriage, smoking, sipping tea, yawning, pressing their noses to the windowglass and seeing there only an unfathomable abyss of darkness outside, they were really not in the carriage at all —they had been home and returned a hundred times since the train left the station. And now they lowered their heads and yawned to conceal the tears in their eyes.

There were not many passengers in the second-class carriage. There was fat Mr. Chang and thin Mr. Chiao, and they sat in the same compartment opposite one another. Whenever they got up, they spread their blankets over their seats to show that intruders would not be welcomed. When the train started they found to their surprise that there were very few passengers indeed, and somehow this led them more than ever to feel grieved at the thought that they were travelling in a train on Christmas

"The Last Train" by Lao Shê, translated by Yuan Chia-hua and Robert Payne from CONTEMPORARY CHINESE SHORT STORIES. Reprinted by permission of Royle Publications Limited.
1. *Lao Shê* (lou shə).

New Year Day.[2] There were other similarities between the two passengers: they were both holding free passes, and both of them had been unable to obtain the pass until the previous day, and they therefore agreed that a man who could give free passes at his will had a perfect right to annoy bona fide travellers by keeping them to the last moment. They were both indignant at this treatment, for in the good old days friends were made of sterner stuff, and so they shook their heads and put the blame on these so-called friends who had prevented them from reaching their homes before the New Year's Day.

Old Mr. Chang removed his fox-fur coat and tucked his legs under his body, but he discovered that the seat was too narrow for sitting comfortably in this posture. Meanwhile, the temperature of the carriage rose and beads of perspiration began to roll down his brow. "Boy, towels!" he shouted, and then to Mr. Chiao he said: "I wonder why they turn so much heat on nowadays." He gasped. "It wouldn't be so hot if we were travelling on an aeroplane."

Old Mr. Chiao had taken off his coat a long while ago, and now he was wearing a robe lined with white sheep's fur, and over that a sleeveless jacket of shining black satin. He showed no sign of feeling faint. He said: "One can get a free pass on an aeroplane, too. It isn't difficult." And he drawled off with a faint smile.

"It's better not to risk travelling by air," Old Mr. Chang said, trying hard to keep his crossed legs under him, but succeeding only with great difficulty. "Boy, towels!"

The "boy" was over forty, and his neck was as thin as a stick, so thin that one imagined that it was quite easy to pluck off his head and plant it back again. You could see him hurrying backwards and forwards along the passageway, his hands full of steaming towels. He was always eager to serve, but really—the way the management made you work on such a sacred day—it was really inconceivable. When he reached the compartment in front, he found Little Tsui and vented his injured feelings on him. "Listen to this! I was on duty on the twenty-seventh and twenty-eighth, and I counted on having today free. Well, at the last moment Mr. Liu comes to me and says, 'Look here, you'll have to have a run on New Year's Day'—that's what he says. There are sixty boys working on this line, and they have to pick on me. I don't care a damn about New Year's Day, but it's lousy all the same!" And saying this, he craned his neck in the direction of fat Mr. Chang, but he remained exactly where he was, and untwining the twisted towels, he offered one of them to Little Tsui. "Have one," he said, and went on with his complaint. "I told Mr. Liu that I didn't care about New Year's Day, but he must understand that it was my turn to

---

2. *Christmas New Year Day*, the New Year of the Gregorian calendar as opposed to the one of the Chinese.

be off duty that evening. I said I had been working the whole year and ought to have a day off." He gulped something down his throat, and his Adam's apple floated up like the bubbles in water when a bottle is suddenly turned upside down. He was so choked that he could not speak for a few moments. "I'm fed up with it all—everything's all wrong nowadays."

From the pale yellow face of Little Tsui something like a smile flowered out. He wanted to incline his head a little to demonstrate his sympathy, but for some reason he found himself unable to do this. He had his own difficulties. Everyone on the railway knew him—even the stationmasters and the mechanics. They were all his friends. His pale yellow face was equivalent to a second-class ticket: the Ministry of Transport itself would not dare to dispute its validity. And everyone knew that he always travelled with one or two hundred ounces of opium in his luggage, and everyone admitted that he was entitled to do this. At the same time Little Tsui was careful never to intimidate anybody, nor to be partial in the distribution of his favours, for fear of arousing people's jealousy, and he understood their sorrows perfectly well and wished to show his sympathy. Because he offended no one, he was afraid of no one; and this, the supreme wisdom of life, could be read on his ticket—or rather, on his face.

"We're all so busy," he complained, hoping in some way that a recital of his troubles would benefit the "boy." And he went on to say that he had had to take this trip entirely against his will, he would have much preferred to remain comfortably at home, but on the very next day he would have to meet a blood-sucking girl who would take all his money away. He smiled, showing darkened teeth, and puffing out his cheeks he spat on the floor.

What he had said began to tell on the "boy," who seemed to be forgetting his own sorrows and nodding appreciatively. The towels in his hand had grown cold and he returned to his cabin to resoak them in water. When he emerged, he passed Little Tsui without saying a word and without looking at him, closing his eyes languidly as though to show that he had not forgotten the injuries done to him in spite of Little Tsui's consolations. Taking advantage of the rocking movement of the train, he swung his body towards a certain Mr. K'ou. "Like a towel, sir? It's trying to travel at this time of the year." He would have liked to vent his feelings on a new audience, but since he did not know Mr. K'ou very well, he went about it in as circuitous a manner as possible.

Mr. K'ou was dressed with considerable éclat. He wore a dark serge overcoat with a beaver collar, with a brand new black satin, melon-shaped hat. He had removed neither his coat nor his hat, and he sat there as rigid as a chairman on a platform waiting solemnly for the moment when he would address a huge audience. He took the towel, stretching out his arm at full length, and taking care not to fold his elbow he described a semicircle with the towel until it reached his face. Then he rubbed his face fastidiously and ostentatiously. When his face emerged from the whirling cloud of the towel it dazzled and lent to his person a renewed splendour and dignity. He nodded to the "boy," without explaining why he was travelling on New Year's Day.

"It's a bad thing—being a waiter," the "boy" said, reluctant to let Mr. K'ou go as easily as that. He knew that it would be inadvisable to repeat what he had said to Little Tsui. It would be necessary to talk with measured deliberation in order to seem both reverent and intimate. "People ought to rest on New Year's Day," he continued, "but there is no rest for us. We can do nothing." And taking back the used towel: "Another one, sir?"

Mr. K'ou shook his head. It was now clear that he was almost touched by the "boy's" misfortunes, but would rather not enter into any conversation. Everyone on the line knew that he was a friend of the manager, and it was his privilege to enjoy a free ride in a second-class carriage any time he pleased. He had only to show his identity, and he could do this by not entering into desultory conversations with a waiter.

And meanwhile the waiter was at a loss to understand why Mr. K'ou had been shaking his head; but he could do nothing, for he knew perfectly well that the man was a friend of the manager. The carriage began to rock again, and the movement of the carriage hurled him into the passageway. Steadying himself, he untwisted a towel and holding it delicately by two corners he offered it to Mr. Chang. "Would you like one, sir?" and the man reached out for it, his thick palm touching the central part of it, which was the hottest. He pressed it to his face, rubbing hard as though he were cleaning a mirror. Then he handed another one to Mr. Chiao, who showed no enthusiasm, but took the towel and with it proceeded to clean his nostrils and fingernails delicately. When he returned it to the waiter, it was all greasy and black.

"The inspectors will soon be coming now," he began, believing that no policy could be worse than that which introduced a conversation with a recital of his own troubles. He decided upon a flank attack. "When they have gone, you will want to have a rest, and if any of you gentlemen would like a cushion, just let me know." And he went on a little later: "There are not many passengers on board, and you'll all be able to have a nap. It's a pity you gentlemen are spending a day like this on a train, but as for us waiters—" He sighed. He realized that he had been talking too much. He should have discovered in which way the wind was blowing. And he handed Mr. Chang another towel. Mr. Chang found that his toilet was taking up too much of his time, but remembered that he had not wiped his hair, which had only recently been cut. Although it was just as hard, or even harder, to rub his scalp, he determined that he would go through with the ordeal, and when he had finished he sighed with relief. However, Mr. Chiao declined a second offer, and gently picked his teeth with his now-clean fingernails.

"What's wrong with the heating system?" Mr. Chang asked, as he tossed back the towel.

"I wouldn't advise you to open the window," the waiter answered. "Nine to ten you'll catch cold. The railway is under a rotten management." The chance lay wide open for him, and he entered quickly. "They make you work all the year round, and don't even let you rest on New Year's Day. Well, all talking is vain."

And so it was, for the train had drawn into a small wayside station.

From the third-class carriages a few passengers stepped down with their bags and baskets, and hurried towards the exit. Some of them stopped and hesitated, as though they were wondering whether they had left anything on the train. Those who remained in the train pressed their noses on the windowpane and looked out, their faces wearing an expression of envy and anxiety. No one in the second-class left the train, but half a dozen soldiers came into the compartment. Their boots thundered on the floor, their leather belts flashed in the light and their luggage consisted of four large cases of fireworks wrapped in scarlet paper and decorated with characters cut out of gold paper. The boxes were so large that for a long time they were undecided what to do with them. Meanwhile, boots crackled, men bustled about, their voices grew louder, and the question where to place the pile of fireworks remained for a long time unsettled. Finally, a man who resembled a battalion commander said that they should be put on the floor. The platoon commander repeated the order, and then all the men bent double and executed the order; afterwards they rose stiffly and clicked their heels. The battalion commander returned the salute and ordered them to dismiss. Boots thundered. A cloud of grey caps, grey uniforms and grey leggings. A moment later someone said: "Hurry!" and they obediently disappeared. A whistle sounded from the train, rather muffled. Lights and shadows flitted about, and the wheels began to rumble and the train to roll out of the station.

The waiter walked from one end of the carriage to the other, looking as though there was something on his mind. He stole a glance at the two soldiers and then at the heap of fireworks which lay so uncompromisingly on the floor, barring his way; but he dare not say anything. He went into a desultory conversation with Little Tsui, harping on the old theme, repeating what he had said a moment before, but adding a more detailed and to him more satisfactory account of his misfortunes. Little Tsui began to talk about his girl friends.

But the waiter was still perturbed by the presence of the fireworks. He left Little Tsui, and resumed his furtive strolling among the compartments. The battalion commander was lying down, tired out, his pistol on the little table at the side of the carriage. The platoon commander had not yet dared to imitate him, but he had removed his cap and was now violently scratching his scalp. The waiter took care not to awaken the senior officer, but he smiled voluminously at the junior. "What was I going to say?" he said in a half-apologetic tone of voice, hesitantly. "Oh yes, I was going to suggest that it might be a better idea to put the crackers up on the shelf."

"Why?" the officer answered, mouth awry with head scratching.

"You know, I was afraid people might step on them," the waiter replied, his head shrinking tortoise-fashion into his shoulders.

"No one would dare to touch them! Why should they touch them?" the officer answered, his little beady eyes askew.

"That's quite all right!" The waiter was all smiles, and his face became smaller as though under the weight of an enormous invisible rock. "It doesn't matter at all. May I know where you are travelling to?"

"If I have any more trouble from you, what about fighting it out?" the officer suddenly shouted. He had been worn thin by the ill-humour of his senior officer, and he was perfectly prepared to fight.

But the waiter was in no need of a fight, and he abruptly disappeared. As he passed Mr. Chang, he said: "The inspectors will be here soon, sir."

Mr. Chang and Mr. Chiao were developing a cordial friendship. The ticket inspection began. There were two inspectors followed by three other men. The first wore a cap with gold braid, was white-skinned, stern, his nose in the air. The second also wore a cap with gold braid, but he was dwarfish, dark, and his face was full of smiles and somehow possessed the power of reconciling all those who were put out by the sternness of the first. As they went through the third-class carriages they pulled long faces, but when they went into the second-class the dwarf inspector was wreathed with smiles, and when they reached the first-class carriages they would both be smiling broadly. The third man was a giant from Tientsin, with a pistol and many rounds of ammunition in his belt. The fourth was a giant from Shantung, and he too carried a belt and a pistol, but he also wore a long sword. And the fifth was the waiter, whose head troubled him—for it was always popping upward and he found the greatest difficulty in maintaining it in its proper position.

The group came to a pause opposite Little Tsui. They all knew him, his pale yellow face and dark teeth, which immediately formed into a smile as between familiar acquaintances. It was an awkward moment.

The first inspector gazed blankly into the distance as though absorbed in meditation; he kept on tapping his ticket-punch gently against his thigh. The second nodded recognition to Little Tsui. The Tientsin giant smiled at him, and immediately afterwards turned off the smile exactly as though he had pressed a switch. The Shantung giant touched the peak of his cap with his hand, and his eloquent eyes seemed to be saying: "I've got a long story to tell you, but wait until all this nonsense is finished." The waiter felt that the inspection had lasted long enough, and as the group moved on he said: "Please sit down. There aren't many passengers —it will be all over in a moment, and then I'll come back to you." Little

Tsui found himself alone, a shadow flitting across his brow. At last he sat down.

The waiter caught them up a little later, but he did not join in their procession. He slipped up to Mr. K'ou. "Mr. K'ou, sir," he said, but the procession leader was slightly irritated by his interference, and giving his hand to Mr. K'ou he said: "How is the manager these days? You know it's late in the year to start on a long journey." Mr. K'ou, his respectability unimpaired and even increased by this encounter, smiled weakly, murmured inaudibly, bowed and smiled again. The two guards stood bolt upright, quite still, feeling that they were outsiders in whatever game was now being employed. Their low positions in life denied them the privilege of entering into the conversation, but they contrived to maintain their dignity by puffing out their chests and standing at attention.

Meanwhile the waiter was taking this opportunity to inform Mr. Chang and Mr. Chiao to get their tickets ready. They gave him their tickets. He was awestruck when he realized that the tickets were free passes, and his reverence for the two gentlemen became even greater than before. He returned Mr. Chang's pass at once, but he ventured to detain Mr. Chiao's for a moment because it was clearly indicated on the pass that the holder was a woman, and there was indisputable evidence that Mr. Chiao was a man. The two inspectors drew apart and began to whisper into each other's ear. A moment later they nodded to one another, and it was clear that they had reached a common understanding that on New Year's Day a man might pass for a woman. The waiter returned Mr. Chiao's ticket with both hands, apologetically.

The battalion commander was now snoring. As soon as he noticed the arrival of the inspectors, the platoon commander put his legs up on the seat and showed every sign of an unwillingness to be disturbed. The inspectors' attention was immediately arrested by the pile of fireworks which littered the passageway. The Shantung giant nodded in admiration, overcome by the length and the solidity of the fireworks. And they passed through the compartment, and it was not until the first inspector reached the door that he turned to the waiter and said: "You'd better tell them to put the fireworks on the shelves," and in order to save the waiter from further embarrassment the second inspector added quickly: "Better still if you did it for them." The waiter nodded his thin neck like a pendulum without saying anything, but all the while he was asking himself: "You haven't the courage to tell them—that's what it is—so what can I do except nod my head?—and besides, there is a great difference between nodding and doing." The truth dawned on his mind. The fireworks must *not* be moved.

When he returned to Little Tsui, he was surprised to find the little fellow sunk in misery and knew at once that he was in need of a cup of water. Without saying anything he brought along the kettle. Little Tsui took something from his pocket—the waiter did not see it, but dimly suspected that it was opium—and pressed it into his left palm with the ball of his thumb, grinning, his face so pale that it resembled paper. He was almost perspiring and something like a faint vapour was rising from his face, which was glazed like an onion in a hothouse. Then he covered his mouth with his cupped hand, and the fingers began to wave in gentle undulations. He closed his eyes, took a sip from the cup and puffed out his cheeks. Afterwards his eyes opened, and an indubitable smile floated over his pale yellow face.

"It's more important than food," Little Tsui said wonderingly.

"Oh yes, far more important," the waiter nodded.

Go-home-go-home-go-home-go-home. The wheels roared in chorus. But they were very slow. The star-strewn sky undulated. Hills, trees, villages, graves, flashed past in clusters. The train dashed on and on in the darkness. Smoke, soot and sparks shot up furiously, and then disappeared. The train ran on, flying breathlessly, one patch of darkness following on another. A stretch of snow and a string of low mounds glowed and darkened and were gone. Go-home-go-home-go-home. The lights were ablaze, the temperature steaming, all the passengers were weary to death, and not one was inclined to sleep. Go-home-go-home-go-home. The farewell rites to the Old Year, the libations to the gods, the offerings to the Ancestors, the writing on the spring scrolls, the firecrackers, the dumplings, the sweetmeats, the dinners and the wine—all these became suddenly very real to them, filling their eyes and their ears, their palates and their nostrils. A smile would light upon their lips and instantly disappear, dying away at the recollection that they were still physically in the train. Go-home-go-home-go-home-go-home. Darkness, darkness, darkness. The starry sky undulated. Patches of snowy ground rose and fell. No human sounds, no traffic, nothing visible. Darkness endlessly receding, an interminable road tightly hugging the brightly lit train which struggled furiously to tear itself away from the menace of the surrounding darkness. And yet the darkness never forsook the train. Go-home-go-home-go-home . . .

Mr. Chang took down from the shelf two bottles of distilled wine, and said to Mr. Chiao: "We're just like old friends now. How about a drop of this? We might as well enjoy New Year's Day—no reason why we shouldn't enjoy ourselves." He handed over a cup of the wine. "Real Yinkow wine. Twenty years old. You can't get it on the market. Bottoms up."

Mr. Chiao was too polite to refuse. He asked himself what he should offer Mr. Chang in return, and all the time he kept his eyes fixed on the cup, and his hands were fidgeting. He reached up to the shelf, took down a large parcel, gently unwrapped it and revealed a number of smaller parcels. He pinched them one by one, and finally removed the three parcels which he felt sure contained dried lichees,[3] preserved dates and spiced

---

3. *lichee*, an Asian fruit which is sweet and jellylike.

bean-curd. He then unwrapped them and offered them to Mr. Chang. "We're like old friends. Don't stand on any ceremony."

Mr. Chang picked a lichee, which burst under the pressure of his fingers. The sound amused him. It was an appropriate sound, reminiscent of New Year's Day. He watched Mr. Chiao sipping the wine and, waiting till his friend had swallowed it all, he asked: "Well, how do you like the stuff?"

"Marvellous!" Mr. Chiao wetted his lips. "Marvellous! Nothing like it anywhere."

They filled up one another's cups, and slowly and imperceptibly their faces turned crimson. Their tongues were unloosened. They talked of their families, their jobs, their friends, the difficulty of earning money, free passes. Their cups clinked, their hearts clinked, their eyes moistened, they were permeated with warmth. It was time for one of them to be generous. Mr. Chiao unwrapped another parcel which contained preserved oranges. Mr. Chang looked at the two remaining bottles and said: "Well, we'll have to finish them. One each. Mustn't leave a drop. We're old friends now. Come on. Bottoms up!"

"I'm not very good at drinking."

"Nonsense. Twenty years old. Mellow. Won't make you drunk. It's God's will that we should become friends. Drink up!"

Mr. Chiao was profoundly honoured. Mr. Chang looked at his bottle—there was not very much left now. He untied his collar. Beads of perspiration stood out on his brow; his eyes were bloodshot and his tongue was stiff. Though still talkative, his talk was reduced to mere babbling; he had not yet completely lost his self-control, he could still put a curb on the curious inner urge which nearly led him to curse in front of his new-found friend, and the resultant of these forces took the form, not of a quarrel, or incivility, but rather of exultation and gaiety. Mr. Chiao, on the other hand, had been able to stomach only half of the bottle assigned to him, but his face was already turning deathly pale. He produced a packet of cigarettes and threw one at Mr. Chang. Both lit their cigarettes. Cigarette in mouth, Mr. Chang reclined along the seat, his legs dangling nonchalantly. He itched to sing, but his throat was scorched and hoarse, and he breathed heavily through his nose like an angry bull. Mr. Chiao also leaned back, cigarette in hand, his eyes fixed on the legs of the seat opposite him, his heart beating wildly. He hiccoughed. His face was pale, and he felt a faint itching all over his body.

Go-home-go-home-go-home-go-home. In Mr. Chang's ears the wheels sounded as though they were going at breakneck speed. His heart beat fast, and suddenly everything began buzzing. His head turned round and round in the air, buzzing like a fly. All objects were dancing and glowing in red circles. When the buzzing ceased, his heart once more began to beat at its accustomed ritual, and he opened his eyes slightly, partially regaining his strength. He pretended that nothing had happened, and groping for the matchbox he relit his extinguished cigarette. Then he threw the match away. Suddenly on the table a greenish flame flared up, smelling of alcohol, spinning among the cups and bottles, fluttering, rising, spreading out. Mr. Chiao was startled out of his dreams as the cigarette which he held in his hand suddenly caught fire. He threw it away. He beat the table with both hands to extinguish the fire, and in doing this he knocked down the cups and bottles. Iridescent tongues licked the unopened parcels. Mr. Chang's face was hidden in flames. Mr. Chiao thought of running away. The flames on the table soared up, and the parcels on the shelf above seemed to reach down to catch the rising columns of flames. Flame linked with flame. Mr. Chiao himself was ablaze. The fire reached his eyebrows, charring them, snapping at his hair, which sizzled, lighting up the alcohol on his lips and turning him into a fire-breathing monster.

Suddenly: pop, pop, pop . . . It sounded like machine-gun fire. The platoon commander had hardly opened his eyes when a cracker exploded on his nose and sent sparks and blood flying in fine sprays. He rose, and began frantically running. There were explosions everywhere, under his feet, all round his body. The noise was deafening as though they had stepped on a land mine. The battalion commander was swallowed up in the fire before he could open his eyes. He was trying to open his eyes when the right eye received a direct hit from one of the exploding crackers.

Mr. K'ou started up. He cast a quick glance at his luggage on the shelf. Some of the parcels were already burning, and the fire was closing in from all sides—from above, from below, and even from a long way away. Flames licked at him, and an idea flashed through his mind. He picked up one of his shoes from the floor and smote at the windowpane. He wanted to jump out of the window. The glass was broken, a gale rushed in, the fire turned wild. His collar of beaver skin, the four bedrolls, the five boxes, his clothes—they were all swallowed up in the flames. The train ran on, the wind was roaring, the firecrackers kept going off. Mr. K'ou ran like a wild animal.

Little Tsui was a seasoned traveller. He had heard the sounds, but he was too lazy to open his eyes. The fire finally reached his feet and spread along his body. He felt hot, and sat up. He saw nothing but smoke and fire. The crackers continued to explode, the opium which he carried on his body began to melt and burn. The delicious smell assailed his nostrils. He felt a scorching heat. His legs could not move. The fire spread over his chest. His huddled body was wrapped in flames, a gigantic bubbling ball of opium paste, until it was reduced to the shape of a cocoon.

So Little Tsui stirred no more. Mr. Chang was dead-drunk, and he lay there like a log. Mr. Chiao, Mr. K'ou and the platoon commander were running about in all directions, stark staring mad. The battalion commander knelt on the bench and wailed. The fire had already penetrated every corner of the carriage; the smell of sulphur was suffocating. The crackers were no longer exploding—they had all been burnt. The noise died away, but the smoke grew thicker. And at last those who were running about no longer ran about, and those who were wailing no longer wailed. The fire began to devour the furniture. The train kept darting forward, the wind kept roaring. Red tongues of flame struggled within the dense clouds of smoke, hoping for an outlet. The smoke turned milky, and the flames began to thrash at the windows. The whole carriage was transparent with light, and tongues of fire streamed away like streamers, a thousand torches burning brightly in the wind.

The train slowed down as it drew near a small station, but it did not stop. The trackman turned the lever and said to himself: "Fire!" The signalman flashed his green lamp and said to himself: "Fire!" The guards stood at attention and said to themselves: "Fire!" The stationmaster was late in arriving, and when he arrived the train had already left, but he saw dimly in his half-drunken stupor that there was a train on fire, and preferred to believe that it was an hallucination. The signalman blew out his lamp, the trackman shifted the lever back by which the rails resumed their normal position; the guards returned with their rifles to their recreation quarters, and each of them retained in his mind a picture of the fire, and yet not one of them was inclined to admit that he had seen it. Gradually the idea of the fire died away in their minds, and they were concerned only about how they could enjoy the festival. They lit firecrackers, drank, played mahjong. Everything was right with the world.

As the train left the station, it gained speed. The wind howled, and the fire crackled. Brilliant rockets shot out in sprays. The night was dark and the train was a chain of lanterns pouring out licking flames. Of the second-class carriage, only a charred skeleton remained. The flames, having nothing to feed on, moved backwards and forwards, and finally entered the third-class carriage. Smoke came first, sending out a pungent, and slightly sweet smell of charred flesh and furniture. Fire followed. "Fire! Fire! Fire!" Everyone was shouting in fearful panic. They lost their heads. They broke the windows in an attempt to leap out, and then hesitated. Some began to run, and then they would fall against one another and fall down. Some sat transfixed to their seats, unable even to cry. Turbulence. Panic. Every effort proved vain. They howled, folded their arms round their heads, beat off the flames with their clothes, ran, jumped out of the carriage. . . .

The fire had discovered a new colony, with rich resources and a great population. It was mad with joy. It licked out with one of its tongues, pawed with another, hid a third in the smoke, and suddenly thrust a fourth through the window. A fifth wandered without any fixed goal. It was the sixth which joined all the others together. Hundreds of flames began dancing in the most fantastic patterns. They rolled themselves up into balls, shot out like meteors, gathered in red-and-green pools of fire. They glowed, dwindled, crept in the wake of the smoke, and then disappeared. Then they burst out of the smoke in torrents. They squeaked and gibbered as they burned human flesh and broiled human hair. The crowd howled, the wind roared, the fire crackled. The whole car was on fire. The smoke was heavy. It was a lovely cremation.

The train arrived at the next station, where it was due to stop. It stopped. Signalmen, ticket-inspectors, guards, the stationmaster and the assistant stationmaster, the clerks and the hangers-on all looked at the burning carriages in amazement, and could do nothing, because there were no fire engines and no implements for putting out fires. The second-class carriage, and the two adjacent third-class carriages in front and behind were silent and still. From them a plume of blue smoke curled up—languidly and leisurely.

It was reported later that fifty-two corpses were found on the train, and the bodies of eleven more, who had jumped off and killed themselves, were found along the line.

After the Lantern Festival—that is, fifteen days after the New Year—an inspector arrived. For the first three days he attended official receptions, and had little time to spare for the investigation. The next three days were spent in looking after some personal affairs which could no longer be laid aside. Then the investigation began.

The guard knew nothing. The first inspector knew nothing. The second inspector knew nothing. Neither the Tientsin giant, nor the Shantung giant, nor the waiter, knew anything about the cause of the fire. Reports from the various stations on the number of tickets sold tallied closely with the number of tickets collected, taking into account the sixty-three tickets which were missing. These corresponded exactly with the number of casualties and so must have been burnt. No station reported the sale of second-class tickets; it followed that the second class must have been empty, and therefore the fire could not have started in the second-class carriage.

Finally, the waiter was re-examined. He declared that he knew nothing about the fire, which must have started when he was in the dining-car. The tribunal decided that he was irrevocably wrong, and should be punished for having left his post of duty. And he was duly discharged from the service.

The inspector submitted his report with a detailed account of the tragedy written in the most admirable style.

"I don't care at all," the waiter said to his wife. "They put you on duty on New Year's Day, and then, when everything goes wrong, they think we will be starved if we leave their wretched railway."

"What nonsense!" his wife answered. "I'm not worried about that. What I am worried about is the cabbage that got burnt."   ✳

Lusin (1881-1936)

THE WIDOW

Translated from the Chinese by
Chi-chen Wang

THE YEAR-END according to the old calendar is, after all, more like what a year-end should be, for the holiday spirit is not only reflected in the life of the people, but seems to pervade the atmosphere itself. Frequent flashes light up the heavy, gray evening clouds, followed by the crisp report of firecrackers set off in honor of the Kitchen God.[1] Those fired in the immediate neighborhood explode, of course, with a louder noise, and before the deafening sound has ceased ringing in one's ears, the air is filled with the acrid aroma of sulphuric smoke. On such an evening I returned for a visit to my native village, Luchen. As we no longer had a house there, I stayed with His Honor Lu the Fourth. He was my kin—my Uncle Four, as he was one generation above me—and a very moral and righteous old graduate. He had not changed much since my previous visit; he had grown a little older, but he did not yet have a beard. After we had exchanged greetings, he remarked that I was stouter, and immediately thereafter launched into a tirade against the reform movement. I knew, however, that his tirade was not directed against me but against the ancient reformers of the nineties, such as K'ang Yu-wei. In any case we could not be said to understand each other, and I was left alone in the study shortly afterwards.

I got up very late the next day. After the midday meal I went out to call on friends and relatives. On the third day I did the same thing. None of them had changed much, they were merely a little older. All were busy with the preparations for the Invocation of Blessings, the most solemn and elaborate ceremony of the year, at which they offered the most generous sacrifices to the God of Blessings and prayed for good luck for the coming

---

1. *Kitchen God*, in Chinese mythology a household god who annually reported to heaven the behavior of every member of the family.

year. Chickens and ducks were killed and pork was bought at the butcher's. Carefully washed by women (whose hands and arms—some adorned with silver bracelets—became red from long immersions in the water), and then boiled and studded with chopsticks, they were offered with candles and incense in the early hour of the fifth watch. Only the male members of the family participated in the ceremony, which was always concluded with firecrackers. Every year it was like this in families that could afford it, and so it was this year.

The overcast sky grew darker and darker, and in the afternoon it began to snow. The dancing snowflakes, as large as plum flowers, the smoke from burning incense and from the chimneys, and the bustle of the people all gave Luchen a festive air. When I returned to Uncle Four's study, the rooftops were white, making the room lighter than usual at that hour. I could make out very clearly the large shou (longevity) character on a scroll hung on the wall, a rubbing based on what was supposed to be the actual handwriting of the Taoist immortal Ch'en T'uan. One of the side scrolls had come off and lay loosely rolled up on the long table against the wall; the one still hanging on the wall expressed the sentiment "Peace comes with understanding." I strolled over to the desk by the window and looked over the books. There were only a few odd volumes of the K'ang Hsi Dictionary and an annotated edition of the Analects.[2]

I decided that I must leave the next day, whatever happened. What had depressed me most was a meeting with Sister Hsiang-lin [3] the day before. I encountered her in the afternoon as I was returning home along the river-bank after visiting some friends in the eastern part of the village, and by the direction of her vacant stare I knew that she was heading for me. Of the people that I had seen at Luchen on this visit no one had changed as much as she. Her gray hair of five years ago had turned entirely white; she was not at all like a woman of only forty. Her face was intolerably drawn and thin; it had lost its sad and sorrowful aspect and was now as expressionless as if carved of wood. Only an occasional movement of her eyes indicated that she was still a living creature. She held in one hand a bamboo basket containing a chipped and empty bowl; with the other hand, she supported herself with a bamboo stick, a little split at the lower end. She had evidently become a beggar.

I stopped, expecting her to ask for money.

"Have you come back?" she asked.

"Yes."

"I am very glad. You are a scholar, and you have been to the outside world and learned of many things. I want to ask you about something." Her lusterless eyes suddenly lighted up as she advanced a few steps towards

---

2. *Analects*, a collection of the teachings and maxims of Confucius (551?–478 B.C.), Chinese philosopher and moral teacher. 3. *Hsiang-lin* (shyäng lin).

me, lowered her voice, and said in a very earnest and confidential manner, "It is this: is there another life after this one?"

I was taken aback by the unexpectedness of the question; the wild look in her eyes, which were fixed on mine, gave me a creepy sensation on my back and made me feel more uncomfortable than I used to at school when an examination was sprung upon us, with the teacher watching vigilantly by our side. I had never concerned myself with the afterlife. How was I to answer her now? Most people here believe in the survival of the soul, I thought rapidly as I considered an answer, but this woman seemed to have her doubts. Perhaps it was a matter of hope with her, the hope that there was an afterlife and that the afterlife would be a better one than this. Why should I add to the unhappiness of this miserable woman? For her sake I had better say that there was another life after this one.

"Maybe there is . . . I think," I said haltingly and without conviction.

"Then there would also be a hell?"

"Oh! Hell?" I was again taken unawares and so I temporized, "Hell?— It would seem logical . . . though it may not necessarily exist . . . but who cares about such things?"

"Then we will meet members of our family after death?"

"Er, er, do we meet them?" I then realized that I was still a very ignorant man and that no amount of temporizing and cogitation would enable me to stand the test of three questions. I became less and less sure of myself and wished to recant all that I had said. "That . . . but really, I cannot say. I cannot really say whether souls survive or not."

Before she could ask any more questions, I fled back to Uncle Four's house very much agitated in spirit. I told myself that my answer to her questions might lead to something unfortunate and that I should be held responsible for what might happen. She probably felt lonely and unhappy at a time when others were celebrating; but was that all, or had she formed a definite plan of action? Then I laughed at myself for taking such a trivial incident so seriously, for pondering upon it and analyzing it. The psychologists would undoubtedly call such a morbid interest or fear pathological. Besides, had I not explicitly said "I cannot really say," thus annulling all my answers and relieving myself of all responsibility?

"I cannot really say" is a very useful sentence. Inexperienced youths are often rash enough to give answers to the difficult problems of life and prescribe remedies for others, and thus lay themselves open to blame when things go wrong. If, however, they qualify their statements by concluding them with "I cannot really say," they will assure themselves of a safe and happy life. I then realized the indispensability of this sentence, indispensable even when one is talking with a beggarwoman.

But my uneasiness persisted; I kept recalling the meeting with a presentiment of evil. On this dark, heavy, snowy afternoon in that dreary study my uneasiness became stronger. I felt I had better go away and spend a day at the county seat. I recalled Fu-hsing-lou's excellent shark's fin cooked in clear broth at only a dollar a plate, and wondered if the price had gone up. Although my friends of former days had scattered hither and yon, I must not fail to feast upon this delicacy, even if I had to eat by myself. Whatever happens, I must leave this place tomorrow, I repeated to myself.

Because I have often seen things happen which I had hoped would not happen, which I had told myself might not necessarily happen, but which had a way of happening just the same, I was very much afraid that it would be so on this occasion. And surely something did happen, for towards evening I overheard a discussion going on in the inner courtyard. Presently it stopped, and after a silence I distinguished the voice of Uncle Four.

"Of course a *thing like that* would choose of all times a time like this."

I was first puzzled and then felt uncomfortable, for the remark sounded as if it might have something to do with me. I looked out the door but did not see anyone that I could ask. Not until the hired man came in to replenish my tea toward suppertime did I have an opportunity to make inquiries.

"With whom was His Honor Four angry a little while ago?" I asked.

"Who else but Sister Hsiang-lin?" he answered very simply.

"Sister Hsiang-lin? What did she do?" I hurriedly pursued.

"She died."

"Died?" My heart sank and I almost jumped. My face must have changed color. But the man did not raise his head and so did not notice it. I calmed myself and continued:

"When did she die?"

"When? Last night or early this morning. I can't really say."

"What did she die of?"

"What did she die of? Why, what else would it be if not poverty?" the man answered in a matter of course way and went out without ever raising his head to look at me.

My terror was transient, for I realized that, since that which was to come to pass had come to pass, there was no longer need for me to worry about my responsibility. Gradually I regained my composure; a sense of regret and disquiet only occasionally intruded. Supper was served, with Uncle Four keeping me company. I wanted to find out more about Sister Hsiang-lin, but I knew that though he had read that "Ghosts and spirits are only the manifestations of the two cardinal principles of nature," he was still subject to many taboos; that such topics as sickness and death should be carefully avoided at a time when New Year blessings were about to be asked; and that if I must satisfy my curiosity, I should resort to some well-considered euphemism. As I unfortunately knew no such euphemisms, I withheld the question I was several times on the point of asking. From the look of displeasure on his face I began to imagine it quite possible that he considered me a "thing like that" for coming to bother him at such a time; thereupon I hastened to set him at ease and told him that I was going to leave Luchen the following day. He did not show much warmth in urging me to stay. Thus we dragged through supper.

Winter days are short at best, and, with snow falling, night soon enveloped the village. Everyone was busy by the lamplight, but outdoors it was quiet and still. Falling upon a thick mattress of snow, the flakes seemed to swish-swish, making one feel all the more lonely and depressed. Sitting alone under the yellow light of the vegetable-oil lamp, I thought of the fate of the poor, forlorn woman who had been cast into the garbage dump like a discarded toy. Hitherto she had continued to remind people of her miserable existence in the garbage dump, much to the surprise and wonder of those who have reason to find life worth living. Now she had at last been swept away clean by the Unpredictable. Whether souls continue to exist or not I do not know, but I did know that at least one who had no reason to find life worth living was at last no longer living and that those who looked upon her as an eyesore no longer had to look at her. It was a good thing, whether looked at from her point of view or from that of others. As I listened to the swish-swishing of the snowflakes outside and pondered along this line of thought I began to take comfort and to feel better.

And I began to put together the fragments that I had heard about her until her story became a fairly coherent whole.

Sister Hsiang-lin was not a native of Luchen. One year in the early part of winter they needed a new maid at Uncle Four's and the middlewoman, old Mrs. Wei, had brought her. She wore a black skirt, a blue, lined coat and light blue vest, and her hair was tied with white strings as a sign of mourning. She was about twenty-six years old, of a dark yellow complexion, with a faint suggestion of color in her cheeks. Old Mrs. Wei called her Sister Hsiang-lin, said that she was a neighbor of her mother's and that as her husband had recently died she had come out to seek employment. Uncle Four frowned and Aunt Four guessed the cause; he did not like the idea of widows. But the woman had regular features and large, strong hands and feet. She was quiet and docile and it appeared that she would make an industrious and faithful servant. Aunt Four kept her in spite of Uncle Four's frown. During the trial period she worked all day as though unhappy without employment. She was strong and could do everything that a man could do. On the third day they decided to keep her, at a monthly wage of 500 *cash*.[4]

---

4. *cash*. The Chinese traditional currency, known as "cash" to foreigners, consisted of copper coins. After European trade began, Mexican silver dollars were used for major transactions. One dollar was worth a thousand cash.

Everyone called her Sister Hsiang-lin; no one asked her surname, but since the middlewoman was from Weichiashan and said that she was a neighbor of her mother's, her name was probably Wei. She was not talkative and spoke only in answer to questions, and that rather briefly. Not until after some ten days did it gradually become known that she had at home a stern mother-in-law, a brother-in-law about ten years old and able to go out to gather fuel, and that her husband who had died in the spring was ten years younger than she and also made his living by cutting firewood. This was all that was known about her.

The days went by quickly and she showed no signs of losing her initial industry; she never complained about her fare or spared her strength. People all talked about the woman help in the house of His Honor Lu who was more capable and industrious than a man. At the year-end she did all the cleaning, sweeping, and killed the chickens and ducks and cooked them; it was actually not necessary to hire temporary help. She seemed happy too; her face grew fuller and traces of smiles appeared around the corners of her mouth.

But shortly after the New Year she returned one day, pale and agitated, from washing rice at the river; she said she had seen a man who looked like an elder cousin-in-law loitering in the distance on the opposite bank, and she feared he was watching her. Aunt Four questioned her but could get no more out of her. When he heard of this incident, Uncle Four knitted his brows and said, "I do not like it. I am afraid that she ran away from home."

As a matter of fact, she had come away without her mother-in-law's permission, and it was not long before this supposition proved to be true.

About ten days later, when the incident had been almost forgotten, old Mrs. Wei suddenly appeared with a woman about thirty years old, whom she introduced as Sister Hsiang-lin's mother-in-law. Though dressed like a woman from the hill villages, she was self-composed and capable of speech. She apologized for her intrusion and said that she had come to take her daughter-in-law home to help with the spring chores, as only she and her young son were at home.

"What else can we do since her mother-in-law wants her back?" Uncle Four said.

Therefore, her wages, which amounted to 1,750 *cash* and of which she had not spent a penny, were handed over to the mother-in-law. The woman took Sister Hsiang-lin's clothes, expressed her thanks, and went away.

Sister Hsiang-lin was not present during this transaction and it did not occur to Aunt and Uncle Four to summon her. It was not until toward noon when she began to feel hungry that Aunt Four suddenly remembered that Sister Hsiang-lin had gone out to wash rice and wondered what had happened to her.

"Aiya! Where is the rice?" she exclaimed. "Did not Sister Hsiang-lin go out to wash the rice?"

She began searching for the washing basket, first in the kitchen, then in the courtyard, then in the bedroom, but there was no trace of it. Uncle Four looked outside the gate but did not see it either, and it was not until he went to the river that he saw the basket resting peacefully on the bank, a head of green vegetable beside it.

Then he learned from eyewitnesses what had happened. A covered boat had been moored in the river all morning, but no one paid any attention to it at the time. When Sister Hsiang-lin came out to wash rice, two men that looked like people from the hills jumped out, seized her as she bent over her task and dragged her into the boat. Sister Hsiang-lin uttered a few cries but was soon silent, probably because she was gagged. Then two women embarked, one a stranger and the other old Mrs. Wei. Some thought that they did see Sister Hsiang-lin lying bound on the bottom of the boat.

"The rascals! But . . . ," Uncle Four said.

That day Aunt Four cooked the midday dinner herself, while her son Niu-erh tended the fire.

Old Mrs. Wei returned after the midday dinner.

"What do you mean by your outrageous behavior? And you have the audacity to come back to see us!" Aunt Four said vehemently over the dishwashing. "You brought her here yourself, and then you conspire with them to kidnap her, causing such a scandal. What will people say? Do you want to make a laughingstock of us?"

"Aiya, aiya! I was duped, really, and I have come back to explain. She came to me and asked me to find a place for her. How was I to know that her mother-in-law knew nothing of it? I beg your forgiveness. It was all my fault, old and weak woman that I am. I should have been more careful. Fortunately, your house has been noted for its generosity and I know you would not return measure for measure with people like us. I shall most certainly find you a good maid to atone for myself."

Thus the episode was closed and shortly afterwards forgotten.

Only Aunt Four, who had difficulty in finding a satisfactory servant, sometimes mentioned Sister Hsiang-lin, whose successors either were lazy or complained of their food, or both. "I wonder what has become of her," Aunt Four would say, hoping that she might come back again. By the beginning of the following year she gave up this hope.

Toward the end of the first month, however, old Mrs. Wei came to offer her New Year's greetings. She was slightly intoxicated with wine and said that she had been late in coming because she had visited her mother at Weichiashan for a few days. The conversation naturally turned to Sister Hsiang-lin.

"That one. She has entered her lucky years," old Mrs. Wei said with pleasure. "When her mother-in-law came to get her, she was already promised to Huo Lao-lui of Huochiatsun and so a few days after her return she was put into a wedding-sedan and carried away."

"Aiya! what a mother-in-law!" Aunt Four said, surprised.

"Aiya! you talk exactly like a lady of a great family. Among us poor people in the hills this is nothing. She has a younger brother-in-law who had to get married. If they did not marry her off where were they to get the money for his wedding? Her mother-in-law was a capable and clever one. She knew how to go about things. She married her off into the hills. In the village, she would not have gotten much for Sister Hsiang-lin, but because there are not many who will marry into the hills, she got 80,000 *cash*. Now her second son is married. She spent only 50,000 and had a clear profit of over 10,000 after expenses. See what a good stroke of business that was?"

"But how could Sister Hsiang-lin ever consent to such a thing?"

"What is there to consent or not to consent? Any bride will make a scene; but all one has to do is bind her up, stuff her into the sedan, carry her to the groom's house, put the bridal hat on her, assist her through the ceremony, put her into the bridal chamber, shut the door—and leave the rest to the groom. But Sister Hsiang-lin was different and unusually difficult. People said it was probably because she had worked in the house of a scholar that she acted differently from the common people. *Tai-tai*,[5] we have seen all sorts of them, these 'again' women; we have seen the kind that weep and cry, the kind that attempt suicide, and the kind that spoil the wedding ceremony by upsetting and breaking things. But Sister Hsiang-lin was worse than any of these. I was told that she bellowed and cursed all the way, so that she had lost her voice when she reached the Huo village. Dragging her out of the sedan, three men were not enough to hold her through the ceremony. Once they loosed their hold on her for a moment, and—*Amitofo*—she dashed her head against the corner of the wedding table, and gave herself a big gash. The blood flowed so freely that two handfuls of incense ash and a bandage could not stop it. She continued to curse after she had been dragged into the wedding chamber and shut in with her man. Aiya-ya, I never . . ." she shook her head, lowered her eyes and was silent for a moment.

"And later?" Aunt Four asked.

"It was said that she did not get up all the next day," she answered, raising her eyes.

"And after that?"

"Well, she got up eventually and by the end of the year she gave birth to a boy. Someone happened to visit the Huo village while I was at my

---

5. *Tai-tai*, mistress. [*Chinese*]

mother's and said on his return that he had seen the mother and the child and that they were both healthy and plump. There is no mother-in-law above her and her man is strong and a willing worker. They have their own house. Ai-ai, she has entered her lucky years."

After that Aunt Four no longer mentioned Sister Hsiang-lin.

But in the fall of one year—it must have been two years after the news of Sister Hsiang-lin's good luck was brought by Mrs. Wei—she reappeared in the courtyard of Uncle Four's house. She put on the table a round basket in the form of a water chestnut and outside under the eaves she left her bundle of bedding. She wore, as on her first visit, white hairstrings, black skirt, blue, lined coat, light blue vest, and her skin was dark yellow as before, but without any trace of color in her cheeks. Instead, traces of tears could be observed around her eyes, which were not as alive as before. Old Mrs. Wei again accompanied her and made this recital to Aunt Four:

"This is truly what is called 'Heaven has unpredictable storms.' Her man was a strong and sturdy one. Who would ever have thought that he would die of influenza? He had gotten well, but he ate a bowl of cold rice and it came back again. Fortunately she had her son and she was capable, could cut firewood, pick tea, or raise silkworms. She was managing all right. Who would ever have thought that her child would be carried off by a wolf? Spring was nearing its end and yet a wolf appeared in the village. Who would have thought of such a thing? Now she is alone. Her elder brother-in-law took possession of her house and put her out. She is now at the end of her road and has no other way except to appeal to her old mistress. Now she has no entanglements and as *tai-tai* happens to be in need of a new maid I have brought her. I think as she is familiar with things here she would be much better than a strange hand."

"I was a fool, really," Sister Hsiang-lin raised her lusterless eyes and said. "I knew that the wild beasts came down to the village to seek food when they couldn't find anything in the hills during the snow season, but I did not know they would come down in the spring. I got up early and opened the door. I gave a basket of beans to our Ah Mao and told him to sit on the gate sill and peel them. He was an obedient child and did everything I told him. He went out and I went behind the house to cut wood and wash rice. After putting the rice in the pot, I wanted to put the beans over it to steam. I called Ah Mao but he did not answer. I went out and looked. I saw beans spilled all over the ground but could not see our Ah Mao. He never went out to play at the neighbors' but I went and looked for him. I did not find him. I was frightened and asked people to go out and search for him. In the afternoon they found one of his shoes in the bramble. They all said that there was no hope, that the wolf must have got him. They went into the bush and sure enough they found him lying in the grass, all his insides gone, his hand still holding on tightly to the handle of the basket . . ."
She broke off sobbing.

Aunt Four hesitated at first, but her eyes reddened after hearing the story. Then she told Sister Hsiang-lin to take the basket and bundle to the maid's room. Old Mrs. Wei sighed with relief, and Sister Hsiang-lin seemed to feel better than when she arrived. As she was familiar with the house, she went and set her things in order without being directed, and thenceforward she again became a maidservant at Luchen.

And everybody called her Sister Hsiang-lin as before.

But this time her fortune had changed considerably. Two or three days later her employers realized that her hands were not as clever and efficient as formerly, her memory failed, her deathlike face never showed the shadow of a smile. Aunt Four could not conceal her displeasure. Uncle Four had frowned as usual when she came, but made no protest as he knew how difficult it was to find a satisfactory servant; he only cautioned Aunt Four, saying that though such people were a pitiable lot, yet she was after all a bane against morality, and that it was all right for her to help in ordinary tasks but she must not touch anything in connection with the ancestral sacrifices. These Aunt Four must prepare herself, else they would be unclean and the ancestors would not touch them.

Preparation of the ancestral sacrifices was the most important event in Uncle Four's house and Sister Hsiang-lin used to be busiest at such a time. Now she had nothing to do. When the table was placed in the center of the hall with a curtain in front of it, she started to arrange the wine cups and chopsticks as she used to do.

"Sister Hsiang-lin, please leave those things alone. I will arrange them," Aunt Four hastened to say.

She drew back her hands in embarrassment and then went to get the candlesticks.

"Sister Hsiang-lin, leave that alone. I'll get it," Aunt Four again said hastily. After hovering around for a little while, Sister Hsiang-lin withdrew in bewilderment. The only thing she was permitted to do that day was to tend the fire in the kitchen.

People in the village still called her Sister Hsiang-lin, but the tone of their voices was different; they still talked with her, but they were scornful of her. She did not seem to notice the change; she only stared vacantly and recited the story that she could not forget, night or day—

"I was a fool, really . . ." Her tears would flow and her voice grow tremulous.

It was a very effective story; men would stop smiling and walk away in confusion; women not only seemed to forgive her and to banish the look of scorn on their faces, but shed tears with her. Some older women, not having heard her own recital, would come to her and listen to her until her voice broke, when they would let fall the tears that had been gradually accumulating in their eyes, heave some sighs and go away satisfied. She was their chief topic of conversation.

Sister Hsiang-lin continued to repeat her story and often attracted three or five listeners. But the story soon became familiar to everyone, and after a while even the kindest and most patient of old ladies ceased to shed any tears. Still later almost everyone in the village could recite her story, and was bored by it.

"I was really a fool, really," she would begin.

"Yes, you knew that wild beasts came down to the village to seek food only when they cannot find anything in the hills," people would thus stop her and walk away.

She would stand gaping and staring for a while and then walk away, a little embarrassed. Still, she tried to bring up the story of Ah Mao by some ruse—a basket, beans, or some other children. For instance, if she saw a child two or three years old, she would say, "Ai-ai, if our Ah Mao were alive he would be as big as that . . ."

The children were afraid of her and of the look in her eyes, and they would tug at their mothers' coats and urge them to go away. And thus Sister Hsiang-lin would be left alone to wander off by herself. Soon people caught on to her new trick; they would forestall her when there were children around by saying, "Sister Hsiang-lin, if your Ah Mao were alive, would he not be as big as that?"

She might not have realized that her sorrow, after having been carefully chewed and relished for so long, had now become insipid dregs, only fit to spit out; but she was able to sense the indifference and the sarcasm in the question and to realize that there was no need of her answering it.

The New Year festivities last a long time in Luchen and begin to occupy people after the twentieth of the last month of the year. At Uncle Four's house they had to hire a temporary man helper, but the work was too much for him and another woman was hired. But she, Liu-ma, was a devout vegetarian and would not kill the chickens and ducks; she only washed dishes. Sister Hsiang-lin had nothing to do but tend the fire. She sat and watched Liu-ma wash the dishes. A light snow was falling outside.

"Ai-ai, I was really a fool," Sister Hsiang-lin soliloquized after looking at the sky, sighing.

"Sister Hsiang-lin, there you go again," Liu-ma looked at her impatiently. "Let me ask you, did you not get your scar when you dashed your head against the table that time?"

"Mmm," she answered evasively.

"Let me ask you, why did you finally give in?"

"I?"

"Yes, you. I think you must have been willing. Otherwise . . ."

"Ah-ah, but you do not know how strong he was."

"I do not believe it. I do not believe that a strong woman like you could not resist him. You must have finally become willing though you now blame it on his strength."

"Ah-ah you . . . you should have tried to resist him yourself," she said with a smile.

Liu-ma laughed, her wrinkled face shriveling up like a peach stone; her tiny dry eyes shifted from the scar on Sister Hsiang-lin's forehead to the latter's eyes, discomforting her and causing her to gather up her smile and turn her eyes to look at the snowflakes.

"Sister Hsiang-lin, you have miscalculated badly," Liu-ma said mysteriously. "You should have resisted to the end, or dashed your head until you were dead. That would have been the thing to do. But now? You lived with your second man only two years and got for it a monstrous evil name. Just think, when you get to the lower world, those two ghost husbands will fight over you. Whom would they give you to? The Great King Yenlo [6] could only have you sawed in two and divided between them . . ."

Sister Hsiang-lin was terrified: this was something that she had not heard about in the hills.

"I think you should atone for your crime while there is still time. Donate a doorsill to the T'u-ti temple as your effigy, so that you might be trampled upon by a thousand men's feet and straddled over by ten thousand men's legs as atonement for your great sin. Then you may escape the tortures in store for you."

Sister Hsiang-lin did not say anything then, but she must have been deeply affected. The next day she got up with black rings around her eyes. After breakfast she went to the T'u-ti temple on the western edge of the village to donate the doorsill. At first the keeper would not accept the gift, but her tears and entreaties finally prevailed and he accepted the offer at the price of 12,000 *cash*.

She had not spoken with anyone for a long time, for she had become an avoided object because of the tiresome story about her Ah Mao; nevertheless, after her conversation with Liu-ma—which seemed to have been broadcast immediately—people began to take a new interest in her and would try to coax her to talk. As to the subject, it was naturally a new one, centering upon the scar on her forehead.

"Sister Hsiang-lin, let me ask you, why did you finally give in?" one would say.

"Ai, too bad you broke your head for nothing," another would echo, looking at her scar.

From their faces and voices she gathered that they were making fun of her; she only stared vacantly and said nothing, later she did not even turn her head. She tightened her mouth and went about her duties—sweeping, washing vegetables and rice, running errands, bearing the scar of her shame. In about a year, she got all the wages that Aunt Four had kept for

6. *King Yenlo*, in Chinese mythology lord of the fifth hell (there are eighteen) and infernal judge.

her, changed them into twelve Mexican dollars, asked for leave to go to the western edge of the village. She soon returned and told Aunt Four that she had donated her doorsill at the T'u-ti temple. She appeared to be in better spirits than she had been for a long time and her eyes showed signs of life.

She worked unusually hard at the ancestral sacrifices at the winter solstice. After watching Aunt Four fill the dishes with the sacrificial things and Ah Niu place the table in the center of the hall, she went confidently to get the wine cups and chopsticks. "Don't you bother, Sister Hsiang-lin!" Aunt Four said in a panicky voice.

She withdrew her hands as if from a hot iron, her face black and pale like burnt coal. She did not try to get the candlesticks. She only stood as if lost, and did not go away until Uncle Four came in to light the incense sticks and dismissed her. This time the change in her was extraordinary. Not only were her eyes sunken the next day, but her wits seemed to have left her entirely. She became terribly afraid, not only of the night and dark corners, but also of people, including her own employers. She would sneak about, trembling like a mouse that had ventured out of its hole in daylight; or she would sit abstractedly like a wooden idol. In less than half a year, her hair became gray, her memory grew worse and worse, until she sometimes forgot to go out to wash rice in the river.

"What is the matter with Sister Hsiang-lin? We should not have kept her in the first place," Aunt Four would say sometimes, in her hearing, as a warning to her.

But she continued in the same condition, and showed no signs of recovering her wits. They began to think of sending her away, to tell her to go back to old Mrs. Wei. When I was still living at Luchen they used to talk of sending her away, but they only talked about it; from what I saw on this visit, it was evident that they did finally carry out their threat. But whether she became a beggar immediately after leaving Uncle Four's house, or whether she first went to old Mrs. Wei and then became a beggar, I could not say.

I was awakened by loud explosions of firecrackers close by. As I blinked at the yellow lamp flame about the size of a bean I heard the crackling of a string of firecrackers—the New Year's ceremony was on at Uncle Four's and I knew that it must be about the fifth watch. With half-shut eyes I heard dreamily the continued crackling in the distance; it seemed to form a thick cloud of festive sounds in the sky, mingling with the snowflakes and enveloping the entire village. In the arms of this festive sound, I felt carefree and comfortable, and the fears and melancholy I had felt all the previous day and the first part of the night were swept away by this atmosphere of joy and blessedness. I fancied that the gods and sages of heaven above and earth below, drunk and satiated with incense and sacrifices of wine and meat, were reeling unsteadily in the sky, ready to confer unlimited blessings upon the inhabitants of Luchen. ✳

Mao Tun (1896-   )

SPRING SILKWORMS

Translated from the Chinese by
Chi-chen Wang

TUNG PAO sat on a rock along the bank of the canal with his back to the sun, his long-stemmed pipe leaning against his side. The sun was already strong, though the period of Clear Bright[1] had just set in, and felt as warm as a brazier of fire. It made him hotter than ever to see the Shaohing trackers pulling hard at their lines, large drops of sweat falling from their brows in spite of their open cotton shirts. Tung Pao was still wearing his winter coat; he had not foreseen the sudden warm spell and had not thought of redeeming his lighter garment from the pawnshop.

"Even the weather is not what it used to be!" muttered Tung Pao, spitting into the canal.

There were not many passing boats, and the occasional ripples and eddies that broke the mirrorlike surface of the greenish water and blurred the placid reflections of the mud banks and neat rows of mulberry trees never lasted long. Presently one could make out the trees again, swaying from side to side at first like drunken men and then becoming motionless and clear and distinct as before, their fistlike buds already giving forth tiny, tender leaves. The fields were still cracked and dry, but the mulberry trees had already come into their own. There seemed to be no end to the rows along the banks and there was another extensive grove back of Tung Pao. They seemed to thrive on the sunlit warmth, their tender leaves growing visibly each second.

Not far from where Tung Pao sat there was a gray white building, used by the cocoon buyers during the season but now quite deserted. There were rumors that the buyers would not come at all this year because the

---

1. *Clear Bright*, the spring season.

Shanghai factories had been made idle by the war, but Tung Pao would not believe this. He had lived sixty years and had yet to see the time when mulberry leaves would be allowed to wither on the trees or be used for fodder, unless of course if the eggs should not hatch, as has sometimes happened according to the unpredictable whims of Heaven.

"How warm it is for this time of the year!" Tung Pao thought again, hopefully, because it was just after a warm spring like this almost two score years ago that there occurred one of the best silk crops ever known. He remembered it well: it was also the year of his marriage. His family fortune was then on the upward swing. His father worked like a faithful old ox, knew and did everything; his grandfather, who had been a Taiping captive [2] in his time, was still vigorous in spite of his great age. At that time too, the house of Chen had not yet begun its decline, for though the old squire had already died, the young squire had not yet taken to opium smoking. Tung Pao had a vague feeling that the fortunes of the Chens and that of his own family were somehow intertwined, though one was about the richest family in town while his was only well-to-do as peasants went.

Both his grandfather and the old squire had been captives of the Taiping rebels and had both escaped before the rebellion was suppressed. Local legend had it that the old squire had made off with a considerable amount of Taiping gold and that it was this gold which enabled him to go into the silk business and amass a huge fortune. During that time Tung Pao's family flourished too. Year after year the silk crops had been good and in ten years his family had been able to acquire twenty mou [3] of rice land and more than ten mou of mulberry trees. They were the most prosperous family in the village, just as the Chens were the richest in the town.

But gradually both families had declined. Tung Pao no longer had any rice land left and was more than three hundred dollars in debt besides. As for the Chen family, it was long ago "finished." It was said that the reason for their rapid decline was that the ghosts of the Taiping rebels had sued in the courts of the nether world and had been warranted by King Yenlo [4] to collect. Tung Pao was inclined to think that there was something to this notion, otherwise why should the young squire suddenly acquire the opium habit? He could not, however, figure out why the fortunes of his own family should have declined at the same time. He was certain that his grandfather did not make away with any Taiping gold. It was true that his grandfather had to kill a Taiping sentinel in making his escape, but had not his family atoned for this by holding services for the dead rebel as long as he could remember? He did not know much about his grandfather, but he knew his father as an honest and hardworking man and could not think

2. *Taiping captive*, a prisoner of the Taiping rebels. The Taiping Rebellion (1851–1864) was the most important of the nineteenth-century revolts against the Manchu dynasty (1644–1912). 3. *mou*, a Chinese land measure, approximately one sixth of an acre. 4. *King Yenlo*, in Chinese mythology lord of the fifth hell (there are eighteen) and infernal judge.

of anything he himself had done that should merit the misfortunes that had befallen him. His older son Ah Ssu [5] and his wife were both industrious and thrifty, and his younger son Ah Dou was not a bad sort, though he was flighty at times as all young people were inclined to be.

Tung Pao sadly lifted his brown, wrinkled face and surveyed the scene before him. The canal, the boats, and the mulberry groves on both sides of the canal—everything was much the same as it was two score years ago. But the world had changed: often they lived on nothing but pumpkins, and he was more than three hundred dollars in debt.

Several blasts from a steam whistle suddenly came from around a bend in the canal. Soon a tug swept majestically into view with a string of three boats in tow. The smaller crafts on the canal scurried out of the way of the puffing monster, but soon they were engulfed in the wide wake of the tug and its train and seesawed up and down as the air became filled with the sound of the engine and the odor of oil. Tung Pao watched the tug with hatred in his eyes as it disappeared around the next bend. He had always entertained a deep enmity against such foreign deviltry as steamboats and the like. He had never seen a foreigner himself, but his father told him that the old squire had seen some, that they had red hair and green eyes and walked with straight knees. The old squire had no use for foreigners either and used to say that it was they that had made off with all the money and made everyone poor. Tung Pao had no doubt that the old squire was right. He knew from his own experience that since foreign yarn and cloth and kerosene appeared in town and the steamer in the river, he got less and less for the things that he produced with his own labor and had to pay more and more for the things that he had to buy. It was thus that he became poorer and poorer until now he had none of his rice land that his father had left him and was in debt besides. He did not hate the foreigners without reason! Even among the villagers he was remarkable for the vehemence of his anti-foreign sentiments.

Five years back someone told him that there had been another change in government and that it was the aim of the new government to rescue the people from foreign oppression. Tung Pao did not believe it, for he had noticed on his trips to town that the youngsters who shouted "Down with the foreigners" all wore foreign clothes. He had a suspicion that these youths were secretly in league with the foreigners and only pretended to be their enemies in order to fool honest people like himself. He was even more convinced that he was right when the slogan "Down with the foreigners" was dropped and things became dearer and dearer and the taxes heavier and heavier. Tung Pao was sure that the foreigners had a hand in these things.

The last straw for Tung Pao was that cocoons hatched from foreign

---

5. *Ah Ssu* (ä szə).

eggs should actually sell for ten dollars more a picul.[6] He had always been on friendly terms with his daughter-in-law, but they quarreled on this score. She had wanted to use foreign eggs the year before. His younger son Ah Dou sided with her, and her husband was of the same mind though he did not say much about it. Unable to withstand their pressure, Tung Pao had to compromise at last and allow them to use one sheet of foreign eggs out of three that they decided to hatch this year.

"The world is becoming worse and worse," he said to himself. "After a few years even the mulberry leaves will have to be foreign! I am sick of it all!"

The weather continued warm and the fingerlike tender leaves were now the size of small hands. The trees around the village itself seemed to be even better. As the trees grew so did the hope in the hearts of the peasants. The entire village was mobilized in preparation for the silkworms. The utensils used in the rearing were taken out from the fuel sheds to be washed and repaired, and the women and children engaged in these tasks lined the brook that passed through the village.

None of the women and children were very healthy looking. From the beginning of spring they had to cut down on their meager food, and their garments were all old and worn. They looked little better than beggars. They were not, however, dispirited; they were sustained by their great endurance and their great hope. In their simple minds they felt sure that so long as nothing happened to their silkworms everything would come out all right. When they thought how in a month's time the glossy green leaves would turn into snow white cocoons and how the cocoons would turn into jingling silver dollars, their hearts were filled with laughter though their stomachs gurgled with hunger.

Among the women was Tung Pao's daughter-in-law Ssu-da-niang [7] with her twelve-year-old boy Hsiao Pao.[8] They had finished washing the feeding trays and the hatching baskets and were wiping their brows with the flap of their coats.

"Ssu-sao, are you using foreign eggs this year?" one of the women asked Ssu-da-niang.

"Don't ask me!" Ssu-da-niang answered with passion, as if ready for a quarrel. "Pa is the one that decides. Hsiao Pao's pa did what he could to persuade the old man, but in the end we are hatching only one sheet of foreign eggs. The doddering old fool hates everything foreign as if it were his sworn foe, yet he doesn't seem to mind at all when it comes to 'foreign money.'"[9]

---

6. *picul*, a Chinese unit of weight, from about 133 to about 143 pounds. 7. *Ssu-da-niang* (szə dä nyäng). 8. *Hsiao Pao* (shyou pou). 9. *'foreign money,'* the Mexican silver dollar, introduced into China by European traders.

The gibe provoked a gale of laughter.

A man walked across the husking field on the other side of the brook. As he stepped on the log bridge, Ssu-da-niang called to him:

"Brother Dou, come and help me take these things home. These trays are as heavy as dead dogs when they are wet."

Ah Dou lifted the pile of trays and carried them on his head and walked off swinging his hands like oars. He was a good-natured young man and was always willing to lend a hand to the women when they had anything heavy to be moved or to be rescued from the brook. The trays looked like an oversize bamboo hat on him. There was another gale of laughter when he wriggled his waist in the manner of city women.

"Ah Dou! Come back here and carry something home for me too," said Lotus, wife of Li Keng-sheng, Tung Pao's immediate neighbor, laughing with the rest.

"Call me something nicer if you want me to carry your things for you," answered Ah Dou without stopping.

"Then let me call you godson!" Lotus said with a loud laugh. She was unlike the rest of the women because of her unusually white complexion, but her face was very flat and her eyes were mere slits. She had been a slave girl in some family in town and was already notorious for her habit of flirting with the menfolk though she had been married to the taciturn Li Keng-sheng only half a year.

"The shameless thing!" someone muttered on the other side of the brook. Thereupon Lotus's pig-like eyes popped open as she shouted:

"Whom are you speaking of? Come out and say it in the open if you dare!"

"It is none of your business! She who is without shame knows best whom I'm speaking of, for 'Even the man who lies dead knows who's kicked his coffin with his toes.' Why should you care?"

They splashed water at each other. Some of the women joined the exchange of words, while the children laughed and hooted. Ssu-da-niang, not wishing to be involved, picked up the remaining baskets and went home with Hsiao Pao. Ah Dou had set down the trays on the porch and was watching the fun.

Tung Pao came out of the room with the tray stands that he had to repair. His face darkened when he caught Ah Dou standing there idle, watching the women. He never approved of Ah Dou's exchanging banter with the women of the village, particularly with Lotus, whom he regarded as an evil thing that brought bad luck to anyone who had anything to do with her.

"Are you enjoying the scenery, Ah Dou?" he shouted at his son. "Ah Ssu is making cocoon trees in the back; go and help him!" He did not take his disapproving eyes off his son until the latter had gone. Then he set to work examining the worm holes on the stands and repaired them wherever necessary. He had done a great deal of carpentering in his time, but his fingers were now stiff with age. After a while he had to rest his aching fingers and as he did so he looked up at the three sheets of eggs hanging from a bamboo pole in the room.

Ssu-da-niang sat under the eaves pasting paper over the hatching baskets. To save a few coppers they had used old newspapers the year before. The silkworms had not been healthy, and Tung Pao had said that it was because it was sacrilegious to use paper with characters on it. In order to buy regular paper for the purpose this year they had all gone without a meal.

"Ssu-da-niang, the twenty-loads of leaves we bought has used up all the thirty dollars that we borrowed through your father. What are we going to do after our rice is gone? What we have will last only two more days." Tung Pao raised his head from his work, breathing hard as he spoke to his daughter-in-law. The money was borrowed at 2½ percent monthly interest. This was considered low, and it was only because Ssu-da-niang's father was an old tenant of the creditor that they had been able to get such a favorable rate.

"It was not such a good idea to put all the money in leaves," complained Ssu-da-niang, setting out the baskets to dry. "We may not be able to use all of them as was the case last year."

"What are you talking about! You would bring ill luck on us before we even got started. Do you expect it to be like last year always? We can only gather a little over ten loads from our own trees. How can that be enough for three sheets of eggs?"

"Yes, yes, you are always right. All I know is that you can cook rice only when there is some to cook and when there isn't you have to go hungry!"

Ssu-da-niang answered with some passion, for she had not yet forgiven her father-in-law for their arguments over the relative merit of foreign and domestic eggs. Tung Pao's face darkened and he said no more.

As the hatching days approached, the entire village of about thirty families became tense with hope and anxiety, forgetting it seemed, even their gnawing hunger. They borrowed and sought credit wherever they could and ate whatever they could get, often nothing but pumpkins and potatoes. None of them had more than a handful of rice stored away. The harvest had been good the year before but what with the landlord, creditors, regular taxes, and special assessments, they had long ago exhausted their store. Their only hope now lay in the silkworms; all their loans were secured by the promise that they would be paid after the "harvest."

As the period of Germinating Rains drew near, the "cloth" in every family began to take on a green hue. This became the only topic of conversation wherever women met.

"Lotus says they will be warming the cloth tomorrow. I don't see how it can be so soon."

"Huang Tao-shih went to the fortune teller. The character he drew indicated that leaves will reach four dollars per picul this year!"

Ssu-da-niang was worried because she could not detect any green on their own three sheets of eggs. Ah Ssu could not find any either when he took the sheets to the light and examined them carefully. Fortunately their anxiety did not last long, for spots of green began to show the following day. Ssu-da-niang immediately put the precious things against her breast to warm, sitting quietly as if feeding an infant. At night she slept with them, hardly daring to stir though the tiny eggs against her flesh made her itch. She was as happy, and as fearful, as before the birth of her first child!

The room for the silkworms had been made ready some days before. On the second day of "warming" Tung Pao smeared a head of garlic with mud and put it in a corner of the room. It was believed that the more leaves there were on the garlic on the day that silkworms were hatched, the better would be the harvest. The entire village was now engaged in this warming of the cloths. There were few signs of women along the brooks or on the husking grounds. An undeclared state of emergency seemed to exist: even the best of friends and the most intimate of neighbors refrained from visiting one another, for it was no joking matter to disturb the shy and sensitive goddess who protected the silkworms. They talked briefly in whispers when they met outside. It was a sacred season.

The atmosphere was even tenser when the "black ladies" began to emerge from the eggs. This generally happened perilously close to the day that ushered in the period of Germinating Rains and it was imperative to time the hatching so that it would not be necessary to gather them on that particular day. In Tung Pao's house, the first grubs appeared just before the tabooed day, but they were able to avoid disaster by transferring the cloths from the warm breast of Ssu-da-niang to the silkworms' room. Tung Pao stole a glance at the garlic and his heart almost stopped beating, for only one or two cloves had sprouted. He did not dare to take another look but only prayed for the best.

The day for harvesting the "black ladies" finally came. Ssu-da-niang was restless and excited, continually watching the rising steam from the pot, for the right moment to start operations was when the steam rose straight up in the air. Tung Pao lit the incense and candles and reverently set them before the kitchen god.[10] Ah Ssu and Ah Dou went out to the fields to gather wild flowers, while Hsiao Pao cut up lampwick grass into fine shreds for the mixture used in gathering the newly hatched worms. Toward noon everything was ready for the big moment. When the pot began to boil vigorously and steam to rise straight up into the air, Ssu-da-

---

10. *kitchen god*, in Chinese mythology a household god who annually reported to heaven the behavior of every member of the family.

niang jumped up, stuck in her hair a paper flower dedicated to the silkworms and a pair of goose feathers and went into the room, accompanied by Tung Pao with a steelyard beam and her husband with the prepared mixture of wild flowers and lampwick grass. Ssu-da-niang separated the two layers of cloth and sprinkled the mixture on them. Then taking the beam from Tung Pao she laid the cloths across it, took a goose feather and began to brush the "black ladies" off gently into the papered baskets. The same procedure was followed with the second sheet, but the last, which contained the foreign eggs was brushed off into separate baskets. When all was done, Ssu-da-niang took the paper flower and the feathers and stuck them on the edge of one of the baskets.

It was a solemn ceremony, one that had been observed for hundreds and hundreds of years. It was as solemn an occasion as the sacrifice before a military campaign, for it was to inaugurate a month of relentless struggle against bad weather and ill luck during which there would be no rest day or night. The "black ladies" looked healthy as they crawled about in the small baskets; their color was as it should be. Tung Pao and Ssu-da-niang both breathed sighs of relief, though the former's face clouded whenever he stole a glance at the head of garlic, for the sprouts had not grown noticeably. Could it be that it was going to be like last year again?

Fortunately the prognostications of the garlic did not prove very accurate this time. Though it was rainy during the first and second molting and the weather colder than around Clear Bright, the "precious things" were all very healthy. It was the same with the "precious things" all over the village. An atmosphere of happiness prevailed, even the brook seemed to gurgle with laughter. The only exception was the household of Lotus, for their worms weighed only twenty pounds at the third "sleep," [11] and just before the fourth Lotus's husband was seen in the act of emptying three baskets into the brooks. This circumstance made the villagers redouble their vigilance against the contamination of the unfortunate woman. They would not even pass by her house and went out of their way to avoid her and her taciturn husband. They did not want to catch a single glance of her or exchange a single word with her for fear that they might catch her family's misfortune. Tung Pao warned Ah Dou not to be seen with Lotus. "I'll lay a charge against you before the magistrate if I catch you talking to that woman," he shouted at his son loud enough for Lotus to hear. Ah Dou said nothing; he alone did not take much stock in these superstitions. Besides, he was too busy to talk to anyone.

Tung Pao's silkworms weighed three hundred pounds after the "great sleep." For two days and two nights no one, not even Hsiao Pao, had a

---

11. *the third "sleep."* The feeding period of the silkworm is interrupted by four 24-hour intervals of sleep.

chance to close his eyes. The worms were in rare condition; in Tung Pao's memory only twice had he known anything equal to it—once when he was married and the other time when Ah Ssu was born. They consumed seven loads of leaves the first day, and it did not take much calculation to know how much more leaf would be needed before the worms were ready to climb up the "mountain."

"The squire has nothing to lend," Tung Pao said to Ah Ssu. "We'll have to ask your father-in-law to try his employers again."

"We still have about ten loads on our own trees, enough for another day," Ah Ssu said, hardly able to keep his eyes open.

"What nonsense," Tung Pao said impatiently. "They have started eating only two days ago. They'll be eating for another three days without counting tomorrow. We need another thirty loads, thirty loads."

The price of leaves had gone up to four dollars a load as predicted by the fortune teller, which meant that it would cost one hundred and twenty dollars to buy enough leaves to see them through. There was nothing to do but borrow the required amount on the only remaining mulberry land that they had. Tung Pao took some comfort in the thought that he would harvest at least five hundred pounds of cocoons and that at fifty dollars a hundred pounds he would get more than enough to pay his debts.

When the first consignment of leaves arrived, the "precious things" had already been without food for more than half an hour and it was heart-breaking to see them raise their heads and swing them hither and yon in search of leaves. A crunching sound filled the room as soon as the leaves were spread on the beds, so loud that those in the room had difficulty in hearing one another. Almost in no time the leaves had disappeared and the beds were again white with the voracious worms. It took the whole family to keep the beds covered with leaves. But this was the last five minutes of the battle; in two more days the "precious things" would be ready to "climb up the mountain" and perform their appointed task.

One night Ah Dou was alone on watch in the room, so that Tung Pao and Ah Ssu could have a little rest. It was a moonlit night and there was a small fire in the room for the silkworms. Around the second watch he spread a new layer of leaves on the beds and then squatted by the fire to wait for the next round. His eyes grew heavy and he gradually dozed off. He was awakened by what he thought was a noise at the door, but he was too sleepy to investigate and dozed off again, though subconsciously he detected an unusual rustling sound amidst the familiar crunching of leaves. Suddenly he awoke with a jerk of his drooping head just in time to catch the swishing of the reed screen against the door and a glimpse of someone gliding away. Ah Dou jumped up and ran out. Through the open gate he could see the intruder walking rapidly toward the brook. Ah Dou flew after him and in another moment he had flung him to the ground.

"Ah Dou, kill me if you want to but don't tell anyone!"

It was Lotus's voice, and it made Ah Dou shudder. Her piggish eyes were fixed on his but he could not detect any trace of fear in them.

"What have you stolen?" Ah Dou asked.

"Your precious things!"

"Where have you put them?"

"I have thrown them into the brook!"

Ah Dou's face grew harsh as he realized her wicked intention.

"How wicked you are! What have we done to you?"

"What have you done? Plenty! It was not my fault that our precious things did not live. Since I did you no harm and your precious things have flourished, why should you look upon me like the star of evil and avoid me like the plague? You have all treated me as if I were not a human being at all!"

Lotus had got up as she spoke, her face distorted with hatred. Ah Dou looked at her for a moment and then said:

"I am not going to hurt you; you can go now!"

Ah Dou went back to the room, no longer sleepy in the least. Nothing untoward happened during the rest of the night. The "precious things" were as healthy and strong as ever and kept on devouring leaves as if possessed. At dawn Tung Pao and Ssu-da-niang came to relieve Ah Dou. They picked up the silkworms that had gradually turned from white to pink and held them against the light to see if they had become translucent. Their hearts overflowed with happiness. When Ssu-da-niang went to the brook to draw water, however, Liu Pao, one of their neighbors, approached her and said to her in a low voice:

"Last night between the Second and Third Watch I saw that woman come out of your house, followed by Ah Dou. They stood close together and talked a long time. Ssu-da-niang, how can you let such things go on in your house?"

Ssu-da-niang rushed home and told her husband and then Tung Pao what had happened. Ah Dou, when summoned, denied everything and said that Liu Pao must have been dreaming. Tung Pao took some consolation in the fact that so far there had been no sign of the curse on the silkworms themselves, but there was Liu Pao's unshakable evidence and she could not have made up the whole story. He only hoped that the unlucky woman did not actually step into the room but had only met Ah Dou outside.

Tung Pao became full of misgivings about the future. He knew well that it was possible for everything to go well all along the way only to have the worms die on the trees. But he did not dare to think of that possibility, for just to think of it was enough to bring ill luck.

The silkworms had at last mounted the trees but the anxieties of the growers were by no means over, for there was as yet no assurance that their labor and investment would be rewarded. They did not, however, let these doubts stop them from their work. Fires were placed under the "mountains" in order to force the silkworms to climb up. The whole family squatted around the trees and listened to the rustling of the straws as the silkworms crawled among them, each trying to find a corner to spin its chamber of silk. They would smile broadly or their hearts would sink according to whether they could hear the reassuring sound or not. If they happened to look up and catch a drop of water from above, they did not mind at all, for that meant that there was at least one silkworm ready to get to work at that moment.

Three days later the fires were withdrawn. No longer able to endure the suspense, Ssu-da-niang drew aside one corner of the surrounding reed screens and took a peep. Her heart leaped with joy, for the entire "mountain" was covered with a snowy mass of cocoons! She had never seen a crop like this in all her life! Joy and laughter filled the household. Their anxieties were over at last. The "precious things" were fair and had not devoured leaves at four dollars a load without doing something to show for it; and they themselves had not gone with practically no food or sleep for nothing; Heaven had rewarded them.

The same sound of joy and laughter rose everywhere in the village. The Goddess of Silkworms [12] had been good to them. Everyone of the twenty or thirty families would gather at least a seventy or eighty percent capacity crop. As for Tung Pao's family they expected a hundred-and-twenty or even a hundred-and-thirty percent crop.

Women and children were again seen on the husking fields and along the brook. They were thinner than a month ago, their eyes more sunken and their voices more hoarse, but they were in high spirits. They talked about their struggles and dreamed of piles of bright silver dollars; some of them looked forward to redeeming their summer garments from the pawnshop, while others watered at the mouth in anticipation of the head of fish that they might treat themselves to at the Dragon Boat Festival.

The actual harvesting of the cocoons followed the next day, attended by visits from friends and relatives bringing presents and their good wishes. Chang Tsai-fa, Ssu-da-niang's father, came to congratulate Tung Pao and brought with him cakes, fruits and salted fish. Hsiao Pao was as happy as a pup frolicking in the snow.

"Tung Pao, are you going to sell your cocoons or reel them yourself?" Chang asked, as the two sat under a willow tree along the brook.

"I'll sell them, of course."

"But the factories are not buying this year," Chang said, standing up and pointing in the direction of the buildings used by the buyers.

Tung Pao would not believe him but when he went to see for himself he

---

12. *The Goddess of Silkworms*, Si Ling Chi, an empress who was deified for discovering the usefulness of silkworms.

found that the buyers' buildings were indeed still closed. For the moment Tung Pao was panic-stricken, but when he went home and saw the basket upon basket of fine, firm cocoons that he had harvested he forgot his worries. He could not believe it that such fine cocoons would find no market.

Gradually, however, the atmosphere of the village changed from one of joy and laughter to one of despair, as news began to arrive that none of the factories in the region were going to open for the season. Instead of the scouts for the cocoon buyers who in other years used to march up and down the village during this season, the village was now crowded with creditors and tax collectors. And none of them would accept cocoons in payment.

Curses and sighs of despair echoed through the entire village. It never occurred to the villagers even in their dreams that the extraordinarily fine crop of cocoons would increase their difficulties. But it did not help to complain and say that the world had changed. The cocoons would not keep and it was necessary to reel them at home if they could not sell them to the factories. Already some of the families had got out their long neglected spinning wheels.

"We'll reel the silk ourselves," Tung Pao said to his daughter-in-law. "We had always done that anyway until the foreigners started this factory business."

"But we have over five hundred pounds of cocoons! How many spinning wheels do you plan to use?"

Ssu-da-niang was right. It was impossible for them to reel all the cocoons themselves and they could not afford to hire help. Ah Ssu agreed with his wife and bitterly reproached his father, saying:

"If you had only listened to us and hatched only one sheet of eggs, we would have had enough leaves from our own land."

Tung Pao had nothing to say to this.

Presently a ray of hope came to them. Huang Tao-shih, one of Tung Pao's cronies, learned from somewhere that the factories at Wusih were buying cocoons as usual. After a family conference it was decided that they would borrow a boat and undertake the journey of around three hundred li [13] in order to dispose of their crop.

Five days later they returned with one basket of cocoons still unsold. The Wusih factory was unusually severe in their selection and paid only thirty dollars a hundred pounds of cocoons from foreign eggs and twelve dollars for the native variety. Though Tung Pao's cocoons were of the finest quality, they rejected almost a hundred pounds of the lot.

Tung Pao got one hundred and eleven dollars in all and had only an even hundred left after expenses of the journey, not enough to pay off

---

13. *li* (lĕ), a Chinese unit of distance, approximately one third of a mile.

the debts they contracted in order to buy leaves. Tung Pao was so mortified that he fell sick on the way and had to be carried home.

Ssu-da-niang borrowed a spinning wheel from Liu Pao's house and set to work reeling the rejected cocoons. It took her six days to finish the work. As they were again without rice, she sent Ah Ssu to the town to sell the silk. There was no market for it at all and even the pawnshop would not loan anything against it. After a great deal of begging and wheedling, he was allowed to use it to redeem the picul of rice that they had pawned before Clear Bright.

And so it happened that everyone in Tung Pao's village got deeper into debt because of their spring silkworm crop. Because Tung Pao had hatched three sheets of eggs and reaped an exceptional harvest, he lost as a consequence a piece of land that produced fifteen loads of mulberry leaves and thirty dollars besides, to say nothing of a whole month of short rations and loss of sleep! ✳

Tuan-mu Hung-liang[1] (c.1900-   )

THE SORROWS
OF THE LAKE OF EGRETS

Translated from the Chinese by
Yuan Chia-hua and Robert Payne

THE MOON WAS SLOWLY RISING, encircled with a halo, like an eye reddened and swollen with weeping. It rose over the luminous bronze mist which hung over the surface of the Lake of Egrets, a mist so suffocating that it was as though a cloud of crystal dust hung dizzily in the air.

A swarm of egrets, stretching their wings and putting out their long necks, flapped slowly over the reeds which border the bean fields. And when they had passed, the air sank once again into its wonted silence, for the kingfishers, with their tiny brilliant emerald headdresses diving and skimming over the surface of the water during the daytime, had long since disappeared. Only a few reddish-brown dragonflies were droning over the rotten rubbish heaps. Meanwhile two men came walking along the shores of the lake.

One, who was tall and swarthy, knelt on his knees and began to lay out a strip of straw matting on the earth. The other, who was slighter and leaner, held in his hand a spear decorated with red fringes, and he gazed into the distance as though trying to discern the boundaries of the vast darkness.

"It's terribly damp," he sighed.

The other paid no attention to him, too occupied with the mat; and now he seated himself unsteadily, grasped his knees in his hands and lifted up his eyes to the moon.

"There will be a full moon soon," he said. "There's no need to sleep in the hut tonight. We can lie here on the ground and look at the moon."

"The Sorrows of the Lake of Egrets" by Tuan-mu Hung-liang, translated by Yuan Chia-hua and Robert Payne from CONTEMPORARY CHINESE SHORT STORIES. Reprinted by permission of Royle Publications Limited.
1. *Tuan-mu Hung-liang* (tɤ än mù hùng lyäng).

"It's a fiendishly red moon tonight," the other answered.

"Yes—ominous."

"They say a red moon like that foretells a war."

"Perhaps."

The two companions were silent for a few moments. On the other side of the lake a gust of gloomy white vapour arose to spread out on the surface of the lake. Far away in the valley, among the young bushy poplars, a glimmering light emerged, but it soon vanished like a will-o'-the-wisp.

"Be careful. It's likely that there will be a thief or two," the stronger man said. "If they come, my nose will be able to smell them out."

"Well, what if they come? We can scare them away. There's always one or two of them every night."

"Scare them away? No, it's better if they have a taste of my fist. The festival day of the Moon Goddess is soon coming."

The younger answered bitterly: "Your fist isn't worth a mooncake!"[2]

"How do you know? At least it will have its fun."

The younger laid his spear on the ground, tore off his wet shoes and crouched down on the mat. "The fog is heavier than before," he muttered, and at the same time an incomprehensible and startling fear began to throb in his heart. He glared into the dusk with his deeply musing eyes; but there was no relief from the pain.

As the moon rose higher, all reality seemed to melt away gradually and distinctly into a smoky haze. Shadows peered out from everywhere, gazing at them. A dark poplar tree cast a shadow almost twice as long as itself over the surface of the water, and a rock, which jutted clear out of the water, lay clad in grey mildew visible still under the great mass of shadow. Over the whole lake there prevailed a mysterious air of disconsolate sadness.

"Brother Lai-pao,[3] how old are you now?"

"Twenty-three—no longer a child," Lai-pao answered.

"I am still sixteen, but mother says that next year I shall no longer be paid as a child worker."

"The less you work the better. Don't be so anxious to work, for everything in the world is wrong. You're not strong enough. If you work too hard, you will get consumption and for the rest of your life you will be miserable."

"How can I avoid it? Father is old—last year he was given three pills by a man who loved charity, but it was all useless. I'll go on contract for a year and earn a hundred dollars, and then everything will be better."

"But who will take you? Who is going to be so generous as to pay you a hundred dollars a year? In the whole place, there were no crops worth a hundred last year. . . . And you are so thin. . . ."

---

2. *mooncake*, a sweet pastry traditionally associated with the Chinese Harvest festival.
3. *Lai-pao* (lī pou).

"I can work hard . . ."

"Well, don't worry about tomorrow. There's some wine here. Won't you have some—it's good wine!" He felt under his girdle and brought out a small jug and a few pieces of bean curd.

The younger one shook his head dreamily, and watched his companion eating.

"Yes, there is something I forgot to tell you, Mah-nao.[4] Changes are going to take place. The little general is going to the capital, and the soldiers will soon be starting for the front. And it's quite true—not just the nonsense that people are always talking. And there's a secret order hidden in someone's shoes, to be delivered to the guerrillas.[5] That's why they never examine the clothes of the people passing through the gates—they only examine the shoes. They say there's no harm in letting the guerrillas try . . ."

"Brother Lai-pao, let's join the guerrillas one day."

"Yes, when the time comes. Yes, everybody has to take his part. We are all Chinese, aren't we?"

Mah-nao, the thinner of the two, sank in deep thought.

"Then we shall own a strip of farmland, eh?"

"No, it will still belong to the landlord, but the crops will be worth more, and besides—more workmen will be wanted."

"I see," Mah-nao sighed. "So we are never going to be prosperous, we'll never be rich."

"Is your mother going to get you a wife?" Lai-pao interrupted bluntly.

Mah-nao blushed and said nothing.

"There's enough bean curd here," Lai-pao said. "I've got enough. Taking a wife is like buying cattle. Your father will soon be retiring. I've seen him walking along the edge of the lake, so bent that his head and his feet almost touch."

"To take a wife, you have to have enough money. Mother gave me two pieces of clothing for my betrothal, but the girl's mother was not satisfied and said that girls are worth more this year. If we had not been engaged since our childhood, they would have done everything they could to cancel it."

"O curse the world—mothers, soldiers, wars—they take everything, even keep their daughters to themselves. Well, why don't you take some bean curd, I can't eat so much?"

"All night my father is coughing, and mother has to get up and bring him some hot water to soothe him."

"It's all a pity. Let's lie down and sleep. We shall have to get up at midnight and look after the thieves."

---

4. *Mah-nao* (mä nou). 5. *the guerrillas*, a reference to Chinese guerrilla activities against the Japanese military occupation of Manchuria in 1931.

Lai-pao laid the spears between them and lifted a ragged cotton-padded coverlet over his head and ears.

"Are you going to sit up for them?" he asked, looking up from under the coverlet.

There was no answer. The other picked up a corner of the coverlet and silently lay down. Dogs could be heard barking from a distant village, but soon the sounds died away. By now the mist had enveloped everything; still more streams of impenetrable vapour arose, rolling in curls like milky smoke, hovering among the reeds which lay before the two companions, congealing into tiny, cold, crystal balls, barely visible. And still the vapour rolled on, scattering its white sticky matter, reaching little by little towards the yellow mist which hung over the lake, pierced by the moonlight and resolving into great masses of boundless vague luminosity.

"Brother Lai-pao, you said that soldiers were starting for the front. Are they starting in the light of the full moon, as in the story of the Tartars?"

". . . ."

"Brother Lai-pao, have you seen my father?"

". . . ."

"Are you asleep—deep in sleep?"

". . . ."

He was turning from side to side, making a little noise.

"Brother Lai-pao . . ."

A pair of disappointed eyes were staring into the thick darkness.

The mist grew heavier; everything was hidden in this veil of obscurity. The two young men lay fast asleep by the water's edge. Behind them lay the bean fields, chequered with ridges and furrows. The plants were already dry, withered. The beans in their shells were waiting for the moment when, fully ripened, they would be reaped and cut. On such a moonlight night the grasshoppers did not chirp, for the damp air clung so tightly to their glassy wings that they could not move them. A faint rustling stirred among the dry leaves, followed by silence.

Mah-nao murmured in his dreams: "Don't beat me—no, don't beat me there—not on my loins." A hedgehog with spotted quivers was aimlessly snuffling around his back; but now, alarmed by the sound of human voices, it withdrew in the direction of the bean fields.

The dry leaves rustled still more, but by now the hedgehog was far away. Then they heard the sound of reaping.

Mah-nao sneezed and woke up. He pressed his ears to the ground and listened attentively. He heard the sound of a sickle, the dry stalks falling to the ground, someone binding them, footsteps, interminable shuffling. His eyes were wide open in the dusk. He looked inquiringly at the moon and thought to discover the time.

He pushed Lai-pao with his arm. "A thief!" he said, his voice almost inaudible. He pushed the boy again, and suddenly Lai-pao rose, waving his arms in bewilderment. He pressed his ears to the ground. He could hear something from the direction of the new fields. He grinned slyly: "Need of a good fist!"

"Shall we catch him?"

"Yes—we want that mooncake?"

So they rose noiselessly and stealthily walked towards the new fields, bending very low lest they should be seen by the crop stealers, who would run away before they could be caught. Mah-nao strode along and then threw himself headlong into the thickly-grown bean field.

"Curse the man!" he thought. "A good fist for a festival present—poor fellow!" Meanwhile he grasped tightly the red-fringed spear.

The fog was so heavy that the two companions soon lost sight of each other, and only by the slight rustling of the leaves could they make out each other's movements. Lai-pao, more experienced than the other, went straight towards the new fields, his fists firmly clenched, creeping forward like a lion through wild jungle, watching eagerly for the approach of his victim. His glaring eyes groped through the reddish mist.

Suddenly Mah-nao heard a yell of pain and the sound of something thumping to the ground. Lai-pao had flung himself on a man, and they were wrestling grimly.

"Curse your hairs! Do you think it all belonged to you?" Lai-pao shouted, and all the while he was showering blows with his fists on the helpless victim. "This time, you old grey-head, shout if you dare!" With all his strength he was holding down the neck of the unfortunate crop-stealer.

"Father, father!" Mah-nao cried out with the voice of a madman, and he suddenly threw himself between the two struggling on the ground.

Lai-pao was stunned. He rubbed his eyes. "Eh, what's that?"

On the ground an old man was writhing, pale, writhing with pain, out of breath, a thin stream of blood on his ash-white face.

The young men were dumbfounded and had no idea what to do.

As the old man made an effort to rise to his feet, he shook his head remorsefully. From his appearance it was clear that he had been a strong workman in his day. Though his back was terribly bent, he had been a good harvester thirty years ago.

"Uncle Mah, Uncle Mah," Lai-pao muttered, wondering how he would ever be able to apologize to the old man.

The old man paid no attention to him. He jumped up, picked up a coil of rope and a sickle and stumbled away. After a while they heard him cursing them over his shoulder.

In silence the two youths wandered back to their resting place.

"There's no more sleep for me," Lai-pao said with ill humour, as he sat down and once again grasped his knees in his hands. "You can sleep if you wish."

"You despise my father, don't you?"

"No, I don't despise him. Go to sleep," he answered, straightening his broad shoulders.

"I shall have to earn more money," he said after a while.

"What's the use of earning more money when you are poor?" Lai-pao snorted contemptuously.

"My father . . . he's an old man . . ."

"But he's strong, anyway."

"Strong?"

"Yes, why not?"

Mah-nao lay on the mat, overcome by a boundless melancholy. His brain was numb with fatigue. Before his eyes there lay only a wasteland, hopeless, silent, except for the ceaseless yell of his father even when at last he fell asleep.

When he woke up, he thought he heard someone talking in the distance. More crop stealers? But perhaps Lai-pao was still sleeping, and it was his own father returning to steal more crops? Suddenly sobering, he realized that Lai-pao had already left him.

On the verge of the western sky the moon was swinging like a great ball of molten fire. It was not long before daybreak. The ghostly crowing of cocks came from a neighbouring village.

"Ah, come now—why are you so shy?"

He could not tell from which direction the voice came.

"All right, strike me—strike on my breast! Swine! But you would like me if you knew how lovely I was!"

Listening to these words, Mah-nao was appalled, overcome by some strange horror which rose up into his consciousness. Meanwhile he heard a sickle rattling, beanstalks were falling, someone was binding them together, and then there were hurrying footsteps, sounds of eagerness, anxiety, coming from a long way away. He was frightened. He felt he would be more comfortable if Lai-pao was with him. He plucked up courage, clutched the red-fringed spear and went straight in the direction of the sounds.

No, he was not accustomed to this kind of thing. With heavily beating heart he imagined a giant, with a great ragged beard, waiting for him, lifting a sickle, striking him over the head. . . . He was nearly crying. He wanted to go back and ask for Lai-pao's assistance. But there was no sign of Lai-pao, only that dim impenetrable yellowish emptiness which surrounded him on all sides.

"Who's there?" he asked, in a loud voice which faltered a little. He felt that if he could threaten his opponent, he would pluck up courage.

Immediately a young girl, lifting her sickle above her head, jumped away from him.

"Go on, go away quickly! Stealing crops, is that what you are up to?"

Now that he knew that his opponent was only a young trembling girl, he became so bold that he could not help wondering why she did not run away as fast as her legs could carry her.

"You are so small, and yet you come stealing?"

"Didn't my mamma—didn't she tell you?"

She was so frightened that she curled up into a little shell, the sickle still in her hand, and she enunciated her words one by one as though they were being choked out by hot smothering air.

Mah-nao never knew why his voice suddenly became kind. Perhaps it was curiosity, perhaps it was because he wanted to pacify the terrified creature standing in front of him.

"Well, who is she—your mamma?"

"Didn't she tell you? Didn't she speak to you?" the girl answered, terrified, trembling from head to foot. She felt that it was all over, her mother had never really seen the man.

"You see, there are two of us. Perhaps she talked it over with the other one. Don't be frightened, I didn't know anything about it—I was sleeping."

She glanced at him doubtfully, and let her sickle hang down. Mah-nao was so uneasy that he wanted to burst out crying. The girl turned her back to him, and began to wield her sickle mechanically over the beanstalks. From time to time she peeped at him slyly from the corners of her eyes.

"Have you a father?" he asked at last, disturbed because he had no idea how to treat her.

The girl shook her head and went on cutting the stalks. Her little hands could barely grasp the bundles she had formed, and she cut them with so much difficulty that he wanted to help her.

"Have you a grandfather?"

"He's coughing. They say he will die very soon."

"Coughing?"

"Yes. At night it's terrible."

"Does your mother boil hot water for him at night?"

"Why?"

"To soothe him."

"No, she has no time."

"Why hasn't she enough time?"

"She has to steal the bean crops."

The girl yawned slightly, and sighed. She had cut down less than a man would cut with a single stroke of his scythe. And yet she went on cutting as though her whole life depended upon it, never becoming exhausted.

"Where is she now?" Mah-nao said, still puzzled.

The girl seemed to be slightly taken aback by the question, and muttered: "I don't know."

"But how can you come out here all alone?"

"My mother said that I can cut the bean crops when she is coughing."

"Oh yes, your mother . . ." he murmured again, and once more sank into deep contemplation. "But aren't you afraid? You know, on misty nights, it is difficult to see clearly."

She looked at him, her eyes glistening, her body growing thinner and smaller.

"Haven't you an elder brother?"

She shook her head sadly.

"And no younger brother?"

She sighed.

Mah-nao looked round in despair. The moon was waning over the western horizon. The bottomless white vapour was still suffocating and spreading out slowly, congealed by the cold morning air into thousands of tiny glistening dewdrops which were gradually sinking into the valley. The reeds, the trees, the hills, all those colourless masses with confused outlines, were lunging out of the dusky twilight. The cocks were crowing again like yearning ghosts.

The girl's hand was bleeding. She wiped it on her clothes, and continued reaping.

"Have you a home?"

"Yes," she said, straightening her back and taking a deep breath. Her ribs protruded out, and she looked weary beyond endurance. "Please don't ask me so many questions." She cast a stealthy glance at him, afraid of having annoyed him. "I've gathered so little, and my mother is coming soon. She'll beat me!"

She muttered these last words reluctantly, and seemed already to be recoiling before the blow.

The thick waves of fog floating over the dim earth were no less smothering than the poison gas that puts people to death. Now, at last, the layers of fog floating over the cloud grew thinner, and were swept away into emptiness.

He left her, unconscious of any aim, staggering like a somnambulist; but after he had gone twenty paces he suddenly decided to return, and he came back to her with long strides. And, seeing him return, the girl was filled with terror.

"I've gathered so little," she complained. "Just a little more. My mother will be coming soon."

Mah-nao seized the sickle, and without saying anything, he began to cut down the bean crops for her.

Cocks were crowing in the distance. Dawn was coming up over the horizon.   ✳

2 BABYLONIAN LITERATURE

Of all the major epics of the Near East, the most important is the Babylonian masterpiece Gilgamesh. *The original poem, some three thousand lines on stone tablets, was written about two thousand* B.C. *The main text, which is now in the British Museum, dates back to the seventh century* B.C. *The present prose version is composed from the poem.*

Like the Iliad *and the* Odyssey, Gilgamesh *originated as a collection of myths and folklore that gradually emerged into a single work. The hero Gilgamesh, it is commonly agreed, is not an entirely mythical figure. As king of Erech, a city in the ancient empire of Babylonia in southwest Asia, a legend grew up around his courageous exploits.*

THE ADVENTURES OF GILGAMESH

Translated from the
Babylonian and retold by
Theodor H. Gaster

ONCE UPON A TIME there lived in the city of Erech a great and terrible being whose name was Gilgamesh. Two-thirds of him were god, and only one-third was human. He was the mightiest warrior in the whole of the East; none could match him in combat, nor could anyone's spear prevail against him. Because of his power and strength all the people of Erech were brought beneath his sway, and he ruled them with an iron hand, seizing youths for his service and taking to himself any maiden he wished.

At length they could endure it no longer, and prayed to heaven for relief. The lord of heaven heard their prayer and summoned the goddess Aruru —that same goddess who, in olden times, had fashioned man out of clay.

"Go," said he, "and mold out of clay a being who will prove the equal of this tyrant, and let him fight with him and beat him, that the people may have relief."

From THE OLDEST STORIES IN THE WORLD, translated & retold by Theodor H. Gaster. Copyright 1952 by Theodor H. Gaster. Reprinted by permission of The Viking Press, Inc.

Thereupon the goddess wetted her hands and, taking clay from the ground, kneaded it into a monstrous creature, whom she named Enkidu. Fierce he was, like the god of battle, and his whole body was covered with hair. His tresses hung long like a woman's, and he was clothed in skins. All day long he roamed with the beasts of the field, and like them he fed on grass and herbs and drank from the brooks.

But no one in Erech yet knew that he existed.

One day a huntsman who had gone out trapping noticed the strange creature refreshing himself beside the herds at the fountain. The mere sight was sufficient to turn the huntsman pale. His face drawn and haggard, his heart pounding and thumping, he rushed home in terror, screaming with dismay.

The next day he went out again into the fields to continue his trapping, only to find that all the pits he had dug had been filled in and all the snares he had laid torn up, and there was Enkidu himself releasing the captured beasts from the toils!

On the third day, when the same thing happened once more, the huntsman went and consulted his father. The latter advised him to go to Erech and report the matter to Gilgamesh.

When Gilgamesh heard what had happened, and learned of the wild creature who was interfering with the labors of his subjects, he instructed the huntsman to choose a girl from the streets and take her with him to the place where the cattle drank. When Enkidu came thither for water she was to strip off her clothing and entice him with her charms. Once he embraced her the animals would recognize that he was not of their kind, and they would immediately forsake him. Thus he would be drawn into the world of men and be forced to give up his savage ways.

The huntsman did as he was ordered and, after three days' journey, arrived with the girl at the place where the cattle drank. For two days they sat and waited. On the third day, sure enough, the strange and savage creature came down with the herd for water. As soon as she caught sight of him the girl stripped off her clothing and revealed her charms. The monster was enraptured and clasped her wildly to his breast and embraced her.

For a whole week he dallied with her, until at last, sated with her charms, he rose to rejoin the herd. But the hinds and gazelles knew him no more for one of their own, and when he approached them they shied away and scampered off. Enkidu tried to run after them, but even as he ran he felt his legs begin to drag and his limbs grow taut, and all of a sudden he became aware that he was no longer a beast but had become a man.

Faint and out of breath, he turned back to the girl. But now it was a changed being who sat at her feet, gazing up into her eyes and hanging intently upon her lips.

Presently she turned toward him. "Enkidu," she said softly, "you have grown handsome as a god. Why should you go on roving with the beasts? Come, let me take you to Erech, the broad city of men. Let me take you to the gleaming temple where the god and goddess sit enthroned. It is there, by the way, that Gilgamesh is rampaging like a bull, holding the people at his mercy."

At these words Enkidu was overjoyed; for, now that he was no longer a beast, he longed for the converse and companionship of men.

"Lead on," said he, "to the city of Erech, to the gleaming temple of the god and goddess. As for Gilgamesh and his rampaging, I will soon alter that. I will fling a challenge in his face and dare him, and show him, once for all, that country lads are no weaklings!"

It was New Year's Eve when they reached the city, and the high point of the festival had now arrived, the moment when the king was to be led to the temple to play the role of bridegroom in a holy marriage with the goddess. The streets were lined with festive throngs, and everywhere the cries of young revelers rang out, piercing the air and keeping their elders from sleep. Suddenly, above the din and hubbub, came a sound of tinkling cymbals and the faint echo of distant flutes. Louder and louder it grew, until at last, around a bend in the road, the great procession wound into sight, with Gilgamesh himself the central figure in its midst. Along the street and into the courtyard of the temple it wove its way. Then it came to a halt, and Gilgamesh strode forward.

But even as he was about to pass within there was a sudden movement in the crowd, and a moment later Enkidu was seen standing in front of the gleaming doors, shouting defiance and barring the way with his foot.

The crowd shrank back amazed, but their amazement was tempered with a secret relief.

"Now at last," each whispered to his neighbor, "Gilgamesh has met his match. Why, this man is his living image! A trifle shorter, perhaps, but just as strong, for he was weaned on the milk of wild beasts! Now we shall see things humming in Erech!"

Gilgamesh, however, was by no means dismayed; for he had been forewarned in dreams of what was about to take place. He had dreamed that he was standing under the stars when suddenly there had fallen upon him from heaven a massive bolt which he could not remove. And then he had dreamed that a huge mysterious ax had suddenly been hurled into the center of the city, no man knew whence. He had related these dreams to his mother, and she had told him that they presaged the arrival of a mighty man whom he would not be able to resist but who would in time become his closest friend.

Gilgamesh strode forward to meet his opponent, and in a few moments they were locked in battle, raging and butting like bulls. At last Gilgamesh sank to the ground and knew that he had indeed met his match.

But Enkidu was chivalrous as well as strong, and saw at once that his opponent was not simply a blustering tyrant, as he had been led to believe, but a brave and stout-hearted warrior, who had courageously accepted his challenge and not flinched from the fight.

"Gilgamesh," said he, "you have proved full well that you are the child of a goddess and that heaven itself has set you on your throne. I shall no longer oppose you. Let us be friends."

And, raising him to his feet, he embraced him.

Now Gilgamesh loved adventure and could never resist a hazard. One day he proposed to Enkidu that they go together into the mountains and, as an act of daring, cut down one of the cedars in the sacred forest of the gods.

"That is not easy," replied his friend, "for the forest is guarded by a fierce and terrible monster called Humbaba. Often, when I lived with the beasts, I beheld his works. His voice is a whirlwind, and he snorts fire, and his breath is the plague."

"For shame!" retorted Gilgamesh. "Should a brave warrior like you be frightened of battle? Only the gods can escape death; and how will you face your children when they ask you what you did in the day when Gilgamesh fell?"

Then Enkidu was persuaded, and, after weapons and axes had been fashioned, Gilgamesh went to the elders of the city and told them of his plan. They warned him against it, but he refused to yield, and promptly repaired to the sun-god and implored his aid. The sun-god, however, was reluctant to help him. So Gilgamesh turned to his mother, the heavenly Queen Ninsun, and begged her to intervene. But when she heard of his plan she too was filled with dismay.

Putting on her finest raiment and her crown, she went up to the roof of the temple and addressed the sun-god. "Sun-God," she said, "you are the god of justice. Why, then, have you allowed me to bear this son, yet made him so restless and wild? Now, dear Sun-God, he has taken it into his head to travel for days on long and perilous paths only to do battle with the monster Humbaba! I beg you to watch over him day and night, and to bring him back to me safe and sound!"

When the sun-god saw her tears, his heart melted with compassion and he promised to help the heroes.

Then the goddess came down from the roof and placed upon Enkidu the sacred badge which all her votaries were wont to wear. "From now on," said she, "you are one of my wards. Go forth unafraid and lead Gilgamesh to the mountain!"

When the elders of the city saw that Enkidu was wearing the sacred badge, they relented of their previous counsel and gave Gilgamesh their blessing.

"Since," they said, "Enkidu is now a ward of the goddess, we will safely entrust our king to his keeping."

Eagerly and impetuously the two stalwarts set out on their journey, covering in three days the distance of six weeks' march. At length they came to a dense forest, and at the entrance of the forest there was a huge door. Enkidu pushed it open a trifle and peered within.

"Hurry," he whispered, beckoning to his companion, "and we can take him by surprise. Whenever he wanders abroad Humbaba always bundles himself up in seven layers of garments. Now he is sitting wearing only his vest. We can get him before he goes out!"

But even as he spoke the huge door swung upon its hinges and slammed shut, crushing his hand.

For twelve days Enkidu lay writhing in anguish, and all the while kept imploring his comrade to give up the wild adventure. But Gilgamesh refused to pay heed to his words.

"Are we such puny weaklings," he cried, "as to be put out by the first mishap? We have traveled a long way. Shall we now turn back defeated? For shame! Your wounds will soon be healed; and if we cannot engage the monster in his house, let us wait for him in the thicket!"

So on they went to the forest and at last they reached the Mountain of Cedars itself—that high and towering mountain on the summit of which the gods held session. Fatigued by the long journey, they lay down beneath the shade of the trees and were soon asleep.

But in the middle of the night Gilgamesh suddenly awoke with a start. "Did you wake me?" he called to his companion. "If not, it must have been the force of my dream. For I dreamed that a mountain was toppling upon me, when all of a sudden there appeared before me the most handsome man in all the world, and he dragged me out from under the weight and raised me to my feet."

"Friend," replied Enkidu, "your dream is an omen, for the mountain which you saw is yon monstrous Humbaba. Now it is clear that even if he falls upon us we shall escape and win!"

Then they turned upon their sides, and sleep fell on them once more. But this time it was Enkidu who woke suddenly with a start.

"Did you wake me?" he called to his companion. "If not, it must have been the force of my dream. For I dreamed that the sky rumbled and the earth shook, and the day grew black and darkness fell, and lightning flashed and a fire blazed, and death poured down. And then, all of a sudden, the glare faded and the fire went out and the sparks which had fallen turned to ashes."

Gilgamesh knew full well that the dream portended ill for his friend. Nevertheless he encouraged him not to give up; and presently they had risen and were deep in the forest.

Then Gilgamesh grasped his ax and felled one of the sacred cedars. The tree fell to earth with a loud crash, and out rushed Humbaba from his house, growling and roaring.

Now the monster had a strange and terrible face, with one eye in the middle, which could turn to stone any upon whom it gazed. As he came storming through the thicket, nearer and nearer, and as the tearing and cracking of branches announced his approach, Gilgamesh for the first time grew truly frightened.

But the sun-god remembered his promise and called to Gilgamesh out of the heavens, bidding him go forth unafraid to the combat. And even as the leaves of the thicket parted and the terrible face bore down upon the heroes, the sun-god sent mighty, searing winds from every quarter of the heavens, and they beat against the eye of the monster until they blinded his vision and he could move neither backward nor forward.

Then, as he stood there, thrashing with his arms, Gilgamesh and Enkidu closed in upon him, until at last he begged for grace. But the heroes would grant him none. They drew their swords and severed the horrible head from his giant frame.

Then Gilgamesh wiped the dust of battle from his brow and shook out the braid of his hair and removed his soiled garments and put on his kingly robe and crown. So wondrous did he appear in his beauty and valor that even a goddess could not resist him, and presently the Lady Ishtar [1] herself was there at his side.

"Gilgamesh," said she, "come, be my lover. I will give you a chariot of gold encrusted with gems, and the mules that draw it shall be swift as the wind. You shall enter our house beneath the fragrance of cedars. Threshold and stoop shall kiss your feet. Kings and princes shall bow before you and bring you the yield of the earth for tribute. Your ewes shall bear twins; your chariot horses shall be chargers; and your oxen shall have no equal."

But Gilgamesh remained unmoved. "Lady," he replied, "you speak of giving me riches, but you would demand far more in return. The food and clothing you would need would be such as befits a goddess; the house would have to be meet for a queen, and your robes of the finest weave. And why should I give you all this? You are but a draughty door, a palace tottering to its ruin, a turban which fails to cover the head, pitch that defiles the hand, a bottle that leaks, a shoe that pinches.

"Have you ever kept faith with a lover? Have you ever been true to your troth? When you were a girl there was Tammuz.[2] But what happened to him? Year by year men mourn his fate! He who comes to you preened like a jaybird ends with broken wings! He who comes like a lion, perfect in strength, you ensnare into pits sevenfold! He who comes like a charger, glorious in battle, you drive for miles with spur and lash, and then give him muddied water to drink! He who comes like a shepherd tending his

---

1. *Lady Ishtar*, a Babylonian goddess of love and war. 2. *Tammuz*, a Babylonian god of the flocks who was confined to the afterworld as a companion for Ishtar.

flock you turn to a ravening wolf, scourged by his own companions and bitten by his own dogs!

"Remember your father's gardener? What happened to *him?* Daily he brought you baskets of fruit, daily bedecked your table. But when he refused your love you trapped him like a spider caught in a spot where it cannot move! You will surely do the same to me."

When Ishtar heard these words she was very angry, and rushed to her father and mother in heaven to complain of the insults which the hero had hurled at her. But the heavenly father refused to interfere, and told her roundly that she had got what she deserved.

Then Ishtar fell to threats. "Father," she cried, "I want you to send against this fellow that mighty heavenly bull whose rampaging brings storms and earthquakes. If you refuse I will break down the doors of hell and release the dead, so that they arise and outnumber the living!"

"Very well," said her father at length, "but remember, whenever the bull comes down from heaven it means a seven-year famine on earth. Have you provided for that? Have you laid up food for men and fodder for beasts?"

"I have thought of all that," replied the goddess. "There is food enough for men and fodder for beasts."

So the bull was sent down from heaven and straightway rushed upon the heroes. But even as it charged, snorting and foaming in their faces, flaying and thrashing with its mighty tail, Enkidu seized its horns and thrust his sword into the back of its neck. Then they plucked out its heart and brought it as an offering to the sun-god.

Meanwhile Ishtar was pacing up and down upon the ramparts of Erech, watching the fight in the valley below. When she saw that the bull had been vanquished she leaped upon the battlements and let out a piercing shriek.

"Woe betide Gilgamesh," she screamed, "who has dared to hold me in contempt and to slay the bull of heaven!"

At these words Enkidu, wishing to make it clear to her that he too had played his part in the victory, tore off the buttocks of the bull and flung them in her face. "Would that I could lay hands on *you*," he cried, "and do the same to you! Would that I could tear out your entrails and hang them up beside this bull's!"

Ishtar was now thoroughly put out, and all that she could do was to prepare to give decent burial to the bull, as befitted a heavenly creature. But even this was denied her, for the two heroes promptly picked up the carcass and carried it in triumph into Erech. So the goddess was left with her maidens, absurdly shedding tears over the animal's buttocks, while Gilgamesh and his comrade went striding merrily into the city, proudly displaying the evidence of their prowess and receiving the plaudits of the people.

But the gods are not mocked; whatsoever a man sows, that shall he also reap.

One night Enkidu had a strange dream. He dreamed that the gods were sitting in council, trying to decide whether he or Gilgamesh was the more to blame for the slaying of Humbaba and the heavenly bull. The more guilty, they had ruled, was to be put to death.

For a long while the debate raged back and forth, but when at length they had still not made up their minds, Anu, the father of the gods, proposed a way out.

"In my opinion," he declared, "Gilgamesh is the greater culprit, for not only did he slay the monster but he also cut down the sacred cedar."

No sooner, however, had he uttered these words than pandemonium broke loose, and soon the gods were at sixes and sevens, each roundly abusing the other.

"Gilgamesh?" screamed the god of the winds. "It is Enkidu who is the real villain, for it was he that led the way!"

"Indeed!" roared the sun-god, wheeling sharply upon him. "What right have *you* to talk? It was *you* who hurled the winds into Humbaba's face!"

"And what about *you?*" retorted the other, shaking with anger. "What about *you?* If it hadn't been for you, neither of them would have done these things! It was *you* that encouraged them and kept coming to their aid!"

Fiercely they argued and fiercely they wrangled, their tempers growing hotter by the minute and their voices louder and louder. But before they could come to a decision—Enkidu woke up.

He was now firmly convinced that he was doomed to die. But when he told the dream to his companion it seemed to Gilgamesh that the real punishment was destined, after all, for himself.

"Dear comrade," he cried, the tears streaming down his cheeks, "do the gods imagine that by killing you they will be letting me go free? Nay, good friend, all my days I shall sit like a beggar on the threshold of death, waiting for the door to open that I may enter and see your face!"

For the rest of the night Enkidu lay awake on his bed, tossing and turning. And as he lay, his whole life seemed to pass before him. He remembered the carefree days of old, when he had roamed the hills with the beasts, and then he bethought him of the huntsman who had found him and of the girl who had lured him to the world of men. He recalled also the adventure in the forest of cedars, and how the door had slammed shut on his hands, inflicting upon him the first and only wound that he had ever suffered. And he cursed the huntsman and the girl and the door with a bitter curse.

At last the first rays of the morning sun came stealing through the window, bathing the room in light and playing against the shadows on the opposite wall. "Enkidu," they seemed to be saying, "not all of your life among men has been darkness, and those whom you are cursing were rays of light. Were it not for the huntsman and the girl, you would still be eating grass and sleeping in cold meadows, but now you feed on the fare of kings and lie on a princely couch. And were it not for them, you would never have met with Gilgamesh, nor found the closest friend of your life!"

Then Enkidu knew that the sun-god had been speaking to him, and he no longer cursed the huntsman and the girl, but called down upon them all manner of blessings.

A few nights later he dreamed a second dream. This time it seemed as though a loud cry went up from heaven and earth, and a strange, grisly creature, with the face of a lion and the wings and talons of an eagle, swooped down from nowhere and carried him off. All of a sudden his arms sprouted feathers, and he became like the monstrous being which had assailed him. Then he knew that he was dead and that one of the harpies of hell was speeding him along the road of no return. At last he reached the house of darkness, where dwelt the shades of the departed. And behold, all the great ones of the earth were around him. Kings and nobles and priests, their crowns and robes put aside forever, sat huddled like hideous demons, covered with birdlike wings; and instead of the roasts and bakemeats of old they now ate dirt and dust. And there, on a lofty throne, sat the queen of hell herself, with her faithful handmaid squatting beside her, reading from a tablet the record of every soul as it passed in the gloom.

When he awoke Enkidu related the dream to his companion; and now they knew for certain which of them was doomed to die.

For nine days Enkidu languished upon his bed, growing weaker and weaker, while Gilgamesh watched beside him, torn with grief.

"Enkidu," he cried in his anguish, "you were the ax at my side, the bow in my hand, the dirk in my belt, my shield, my robe, my chiefest delight! With you I braved and endured all things, scaled the hills and hunted the leopard! With you I seized the heavenly bull and came to grips with the ogre of the forest! But now, behold, you are wrapped in sleep and shrouded in darkness, and hear not my voice!"

And even as he cried he saw that his companion no longer stirred nor opened his eyes; and when he felt Enkidu's heart it was beating no more.

Then Gilgamesh took a cloth and veiled the face of Enkidu, even as men veil a bride on the day of her espousal. And he paced to and fro and cried aloud, and his voice was the voice of a lioness robbed of her whelps. And he stripped off his garments and tore his hair and gave himself up to mourning.

All night long he gazed upon the prostrate form of his companion and saw him grow stiff and wizened, and all the beauty was departed from him. "Now," said Gilgamesh, "I have seen the face of death and am sore afraid. One day I too shall be like Enkidu."

When morning came he had made a bold resolve.

On an island at the far ends of the earth, so rumor had it, lived the only mortal in the world who had ever escaped death—an old, old man, whose name was Utnapishtim. Gilgamesh decided to seek him out and to learn from him the secret of eternal life.

As soon as the sun was up he set out on his journey, and at last, after traveling long and far, he came to the end of the world and saw before him a huge mountain whose twin peaks touched the sky and whose roots reached down to nethermost hell. In front of the mountain there was a massive gate, and the gate was guarded by fearsome and terrible creatures, half man and half scorpion.

Gilgamesh flinched for a moment and screened his eyes from their hideous gaze. Then he recovered himself and strode boldly to meet them.

When the monsters saw that he was unafraid, and when they looked on the beauty of his body, they knew at once that no ordinary mortal was before them. Nevertheless they challenged his passage and asked the purpose of his coming.

Gilgamesh told them that he was on his way to Utnapishtim, to learn the secret of eternal life.

"That," replied their captain, "is a thing which none has ever learned, nor was there ever a mortal who succeeded in reaching that ageless sage. For the path which we guard is the path of the sun, a gloomy tunnel twelve leagues long, a road where the foot of man may not tread."

"Be it never so long," rejoined the hero, "and never so dark, be the pains and the perils never so great, be the heat never so searing and the cold never so sharp, I am resolved to tread it!"

At the sound of these words the sentinels knew for certain that one who was more than a mortal was standing before them, and at once they threw open the gate.

Boldly and fearlessly Gilgamesh entered the tunnel, but with every step he took the path became darker and darker, until at last he could see neither before nor behind. Yet still he strode forward, and just when it seemed that the road would never end, a gust of wind fanned his face and a thin streak of light pierced the gloom.

When he came out into the sunlight a wondrous sight met his eyes, for he found himself in the midst of a faery garden, the trees of which were hung with jewels. And even as he stood rapt in wonder the voice of the sun-god came to him from heaven.

"Gilgamesh," it said, "go no farther. This is the garden of delights. Stay awhile and enjoy it. Never before have the gods granted such a boon to a mortal, and for more you must not hope. The eternal life which you seek you will never find."

But even these words could not divert the hero from his course and, leaving the earthly paradise behind him, he proceeded on his way.

Presently, footsore and weary, he saw before him a large house which had all the appearance of being a hospice.[3] Trudging slowly toward it, he sought admission.

But the alewife, whose name was Siduri, had seen his approach from afar and, judging by his grimy appearance that he was simply a tramp, she had ordered the postern barred in his face.

Gilgamesh was at first outraged and threatened to break down the door, but when the lady called from the window and explained to him the cause of her alarm his anger cooled, and he reassured her, telling her who he was and the nature of his journey and the reason he was so disheveled. Thereupon she raised the latch and bade him welcome.

Later in the evening they fell to talking, and the alewife attempted to dissuade him from his quest. "Gilgamesh," she said, "that which you seek you will never find. For when the gods created man they gave him death for his portion; life they kept for themselves. Therefore enjoy your lot. Eat, drink, and be merry; for *that* were you born!"

But still the hero would not be swerved, and at once he proceeded to inquire of the alewife the way to Utnapishtim.

"He lives," she replied, "on a faraway isle, and to reach it you must cross an ocean. But the ocean is the ocean of death, and no man living has sailed it. Howbeit, there is at present in this hospice a man named Urshanabi. He is the boatman of that aged sage, and he has come hither on an errand. Maybe you can persuade him to ferry you across."

So the alewife presented Gilgamesh to the boatman, and he agreed to ferry him across.

"But there is one condition," he said. "You must never allow your hands to touch the waters of death, and when once your pole has been dipped in them you must straightway discard it and use another, lest any of the drops fall upon your fingers. Therefore take your ax and hew down six-score poles; for it is a long voyage, and you will need them all."

Gilgamesh did as he was bidden, and in a short while they had boarded the boat and put out to sea.

But after they had sailed a number of days the poles gave out, and they had well nigh drifted and foundered had not Gilgamesh torn off his shirt and held it aloft for a sail.

Meanwhile, there was Utnapishtim, sitting on the shore of the island, looking out upon the main, when suddenly his eyes descried the familiar craft bobbing precariously on the waters.

"Something is amiss," he murmured. "The gear seems to have been broken."

And as the ship drew closer he saw the bizarre figure of Gilgamesh holding up his shirt against the breeze.

---

3. *hospice,* a house of rest for travelers.

"That is not my boatman," he muttered. "Something is surely amiss."

When they touched land Urshanabi at once brought his passenger into the presence of Utnapishtim, and Gilgamesh told him why he had come and what he sought.

"Young man," said the sage, "that which you seek you will never find. For there is nothing eternal on earth. When men draw up a contract they set a term. What they acquire today, tomorrow they must leave to others. Age-long feuds in time die out. Rivers which rise and swell, in the end subside. When the butterfly leaves the cocoon it lives but a day. Times and seasons are appointed for all."

"True," replied the hero. "But you yourself are a mortal, no whit different from me; yet you live forever. Tell me how you found the secret of life, to make yourself like the gods."

A faraway look came into the eyes of the old man. It seemed as though all the days of all the years were passing in procession before him. Then, after a long pause, he lifted his head and smiled.

"Gilgamesh," he said slowly, "I will tell you the secret—a secret high and holy, which no one knows save the gods and myself." And he told him the story of the great flood which the gods had sent upon the earth in the days of old, and how Ea, the kindly lord of wisdom, had sent him warning of it in the whistle of the wind which soughed through the wattles of his hut. At Ea's command he had built an ark, and sealed it with pitch and asphalt, and loaded his kin and his cattle within it, and sailed for seven days and seven nights while the waters rose and the storms raged and the lightnings flashed. And on the seventh day the ark had grounded on a mountain at the end of the world, and he had opened a window in the ark and sent out a dove, to see if the waters had subsided. But the dove had returned, for want of place to rest. Then he had sent out a swallow, and the swallow too had come back. And at last he had sent out a raven, and the raven had not returned. Then he had led forth his kinsmen and his cattle and offered thanksgiving to the gods. But suddenly the god of the winds had come down from heaven and led him back into the ark, along with his wife, and set it afloat upon the waters once more, until it came to the island on the far horizon, and there the gods had set him to dwell forever.

When Gilgamesh heard the tale he knew at once that his quest had been vain, for now it was clear that the old man had no secret formula to give him. He had become immortal, as he now revealed, by special grace of the gods and not, as Gilgamesh had imagined, by possession of some hidden knowledge. The sun-god had been right, and the scorpion-men had been right, and the alewife had been right: that which he had sought he would never find—at least on this side of the grave.

When the old man had finished his story he looked steadily into the drawn face and tired eyes of the hero. "Gilgamesh," he said kindly, "you must rest awhile. Lie down and sleep for six days and seven nights." And no sooner had he said these words than, lo and behold, Gilgamesh was fast asleep.

Then Utnapishtim turned to his wife. "You see," said he, "this man who seeks to live forever cannot even go without sleep. When he awakes he will, of course, deny it—men were liars ever—so I want you to give him proof. Every day that he sleeps bake a loaf of bread and place it beside him. Day by day those loaves will grow staler and moldier, and after seven nights, as they lie in a row beside him, he will be able to see from the state of each how long he has slept."

So every morning Utnapishtim's wife baked a loaf, and she made a mark on the wall to show that another day had passed; and naturally, at the end of six days, the first loaf was dried out, and the second was like leather, and the third was soggy, and the fourth had white specks on it, and the fifth was filled with mold, and only the sixth looked fresh.

When Gilgamesh awoke, sure enough, he tried to pretend that he had never slept. "Why," said he to Utnapishtim, "the moment I take a nap you go jogging my elbow and waking me up!" But Utnapishtim showed him the loaves, and then Gilgamesh knew that he had indeed been sleeping for six days and seven nights.

Thereupon Utnapishtim ordered him to wash and cleanse himself and make ready for the journey home. But even as the hero stepped into his boat to depart Utnapishtim's wife drew near.

"Utnapishtim," said she, "you cannot send him away empty-handed. He has journeyed hither with great effort and pain, and you must give him a parting gift."

The old man raised his eyes and gazed earnestly at the hero. "Gilgamesh," he said, "I will tell you a secret. In the depths of the sea lies a plant. It looks like a buckthorn and pricks like a rose. If any man come into possession of it, he can, by tasting it, regain his youth!"

When Gilgamesh heard these words he tied heavy stones to his feet and let himself down into the depths of the sea; and there, on the bed of the ocean, he espied the plant. Caring little that it pricked him, he grasped it between his fingers, cut the stones from his feet, and waited for the tide to wash him ashore.

Then he showed the plant to Urshanabi the boatman. "Look," he cried, "it's the famous plant called Graybeard-grow-young! Whoever tastes it, gets a new lease on life! I will carry it back to Erech and give it to the people to eat. So will I at least have some reward for my pains!"

After they had crossed the perilous waters and reached land, Gilgamesh and his companion began the long journey on foot to the city of Erech. When they had traveled fifty leagues the sun was already beginning to set, and they looked for a place to pass the night. Suddenly they came upon a cool spring.

"Here let us rest," said the hero, "and I will go bathe."

So he stripped off his clothes and placed the plant on the ground and went to bathe in the cool spring. But as soon as his back was turned a serpent came out of the waters and, sniffing the fragrance of the plant, carried it away. And no sooner had it tasted of it than at once it sloughed off its skin and regained its youth.

When Gilgamesh saw that the precious plant had now passed from his hands forever he sat down and wept. But soon he stood up and, resigned at last to the fate of all mankind, he returned to the city of Erech, back to the land whence he had come.　　　　　　　　　　　　　✳

3 HEBREW LITERATURE

from *THE BIBLE*

King James Version

The Story of Samson (Judges 13-16)

CHAPTER 13

ISRAEL UNDER THE PHILISTINES; SAMSON BORN.

AND THE CHILDREN OF ISRAEL did evil again in the sight of the Lord; and the Lord delivered them into the hand of the Philistines forty years.

2 And there was a certain man of Zorah, of the family of the Danites, whose name was Manoah; and his wife was barren, and bare not.

3 And the angel of the Lord appeared unto the woman, and said unto her, Behold now, thou art barren, and bearest not: but thou shalt conceive, and bear a son.

4 Now therefore beware, I pray thee, and drink not wine nor strong drink, and eat not any unclean thing [1]:

5 For, lo, thou shalt conceive, and bear a son; and no razor shall come on his head: for the child shall be a Nazarite [2] unto God from the womb: and he shall begin to deliver Israel out of the hand of the Philistines.

6 Then the woman came and told her husband, saying, A man of God came unto me, and his countenance was like the countenance of an angel of God, very terrible: but I asked him not whence he was, neither told he me his name:

7 But he said unto me, Behold, thou shalt conceive, and bear a son; and now drink no wine nor strong drink, neither eat any unclean thing: for the child shall be a Nazarite to God from the womb to the day of his death.

---

1. *eat . . . thing*, a reference to the Hebrew dietary laws which prohibit the Jews from eating certain foods. 2. *Nazarite*, among the ancient Hebrews, one who had taken strict religious vows.

8 Then Manoah entreated the Lord, and said, O my Lord, let the man of God which thou didst send come again unto us, and teach us what we shall do unto the child that shall be born.

9 And God hearkened to the voice of Manoah; and the angel of God came again unto the woman as she sat in the field: but Manoah her husband was not with her.

10 And the woman made haste, and ran, and shewed her husband, and said unto him, Behold, the man hath appeared unto me, that came unto me the other day.

11 And Manoah arose, and went after his wife, and came to the man, and said unto him, Art thou the man that spakest unto the woman? And he said, I am.

12 And Manoah said, Now let thy words come to pass. How shall we order the child, and how shall we do unto him?

13 And the angel of the Lord said unto Manoah, Of all that I said unto the woman let her beware.

14 She may not eat of any thing that cometh of the vine, neither let her drink wine nor strong drink, nor eat any unclean thing: all that I commanded her let her observe.

15 And Manoah said unto the angel of the Lord, I pray thee, let us detain thee, until we shall have made ready a kid for thee.

16 And the angel of the Lord said unto Manoah, Though thou detain me, I will not eat of thy bread: and if thou wilt offer a burnt offering, thou must offer it unto the Lord. For Manoah knew not that he was an angel of the Lord.

17 And Manoah said unto the angel of the Lord, What is thy name, that when thy sayings come to pass we may do thee honor?

18 And the angel of the Lord said unto him, Why askest thou thus after my name, seeing it is secret?

19 So Manoah took a kid with a meat offering, and offered it upon a rock unto the Lord: and the angel did wondrously; and Manoah and his wife looked on.

20 For it came to pass, when the flame went up toward heaven from off the altar, that the angel of the Lord ascended in the flame of the altar. And Manoah and his wife looked on it, and fell on their faces to the ground.

21 But the angel of the Lord did no more appear to Monoah and to his wife. Then Manoah knew that he was an angel of the Lord.

22 And Manoah said unto his wife, We shall surely die, because we have seen God.

23 But his wife said unto him, If the Lord were pleased to kill us, he would not have received a burnt offering and a meat offering at our hands, neither would he have shewed us all these things, nor would as at this time have told us such things as these.

24 And the woman bare a son, and called his name Samson: and the child grew, and the Lord blessed him.

25 And the Spirit of the Lord began to move him at times in the camp of Dan between Zorah and Eshtaol.

CHAPTER 14

SAMSON'S MARRIAGE; HE IS BETRAYED.

AND SAMSON went down to Timnath, and saw a woman in Timnath of the daughters of the Philistines.

2 And he came up, and told his father and his mother, and said, I have seen a woman in Timnath of the daughters of the Philistines: now therefore get her for me to wife.

3 Then his father and his mother said unto him, Is there never a woman among the daughters of thy brethren, or among all my people, that thou goest to take a wife of the uncircumcised Philistines? And Samson said unto his father, Get her for me; for she pleaseth me well.

4 But his father and his mother knew not that it was of the Lord, that he sought an occasion against the Philistines: for at that time the Philistines had dominion over Israel.

5 Then went Samson down, and his father and his mother, to Timnath, and came to the vineyards of Timnath: and, behold, a young lion roared against him.

6 And the Spirit of the Lord came mightily upon him, and he rent him as he would have rent a kid, and he had nothing in his hand: but he told not his father or his mother what he had done.

7 And he went down, and talked with the woman; and she pleased Samson well.

8 And after a time he returned to take her, and he turned aside to see the carcass of the lion: and, behold, there was a swarm of bees and honey in the carcass of the lion.

9 And he took thereof in his hands, and went on eating, and came to his father and mother; and he gave them, and they did eat: but he told not them that he had taken the honey out of the carcass of the lion.

10 So his father went down unto the woman: and Samson made there a feast; for so used the young men to do.

11 And it came to pass, when they saw him, that they brought thirty companions to be with him.

12 And Samson said unto them, I will now put forth a riddle unto you: if ye can certainly declare it me within the seven days of the feast, and find it out, then I will give you thirty sheets and thirty change of garments:

13 But if ye cannot declare it me, then shall ye give me thirty sheets and thirty change of garments. And they said unto him, Put forth thy riddle, that we may hear it.

14 And he said unto them, Out of the eater came forth meat, and out of the strong came forth sweetness. And they could not in three days expound the riddle.

15 And it came to pass on the seventh day, that they said unto Samson's wife, Entice thy husband, that he may declare unto us the riddle, lest we burn thee and thy father's house with fire: have ye called us to take that we have? is it not so?

16 And Samson's wife wept before him, and said, Thou dost but hate me, and lovest me not: thou hast put forth a riddle unto the children of my people, and hast not told it me. And he said unto her, Behold, I have not told it my father nor my mother, and shall I tell it thee?

17 And she wept before him the seven days, while their feast lasted: and it came to pass on the seventh day, that he told her, because she lay sore upon him: and she told the riddle to the children of her people.

18 And the men of the city said unto him on the seventh day before the sun went down, What is sweeter than honey? and what is stronger than a lion? And he said unto them, If ye had not plowed with my heifer, ye had not found out my riddle.

19 And the Spirit of the Lord came unto him, and he went down to Ashkelon, and slew thirty men of them, and took their spoil, and gave change of garments unto them which expounded the riddle. And his anger was kindled, and he went up to his father's house.

20 But Samson's wife was given to his companion, whom he had used as his friend.

CHAPTER 15

SAMSON'S CONFLICTS WITH THE PHILISTINES.

But it came to pass within a while after, in the time of wheat harvest, that Samson visited his wife with a kid; and he said, I will go in to my wife into the chamber. But her father would not suffer him to go in.

2 And her father said, I verily thought that thou hadst utterly hated her; therefore I gave her to thy companion: is not her younger sister fairer than she? take her, I pray thee, instead of her.

3 And Samson said concerning them, Now shall I be more blameless than the Philistines, though I do them a displeasure.

4 And Samson went and caught three hundred foxes, and took fire-brands, and turned tail to tail, and put a firebrand in the midst between two tails.

5 And when he had set the brands on fire, he let them go into the standing corn of the Philistines, and burnt up both the shocks, and also the standing corn, with the vineyards and olives.

6 Then the Philistines said, Who hath done this? And they answered, Samson, the son-in-law of the Timnite, because he had taken his wife, and given her to his companion. And the Philistines came up, and burnt her and her father with fire.

7 And Samson said unto them, Though ye have done this, yet will I be avenged of you, and after that I will cease.

8 And he smote them hip and thigh with a great slaughter: and he went down and dwelt in the top of the rock Etam.

9 Then the Philistines went up, and pitched in Judah, and spread themselves in Lehi.

10 And the men of Judah said, Why are ye come up against us? And they answered, To bind Samson are we come up, to do to him as he hath done to us.

11 Then three thousand men of Judah went to the top of the rock Etam, and said to Samson, Knowest thou not that the Philistines are rulers over us? what is this that thou hast done unto us? And he said unto them, As they did unto me, so have I done unto them.

12 And they said unto him, We are come down to bind thee, that we may deliver thee into the hand of the Philistines. And Samson said unto them, Swear unto me, that ye will not fall upon me yourselves.

13 And they spake unto him, saying, No; but we will bind thee fast, and deliver thee into their hand: but surely we will not kill thee. And they bound him with two new cords, and brought him up from the rock.

14 And when he came unto Lehi, the Philistines shouted against him: and the Spirit of the Lord came mightily upon him, and the cords that were upon his arms became as flax that was burnt with fire, and his bands loosed from off his hands.

15 And he found a new jawbone of an ass, and put forth his hand and took it, and slew a thousand men therewith.

16 And Samson said, With the jawbone of an ass, heaps upon heaps, with the jaw of an ass have I slain a thousand men.

17 And it came to pass, when he had made an end of speaking, that he cast away the jawbone out of his hand, and called that place Ramath-lehi.

18 And he was sore athirst, and called on the Lord, and said, Thou hast given this great deliverance into the hand of thy servant: and now shall I die for thirst, and fall into the hand of the uncircumcised?

19 But God clave a hollow place that was in the jaw, and there came water thereout; and when he had drunk, his spirit came again, and he revived: wherefore he called the name thereof Enhakkore, which is in Lehi unto this day.

20 And he judged Israel in the days of the Philistines twenty years.

CHAPTER 16

THEN WENT Samson to Gaza, and saw there a harlot, and went in unto her.

2 And it was told the Gazites, saying, Samson is come hither. And they compassed him in, and laid wait for him all night in the gate of the city, and were quiet all the night, saying, In the morning, when it is day, we shall kill him.

3 And Samson lay till midnight, and arose at midnight, and took the doors of the gate of the city, and the two posts, and went away with them, bar and all, and put them upon his shoulders, and carried them up to the top of a hill that is before Hebron.

4 And it came to pass afterward, that he loved a woman in the valley of Sorek, whose name was Delilah.

5 And the lords of the Philistines came up unto her, and said unto her, Entice him, and see wherein his great strength lieth, and by what means we may prevail against him, that we may bind him to afflict him: and we will give thee every one of us eleven hundred pieces of silver.

6 And Delilah said to Samson, Tell me, I pray thee, wherein thy great strength lieth, and wherewith thou mightest be bound to afflict thee.

7 And Samson said unto her, If they bind me with seven green withes that were never dried, then shall I be weak, and be as another man.

8 Then the lords of the Philistines brought up to her seven green withes which had not been dried, and she bound him with them.

9 Now there were men lying in wait, abiding with her in the chamber. And she said unto him, The Philistines be upon thee, Samson. And he brake the withes, as a thread of tow is broken when it toucheth the fire. So his strength was not known.

10 And Delilah said unto Samson, Behold, thou hast mocked me, and told me lies: now tell me, I pray thee, wherewith thou mightest be bound.

11 And he said unto her, If they bind me fast with new ropes that never were occupied, then shall I be weak, and be as another man.

12 Delilah therefore took new ropes, and bound him therewith, and said unto him, The Philistines be upon thee, Samson. And there were liers in wait abiding in the chamber. And he brake them from off his arms like a thread.

13 And Delilah said unto Samson, Hitherto thou hast mocked me, and told me lies: tell me wherewith thou mightest be bound. And he said unto her, If you weavest the seven locks of my head with the web.[3]

---

3. *weavest . . . web.* The web refers to a horizontal loom in which the material being woven was stretched between supports fixed in the ground. Samson suggests that Delilah weave his hair into the warp of the loom and fasten it with the pin, or peg.

14 And she fastened it with the pin, and said unto him, The Philistines be upon thee, Samson. And he awaked out of his sleep, and went away with the pin of the beam, and with the web.

15 And she said unto him, How canst thou say, I love thee, when thine heart is not with me? thou hast mocked me these three times, and hast not told me wherein thy great strength lieth.

16 And it came to pass, when she pressed him daily with her words, and urged him, so that his soul was vexed unto death;

17 That he told her all his heart, and said unto her, There hath not come a razor upon mine head: for I have been a Nazarite unto God from my mother's womb: if I be shaven, then my strength will go from me, and I shall become weak, and be like any other man.

18 And when Delilah saw that he had told her all his heart, she sent and called for the lords of the Philistines, saying, Come up this once, for he hath shewed me all his heart. Then the lords of the Philistines came up unto her, and brought money in their hand.

19 And she made him sleep upon her knees; and she called for a man, and she caused him to shave off the seven locks of his head; and she began to afflict him, and his strength went from him.

20 And she said, The Philistines be upon thee, Samson. And he awoke out of his sleep, and said, I will go out as at other times before, and shake myself. And he wist not that the Lord was departed from him.

21 But the Philistines took him, and put out his eyes, and brought him down to Gaza, and bound him with fetters of brass; and he did grind in the prison house.

22 Howbeit the hair of his head began to grow again after he was shaven.

23 Then the lords of the Philistines gathered them together for to offer a great sacrifice unto Dagon their god, and to rejoice: for they said, Our god hath delivered Samson our enemy into our hand.

24 And when the people saw him, they praised their god: for they said, Our god hath delivered into our hands our enemy, and the destroyer of our country, which slew many of us.

25 And it came to pass, when their hearts were merry, that they said, Call for Samson, that he may make us sport. And they called for Samson out of the prison house; and he made them sport: and they set him between the pillars.

26 And Samson said unto the lad that held him by the hand, Suffer me that I may feel the pillars whereupon the house standeth, that I may lean upon them.

27 Now the house was full of men and women; and all the lords of the Philistines were there; and there were upon the roof about three thousand men and women, that beheld while Samson made sport.

28 And Samson called unto the Lord, and said, O Lord God, remember

me, I pray thee, and strengthen me, I pray thee, only this once, O God, that I may be at once avenged of the Philistines for my two eyes.

29 And Samson took hold of the two middle pillars upon which the house stood, and on which it was borne up, of the one with his right hand, and of the other with his left.

30 And Samson said, Let me die with the Philistines. And he bowed himself with all his might; and the house fell upon the lords, and upon all the people that were therein. So the dead which he slew at his death were more than they which he slew in his life.

31 Then his brethren and all the house of his father came down, and took him, and brought him up, and buried him between Zorah and Eshtaol in the buryingplace of Manoah his father. And he judged Israel twenty years.   ✕

Psalm 8

O LORD our Lord, how excellent is thy name in all the earth! who hast set thy glory above the heavens.

2 Out of the mouth of babes and sucklings hast thou ordained strength because of thine enemies, that thou mightest still the enemy and the avenger.

3 When I consider thy heavens, the work of thy fingers, the moon and the stars, which thou hast ordained;

4 What is man, that thou art mindful of him? and the son of man, that thou visitest him?

5 For thou has made him a little lower than the angels, and hast crowned him with glory and honor.

6 Thou madest him to have dominion over the works of thy hands; thou hast put all things under his feet:

7 All sheep and oxen, yea, and the beasts of the field;

8 The fowl of the air, and the fish of the sea, and whatsoever passeth through the paths of the seas.

9 O Lord our Lord, how excellent is thy name in all the earth!

Psalm 19

THE HEAVENS declare the glory of God; and the firmament sheweth his handywork.

2 Day unto day uttereth speech, and night unto night sheweth knowledge.

3 There is no speech nor language, where their voice is not heard.

4 Their line is gone out through all the earth, and their words to the end of the world. In them hath he set a tabernacle for the sun,

5 Which is as a bridegroom coming out of his chamber, and rejoiceth as a strong man to run a race.

6 His going forth is from the end of the heaven, and his circuit unto the ends of it: and there is nothing hid from the heat thereof.

7 The law of the Lord is perfect, converting the soul: the testimony of the Lord is sure, making wise the simple.

8 The statutes of the Lord are right, rejoicing the heart: the commandment of the Lord is pure, enlightening the eyes.

9 The fear of the Lord is clean, enduring for ever: the judgments of the Lord are true and righteous altogether.

Psalm 23

THE LORD is my shepherd; I shall not want.

2 He maketh me to lie down in green pastures: he leadeth me beside the still waters.

3 He restoreth my soul: he leadeth me in the paths of righteousness for his name's sake.

4 Yea, though I walk through the valley of the shadow of death, I will fear no evil: for thou art with me; thy rod and thy staff they comfort me.

5 Thou preparest a table before me in the presence of mine enemies: thou anointest my head with oil; my cup runneth over.

6 Surely goodness and mercy shall follow me all the days of my life: and I will dwell in the house of the Lord for ever.

Psalm 45

MY HEART is inditing a good matter: I speak of the things which I have made touching the king: my tongue is the pen of a ready writer.

2 Thou art fairer than the children of men: grace is poured into thy lips: therefore God hath blessed thee for ever.

3 Gird thy sword upon thy thigh, O most mighty, with thy glory and thy majesty.

4 And in thy majesty ride prosperously because of truth and meekness and righteousness; and thy right hand shall teach thee terrible things.

5 Thine arrows are sharp in the heart of the king's enemies; whereby the people fall under thee.

6 Thy throne, O God, is for ever and ever: the sceptre of thy kingdom is a right sceptre.

7 Thou lovest righteousness, and hatest wickedness: therefore God, thy God, hath anointed thee with the oil of gladness above thy fellows.

8 All thy garments smell of myrrh, and aloes, and cassia,[2] out of the ivory palaces, whereby they have made thee glad.

9 King's daughters were among thy honorable women: up thy right hand did stand the queen in gold of Ophir.[3]

10 Hearken, O daughter, and consider, and incline thine ear; forget also thine own people, and thy father's house;

11 So shall the king greatly desire thy beauty: for he is thy Lord; and worship thou him.

12 And the daughter of Tyre [4] shall be there with a gift; even the rich among the people shall entreat thy favor.

13 The king's daughter is all glorious within: her clothing is of wrought gold.

14 She shall be brought unto the king in raiment of needlework: the virgins her companions that follow her shall be brought unto thee.

15 With gladness and rejoicing shall they be brought: they shall enter into the king's palace.

16 Instead of thy fathers shall be thy children, whom thou mayest make princes in all the earth.

17 I will make thy name to be remembered in all generations: therefore shall the people praise thee for ever and ever.

---

1. *Maschil*, from the Hebrew *maskil*, meaning a poem. 2. *cassia*, a variety of cinnamon. 3. *Ophir*, a country of unsure location, possibly in southern Arabia or the eastern coast of Africa, famous for its precious stones. 4. *Tyre*, an ancient seaport in Phoenicia.

Psalm 95

OH COME, let us sing unto the Lord: let us make a joyful noise to the rock of our salvation.

2 Let us come before his presence with thanksgiving, and make a joyful noise unto him with psalms.

3 For the Lord is a great God, and a great King above all gods.

4 In his hand are the deep places of the earth: the strength of the hills is his also.

5 The sea is his, and he made it: and his hands formed the dry land.

6 O come, let us worship and bow down: let us kneel before the Lord our maker.

7 For he is our God; and we are the people of his pasture, and the sheep of his hand. To-day if ye will hear his voice,

8 Harden not your heart, as in the provocation, and as in the day of temptation in the wilderness:

9 When your fathers tempted me, proved me, and saw my work.

10 Forty years long was I grieved with this generation, and said, It is a people that do err in their heart, and they have not known my ways:

11 Unto whom I sware in my wrath that they should not enter into my rest.

Psalm 98

OH SING unto the Lord a new song; for he hath done marvellous things: his right hand, and his holy arm, hath gotten him the victory.

2 The Lord hath made known his salvation: his righteousness hath he openly shewed in the sight of the heathen.

3 He hath remembered his mercy and his truth toward the house of Israel: all the ends of the earth have seen the salvation of our God.

4 Make a joyful noise unto the Lord, all the earth: make a loud noise, and rejoice, and sing praise.

5 Sing unto the Lord with the harp; with the harp, and the voice of a psalm.

6 With trumpets and sound of cornet make a joyful noise before the Lord, the King.

7 Let the sea roar, and the fulness thereof; the world, and they that dwell therein.

8 Let the floods clap their hands: let the hills be joyful together

9 Before the Lord; for he cometh to judge the earth: with righteousness shall he judge the world, and the people with equity.

THE VAIN PHILOSOPHY OF TIMES AND SEASONS.

To EVERY THING there is a season, and a time to every purpose under the heaven:

2 A time to be born, and a time to die; a time to plant, and a time to pluck up that which is planted;

3 A time to kill, and a time to heal; a time to break down, and a time to build up;

4 A time to weep, and a time to laugh; a time to mourn, and a time to dance;

5 A time to cast away stones, and a time to gather stones together; a time to embrace, and a time to refrain from embracing;

6 A time to get, and a time to lose; a time to keep, and a time to cast away;

7 A time to rend, and a time to sew; a time to keep silence, and a time to speak;

8 A time to love, and a time to hate; a time of war, and a time of peace.

9 What profit hath he that worketh in that wherein he laboreth?

10 I have seen the travail, which God hath given to the sons of men to be exercised in it.

11 He hath made every thing beautiful in his time: also he hath set the world in their heart, so that no man can find out the work that God maketh from the beginning to the end.

12 I know that there is no good in them, but for a man to rejoice, and to do good in his life.

13 And also that every man should eat and drink, and enjoy the good of all his labor, it is the gift of God.

14 I know that, whatsoever God doeth, it shall be for ever: nothing can be put to it, nor any thing taken from it: and God doeth it, that men should fear before him.

15 That which hath been is now; and that which is to be hath already been; and God requireth that which is past.

16 And moreover I saw under the sun the place of judgment, that wickedness was there; and the place of righteousness, that iniquity was there.

17 I said in mine heart, God shall judge the righteous and the wicked: for there is a time there for every purpose and for every work.

18 I said in mine heart concerning the estate of the sons of men, that God might manifest them, and that they might see that they themselves are beasts.

19 For that which befalleth the sons of men befalleth beasts; even one thing befalleth them: as the one dieth, so dieth the other; yea, they have all one breath; so that a man hath no preeminence above a beast: for all is vanity.

20 All go unto one place; all are of the dust, and all turn to dust again.

21 Who knoweth the spirit of man that goeth upward, and the spirit of the beast that goeth downward to the earth?

22 Wherefore I perceive that there is nothing better, than that a man should rejoice in his own works; for that is his portion: for who shall bring him to see what shall be after him?

Aharon Amir [1] (1923–   )

Nothingness

Translated from the Hebrew by
Abraham Birman

I woke up at night and my language was gone
no sign of language no writing no alphabet
nor symbol nor word in any tongue
and raw was my fear—like the terror perhaps
of a man flung from a treetop far above the ground   5
a shipwrecked person on a tide-engulfed sandbank
a pilot whose parachute would not open
or the fear of a stone in a bottomless pit
and the fright was unvoiced unlettered unuttered
and inarticulate O how inarticulate   10
and I was alone in the dark
a non-I in the all-pervading gloom
with no grasp no leaning point
everything stripped of everything
and the sound was speechless and voiceless   15
and I was naught and nothing
without even a gibbet to hang onto
without a single peg to hang onto
and I no longer knew who or what I was—
and I was no more   20

1. *Aharon Amir* (ă hä rôn′ ă mĕr′).

David Avidan [1] (1934-   )

Preliminary Challenge

Translated from the Hebrew by
Abraham Birman

An elderly couple bent over their cold supper, viewing
the dry wind with two pairs of moist eyes, awaiting
Death who is expecting
me.
Today I managed, at long last, to take off four pounds, after   5
five days of culpable negligence, and I'm perfectly ready
for the preliminary signs. Everything becomes
so frightening, yet so mollifying, when the
preliminary, not imaginary, signs have replaced
the dilatory disaster, when petty warfare has forever procrastinated   10
the final battle.
I think a great deal about Death. When one thinks of him,
he relaxes, watches from a distance. He has some highly developed
narcissistic qualities. Hence the interplay and interdependence between
us.
He likes attention, so I'm giving it to him with the full endeavour of   15
a resolute mortal inclined at times to believe that a totally different race
has conceived and borne him. I am not from here, not from here, but
not from there either. For example, which of the following
four possibilities is more convenient, more pleasant or more
correct: For dust thou art and unto   20
dust shalt thou return. For dust thou art not and unto
dust shalt thou return. For dust thou art and unto
dust thou shalt not

1. *David Avidan* (dä vēd′ ä vē dän′).

return. For dust thou art not and unto
dust thou shalt not return.   25
I am misleading Death with the aid of
a complex system of alternatives, yet
because of our intrinsic relationship I only
seem to mislead myself. Any other way out is better than
any other way out, bypassing with a pathetic gesture the only   30
way out that I do not wish to know within the present framework
of my ingresses and egresses, through which I have been preparing
not to pass since the dawn of my youth, since the dawn of
my self-defending consciousness, commander-in-chief of
the most active private army in my vicinity. Don't go   35
home this evening, girl. It is, after all, an evening
destined to last forever. It is, in fact, the first
and last evening destined for anything
at all. The inevitable hootings
are already chasing it. Something   40
transpires in the bowels of the earth, aspires to
something darker than itself though
brighter than itself. Nothing will change, of course, but
I am still, as always, tensed towards the other way out, finally prepared
for the takeoff. When the chariot-of-fire [2]   45
has landed, I wouldn't wish to be found
in a better or worse state than the one I'm in
at this singular hour.

2. *chariot-of-fire*. According to the Old Testament the Prophet Elijah departed from the
earth in a chariot of fire.

Avraham Ben-Itzhak[1] (1883–1950)

Blessing

Translated from the Hebrew by
Arthur Jacobs

Blessed are those who sow and do not reap
Because they wander far.

Blessed are those who give themselves freely, the splendour
Of whose youth has added to daylight
Though they flung off their glory where roads part.   5

Blessed are those whose pride crosses the borders of their souls
And becomes a white humility
After the rainbow's rising in the cloud.

Blessed are those who know what their heart cries out in desert
And on their lips silence flowers.   10

Blessed are they, for they will be taken into the heart of the world
Wrapped in a cloak of unremembrance,
Speechless for ever.

"Blessing" by Avraham Ben-Itzhak, translated by Arthur Jacobs. Reprinted from AN ANTHOLOGY OF MODERN HEBREW POETRY, edited by Abraham Birman. By permission of Abelard-Schuman Ltd. All Rights Reserved. Copyright year 1968.
1. *Avraham Ben-Itzhak* (äv rä häm′ ben ēts häk′).

Avenue in Ellul[1]

Translated from the Hebrew by
Arthur Jacobs

Lights that are dreaming,
Lights whitening,
At my feet are falling,
Shadows that are soft,
Tired shadows,   5
Fondle my path.

        Between bared tree heights
        A little wind
        Moves sound
        And hushes.   10
        A last leaf
        Floats downwards,
        Trembles for one moment—
        Then turns to silence.

1. *Ellul*, the last month in the Jewish calendar. It has twenty-nine days and corresponds to August-September.

Ory Bernstein (1936-   )

Birds Have Thoughts

Translated from the Hebrew by
Abraham Birman

Birds have thoughts
when passing from wind to wind.
How they would like to rescind
their motion! But fraught
with their own self-importance   5
and their soaring prestige
in the nubilous sphere,
they fly. At the tip of their wing, though,
tiredness flits like a portent.
Birds have thoughts   10
expressed in flight
not in speech.
And when they give up the sky
and lie
among the stones   15
and chill sprouts in their bones,
a sharp thought pecks at each
tiny brain: if they can make up a system
maybe those wings won't be so heavy
when the winds twist them.   20
Celestial stability
demands ever-young wings—
a thought beyond the scope
of birdlike ability,
a thought with which they can't cope.   25
So the birds are assailed
by the light where everything might happen,
so their bodies grow cold and misshapen,
and all their thoughts are of no avail
against death.   30

Hayyim Nahman Bialik [1] (1873–1934)

Summer Is Dying

Translated from the Hebrew by
L. V. Snowman

Summer is dying, woven in fine gold,
    Couched on a purple bed
Of falling garden leaves and twilight clouds
    That lave their hearts in red.

The garden is deserted, save where a youth   5
    Saunters, or a maiden walks,
Casting an eye and a sigh after the flight
    Of the last and lingering storks.

The heart is orphaned. Soon a rainy day
    Will softly tap the pane.   10
"Look to your boots, patch up your coats, go fetch
    The potatoes in again."

"Summer Is Dying" by Hayyim Nahman Bialik, translated by L. V. Snowman. Reprinted from AN ANTHOLOGY OF MODERN HEBREW POETRY, edited by Abraham Birman. By permission of Abelard-Schuman Ltd. All Rights Reserved. Copyright year 1968.
1. *Hayyim Nahman Bialik* (hī′im näH′män bē ä′lik).

On My Return

Translated from the Hebrew by
L. V. Snowman

Here again is the wizened man
    With shrunk and shrivelled look,
Shade of dry stubble, wandering leaf
    That strays from book to book.

Here again is the wizened hag,   5
    Knitting socks and fumbling,
Her mouth with oaths and curses filled,
    Her lips for ever mumbling.

Our cat is there: he has not stirred
    From his quarters in the house,   10
But in his oven dream he makes
    A treaty with a mouse.

The rows of spiders' webs are there,
    As of old in darkness, spread
In the western corner, choked with flies,   15
    Their bodies blown out, dead.

You have not changed, you're antic old,
    There's nothing new I think;
Friends, let me join your club, we'll rot
    Together till we stink.   20

"On My Return" by Hayyim Nahman Bialik, translated by L. V. Snowman. Reprinted from AN ANTHOLOGY OF MODERN HEBREW POETRY, edited by Abraham Birman. By permission of Abelard-Schuman Ltd. All Rights Reserved. Copyright year 1968.

Maxim Ghilan[1] (1931-   )

Ars Po [2]

Translated from the Hebrew by
the author

Poetry
Is the infirm's glass, the oldster's staff
The quilt
Across the legs, drawn tight,
The light   5
Of candles held aloft. The soft
Cry in the night. The knee
Bent against stone, a silent ballad
Below the weight. The sleight
Of hands that must grasp rain   10
The hidden spatter of furtive, grass-grained
Sheets of pain.

"Ars Po" by Maxim Ghilan, translated by Maxim Ghilan. Reprinted from AN ANTHOL-
OGY OF MODERN HEBREW POETRY, edited by Abraham Birman. By permission of
Abelard-Schuman Ltd. All Rights Reserved. Copyright year 1968.
1. *Ghilan* (gi län'). 2. *Ars Po*, shortened form of *Ars Poetica* (*The Art of Poetry*), the
title given to an epistle by the Roman poet Horace (65–8 B.C.) dealing with technical
points relating to poetic composition as well as giving a basic approach to poetic art in
general.

Ka-Tzetnik 135633[1] (? -   )

from *THE CLOCK OVERHEAD*

Translated from the Hebrew by
Nina De-Nur and Chayym Zeldis

FACE TO FACE

NAKED MARCH INTO the night.

Midnight silence of Auschwitz.

You cannot hear a single step from all the bare feet marching on the ground.

You do not know the length of the column in which you march, where it begins, where it ends.

Around you breathe naked human bodies, marching six abreast. Six abreast.

A transport is being led to the Auschwitz "Bath House."[2]

Over your head vaults a star-sprinkled sky. Before your eyes a smokestack thrusts skywards. Thick, fatty smoke gushes out.

Sparks beyond count. Sparks scatter and flash across the starry sky, mingle with the stars, and you cannot tell whose light is the brighter.

Unnumbered naked bodies. Auschwitz under your bare feet. The column marches towards the smokestack.

Night about you. Auschwitz about you. Death holds your life between his hands—a circular mirror held up to your eyes. You don't see Death in

"The Clock Overhead" (four excerpts), by Ka-Tzetnik 135633, translated by Nina De-Nur & Chayym Zeldis. Reprinted from AN ANTHOLOGY OF MODERN HEBREW POETRY, edited by Abraham Birman. By permission of Abelard-Schuman Ltd. All Rights Reserved. Copyright year 1968.

1. *Ka-Tzetnik 135633* (kä'tset nik). Ka-Tzetnik, the author's pseudonym, was a German slang term used to designate an inmate in a Nazi death camp; 135633 was the author's number when he was imprisoned in Auschwitz, a Nazi concentration camp in Poland during World War II. 2. *"Bath House."* A term for the gas chamber, a building usually disguised as a bathhouse, used by the Nazis for the mass extermination of their victims by means of poisonous gas.

person—not yet. His face is hidden behind the mirror. His breath alone blows on you, the way wind blows on a spark in ashes—

The better to see it go out.

On both sides walk SS Germans,[3] silhouettes of silence mantled in night. You are no longer free to choose your own death. You have already been handed over. Death, your master, is taking you to his abode.

Walking under his long cloak, you scent his smell. You can no longer change places with anyone. He knows your flesh by now. He has seen you. Naked, you come unto him.

No longer are you free to choose your own death. This is—Auschwitz. Already your feet tread the corridor of your death. In a moment, you'll go inside and see him face to face; your lord and master, Death-of-Auschwitz.

Hush. No one here dares breathe a word. Words are no more. Sparks slip out of the smokestack. You squeeze the bit of soap in your fist. Countless feet. Naked feet. You can't hear their steps. Night leads you unto itself. Stars vanish over your head. Nothing is yours anymore. Even your head's hair has been taken away from you. This hair is still worth something, you are shorn of all. Except for a single spark you still carry within you. Death has bought it on the Jew-market. It belongs to him. Soon it will shoot out of the smokestack.

Auschwitz.

What kind of factory has death established here? Of what use to him can be the sparks leaping from the smokestack?

INSIDE

A network of pipes above your head. From the pipes jut shower sprinklers. Row upon row of sprinklers. And in the sprinklers—pores.

From somewhere in among the sprinklers, rusted opaque light drains down, illuminating what is imminent.

The open gate thrusts into the night. Still they keep coming in, an unbroken stream: naked bodies. More and more. Human beings. All of them looking alike. More, still more.

It's getting packed. Bodies, nude and clammy, around you. Naked skin on naked skin. At each contact your body shudders. But as the shudder runs over you, you suddenly thrill to a feeling of reprieve. It wakens a sense of life in you. You still have a body! A body of your own. As if you had it thrust anew into your arms. Never did you love your body so. You feel: fear whetting knife-blades on it. Soon it must grapple with a faceless death. Soon death will make his appearance. Soon you will see him, face to face. He sits on high, inside the sprinkler-pores. Any second now—

---

3. *SS Germans*, members of an elite military corps of the Nazi party, notorious for their calculated brutality.

All eyes are fixed on the sprinkler-pores overhead.

The gates of the "Bath House" lock. Even night is no more.

Naked bodies enclose your body. Trembling, the way your body trembles. The tremor runs from end to end, like wind through cornstalks in a field. The ends you cannot see, but you can feel the shudder of all the bodies through your own. The gates are sealed. Even night is gone. Nothing but bodies. All bodies are now—your body, just as the death of any body is now—the death of your own.

Inch by inch all bodies turn to stone. A crust of hoarfrost jells over all. Petrified, all.

Necks.

Not a head to be seen. Not a face. Nothing but necks. Necks thrown back. A plateau of necks flung back. Headless.

To start with—a torso; on top of it—shoulders; on top of the shoulders —a neck. And atop the neck—pores. Dark pores.

Sprinkler-pores of the Auschwitz "Bath House."

Rust-clotted light eddies between the necks and the shower-pores. In this light, death hovers. About to swoop.

Necks like cobblestones. Death stomps upon them as on stones of a deserted street. Here he is all by himself. Here he is on his own grounds, alone. This is his abode. Here he casts off his veils and his face shows. Here, in the sealed "Bath House"; here, in this inner sanctum of the Temple of Auschwitz.

And you see him.

Heads flung back to the nape, like chickens' heads in the slaughterer's grip. Mouths wide open. Necks stretched out. To the slaughtering knife on high.

You see his face.

Death's face.

The necks take no breath.

Suddenly—

A wisp of white steam. Unhurrying. Leisurely. Lightly twisting and weaving. Gracefully curling against the sprinkler-pores as if circling a floor in dance. And gone.

The necks take no breath.

Then from the pores swell—drops. Single drops. Pendulous. Pear-shaped. Unfalling. Suspended above the eyes—

The necks take no breath. Petrified.

Suddenly:

Thin, scalding streaks, vapor-encoiled. White-hot whips. A moment— and off they break in mid-air. Gone.

Once again empty pores, dark and secretive. Shower-pores of the Auschwitz "Bath House."

Suddenly:

Thin, freezing streaks. Biting whips of frost. A moment—and off they break in mid-air. Gone.

Empty pores, dark and secretive. The shower-pores of the Auschwitz "Bath House."

Over again

again,

and again,

All at once a wailing shriek crashes out:

"Water!!!"

"Water!!!"

"Water!!!"

Bodies leap up into the air, howling and screaming, tearing their scalps as they would tear hair. Drenched in tears they bawl out their happiness in wild uncontrollable weeping:

"W—a—t—er!!!"

At the walls, fingers pinch their own body; raving mad they scratch and grovel at the blank walls: *Water!!!*

As if corks had all at once blasted from their stoppered throats. All as one, they wail with twisted mouths, weeping and flailing arms gone crazy with joy:

"W—a—t—er!!!"

One, the Know-it-all in every crowd, shouts back at them: "Shut up! Of course it's water! That's all it is—water!"

But not one of them pays him any attention. The mouths sob at him, shrieking insanely: W—a—t—e—r!!!

Until the gates unlock.

Outside, the night foams and bubbles with the mirthsome guffaws of SS Germans; it rolls on the waves of their laughter, breaking over black-horizoned shores. The Germans stand in the dark and look on, the way spectators watch a comedy enacted on a brightly-lit screen—and double up in laughter.

The naked bodies stream out, as if spewed onto an unfamiliar shore. Opposite them, the sparks stream from the smokestack and vanish over the starry sky. Stupefied, they stare at the laughing maws and do not understand—

They don't understand that truly happy were those who got, not water out of sprinklers, but Zyklon [4] cans jetting blue gas into their lungs, instead.

They don't understand that truly happy were those who at the very threshold of Auschwitz were turned into these sparks now spraying out of the smokestack opposite—

W—a—t—e—r!

They are alive—

And they go marching, drunk with joy, towards the blocks of the camp called "Auschwitz."

DAWN IN AUSCHWITZ

Backs.

Backs and eyes—

In Auschwitz, everyone tries to draw his back as high up as he can, as if the back were a woolen blanket you could pull over your head to keep warm.

On the narrow backpath running along the blocks.

More than ten thousand shadow-men.

No beginning, no end to them. There is no beginning, no end in Auschwitz. Everywhere around, beyond the walls of barbed wire surrounding your camp, range more camps. No end of camps. Isolated from each other, like stars. A galaxy as yet beyond human ken and exploration. To the right—"B" Camp, to the left—Quarantine Camp. Behind—Women's Camp. In front—the milky way, down which the packed vans roll without cease, without cease, to the crematorium.

And above all—the final hour.

The final hour of the night. Ten thousand pairs of eyes spill out of the blocks every day at this hour, the hour before dawn, into the backpath. Cleanliness. The German loves cleanliness, so now the block orderlies "clean out" the blocks—they are apportioning out the bread rations. Instead of four, they'll cut eight and ten rations from each loaf. The loaves they gain in this way will soon be on their way to the latrine—the camp stock-exchange—to be traded for cigarettes for the Block Chiefs. Four cigarettes to the loaf. And outside, on the backpath running along the blocks, ten thousand and more shadow-men hop a hypnotic jungle dance, foot up, foot down—

The cold earth of Auschwitz sucks through the soles of bare feet the last remains of marrow from the bones.

Eyes—

A river, over which rain whips endlessly, trace enormous, gaping

---

4. *Zyklon*, the name of a gas used by the Nazis for the mass extermination of their victims.

water-eyes. A stream which flows from the railroad platform to the crematorium. Ever the same stream, never the same drops. Drops ever changing,
ever new. You see them in their sluggish, silent flow as they look at you
with glass-sheened gazes, probing your face for some stir of their own lives
which stream by—out of their reach—and see naught. Not even the camp
they're passing through.

Eyes—

Eyes that for fifty years struck foundations for generations to come; and
eyes of fifteen years, in first beauty of flowering, brimming with sap and
vitality, finest of mankind, the crown of creation.

Eyes—of lords of wealth, ruthless tyrants of international trade-marts;
and eyes of careworn shopkeepers, harassed and cowed, penniless trades-
men whose worries have been handed down to them at birth: where will
food for the Sabbath come from? Who will pay the teacher's wages?

Eyes—of seekers, men of science, artists anointed with divine gifts of
genius; and eyes of thick-tongued labourers, prayerbooks clasped in blackened, calloused hands. Grey as the days of the week, nondescript as the
chemicals fructifying our earth.

Eyes—of self-designated lordlings, society's upper crust, whose names
by the clash of cymbals were always heralded; yet miserly, insatiable,
enviously ill-willed if ever success shone in through another's window. And
eyes of men of soul, delicate spirits, noble, modest—the sweet fragrance of
our lives.

All along the road, from the Auschwitz railroad platform to the crematorium, these eyes all now beg the answer to one question:

When will the soup ration ever be handed out?

O Night-of-Auschwitz on backs and eyes!

Hour of awful despair and pity.

Enigma of an hour when night wraps in one black robe SS man and
campling alike.

Far, far off, lights speed down the main road. You know: each pair of
lights—a packed van heading for the crematorium. Many a time you have
wished to be taken to the crematorium at night. Better by night than by
day. At night you can cry. Never did anyone weep on his way to the
crematorium by day. At night, tears come from your eyes.

Awesome mystery of Night-of-Auschwitz, never to be fathomed by
mortal man.

Until night is drawn from your lids, like black scabbard slipped from
sword. Slowly the chill blade of Auschwitz day gleams bare.

To the west, the red bulbs still glow along the barbed wire—a coral
necklace on the flesh of Auschwitz night.

To the east, the new day already shows ashen-grey among the block-
roofs, as if the mounds of ash had quit their posts by the crematorium,
falling into line here between one roof and the next.

The SS sentry climbs down the watchtower ladder, rung by rung: first, the black boots, then the rifle slung across back. He carries the night with him, folded and shrivelled. Like a black crow night roosts on his shoulder. He turns over his post to his *Kamerad*, the day-sentry, who climbs up the ladder, rung by rung: first the hands, white hands, soaking in the new day—your day. Every hunched-up back in Auschwitz now proffers your eyes your own loneliness. Each pair of eyes gazes at you with the pity for a life that once bore your name—

Dawn of Auschwitz on backs and eyes.

"WIEDERGUTMACHUNG" [5]

I

My mother was—my mother.

How can I describe you, Mother?

My mother was the most beautiful of all mothers in the world.

My mother said:

"No! My little boy didn't do this naughty thing . . ." Lovingly she pressed the profiles of my head between her open palms, her fingers long and parted. Her eyes plumbed the depths of my own as she said, "I! I did the naughty thing! Because I am my little boy!"

Afterwards, I was always very careful to behave, because I couldn't bear for my mother to do a naughty thing.

My mother!

Of all mothers in the world mine was the most beautiful.

On her way to the crematorium my mother saw my face. I know it. Because I, too, on my way to the crematorium, saw my mother's face.

Mother, now they want to give me money to make up for you.

I still can't figure how many German marks a burnt mother comes to.

"My little boy couldn't have done this naughty thing . . ."

Mother, I feel your open palms touching the profiles of my head. My eyes sink into yours: Isn't it true, Mother, you wouldn't take money for your little one, burnt?

---

5. *"Wiedergutmachung,"* literally, "setting things right": reparations paid by the West German government to the victims of Nazi persecution or to their families. [*German*]

II

My sister's hair was long and curly, the colour of ripe gold. Mother's hands vanished in white-gold foam every time she washed it. Whenever she rinsed it, sheer gold cascaded down my sister's nape like a waterfall all the way to the bottom of the tub.

My mother loved to plait ribbons into her tiny daughter's hair. She would sort them out, singing soft to herself as she did:

> "Ribbon green for hair's gold sheen,
> Ribbon pink for chocolate skin,
> Ribbon blue for the eyes . . ."

My sister's eyes were blue like sky.

Sabbath morning, in front of the house, when the sun met my sister's hair, neighbours at their windows would call:
"Whose hair is that, little Goldilocks?"
"My mother's," answered my sister.
I loved my sister's hair. She never lifted scissors to it. She said "My mother's . . ."
Before my sister was burned in the crematorium of Auschwitz they shaved off her hair. Seventeen years the golden locks lengthened on my sister's head. Long locks of gold. Seventeen years.

In a shipment of hair, in sacks, or in rectangular bales, tight-pressed like cotton from rich plantations, my sister's hair was sent to Germany. It was unloaded at a factory, to make:

blankets—

soft club-chairs—

upholstery—

Somewhere, in Germany, a young Fräulein now covers herself with a blanket. A single hair of gold, unprocessed, thrusts out of the blanket's weave. The Fräulein stretches out a bare arm, pulls, pulls . . .
"Fräulein! Give me back that hair! It's out of my sister's golden locks . . ."

My sister, now they want to give me money for you. But I don't know how many German marks your curls should bring.
"Whose hair is it, little Goldilocks?"
"My mother's . . ."

Mother, Mother, what do you say—how much is your little Goldilocks'
hair worth?

My mother croons to herself:

> "Ribbon green for hair's gold sheen,
> Ribbon pink for chocolate skin,
> Ribbon blue for the eyes . . ."

My sister had eyes like the blue sky.

III

Among tens of thousands of shoes I'd recognize a shoe of yours, Father!
Your heels were never crooked.

Father, your step was always straight.

Each day a new mountain of shoes piles up on the compound of the
crematorium. Remember when I was little? The first time you let me shine
your shoes, I polished them tops and bottoms. Oh how you laughed at me
then!

"There is, sonny, a dirty side as well, on which a man must tread.
When you're big you'll understand."

Father, I'm big now.

The sun bends over the slope of the tall shoe-mountain, illuminating it
for me as with a flashlight:

Shoes!

Shoes without end!

A torn baby-shoe—like an infant's open mouth, eager for the full spoon
in mother's hand; a torn baby-shoe—an infant's head, eyes bugging from
the shoe-mountain to the sun shining on earth.

Nearby—

A narrow, delicate woman's shoe, high and slender-heeled, brown-
scaled. Open on all sides. Several entwined leather straps on top. The gold
imprint on the steep arch glitters in the face of the sun.

Nearby—

A lime-spattered workman's shoe. The sun peers into it as into the
mouth of a cavern hacked into barren mountain rock.

Nearby—

A mountaineer's shoe, its toe wedged in the side of the mountain, as if
the climber had paused in mid-ascent, breathless: "Oh, what a
view! . . ."

Nearby—

A leg with a shoe on its foot—prosthesis [6] to the groin. Trouserless, naked to the sun.

Shoes!

Shoes beyond count!

Father, among tens of thousands of shoes I would recognize yours!

Your heels were never crooked—

Father, your step was straight.

IV

How can I take money for my sister the "Field Whore" from you—and not be a pimp?

Give me—

Give me back one single hair of my sister's golden curls!

Give me back one shoe of my father's;

A broken wheel from my little brother's skates;

And a mote of dust that on my mother rested—

---

6. *prosthesis*, addition of an artificial part to the body.

Yehudah Karni (1884–1948)

Evening in Jerusalem

Translated from the Hebrew by
Abraham Birman

The evening here does not approach in stealth,
  With feline bounds;
Night is no velvet of luxurious wealth
  To wrap you round.

The evening never oozes from the soul   5
  Until the last small drop is gone,
Nor does Night's curtain slowly fall
  Between the bright and dun.

The evening seizes, fetters,
  Hands on to the night;   10
The latter clutches, batters,
  Kills and buries tight.

Aharon Megged [1] (1920-   )

THE NAME

Translated from the Hebrew by
Minna Givton

GRANDFATHER ZISSKIND LIVED IN a little house in a southern suburb of
the town. About once a month, on a Saturday afternoon, his granddaughter
Raya and her young husband Yehuda would go and pay him a visit.

Raya would give three cautious knocks on the door (an agreed signal
between herself and her grandfather ever since her childhood, when he had
lived in their house together with the whole family) and they would wait
for the door to be opened. "Now he's getting up," Raya would whisper to
Yehuda, her face glowing, when the sound of her grandfather's slippers
was heard from within, shuffling across the room. Another moment, and
the key would be turned and the door opened.

"Come in," he would say somewhat absently, still buttoning up his
trousers, with the rheum of sleep in his eyes. Although it was very hot he
wore a yellow winter vest with long sleeves, from which his wrists stuck
out—white, thin, delicate as a girl's, as was his bare neck with its taut
skin.

After Raya and Yehuda had sat down at the table, which was covered
with a white cloth showing signs of the meal he had eaten alone—crumbs
from the Sabbath loaf, a plate with meat leavings, a glass containing some
grape pips, a number of jars and so on—he would smooth the crumpled
pillows, spread a cover over the narrow bed and tidy up. It was a small
room, and its obvious disorder aroused pity for the old man's helplessness
in running his home. In the corner was a shelf with two sooty kerosene
burners, a kettle and two or three saucepans, and next to it a basin
containing plates, knives and forks. In another corner was a stand holding
books with thick leather bindings, leaning and lying on each other. Some

Reprinted by permission of Schocken Books Inc. from ISRAELI STORIES, edited by Joel
Blocker. Copyright © 1962 by Schocken Books Inc.
1. *Aharon Megged* (ä hä rôn′ me′ ged).

of his clothes hung over the backs of the chairs. An ancient walnut cupboard with an empty buffet stood exactly opposite the door. On the wall hung a clock which had long since stopped.

"We ought to make Grandfather a present of a clock," Raya would say to Yehuda as she surveyed the room and her glance lighted on the clock; but every time the matter slipped her memory. She loved her grandfather, with his pointed white silky beard, his tranquil face from which a kind of holy radiance emanated, his quiet, soft voice which seemed to have been made only for uttering words of sublime wisdom. She also respected him for his pride, which had led him to move out of her mother's house and live by himself, accepting the hardship and trouble and the affliction of loneliness in his old age. There had been a bitter quarrel between him and his daughter. After Raya's father had died, the house had lost its grandeur and shed the trappings of wealth. Some of the antique furniture which they had retained—along with some crystalware and jewels, the dim lustre of memories from the days of plenty in their native city—had been sold, and Rachel, Raya's mother, had been compelled to support the home by working as a dentist's nurse. Grandfather Zisskind, who had been supported by the family ever since he came to the country, wished to hand over to his daughter his small capital, which was deposited in a bank. She was not willing to accept it. She was stubborn and proud like him. Then, after a prolonged quarrel and several weeks of not speaking to each other, he took some of the things in his room and the broken clock and went to live alone. That had been about four years ago. Now Rachel would come to him once or twice a week, bringing with her a bag full of provisions, to clean the room and cook some meals for him. He was no longer interested in expenses and did not even ask about them, as though they were of no more concern to him.

"And now . . . what can I offer you?" Grandfather Zisskind would ask when he considered the room ready to receive guests. "There's no need to offer us anything, Grandfather; we didn't come for that," Raya would answer crossly.

But protests were of no avail. Her grandfather would take out a jar of fermenting preserves and put it on the table, then grapes and plums, biscuits and two glasses of strong tea, forcing them to eat. Raya would taste a little of this and that just to please the old man, while Yehuda, for whom all these visits were unavoidable torment, the very sight of the dishes arousing his disgust, would secretly indicate to her by pulling a sour face that he just couldn't touch the preserves. She would smile at him placatingly, stroking his knee. But Grandfather insisted, so he would have to taste at least a teaspoonful of the sweet and nauseating stuff.

Afterwards Grandfather would ask about all kinds of things. Raya did her best to make the conversation pleasant, in order to relieve Yehuda's boredom. Finally would come what Yehuda dreaded most of all and on account of which he had resolved more than once to refrain from these visits. Grandfather Zisskind would rise, take his chair and place it next to the wall, get up on it carefully, holding on to the back so as not to fall, open the clock and take out a cloth bag with a black cord tied round it. Then he would shut the clock, get off the chair, put it back in its place, sit down on it, undo the cord, take out of the cloth wrapping a bundle of sheets of paper, lay them in front of Yehuda and say:

"I would like you to read this."

"Grandfather," Raya would rush to Yehuda's rescue, "but he's already read it at least ten times. . . ."

But Grandfather Zisskind would pretend not to hear and would not reply, so Yehuda was compelled each time to read there and then that same essay, spread over eight, long sheets in a large, somewhat shaky handwriting, which he almost knew by heart. It was a lament for Grandfather's native town in the Ukraine [2] which had been destroyed by the Germans, and all its Jews slaughtered. When he had finished, Grandfather would take the sheets out of his hand, fold them, sigh and say:

"And nothing of all this is left. Dust and ashes. Not even a tombstone to bear witness. Imagine, of a community of twenty thousand Jews not even one survived to tell how it happened . . . Not a trace."

Then out of the same cloth bag, which contained various letters and envelopes, he would draw a photograph of his grandson Mendele,[3] who had been twelve years old when he was killed; the only son of his son Ossip, chief engineer in a large chemical factory. He would show it to Yehuda and say:

"He was a genius. Just imagine, when he was only eleven he had already finished his studies at the Conservatory, won a scholarship from the Government and was considered an outstanding violinist. A genius! Look at that forehead. . . ." And after he had put the photograph back he would sigh and repeat "Not a trace."

A strained silence of commiseration would descend on Raya and Yehuda, who had already heard these same things many times over and no longer felt anything when they were repeated. And as he wound the cord round the bag the old man would muse: "And Ossip was also a prodigy. As a boy he knew Hebrew well, and could recite Bialik's poems [4] by heart. He studied by himself. He read endlessly, Gnessin, Frug, Bershadsky . . . You didn't know Bershadsky; he was a good writer . . . He had a warm heart, Ossip had. He didn't mix in politics, he wasn't even a Zionist,[5] but even when they promoted him there he didn't forget that he was a Jew

---

2. *Ukraine*, a Soviet republic in the southwest of the U.S.S.R. During World War II the Ukraine was occupied by German forces who, according to most estimates, rounded up and massacred 250,000 Jews. 3. *Mendele* (men'də lə). 4. *Bialik's poems*. See page 144. 5. *Zionist*, a member of the Zionist movement founded during the nineteenth century to secure the Jewish return to Palestine (Israel).

. . . He called his son Mendele, of all names, after his dead brother, even though it was surely not easy to have a name like that among the Russians . . . Yes, he had a warm Jewish heart . . ."

He would turn to Yehuda as he spoke, since in Raya he always saw the child who used to sit on his knee listening to his stories, and for him she had never grown up, while he regarded Yehuda as an educated man who could understand someone else, especially inasmuch as Yehuda held a government job.

Raya remembered how the change had come about in her grandfather. When the war was over he was still sustained by uncertainty and hoped for some news of his son, for it was known that very many had succeeded in escaping eastwards. Wearily he would visit all those who had once lived in his town, but none of them had received any sign of life from relatives. Nevertheless he continued to hope, for Ossip's important position might have helped to save him. Then Raya came home one evening and saw him sitting on the floor with a rent in his jacket.[6] In the house they spoke in whispers, and her mother's eyes were red with weeping. She, too, had wept at Grandfather's sorrow, at the sight of his stricken face, at the oppressive quiet in the rooms. For many weeks afterwards it was as if he had imposed silence on himself. He would sit at his table from morning to night, reading and re-reading old letters, studying family photographs by the hour as he brought them close to his shortsighted eyes, or leaning backwards on his chair, motionless, his hand touching the edge of the table and his eyes staring through the window in front of him, into the distance, as if he had turned to stone. He was no longer the same talkative, wise and humorous grandfather who interested himself in the house, asked what his granddaughter was doing, instructed her, tested her knowledge, proving boastfully like a child that he knew more than her teachers. Now he seemed to cut himself off from the world and entrench himself in his thoughts and his memories, which none of the household could penetrate. Later, a strange perversity had taken hold of him which it was hard to tolerate. He would insist that his meals be served at his table, apart, that no one should enter his room without knocking at the door, or close the shutters of his window against the sun. When any one disobeyed these prohibitions he would flare up and quarrel violently with his daughter. At times it seemed that he hated her.

When Raya's father died, Grandfather Zisskind did not show any signs of grief, and did not even console his daughter. But when the days of mourning were past it was as if he had been restored to new life, and he emerged from his silence. Yet he did not speak of his son-in-law, nor of his son Ossip, but only of his grandson Mendele. Often during the day he would mention the boy by name as if he were alive, and speak of him

---

6. *rent in his jacket.* In Judaism it is customary for a mourner to rend a garment.

familiarly, although he had seen him only on photographs—as though deliberating aloud and turning the matter over, he would talk of how Mendele ought to be brought up. It was hardest of all when he started criticizing his son and his son's wife for not having foreseen the impending disaster, for not having rushed the boy away to a safe place, not having hidden him with non-Jews, not having tried to get him to the Land of Israel in good time. There was no logic in what he said; this would so infuriate Rachel that she would burst out with, "Oh, do stop! Stop it! I'll go out of my mind with your foolish nonsense!" She would rise from her seat in anger, withdraw to her room, and afterwards, when she had calmed down, would say to Raya, "Sclerosis, apparently. Loss of memory. He no longer knows what he's talking about."

One day—Raya would never forget this—she and her mother saw that Grandfather was wearing his best suit, the black one, and under it a gleaming white shirt; his shoes were polished, and he had a hat on. He had not worn these clothes for many months, and the family was dismayed to see him. They thought that he had lost his mind. "What holiday is it today?" her mother asked. "Really, don't you know?" asked her grandfather. "Today is Mendele's birthday!" Her mother burst out crying. She too began to cry and ran out of the house.

After that, Grandfather Zisskind went to live alone. His mind, apparently, had become settled, except that he would frequently forget things which had occurred a day or two before, though he clearly remembered, down to the smallest detail, things which had happened in his town and to his family more than thirty years ago. Raya would go and visit him, at first with her mother and, after her marriage, with Yehuda. What bothered them was that they were compelled to listen to his talk about Mendele his grandson, and to read that same lament for his native town which had been destroyed.

Whenever Rachel happened to come there during their visit, she would scold Grandfather rudely. "Stop bothering them with your masterpiece," she would say, and herself remove the papers from the table and put them back in their bag. "If you want them to keep on visiting you, don't talk to them about the dead. Talk about the living. They're young people and they have no mind for such things." And as they left his room together she would say, turning to Yehuda in order to placate him, "Don't be surprised at him. Grandfather's already old. Over seventy. Loss of memory."

When Raya was seven months pregnant, Grandfather Zisskind had in his absent-mindedness not yet noticed it. But Rachel could no longer refrain from letting him share her joy and hope, and told him that a great-grandchild would soon be born to him. One evening the door of Raya and Yehuda's flat opened, and Grandfather himself stood on the threshold in his holiday clothes, just as on the day of Mendele's birthday. This was the first time he had visited them at home, and Raya was so surprised that she hugged and kissed him as she had not done since she was a child. His face shone, his eyes sparkled with the same intelligent and mischievous light they had in those far-off days before the calamity. When he entered he walked briskly through the rooms, giving his opinion on the furniture and its arrangement, and joking about everything around him. He was so pleasant that Raya and Yehuda could not stop laughing all the time he was speaking. He gave no indication that he knew what was about to take place, and for the first time in many months he did not mention Mendele.

"Ah, you naughty children," he said, "is this how you treat Grandfather? Why didn't you tell me you had such a nice place?"

"How many times have I invited you here, Grandfather?" asked Raya.

"Invited me? You ought to have *brought* me here, dragged me by force!"

"I wanted to do that too, but you refused."

"Well, I thought that you lived in some dark den, and I have a den of my own. Never mind, I forgive you."

And when he took leave of them he said:

"Don't bother to come to me. Now that I know where you're to be found and what a palace you have, I'll come to you . . . if you don't throw me out, that is."

Some days later, when Rachel came to their home and they told her about Grandfather's amazing visit, she was not surprised:

"Ah, you don't know what he's been contemplating during all these days, ever since I told him that you're about to have a child . . . He has one wish—that if it's a son, it should be named . . . after his grandson."

"Mendele?" exclaimed Raya, and involuntarily burst into laughter. Yehuda smiled as one smiles at the fond fancies of the old.

"Of course, I told him to put that out of his head," said Rachel, "but you know how obstinate he is. It's some obsession and he won't think of giving it up. Not only that, but he's sure that you'll willingly agree to it, and especially you, Yehuda."

Yehuda shrugged his shoulders. "Crazy. The child would be unhappy all his life."

"But he's not capable of understanding that," said Rachel, and a note of apprehension crept into her voice.

Raya's face grew solemn. "We have already decided on the name," she said. "If it's a girl she'll be called Osnath, and if it's a boy—Ehud."

Rachel did not like either.

The matter of the name became almost the sole topic of conversation between Rachel and the young couple when she visited them, and it infused gloom into the air of expectancy which filled the house.

Rachel, midway between the generations, was of two minds about the matter. When she spoke to her father she would scold and contradict him, flinging at him all the arguments she had heard from Raya and Yehuda as though they were her own, but when she spoke to the children she sought to induce them to meet his wishes, and would bring down their anger on herself. As time went on, the question of a name, to which in the beginning she had attached little importance, became a kind of mystery, concealing something preordained, fearful, and pregnant with life and death. The fate of the child itself seemed in doubt. In her innermost heart she prayed that Raya would give birth to a daughter.

"Actually, what's so bad about the name Mendele?" she asked her daughter. "It's a Jewish name like any other."

"What are you talking about, Mother"—Raya rebelled against the thought—"a Ghetto name, ugly, horrible! I wouldn't even be capable of letting it cross my lips. Do you want me to hate my child?"

"Oh, you won't hate your child. At any rate, not because of the name . . ."

"I should hate him. It's as if you'd told me that my child would be born with a hump! And anyway—why should I? What for?"

"You have to do it for Grandfather's sake," Rachel said quietly, although she knew that she was not speaking the whole truth.

"You know, Mother, that I am ready to do anything for Grandfather," said Raya. "I love him, but I am not ready to sacrifice my child's happiness on account of some superstition of his. What sense is there in it?"

Rachel could not explain the "sense in it" rationally, but in her heart she rebelled against her daughter's logic which had always been hers too and now seemed very superficial, a symptom of the frivolity afflicting the younger generation. Her old father now appeared to her like an ancient tree whose deep roots suck up the mysterious essence of existence, of which neither her daughter nor she herself knew anything. Had it not been for this argument about the name, she would certainly never have got to meditating on the transmigration of souls and the eternity of life. At night she would wake up covered in cold sweat. Hazily, she recalled frightful scenes of bodies of naked children, beaten and trampled under the jackboots of soldiers, and an awful sense of guilt oppressed her spirit.

Then Rachel came with a proposal for a compromise: that the child should be named Menachem.[7] A Hebrew name, she said; an Israeli one, by all standards. Many children bore it, and it occurred to nobody to make fun of them. Even Grandfather had agreed to it after much urging.

Raya refused to listen.

"We have chosen a name, Mother," she said, "which we both like, and we won't change it for another. Menachem is a name which reeks of old age, a name which for me is connected with sad memories and people I don't like. Menachem you could call only a boy who is short, weak and not good-looking. Let's not talk about it any more, Mother."

---

7. *Menachem* (me nä ḤEM').

Rachel was silent. She almost despaired of convincing them. At last she said:

"And you are ready to take the responsibility of going against Grandfather's wishes?"

Raya's eyes opened wide, and fear was reflected in them:

"Why do you make such a fateful thing of it? You frighten me!" she said, and burst into tears. She began to fear for her offspring as one fears the evil eye.[8]

"And perhaps there *is* something fateful in it . . ." whispered Rachel without raising her eyes. She flinched at her own words.

"What is it?" insisted Raya, with a frightened look at her mother.

"I don't know . . ." she said. "Perhaps all the same we are bound to retain the names of the dead . . . in order to leave a remembrance of them . . ." She was not sure herself whether there was any truth in what she said or whether it was merely a stupid belief, but her father's faith was before her, stronger than her own doubts and her daughter's simple and understandable opposition.

"But I don't always want to remember all those dreadful things, Mother. It's impossible that this memory should always hang about this house and that the poor child should bear it!"

Rachel understood. She, too, heard such a cry within her as she listened to her father talking, sunk in memories of the past. As if to herself, she said in a whisper:

"I don't know . . . at times it seems to me that it's not Grandfather who's suffering from loss of memory, but ourselves. All of us."

About two weeks before the birth was due, Grandfather Zisskind appeared in Raya and Yehuda's home for the second time. His face was yellow, angry, and the light had faded from his eyes. He greeted them, but did not favor Raya with so much as a glance, as if he had pronounced a ban upon the sinner. Turning to Yehuda he said, "I wish to speak to you."

They went into the inner room. Grandfather sat down on the chair and placed the palm of his hand on the edge of the table, as was his wont, and Yehuda sat, lower than he, on the bed.

"Rachel has told me that you don't want to call the child by my grandchild's name," he said.

"Yes . . ." said Yehuda diffidently.

"Perhaps you'll explain to me why?" he asked.

"We . . ." stammered Yehuda, who found it difficult to face the piercing gaze of the old man. "The name simply doesn't appeal to us."

Grandfather was silent. Then he said, "I understand that Mendele doesn't appeal to you. Not a Hebrew name. Granted! But Menachem—

---

8. *evil eye*, a superstition, still prevalent in the Near East, that certain individuals can harm by an envious or malicious glance.

what's wrong with Menachem?" It was obvious that he was controlling his feelings with difficulty.

"It's not . . ." Yehuda knew that there was no use explaining; they were two generations apart in their ideas. "It's not an Israeli name . . . it's from the *Golah*." [9]

"*Golah*," repeated Grandfather. He shook with rage, but somehow he maintained his self-control. Quietly he added, "We all come from the *Golah*. I, and Raya's father and mother. Your father and mother. All of us."

"Yes . . ." said Yehuda. He resented the fact that he was being dragged into an argument which was distasteful to him, particularly with this old man whose mind was already not quite clear. Only out of respect did he restrain himself from shouting: That's that, and it's done with! . . . "Yes, but we were born in this country," he said aloud; "that's different."

Grandfather Zisskind looked at him contemptuously. Before him he saw a wretched boor, an empty vessel.

"You, that is to say, think that there's something new here," he said, "that everything that was there is past and gone. Dead, without sequel. That you are starting everything anew."

"I didn't say that. I only said that we were born in this country. . . ."

"You were born here. Very nice . . ." said Grandfather Zisskind with rising emotion. "So what of it? What's so remarkable about that? In what way are you superior to those who were born *there?* Are you cleverer than they? More cultured? Are you greater than they in Torah [10] or good deeds? Is your blood redder than theirs?" Grandfather Zisskind looked as if he could wring Yehuda's neck.

"I didn't say that either, I said that *here* it's different. . . ."

Grandfather Zisskind's patience with idle words was exhausted.

"You good-for-nothing!" he burst out in his rage. "What do you know about what was there? What do you know of the *people* that were there? The communities? The cities? What do you know of the *life* they had there?"

"Yes," said Yehuda, his spirit crushed, "but we no longer have any ties with it."

"You have no ties with it?" Grandfather Zisskind bent towards him. His lips quivered in fury. "With what . . . with what *do* you have ties?"

"We have . . . with this country," said Yehuda and gave an involuntary smile.

"Fool!" Grandfather Zisskind shot at him. "Do you think that people come to a desert and make themselves a nation, eh? That you are the first

9. *Golah*, a term applied to all geographical locations outside Israel where Jews have settled. 10. *Torah*, the fundamental laws of Judaism.

of some new race? That you're not the son of your father? Not the grandson of your grandfather? Do you want to forget them? Are you ashamed of them for having had a hundred times more culture and education than you have? Why . . . why, everything here"—he included everything around him in the sweep of his arm—"is no more than a puddle of tapwater against the big sea that was there! What have you here? A mixed multitude! Seventy languages! Seventy distinct groups! Customs? A way of life? Why, every home here is a nation in itself, with its own customs and its own names! And with this you have ties, you say . . ."

Yehuda lowered his eyes and was silent.

"I'll tell you what ties are," said Grandfather Zisskind calmly. "Ties are remembrance! Do you understand? The Russian is linked to his people because he remembers his ancestors. He is called Ivan, his father was called Ivan and his grandfather was called Ivan, back to the first generation. And no Russian has said: From today onwards I shall not be called Ivan because my fathers and my fathers' fathers were called that; I am the first of a new Russian nation which has nothing at all to do with the Ivans. Do you understand?"

"But what has that got to do with it?" Yehuda protested impatiently. Grandfather Zisskind shook his head at him.

"And you—you're ashamed to give your son the name Mendele lest it remind you that there were Jews who were called by that name. You believe that his name should be wiped off the face of the earth. That not a trace of it should remain . . ." He paused, heaved a deep sigh and said:

"O children, children, you don't know what you're doing . . . You're finishing off the work which the enemies of Israel began. They took the bodies away from the world, and you—the name and the memory . . . No continuation, no evidence, no memorial and no name. Not a trace . . ."

And with that he rose, took his stick and with long strides went towards the door and left.

The new-born child was a boy and he was named Ehud, and when he was about a month old, Raya and Yehuda took him in the carriage to Grandfather's house.

Raya gave three cautious knocks on the door, and when she heard a rustle inside she could also hear the beating of her anxious heart. Since the birth of the child Grandfather had not visited them even once. "I'm terribly excited," she whispered to Yehuda with tears in her eyes. Yehuda rocked the carriage and did not reply. He was now indifferent to what the old man might say or do.

The door opened, and on the threshold stood Grandfather Zisskind, his face weary and wrinkled. He seemed to have aged. His eyes were sticky with sleep, and for a moment it seemed as if he did not see the callers.

"Good Sabbath, Grandfather," said Raya with great feeling. It seemed to her now that she loved him more than ever.

Grandfather looked at them as if surprised, and then said absently, "Come in, come in."

"We've brought the baby with us!" said Raya, her face shining, and her glance traveled from Grandfather to the infant sleeping in the carriage.

"Come in, come in," repeated Grandfather Zisskind in a tired voice. "Sit down," he said as he removed his clothes from the chairs and turned to tidy the disordered bedclothes.

Yehuda stood the carriage by the wall and whispered to Raya, "It's stifling for him here." Raya opened the window wide.

"You haven't seen our baby yet, Grandfather!" she said with a sad smile.

"Sit down, sit down," said Grandfather, shuffling over to the shelf, from which he took the jar of preserves and the biscuit tin, putting them on the table.

"There's no need, Grandfather, really there's no need for it. We didn't come for that," said Raya.

"Only a little something. I have nothing to offer you today. . . ." said Grandfather in a dull, broken voice. He took the kettle off the kerosene burner and poured out two glasses of tea which he placed before them. Then he too sat down, and said "Drink, drink," and softly tapped his fingers on the table.

"I haven't seen your Mother for several days now," he said at last.

"She's busy . . ." said Raya in a low voice, without raising her eyes to him. "She helps me a lot with the baby. . . ."

Grandfather Zisskind looked at his pale, knotted and veined hands lying helplessly on the table; then he stretched out one of them and said to Raya, "Why don't you drink? The tea will get cold."

Raya drew up to the table and sipped the tea.

"And you—what are you doing now?" he asked Yehuda.

"Working as usual," said Yehuda, and added with a laugh, "I play with the baby when there's time."

Grandfather again looked down at his hands, the long thin fingers of which shook with the palsy of old age.

"Take some of the preserves," he said to Yehuda, indicating the jar with a shaking finger. "It's very good." Yehuda dipped the spoon in the jar and put it to his mouth.

There was a deep silence. It seemed to last a very long time. Grandfather Zisskind's fingers gave little quivers on the white tablecloth. It was hot in the room, and the buzzing of a fly could be heard.

Suddenly the baby burst out crying, and Raya started from her seat and hastened to quiet him. She rocked the carriage and crooned, "Quiet, child, quiet, quiet . . ." Even after he had quieted down she went on rocking the carriage back and forth.

Grandfather Zisskind raised his head and said to Yehuda in a whisper:

"You think it was impossible to save him . . . it was possible. They had many friends. Ossip himself wrote to me about it. The manager of the factory had a high opinion of him. The whole town knew them and loved them. . . . How is it they didn't think of it . . . ?" he said, touching his forehead with the palm of his hand. "After all, they knew that the Germans were approaching . . . It was still possible to do something . . ." He stopped a moment and then added, "Imagine that a boy of eleven had already finished his studies at the Conservatory—wild beasts!" He suddenly opened eyes filled with terror. "Wild beasts! To take little children and put them into wagons and deport them . . ."

When Raya returned and sat down at the table, he stopped and became silent; and only a heavy sigh escaped from deep within him.

Again there was a prolonged silence, and as it grew heavier Raya felt the oppressive weight on her bosom increasing till it could no longer be contained. Grandfather sat at the table tapping his thin fingers, and alongside the wall the infant lay in his carriage; it was as if a chasm gaped between a world which was passing and a world that was born. It was no longer a single line to the fourth generation. The aged father did not recognize the great-grandchild whose life would be no memorial.

Grandfather Zisskind got up, took his chair and pulled it up to the clock. He climbed on to it to take out his documents.

Raya could no longer stand the oppressive atmosphere.

"Let's go," she said to Yehuda in a choked voice.

"Yes, we must go," said Yehuda, and rose from his seat. "We have to go," he said loudly as he turned to the old man.

Grandfather Zisskind held the key of the clock for a moment more, then he let his hand fall, grasped the back of the chair and got down.

"You have to go. . . ." he said with a tortured grimace. He spread his arms out helplessly and accompanied them to the doorway.

When the door had closed behind them the tears flowed from Raya's eyes. She bent over the carriage and pressed her lips to the baby's chest. At that moment it seemed to her that he was in need of pity and of great love, as though he were alone, an orphan in the world.

Dan Paggis (1930-   )

Epilogue to Robinson Crusoe

Translated from the Hebrew by
Dennis Silk

From an island heavy with parrots and forgotten by speech
He's back, as if he'd paused for a day
Till the lucky wind came. He's back and here he is.
But at the door
The years turned suddenly on hinges. And then,   5
Between empty chairs, he knew
What had happened in the meantime, and grew wise
Like someone who has no return.
Too wise to live, gray-haired and dry he lived
With the clay-pipe of his stories, and he spoke—   10
To dull the ticking of his dead
And their chiming—he spoke and spoke
Of an island unchanged and still waiting for shipwrecks.

Shin Shalom[1] (1905-   )

The Dance of the Torches

Translated from the Hebrew by
Abraham Birman

*"They say that on every Simkhat
Beth Ha'shoëvá [Libation Festival],
Rabbán Shimon Ben Gamliël used to juggle
eight lighted torches in the air, throwing
one torch and catching another,
and they never touched."*
SUKKAH,[2] 53

Forward, honest torch; backward, fulsome torch;
    onward, sober torch; glory is a torch.
Justice is a torch; kindness is a torch;
    nothingness a torch; everything a torch.
Throw the shackled one; catch the tackled one;   5
    summon glow and fun to the blazing pyre;
Crookedness is fair; circle is a square;
    sacrilege a snare; boulders—seas of fire.
Volatile and deep; diving bold and steep;

---

1. *Shin Shalom* (shin shä lôm'). 2. *Sukkah*, a book explaining the laws and customs connected with the Feast of Tabernacles (Sukkot). In Biblical times the feast marked the autumn harvest.

lucid and opaque; manacled and free.   10
Sluggish and alert; dashing and inert;
    with discretion girt to control the spree.

    Up goes the glance,
    Down goes the dance.
    Thrill with mildness blended,   15
    Swing by sloth amended.
    If one torch should drop
    The whole dance will flop.

Hearts with pride will swell; hosts of Israel;
    flocks of Miriam's Well,[3] with my heartblood watered.   20
Stigma, stain and stitch; arrows' flight and swish;
    tone and sound and pitch all around me quartered.
Loads of water tote for the lambs and goats;
    soon my burning throat rabid flames will swallow.
Clapping hand to hand; wielding magic wands;   25
    tears in silent lands with a star to follow.
Worlds to pieces fall; light disperses all;
    sparks demurely call at eternal gates.
Countless battles won; countless flickers gone;
    only Love is one, but the torches—eight!   30

---

3. *Miriam's Well*, a well named after Miriam, a sister of Moses, who, according to the Old Testament, led the Israelite women in a triumphal dance, after the exodus from Egypt.

The Cat

Translated from the Hebrew by
Abraham Birman

In my dream I dropped a ponderous weight
On the paw of a cat.
It yelled from the smart,
It clawed my lost heart.
In my dream I dropped a ponderous weight   5
On the paw of a cat.

In a dream none can tell
A man from a cat,
A heart from a weight.
Thus I was: 10
The weight that fell,
The paw,
The pain,
The pounce into space,
The terrified yell.   15
In a dream none can tell
A weight from a heart,
A cat from a man.

Yaakov Shteinberg (1887–1947)

THE BLIND GIRL

Translated from the Hebrew by
Curt Leviant

CHANA, THE BLIND BRIDE-TO-BE, listened to her mother enumerating the groom's qualities: he was a widower; he was in the tobacco business; and he had no children from his first wife. Mindful of her daughter's angry aversion to lies, the mother added, "I mean his place is so huge the two little ones will hardly be noticed at all. They're as quiet as a pair of doves. As for the house, it's really a mansion, and has a large courtyard. When you first get there don't stray too far from the house by yourself. Remember, he's a tobacco merchant and he lives among gentiles at the edge of town. So you better stay at home."

The blind girl listened silently, unseeing eyes opened wide, but a terrible rage stormed within her. She tapped the table twice, then asked with repressed anger: "How old is he?"

"I swear he's only thirty," her mother said quickly. "And so does the matchmaker. Anyway, what's a year more or less?"

The blind girl, skeptical and rankled, stood motionless, tapping the table occasionally. The mother said no more, but a scarcely audible whisper escaped her thin, grieving lips, and she tenderly removed her daughter's trembling hands from the edge of the table.

On the wedding night the blind girl waited until her husband was asleep and then gingerly ran her fingertips over his beard. She realized at once that she had been deceived. The old man would never see thirty again. Her heart pounded in vexation. For a long while she lay awake, listening to her husband coughing, and speculating about his occupation. Was he a water carrier? A rag peddler? A carpenter? A tobacco merchant did not cough like that. Furious, Chana tossed from side to side.

"The Blind Girl" by Yaakov Shteinberg, translated by Curt Leviant, from THE JEWISH SPECTATOR. Reprinted by permission of *The Jewish Spectator*.

Suddenly she slipped off her bed and crawled along the familiar floor of her room until her hands touched her husband's huge boots. She felt the rough and wrinkled footgear for a moment and then cast them aside. The boots told much to the blind girl and she spent a long, sleepless night drawing a mental image of her husband: she pictured a tall, thin man who walked with a stoop and wore an old skull-cap and a long patched kaftan.[1]

In the morning she listened for the sounds of her husband's footsteps. When he left the house she followed him noiselessly and heard him rhythmically pounding the hard courtyard with his heavy staff. The blind girl knew that only old men walk so deliberately. Who her husband was and what he did still puzzled her. But she was certain she had been deceived. Her husband was not in the tobacco business.

Months later, after Sukkot,[2] the rains came. Chana was told that, due to her pregnancy, she would soon find it difficult to travel, and she agreed to journey to her husband's house immediately.

The wagon entered the village at night, passed the houses of sleeping Jews and slowly slogged through the mud of the market place. Not even a barking dog broke the stillness; only the measured sound of the watch-man's tread was audible. The blind girl guessed that this was the village square where all the shops were located. Then the wagon gained speed on a straight road. Hearing dogs barking on all sides, Chana assumed they were passing through the gentile neighborhood and recalled that her husband's house was located at the edge of town. But she wondered—why was the trip taking so long?

The wind blew stronger. The horses plodded uphill past the town limits and finally stopped. The driver stepped down and told Chana to wait. She remained seated and listened to the receding sounds of his footsteps. Then, wearily, she closed her eyelids . . .

She woke with a start. The horses had not budged. The wind was howling from all sides. Where was the wagon standing, she wondered, in a field? In the distance she heard the driver knocking on a window. The blind girl turned her head and listened to the sounds in the night. It seemed as though he were knocking at a gentile's window. On a Jew's window one knocked in an entirely different manner. Her husband, then, lived like a gentile . . . What sort of man was he really?

She heard the driver calling: "Reb [3] Yisroel! Reb Yisroel!"

Finally her husband came. He helped his wife down from the wagon, took her arm, and led her to the house. Passing through the hallway, the blind girl concluded that it was quite wide, like those in peasant houses. A

---

1. *kaftan*, a long garment girdled at the waist and worn under a coat. 2. *Sukkot*, the Feast of Tabernacles, originally a Jewish harvest festival. 3. *Reb*, a Yiddish term for Rabbi, usually applied to a teacher; a term of respect.

door was opened and a blast of warm air enveloped her. She realized that the cooking stove was in the living room—another gentile custom. Then she heard the cry of a child.

"That's the little one," said her husband and went to prepare tea.

The blind girl explored the room. She felt two beds. One was cold and unmade; in the other lay a small child who started to wail. The father came over, pacified the boy, and led Chana to the table.

As the house quieted down the blind girl heard sounds of trees rustling in the autumn wind, and wondered if the house had a garden. She closed her eyes and wrinkled her brow, her characteristic gesture when she could not picture a scene.

Meanwhile her husband had brought the tea kettle and a knife to cut the loaf of sugar. As he worked, a small piece of sugar fell to the floor. Reb Yisroel bent to pick it up, groaning like an old man. At that moment the blind girl slid her hand along the table until she found the knife. She tested it with her fingers to see if, like knives found in Jewish homes, it had a thick bone handle.

Reb Yisroel poured some tea into a dish and asked his wife, "Shall I help you?"

Chana blushed and replied, "I can drink by myself."

Heart pounding, the dish shaking in her hand, the blind girl swallowed a mouthful. She knew that her husband was watching her. A moment later, her hand still shaking, she spilled some tea and scalded herself. Chana then agreed to accept her husband's assistance.

As Yisroel began to make the bed, someone knocked loudly on the window and called, "Reb Yisroel! Reb Yisroel!"

Chana, who had already started to undress, turned pale and stood immobile. She could not understand how her husband could open the door so serenely. Surely this nighttime knocking portended some misfortune. She tried to listen, but the conversation between her husband and the stranger was inaudible. Finally she heard her husband groan and the door slam.

"What happened?" the blind girl asked, shivering in her scanty night clothes.

Reb Yisroel told her his aunt had just taken sick. Chana remained silent. Her face expressed wide-eyed amazement, a common reaction of hers. She went to bed and immediately covered herself with the warm blankets. But they did not dispel the cold shivers coursing through her body.

Yosele,[4] the older child, rapped on the window with his little hands. The blind girl left her work and hurried to him. She placed her hand on the four-year-old's shoulder, but the boy could not tell her what had excited him because he could not yet speak clearly.

---

4. *Yosele* (yo′sə lə).

Standing there, Chana feared that the child had suddenly become ill and was pounding on the window out of pain. But passing her hand over his head and cheeks she was assured that he was well. Fleetingly she considered the reasons for Yosele's difficulty in speaking. There were no other houses nearby and no one to speak to him. Even his taciturn father spoke only to gentiles, and the few words he uttered emerged as groans.

What, she wondered, had drawn the child to the window? Did he see something outside? Chana went to the window and pressed her ear to the glass. She was aware only of a silence so deep that she could hear the wing beat and the cawing of a crow flying by. Minutes passed and Chana did not stir. It seemed to her that something had changed outside. Everything was silent. It was like the peaceful calm of a Friday afternoon after her mother's house had been cleaned for the Sabbath. At length she seemed to understand what the child was trying to say: the first snow of the season was falling.

Chana wanted to ask her husband, but he was out. Although Yisroel was generally at home, he would sometimes be called away for hours. Upon his return he would wash his hands carefully. Chana never asked him where he had gone. She rarely spoke to him, or for that matter, to anyone, because Yisroel did all the marketing himself. In any case, what was there to talk about?

On her way to taste the stew, Chana heard a noise outside. She stood rooted in place, listening to the sound of approaching footsteps, wondering if it were her husband. But there was a shuffling of many feet, the sound of many people. Why had such a large group come? Were these village bound gentiles returning from town? No . . . The gentiles had a recognizable heavy, measured tread of their own. The blind girl continued to listen. She could have sworn the people outside were Jews and recalled that on previous occasions she had heard groups of people outside the house. What did it all mean? Chana lifted the boy up to the window and asked, "Yosele, tell me, who's walking out there?"

The boy was pleased and banged on the window. But he said nothing. Chana realized that if she were sensitive to them, Yosele's reactions could be her guide to events outside the house. For many days she had been longing to hear a human footfall. She yearned to step into the fresh air. But walking was cumbersome. She was nearing the term of her pregnancy and had ceased going outdoors.

Chana stood by the window, desperate for the sound of a human voice. She heard the door open and her husband enter. Without a word to his wife, he removed a handful of copper coins from his pocket, spread them on the table, and began counting them one by one, breathing heavily as usual.

By their ring the blind girl knew that he was counting pennies. Chana waited until her husband had finished and then asked, "Yisroel! Do you know those people moving about outside?"

"What do you care?" he groaned.

But the blind girl insisted, "There was such a great tumult out there. Was there a fire?"

"None of your business," her husband answered angrily. "You just stay in the house and pay attention to your own affairs."

Chana lowered her head—her characteristic gesture for repressed anger. She said nothing, but seethed inwardly. However, when she heard her husband walking toward the door, she asked, "When will you eat lunch?"

"I've got more important things than lunch to worry about," Yisroel shouted from the doorway, and slammed the door behind him.

Chana groped her way to the corner and after a brief search found her husband's staff. Evidently he was not going very far; merely to a Jewish neighbor. With head lowered and brow furrowed, Chana ran her hand over the heavy staff and wondered what use Yisroel made of it.

During the first cold spell of winter Chana gave birth to a girl. Each night the midwife would take the baby from Chana's bed and place her elsewhere. After a few days the blind girl understood the reason. She feared Chana would smother the infant while she slept. But Chana laughed to herself. Wasn't she aware of everything taking place in the house?

When the baby was three days old the midwife gave Chana a bowl of hot soup. Before eating, Chana picked the infant up and moved her away. The old woman noticed this and assumed that Chana was not totally blind, but could dimly discern the light of day.

After her confinement Chana's face shone with a new glow. An aura of contentment suffused her. She became more silent than ever, except when she sang lullabies to the baby. Whenever she sat by the cradle her two stepsons would rush to her side. She would embrace them both and sing for an hour or so, until her husband's return. Hearing his groaning, Chana would wrinkle her brow slightly, for she could not sense from afar whether or not he was angry.

Just before Purim [5] the cold became more severe. One morning Chana went to the hallway for some firewood. A strong wind blew the outer door open and blustered icily over the young woman as she gathered the chunks of wood with frozen hands. The instant the cold bit into her flesh the blind girl realized why the wind was so strong. Their house stood in an open field with nothing to block its passage. Holding the wood in her arms, Chana walked toward the open door and carefully listened to the wind whistling over the field.

---

5. *Purim*, a joyous Jewish festival celebrated on the fourteenth day of the Hebrew month of Adar (February-March) to commemorate the deliverance of Persian Jewry from a plot to destroy them. According to the Old Testament, Haman, adviser to King Ahasuerus of Persia, persuaded the king to annihilate all the Jews in his kingdom. However, Esther, Ahasuerus' beautiful Jewish queen, pleaded with the king and succeeded in saving her people.

She heard the gentle, soughing sounds of the snowflakes, spattering against her face and the drone of the wind blowing the snow about. After each gust the blind girl inclined her head and listened. She sensed that something in front of the house did stop the wind. Chana could not tell exactly what it was, but now that milder weather was approaching she planned to explore the area around the house.

The thaw came. All day long Chana heard the water dripping from the roofing. One day Reb Yisroel, groaning as usual, told his wife "There's a diphtheria epidemic in town." At lunchtime, a few days later, he told her, "Every day babies are dying."

The piece of bread Chana was chewing stuck in her throat. Terror-stricken, she wondered why he had told her such somber news.

After that the blind girl paid less and less attention to her household chores. She spent her day beside the cradle, constantly touching the baby's face and checking its breathing. She felt certain she would easily be able to detect the slightest ailment.

Each day when her husband came back from town she asked him about the children's epidemic raging there. Reb Yisroel would groan and answer, "The babies are dropping like flies."

Her husband's careless answer sent a chill through Chana, which penetrated to her bones. What caused him to sigh so piteously?

The warm weather set in. Puddles of water gathered outside. From Yisroel's heavy tread the blind girl guessed that his boots were knee-deep in mud. Each morning birds chirped in front of the window. Seeing this, the older boy began to prance and shout. But Chana remained gloomy as she sat by her little daughter's cradle. She had not told her husband of the strange foreboding in her heart. But one day, after he had entered and had wiped the mud from his boots, the words long trapped within her burst forth: "Look at the baby, Yisroel! I think her breathing is heavy."

As soon as she had said this a deep fear pierced her heart. Transfixed, her head bowed, her fingers tightly interlocked, she understood that her baby was sick.

Yisroel did not reply. He stood his staff in the corner and began to wash his hands thoroughly. Chana felt relieved when she saw that the child's illness had not alarmed her husband.

The baby was ill for some days. But Reb Yisroel came and went as usual. He busied himself with trivial things and spent much time cutting the loaf of sugar into little pieces. The blind girl, immersed in her sorrow, neither cooked nor ate. She felt a burgeoning hatred for her husband. Why did he maintain his indifferent calm? Why were his footsteps so measured and heavy?

Finally, Chana could no longer withhold her anger. "Murderer!" she screamed at Yisroel. "You have eyes, don't you? Tell me what is wrong with the child!"

With a groan the man evaded his wife. She listened silently. Was he going toward the cradle and the gasping baby? No. Yisroel had turned away, taking his staff from the corner, and left the house.

During the night, while Yisroel's snores filled the house and the water dripped from the roof, Chana sat for endless hours near the cradle, listening to the child's labored breathing. She knew that her daughter would die, but had no strength left to weep. Her lips moved ceaselessly in a silent whisper: "Let the grave digger try to come! I won't give him my baby. Just let him try." As she sat beside the cradle, her head bowed and her lips moving, she imagined that many years had passed and that she would sit there forever.

Outside the water continued to drip, but the man's snoring had ceased. Her mind empty of all thoughts, her heart stony and cold, the blind girl lowered her head still further and slowly sank into sleep.

She awoke and bent over the cradle. Silence. She could not hear the little girl's breathing. She listened for a few moments, then jumped up and began to scream.

All night long she wailed and wept, sitting alone, unaware that her husband had gone out. Toward dawn, exhausted, Chana stopped crying, but still she did not stir from the cradle. Her hair was disheveled, her head nodded ceaselessly, and she whispered from time to time: "Let the grave digger try to come. Just let him."

She reached into the cradle to touch the dead child once more. But it was gone. A terrible shriek burst from the blind girl's throat: "Yisroel! Where is the baby?"

There was no reply. Her body racked with agony, Chana groped her way to the door, screaming. "Yisroel! Where is the baby?"

On the doorstep she stopped and waited silently. A drop of water from the roof splashed on her face, rousing her. The blind girl cocked her ear toward the field.

Chana followed the sounds, walking at first, then running. She tripped, rose, then proceeded forward more slowly. Her feet stumbled over some stones; she ran up against a huge rock. Without thinking, she spread her hands and began to run her sensitive fingers over the stone. Stunned by her discovery, the blind girl gave voice to a heart-rending wail that echoed through the graveyard. ✕

Mulk Raj Anand (1905-   )

THE GOLD WATCH

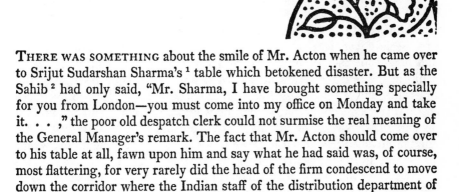

THERE WAS SOMETHING about the smile of Mr. Acton when he came over to Srijut Sudarshan Sharma's [1] table which betokened disaster. But as the Sahib [2] had only said, "Mr. Sharma, I have brought something specially for you from London—you must come into my office on Monday and take it. . . ," the poor old despatch clerk could not surmise the real meaning of the General Manager's remark. The fact that Mr. Acton should come over to his table at all, fawn upon him and say what he had said was, of course, most flattering, for very rarely did the head of the firm condescend to move down the corridor where the Indian staff of the distribution department of the great Marmalade Empire of Henry King & Co. worked.

But that smile on Mr. Acton's face! Specially as Mr. Acton was not known to smile too much, being a morose old Sahib, hard working, conscientious, and a slave driver, famous as a shrewd businessman, so devoted to the job of spreading the monopoly of King's Marmalade and sundry other products that his wife had left him after a three months' spell of marriage and never returned to India, though no one quite knew whether she was separated or divorced from him or merely preferred to stay away. So the fact that Acton Sahib should smile was enough to give Srijut Sharma cause for thought. But then Srijut Sharma was, in spite of his nobility of soul and fundamental innocence, experienced enough in his

"The Gold Watch" by Mulk Raj Anand from MODERN STORIES FROM MANY LANDS, edited by Decker and Angoff. Originally appeared in *The Literary Review*, Vol. 4, No. 4 (Summer, 1961). Reprinted by permission of the author, Manyland Books, Inc. and *The Literary Review*.
1. *Srijut Sudarshan Sharma* (srē jŭt′ sŭ′där shän shär′mä). *Srijut* is the equivalent of Mr.
2. *Sahib*, a term of respect used during the colonial era by Indians when addressing Europeans; also by Hindus and Moslems for people of rank.

study of the vague, detached faces of the white Sahibs by now and had clearly noticed the slight awkward curl of the upper lip, behind which the determined tobacco-stained long teeth showed for the briefest moment a snarl suppressed by the deliberation which Acton Sahib had brought to the whole operation of coming over and pronouncing those kind words. And what could be the reason for his having been singled out from among the twenty-five odd members of the distribution department? In the usual way, he, the despatch clerk, only received an occasional greeting: "Hello, Sharma—how you getting on?" from the head of his own department, Mr. West Sahib, or a reprimand because some letters or packets had gone astray; otherwise, he himself being the incarnation of clockwork efficiency and well-versed in the routine of his job, there was no occasion for any break in the monotony of that anonymous, smooth-working Empire, so far at least as he was concerned.

To be sure, there was the continual gossip of the clerks and the account-ants, the bickerings and jealousies of the people above him for grades and promotions and pay, but he, Sharma, had been employed twenty years ago as a special favor, was not even a matriculate, but had picked up the work somehow and, though unwanted and constantly reprimanded by West Sahib in the first few years, had been retained in his job because of the general legend of saintliness which he had acquired . . . He had five more years of service to do, because then he would be fifty-five and the family-raising, *grhst* portion of his life in the fourfold scheme,[3] prescribed by religion, finished. He hoped to retire to his home town, Jullundhur, where his father still ran the confectioner's shop off the Mall Road.

"And what did Acton Sahib have to say to you, Mr. Sharma?" asked Miss Violet Dixon, the plain snub-nosed Anglo-Indian typist in her sing-song.

Since he was an old family man of fifty who had greyed prematurely, she considered her virginity safe enough with this "gentleman" and freely conversed with him, specially during the lunch hour.

"Han," he said, "he has brought something for me from England," Srijut Sharma answered.

"There are such pretty things in U.K.," she said. "My! I wish I could go there! . . . My sister is there, you know! Married! . . ."

She had told Sharma all these things before. So he was not interested. Specially today, because all his thoughts were concentrated on the inner meaning of Mr. Acton's sudden visitation and the ambivalent smile.

---

3. *grhst . . . fourfold scheme.* In Hinduism, the common religion of India, adherents are divided into four hereditary castes (classes), with members of one having no social inter-course with those of another. The Brahmins, or Brahmans, belong to the highest caste, which includes priests, scholars, and government officials. The *grhst* (*grihastha*) is the second of four stages in the Brahminic scheme of life. In this stage the man assumes the responsibilities of a married householder.

"Well, half day today, I am off," said Violet and moved away with the peculiar snobbish agility of the Mem Sahib [4] she affected to be.

Srijut Sharma stared at her blankly, though taking her regular form into his subconscious with more than the old uncle's interest he had always pretended. It was only her snub nose, like that of Sarup-naka, the sister of the demon king, Ravana, that stood in the way of her being married, he felt sure, for otherwise she had a tolerable figure. And his obsession about the meaning of Acton Sahib's words returned, from the pent-up curiosity, with greater force now that he realized the vastness of the space of time during which he would have to wait in suspense before knowing what the boss had brought for him and why.

He took up his faded sola topee,[5] which was, apart from the bush shirt and trousers, one of the few concessions to modernity which he had made throughout his life as a good Brahmin,[6] got up from his chair, beckoned Dugdu from the verandah on his way out and asked: "Has Acton Sahib gone you know?"

"Abhi-Sahib in lift, going down," Dugdu said.

Srijut Sharma made quickly for the stairs and, throwing all caution about slipping on the polished marble steps to the winds, hurtled down. There were three floors below him and he began to sweat, both through fear of missing the Sahib and the heat of mid-April. As he got to the ground floor he saw Acton Sahib already going out of the door.

It was now or never.

Srijut Sharma rushed out. But he was conscious that quite a few employees of the firm would be coming out of the two lifts and he might be seen talking to the Sahib. And that was not done—outside the office. The Sahibs belonged to their private world where no intrusion was tolerated, for they refused to listen to pleas for advancement through improper channels.

Mr. Acton's uniformed driver opened the door of the polished Buick and the Sahib sat down, spreading the shadow of grimness all around him.

Srijut Sharma hesitated, for the demeanor of the Goanese chauffeur was frightening.

By now the driver had smartly shut the back door of the car and was proceeding to his seat.

That was his only chance.

Taking off his hat, he rushed up to the window of the car and rudely thrust his face into the presence of Mr. Acton.

Luckily for him the Sahib did not brush him aside, but smiled a broader smile than that of a few minutes ago and said: "You want to know what I have brought for you—well, it is a gold watch with an inscription on it.

---

4. *Mem Sahib*, the feminine of *Sahib*. See footnote 2. 5. *sola topee*, Indian sun helmet. 6. *Brahmin*. See footnote 3.

See me Monday morning . . ." The Sahib's initiative in anticipating his question threw Srijut Sharma further off his balance. The sweat just poured down from his forehead, even as he mumbled, "Thank you, Sir, thank you . . ."

"Chalo, driver!" the Sahib ordered.

And the chauffeur turned and looked hard at Srijut Sharma.

The despatch clerk withdrew with a sheepish, abject smile on his face and stood, hat in left hand, the right hand raised to his forehead in the attitude of a nearly military salute.

The motor car moved off.

But Srijut Sharma stood still, as though he had been struck dumb. He was neither happy nor sad at this moment—only numbed by the shock of surprise. Why should he be singled out from the whole distribution department of Henry King & Co. for the privilege of the gift of a gold watch! . . . He had done nothing brave that he could remember. "A gold watch, with an inscription on it!" Oh, he knew now—the intuitive truth rose inside him—the Sahib wanted him to retire . . .

The revelation rose to the surface of his awareness from the deep obsessive fear which had possessed him for nearly half an hour, and his heart began to palpitate against his will, and the sweat sozzled his body. He reeled a little, then adjusted himself and got onto the pavement, looking after the car which had already turned the corner into Nicol Road.

He turned and began to walk towards Victoria Terminus Station to take his train to Thana, thirty miles out, where he had resided for cheapness almost all the years he had been in Bombay. His steps were heavy, for he was reasonably sure now that he would get notice of retirement on Monday. He tried to think of some other possible reason why the Sahib may have decided to give him the gift of a gold watch with an inscription. There was no other explanation. His doom was sealed. What would he say to his wife? And his son had still not passed his Matric.[7] How would he support the family? The provident fund would not amount to very much, specially in these days of rising prices . . .

He felt a pull at his heart. He paused for breath and tried to calm himself. The old blood pressure! Or was it merely wind? . . . He must not get into a panic at any cost. He steadied his gait and walked along muttering to himself, "Shanti! Shanti! Shanti!" as though the very incantation of the formula of peace would restore him to calm and equanimity.

During the weekend, Srijut Sharma was able to conceal his panic and confusion behind the façade of an exaggerated *bonhomie* [8] with the skill of an accomplished actor. On Saturday night he went with his wife and son to see Professor Ram's circus which was performing opposite the Portuguese

---

7. *Matric*, an abbreviation for Matriculation, a British examination held at the end of secondary school. 8. *bonhomie*, a genial manner.

Church. He spent a little longer on his prayers, but otherwise seemed normal enough on the surface. Only he ate very little of the gala meal of the rice kichri put before him by his wife and seemed lost in thought for a few moments at a time. And his illiterate but shrewd wife noticed that there was something on his mind.

"Thou has not eaten at all today," she said as he left the tasty papadum and the mango pickle untouched. "Look at Hari! He has left nothing in his thali!"

"Hoon," he answered abstractedly. And then, realizing that he might be found out for the worried, unhappy man he was, he tried to bluff her. "As a matter of fact, I was thinking of some happy news that the Sahib gave me yesterday: he said he had brought a gold watch as a gift for me from Vilayat . . ."

"Then, Papaji,[9] give me the silver watch you are using now," said Hari, his young son, impetuously. "I have no watch at all and am always late everywhere."

"Not so impatient, son!" counseled Hari's mother. "Let your father get the gold watch first and then . . . he will surely give you his silver watch!"

In the ordinary way, Srijut Sharma would have endorsed his wife's sentiments. But today he felt that, on the face of it, his son's demand was justified. How should Hari know that the silver watch, the gold watch and a gold ring would be all the jewelry he, the father, would have for security against hard days if the gold watch was, as he prognosticated, only a token being offered by the firm to sugarcoat the bitter pill they would ask him to swallow—retirement five years before the appointed time! He hesitated, then lifted his head, smiled at his son and said:

"Acha, Kaka, you can have my silver watch . . ."

"Can I have it really, Papaji, hurry!" the boy said, getting up to fetch it from his father's pocket. "Give it to me now, today!"

"Vay, son, you are so selfish!" his mother exclaimed. For, with the peculiar sensitiveness of the woman, she had surmised from the manner in which her husband had hung his head and then tried to smile as he lifted his face to his son that the father of Hari was upset inside him or at least not in his usual mood of accepting life evenly, accompanying this acceptance with the pious invocation, "Shanti! Shanti! Shanti!"

Hari brought the silver watch, adjusted it to his left ear to see if it ticked and, happy in the possession of it, capered a little caper.

Srijut Sharma did not say anything, but pushing his thali away got up to wash his hands.

The next day it happened as Srijut Sharma had anticipated.

He went in to see Mr. Acton as soon as the Sahib came in, for the

---

9. *Papaji.* In India the suffix *ji* is added as a token of respect.

suspense of the weekend had mounted to a crescendo by Monday morning and he had been trembling with trepidation, pale and completely unsure of himself. The General Manager called him in immediately and the peon Dugdu presented the little slip with the despatch clerk's name on it.

"Please sit down," said Mr. Acton, lifting his grey-haired head from the papers before him. And then, pulling his keys from his trousers pocket by the gold chain to which they were adjusted, he opened a drawer and fetched out what Sharma thought was a beautiful red case.

"Mr. Sharma, you have been a loyal friend of this firm for many years . . . and . . . you know, your loyalty has been your greatest asset here . . . because . . . er . . . otherwise, we could have got someone with better qualifications to do your work! Now . . . we are thinking of increasing the efficiency of the business all around! And, well, we feel that you would also like, at your age, to retire to your native Punjab . . . So, as a token of our appreciation for your loyalty to Henry King & Co., we are presenting you this gold watch . . ." And he pushed the red case towards him.

"Sahib! . . ." Srijut Sharma began to speak, but though his mouth opened, he could not go on. "I am only fifty years old," he wanted to say, "and I still have five years to go." His facial muscles seemed to contract, his eyes were dimmed with the fumes of frustration and bitterness, his forehead was covered with sweat. At least they might have made a little ceremony of the presentation. He could not even utter the words, "Thank you, Sir."

"Of course, you will also have your provident fund and one month's leave with pay before you retire . . ."

Again Srijut Sharma tried to voice his inner protest in words which would convey his meaning without seeming to be disloyal, for he did not want to obliterate the one concession the Sahib had made to the whole record of his service with his firm. It was just likely that Mr. Acton might remind him of his failings as a despatch clerk if he should as much as indicate that he was unamenable to the suggestion made by the Sahib on behalf of Henry King & Co.

"Look at the watch—it has an inscription on it which will please you," said Mr. Acton to get over the embarrassment created by the silence of the despatch clerk.

These words hypnotized Sharma and, stretching his hands across the large table, he reached out heavily for the gift.

Mr. Acton noticed the unsureness of his hand and pushed it gently forward.

Srijut Sharma picked up the red box, but, in his eagerness to follow the Sahib's behests, dropped it even as he had held it aloft and tried to open it.

The Sahib's face was livid as he picked up the box and hurriedly opened it. Then, lifting the watch from its socket, he wound it and applied it to his ear. It was ticking. He turned it round and showed the inscription to the despatch clerk.

Srijut Sharma put both his hands out, more steadily this time, and took the gift in the manner in which a beggar receives alms. He brought the glistening object within the orbit of his eyes, but they were dimmed with tears and he could not read anything. He tried to smile, however, and then, with a great heave of his will which rocked his body from side to side, pronounced the words, "Thank you, Sir . . ."

Mr. Acton got up, took the gold watch from Srijut Sharma's hands and put it back in the socket of the red case. Then he stretched his right hand towards the despatch clerk with a brisk shake-hand gesture and offered the case to him with his left hand.

Srijut Sharma instinctively took the Sahib's right hand gratefully in his two sweating hands and then opened the palms out to receive the case.

"Good luck, Sharma," Mr. Acton said. "Come and see me after your leave is over. And when your son matriculates let me know if I can do something for him . . ."

Dumb and with bent head, the fumes of his violent emotions rising above the mouth which could have expressed them, he withdrew in the abject manner of his ancestors going out of the presence of a feudal lord.

Mr. Acton saw the danger to the watch and went ahead to open the door so that the clerk could go out without knocking his head against the door or falling down.

As Srijut Sharma emerged from the General Manager's office, tears involuntarily flowed from his eyes and his lower lip fell in a pout that somehow controlled him from breaking down completely.

The eyes of the whole office staff were on him. In a moment, a few of the men clustered around his person. One of them took the case from his hands, opened it and read the inscription out loud: "In appreciation of the loyal service of Mr. Sharma to Henry King & Co. on his retirement."

The curiosity of his colleagues became a little less enthusiastic though the watch passed from hand to hand.

Unable to stand because of the waves of dizziness that swirled in his head, Srijut Sudarshan Sharma sat down on his chair with his head hidden in his hands and allowed the tears to roll down. One of his colleagues, Mr. Banaji, the accountant, patted his back understandingly. But the pity was too much for him.

"To be sure, Seth Makanji, the new partner, has a relation to fill Sharma's position," one said.

"No, no," another refuted him. "No one is required to kill himself with work in our big concern . . . We are given the Sunday off! And a fat pension years before it is due. The bosses are full of love for us! . . ."

"Damn fine gold watch, but it does not go!" said Shri Raman the typist.

Mr. Banaji took the watch from Srijut Raman and, putting it in the case, placed it before Srijut Sharma as he signed the others to move away.

As Srijut Sharma realized that his colleagues had drifted away, he lifted his morose head, took the case, as well as his hat, and began to walk away. Mr. Banaji saw him off to the door, his hand on Sharma's back. "Sahibji," the parsi [10] accountant said as the lift came up and the liftman took Sharma in.

On the way home he found that the gold watch only went when it was shaken. Obviously some delicate part had broken when he had dropped it on Mr. Acton's table. He would get it mended, but he must save all the cash he could get hold of and not go spending it on the luxury of having a watch repaired now. He shouldn't have been weak with his son and given him his old silver watch. But as there would be no office to attend, he would not need to look at the time very much, specially in Jullundhur where time just stood still and no one bothered about keeping appointments.   ✗

---

10. *parsi,* a member of a Zoroastrian religious sect in India, descended from a group of Persian refugees who fled from religious persecution by the Moslems in the 7th and 8th centuries. Zoroastrianism, founded about 600 B.C. by Zoroaster, includes belief in an afterlife and in the continuous struggle between the universal spirit of good and the spirit of evil, with the good finally triumphing.

Anonymous

from the *Mahabharata* [1]

SAVITRI'S LOVE

Adapted from a translation from the Sanskrit by Romesh Dutt

THERE WAS A KING in India named Aswapati, and his people loved him, for he helped all in need and served the shining gods with prayer and sacrifice.

But the king had no child in whom his name and line could live on, and his heart was very sad. So he fasted often, and he said hymns to the shining gods, hoping they would grant this one wish. After sixteen years his prayers were heard. In the red fire of the altar he saw a woman, fair of face and manner.

"Your devotions have pleased me," she said. "State your wish and it will be granted."

"My wish is to be blessed with a child who will live after I am gone," the king replied.

"The gods will grant you that wish," she said, and then she was gone and the king saw only the red flame.

A child was born—a girl with bright eyes, bright as the lotus lily—and she was the pride of her mother and father. Eventually she grew into a beautiful woman; so beautiful in fact that her father was sure other kings would come to seek her hand from near and far. But none came, for this lotus-eyed one was blessed with a soul too magnificent even for royalty, and her serious ways and mystic speech made men stand back in awe.

One day this maiden of grace—Savitri by name—knelt at the altar of Agni, god of the red flame. She asked the god's blessings and laid before it an offering of cakes and drink. Then she gathered a bunch of flowers to take to her father. Aswapati looked at her with tender eyes.

"Savitri's Love" from the *Mahabharata* (adapted from the prose translation by Romesh Dutt).

1. *Mahabharata.* The *Mahabharata*, or *Stream of Stories*, is an epic poem of India, which dates from the centuries just preceding the Christian era. It was converted into prose during the nineteenth century.

"My daughter, it is time you were married as is the fashion of all high-born ladies. We must lose no time as people might think it is my fault that no husband has been chosen for you. Since no one has come to seek your hand, I suggest you travel and select one for yourself."

So Savitri began her search. She traveled in a splendid train, accompanied by nobles and wise men. The royal procession passed through forests and moved along streets of great cities, and journeyed even through the small villages in the hills. Wherever Savitri went she gave alms to the poor, and greeted the mighty and the lowly, and the people all blessed her.

One day she finally returned. The king greeted her from the throne. At his side sat Narad, the wise man. "I have found my husband," the princess said. "He is the Prince Satyavan.[2] Even though he does not live in a palace, still he is a noble of royal blood."

"What land does he rule?" the king asked.

"He has no kingdom, but lives in a cottage in the woods with his father and mother. Their lot is not a happy one. The old man is blind, and he and his queen have lived in the jungle since their son was an infant. Many years ago, the king's enemies drove him from his rightful throne and took away his lands. Ah, but my prince is as noble as his name; at his birth the Brahmans [3] called him Satyavan, or Truth Lover. He is manly and full of laughter, an excellent horseman, and he can paint pictures of horses that are a wonder to behold."

"What do you think?" the king asked the wise man, Narad.

"She has chosen badly," Narad answered. "The old king is indeed a just man, and the Prince Satyavan a noble youth. But I see a dark fate awaiting them, for it has been shown to me by the shining gods that the prince will die a year from this very day."

"Do you hear that, my daughter? I beg you to select another. It would be foolish to go ahead with your marriage since Yama, the god of death, will come in a year to claim your husband for his own."

"I can't choose another, dear father. My heart belongs to Satyavan alone. Whether he is taken from me or not, I will marry only him."

"You may do as you want, my child. But it is a strange wish you have shown. You ask to live in the wilds for twelve months, then to spend the rest of your years in mourning."

The next day the king and his daughter went into the jungle, accompanied by courtiers and priests, and carrying with them a great treasure. They found the blind old king seated on a grass mat beside a *sal* tree.

At the blind king's request, Aswapati and his daughter sat down on the grass mat. The host offered his honored guests some water, for he was too

---

2. *Satyavan* (sä tä′vän). 3. *Brahmans*. In Hinduism, the common religion of India, adherents are divided into four hereditary castes (classes), with members of one having no social intercourse with those of another. The Brahmans belong to the highest caste, which includes priests, scholars, and government officials.

poor to afford the customary wine. After cordialities, the two kings agreed upon the marriage, and not long afterwards the prince and princess were married. The lovely maiden thus became the queen of a small cottage nestled in the trees of a vast jungle. Once the wedding was concluded, her friends and father said their farewells amid many tears.

After her parents had gone, Savitri removed her sparkling jewels and her beautiful dress, and put on a plain robe fashioned from the bark of trees. This she bound around her with a cord of cheap yellow cloth. She would be a queen, not by her jewels or dress, but by serving the blind old king and his wife, and by her love and obedience to the prince of her choice.

So passed the happy year.

Now only four days remained before the Shadow of Death would glide into the forest kingdom. For three of these days Savitri fasted and went without sleep. Her heart was pained with the dread of that which had been preordained. But she told her story to no one, so neither the blind king nor the noble prince knew of the fate that lay ahead.

On the morning of that fatal day Satyavan arose in a joyful mood. He took his woodsman's axe and smiled at his princess. "I'm off to cut some wood," he announced. "I will be home again at the setting of the sun."

The prince's words broke Savitri's heart. She knew too well how the black-robed Yama would lay his thin hand upon her lover and so take him from her. "Let me go with you today," she said.

"No. The ground is too rugged for your dainty feet, and the way will be long, and the trip will be too exhausting. . . ."

"Please," she begged.

This plea Satyavan could not deny, and the prince and the princess set out for the depths of the jungle forest. They came to a distant place where there were many high trees for cutting and much fruit that could be gathered. The hour of noon had passed and dusk began to creep through the great forest. The sound of the axe echoed in the grove. Basket in hand, Savitri picked ripe berries from the shrubs. Again and again she would stop to look over at her husband.

Suddenly he cried out: "Oh, my wife!"

Savitri threw down her basket and rushed to his side.

"It's my head. A sharp pain is stabbing at my brain. Look, now my blood is hot. Oh, I must lie down."

Savitri helped him to a tree. Beneath the limbs she laid his head in her lap and fanned his face. His eyes had been closed for many moments when at last he fell silent. Then his pulse slowed and, finally, it was still.

The year had passed. The heartbroken Savitri looked up to see a huge shadow in the shape of a man. Its robe was black, its eyes shone like red lights, and it wore a strange crown on its head.

"Are you one of the gods?" she asked in a whisper.

"Princess, I am Yama, the god of Death. I have come this day for your husband, the prince."

At these words Yama raised his hands and threw a cord at the still form of Satyavan. The cord caught the life of the prince in its noose and drew it from his body. Then Yama turned towards his kingdom in the south.

The jungle became dark. And the power of Yama was strong. But the princess was brave. She got up and followed in the footsteps of Yama. After a short time the black god heard her; he turned.

"Go back. You have come too far. Go back and begin those sad rites which mourners make to show their sorrow for the dead."

"I follow my husband. It is my duty. The wise men say that to walk seven steps with another makes friendship. So let me walk more than seven steps with you. Besides the wise men tell that the way of righteousness is the way for all, and so it must be my way."

"Your loyalty and fidelity are great," Yama replied. "In return for these I will grant you one wish, any wish—except for the soul of the dead Satyavan."

"Then give me this. Let the eyes of my prince's father once again see the light of day, and let his strength be as the strength of the sun itself."

"It shall be done. Now turn back. You must return home. My way leads only to doom."

"Sad indeed will be the path home without my husband's guiding hand. There is no sweeter fruit on earth than the company of those we love."

The black god smiled, for Savitri's words were good and wise.

"I give you one more wish—except the soul of Satyavan."

"Then I ask that the kingdom of the old king be restored so that he may have his lands as well as his sight."

"It shall happen as you say. And now go back. The forest is wide and your home is far off."

"Yama, hear me once more. What is the goodness of a good man? Is it kindness to all things on earth, in the air or on the sea? It is indeed. So even if your enemy seeks help, grant him that help for by so doing you become good."

"Your words are the words of wisdom, princess. And for these last words I promise you still another wish. What will it be?"

"Oh, Yama, I only want to be the mother of noble children so that I can teach them to walk in the footsteps of their dear father, Satyavan. And for that—return my prince."

The god of death shook his cord. "Woman, your husband shall reign with you for many years, and you shall have sons to reign after you."

The dark shadow of Yama then floated off into the gloom of the jungle.

With quick feet Savitri ran. Breathless she flew. And when she reached the tree where the body of Satyavan lay she knelt. After putting his head on her lap, she waited and watched. At last the prince opened his eyes.

"I must have overslept. Strange, just as I was falling asleep I thought I saw something like a shadow. It reached out and grasped my life in some kind of magic noose. Then I was carried away into the darkness—"

"That was Yama, the god of death. But he is gone. Get up now, Satyavan. It is dark and we must go home."

"Ah, now I remember—a sharp pain was piercing my brain."

"We'll talk about it tomorrow. It's time to go."

"It's too dark. We'll never find the path."

"Look," she said. "There is a fire burning in the forest a long way off. Perhaps it's the work of the blazing mid-day sun. We will head towards it. You can use the burning wood to make a torch so that we can drive off the wild beasts as we walk. But if your pain is still present, we can remain here until you recover."

"The pain is gone, Savitri. I am strong again. You are right, father and mother will be worried by our absence."

As he spoke of his blind father, tears filled the prince's eyes. He jumped to his feet, brushing the dry leaves from his clothes.

"Get your basket of fruit."

"We'll get it tomorrow, Satyavan. We have enough to do to find our way in the darkness. Here, let me carry the axe."

Savitri carried the axe in her left hand and put her right arm about her husband. In this way they traveled through the jungle, harmed neither by bear nor tiger.

The sky had turned to grey by the time Savitri and Satyavan reached the cottage. As they approached, they heard voices, and a shout arose as the prince and princess broke through the clearing.

"My children," cried the king.

"Father," shouted Satyavan. "How are you able to see me?"

"I do not know how this miracle came about, but I do know that I can see you, my son. And you, dearest Savitri, now I can look upon my faithful daughter for the first time."

The old king embraced his son and daughter-in-law.

"Now tell me," he asked. "Where have you two been all night?"

After Satyavan explained their delay, Savitri told of the evil prophesy and of her encounter with Yama, the god of death. No sooner had she finished than a jumble of noises came from the forest and a crowd of people approached.

"Good news," they cried. "The tyrant who captured the old king's throne has been overthrown. Return to your kingdom, dear ruler. Even though you are blind, your loyal subjects stand by your side."

"But the shining gods have cleared my eyes," the old king announced. "Come, let us all return to the lands and people of my birth."

And that is the story of Savitri, of her meeting with the black god of death, and of her great love.   ✳

Chauras[1] (11th–12th centuries)

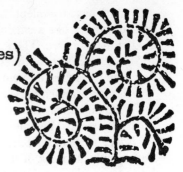

from *BLACK MARIGOLDS*

Translated from the Sanskrit by
E. Powys Mathers

Hundreds of years ago Chauras, a young Brahman poet, lived at the court of the king and loved Vidya, the king's daughter. Upon discovery of their love, Chauras was imprisoned and sentenced to death. During his time in prison he composed the Chauraspanchasika, *"The Fifty Stanzas of Chauras." Legend has it that Vidya's father was so moved by the poem that he released the poet, but in actual fact he was not so kind: Chauras was executed within hours of completing his stanzas.*

> EVEN now
> My thought is all of this gold-tinted king's daughter
> With garlands tissue and golden buds,
> Smoke tangles of her hair, and sleeping or waking
> Feet trembling in love, full of pale languor;   5
> My thought is clinging as to a lost learning
> Slipped down out of the minds of men,
> Laboring to bring her back into my soul.
>
> Even now
> If I see in my soul the citron-breasted fair one   10
> Still gold-tinted, her face like our night stars,
> Drawing unto her; her body beaten about with flame,
> Wounded by the flaring spear of love,
> My first of all by reason of her fresh years,
> Then is my heart buried alive in snow.   15

"Bilhana: Black Marigolds" translated by E. Powys Mathers (a free interpretation of the Chauraspanchasika). Published in 1919 by Houghton Mifflin Company.
1. *Chauras* (chō′ras).

Even now
I bring her back, ah, wearied out with love
So that her slim feet could not bear her up;
Curved falls of her hair down on her white cheeks;
In the confusion of her colored vests   20
Speaking that guarded giving up, and her scented arms
Lay like cool bindweed over against my neck.

Even now
If I saw her lying all wide eyes
And with collyrium [2] the indent of her cheek   25
Lengthened to the bright ear and her pale side
So suffering the fever of my distance,
Then would my love for her be ropes of flowers, and night
A black-haired lover on the breasts of day.

Even now   30
She is art-magically present to my soul,
And that one word of strange heart's ease, good-by,
That in the night, in loth moving to go,
And bending over to a golden mouth,
I said softly to the turned away   35
Tenderly tied hair of this king's daughter.

Even now
My eyes that hurry to see no more are painting, painting
Faces of my lost girl. O golden rings
That tap against cheeks of small magnolia leaves,   40
O whitest so soft parchment where
My poor divorcèd lips have written excellent
Stanzas of kisses, and will write no more.

Even now
When all my heavy heart is broken up   45
I seem to see my prison walls breaking
And then a light, and in that light a girl
Her fingers busied about her hair, her cool white arms
Faint rosy at the elbows, raised in the sunlight,
And temperate eyes that wander far away.   50

---

2. *collyrium*, a medication for the eyes, probably used as a cosmetic.

Even now
I seem to see my prison walls come close,
Built up of darkness, and against that darkness
A girl no taller than my breast and very tired,
Leaning upon the bed and smiling, feeding   55
A little bird and lying slender as ash trees,
Sleepily aware as I told of the green
Grapes and the small bright-colored river flowers.

Even now
I see her, as I used, in her white palace   60
Under black torches throwing cool red light,
Woven with many flowers and tearing the dark.
I see her rising, showing all her face
Defiant timidly, saying clearly:
Now I shall go to sleep, good-night, my ladies.   65

Even now
Though I am so far separate, a flight of birds
Swinging from side to side over the valley trees,
Passing my prison with their calling and crying,
Bring me to see my girl. For very bird-like   70
Is her song singing, and the state of a swan
In her light walking, like the shaken wings
Of a black eagle falls her nightly hair.

Even now
I know my princess was happy. I see her stand   75
Touching her breasts with all her flower-soft fingers,
Looking askance at me with smiling eyes.
There is a god that arms him with a flower
And she was stricken deep. Here, oh die here.
Kiss me and I shall be purer than quick rivers.   80

Even now
They chatter her weakness through the two bazaars
Who was so strong to love me. And small men
That buy and sell for silver being slaves
Crinkle the fat about their eyes; and yet   85
No Prince of the Cities of the Sea has taken her,
Leading to his grim bed. Little lonely one,
You clung to me as a garment clings; my girl.

Even now
Only one dawn shall rise for me. The stars   90
Revolve to-morrow's night and I not heed.
One brief cold watch beside an empty heart
And that is all. This night she rests not well;
Oh, sleep; for there is heaviness for all the world
Except for the death-lighted heart of me.   95

Even now
I mind the coming and talking of wise men from towers
Where they had thought away their youth. And I, listening,
Found not the salt of the whispers of my girl,
Murmur of confused colors, as we lay near sleep;   100
Little wise words and little witty words,
Wanton as water, honied with eagerness.

Even now
The woodcutter and the fisherman turn home,
With on his axe the moon and in his dripping net   105
Caught yellow moonlight. The purple flame of fires
Calls them to love and sleep. From the hot town
The maker of scant songs for bread wanders
To lie under the clematis with his girl.
The moon shines on her breasts, and I must die.   110

Even now
I seem to see the face of my lost girl
With frightened eyes, like a wood wanderer,
In travail with sorrowful waters, unwept tears
Laboring to be born and fall; when white face turned   115
And little ears caught at the far murmur,
The pleased snarling of the tumult of dogs
When I was hurried away down the white road.

Even now
When slow rose-yellow moons looked out at night   120
To guard the sheaves of harvest and mark down
The peach's fall, how calm she was and love worthy.
Glass-colored starlight falling as thin as dew
Was wont to find us at the spirit's starving time
Slow straying in the orchard paths with love.   125

Even now
I marvel at the bravery of love,
She, whose two feet might be held in one hand
And all her body on a shield of the guards,
Lashed like a gold panther taken in a pit   130
Tearfully valiant, when I too was taken;
Bearding her black beard father in his wrath,
Striking the soldiers with white impotent hands.

Even now
Sleep left me all these nights for your white bed   135
And I am sure you sistered lay with sleep
After much weeping. Piteous little love,
Death is in the garden, time runs down,
The year that simple and unexalted ran till now
Ferments in winy autumn, and I must die.   140

Even now
I mind our going, full of bewilderment
As who should walk from sleep into great light,
Along the running of the winter river,
A dying sun on the cool hurrying tide   145
No more by green rushes delayed in dalliance,
With a clear purpose in his flower-flecked length
Informed, to reach Nirvana [3] and the sea.

Even now
The stainless fair appearance of the moon   150
Rolls her gold beauty over an autumn sky
And the stiff anchorite [4] forgets to pray;
How much the sooner I, if her wild mouth
Tasting of the taste of manna [5] came to mine
And kept my soul at balance above a kiss.   155

---

3. *Nirvana*, in Hinduism, the common religion in India, the salvation of the individual soul through union with Brahma, the god of creation. 4. *anchorite*, hermit. 5. *manna*, divine food.

Even now
She with young limbs as smooth as flower pollen,
Whose swaying body is laved in the cool
Waters of languor, this dear bright-colored bird,
Walks not, changes not, advances not   160
Her weary station by the black lake
Of Gone Forever, in whose fountain vase
Balance the water lilies of my thought.

Even now
Spread we our nets beyond the farthest rims   165
So surely that they take the feet of dawn
Before you wake and after you are sleeping
Catch up the visible and invisible stars
And web the ports the strongest dreamer dreamed,
Yet is it all one, Vidya,[6] yet is it nothing.   170

Even now
The night is full of silver straws of rain,
And I will send my soul to see your body
This last poor time. I stand beside our bed;
Your shadowed head lies leaving a bright space   175
Upon the pillow empty, your sorrowful arm
Holds from your side and clasps not anything.
There is no covering upon you.

Even now
I think your feet seek mine to comfort them.   180
There is some dream about you even now
Which I'll not hear at waking. Weep not at dawn,
Though day brings wearily your daily loss
And all the light is hateful. Now is it time
To bring my soul away.   185

_____

6. *Vidya*, the king's daughter whom Chauras loves.

Even now
I mind that I went round with men and women,
And underneath their brows, deep in their eyes,
I saw their souls, which go slipping aside
In swarms before the pleasure of my mind; 190
The world was like a flight of birds, shadow or flame
Which I saw pass above the engraven hills.
Yet was there never one like to my woman.

Even now
Death I take up as consolation. 195
Nay, were I free as the condor with his wings
Or old kings throned on violet ivory,
Night would not come without beds of green floss
And never a bed without my bright darling.
It is most fit that you strike now, black guards, 200
And let this fountain out before the dawn.

Even now
I know that I have savored the hot taste of life
Lifting green cups and gold at the great feast.
Just for a small and a forgotten time 205
I have had full in my eyes from off my girl
The whitest pouring of eternal light.
The heavy knife. As to a gala day.

Dhumketu [1] (1892–)

THE LETTER

Translated from the Gujerati [2] by
the author

IN THE GREY SKY of early dawn stars still glowed, as happy memories light up a life that is nearing its close. An old man was walking through the town, now and again drawing his tattered cloak tighter to shield his body from the cold and biting wind. From some houses standing apart came the sound of grinding mills and the sweet voices of women singing at their work, and these sounds helped him along his lonely way. Except for the occasional bark of a dog, the distant steps of a workman going early to work or the screech of a bird disturbed before its time, the whole town was wrapped in deathly silence. Most of its inhabitants were still in the arms of sleep, a sleep which grew more and more profound on account of the intense winter cold; for the cold used sleep to extend its sway over all things even as a false friend lulls his chosen victim with caressing smiles. The old man, shivering at times but fixed of purpose, plodded on till he came out of the town gate to a straight road. Along this he now went at a somewhat slower pace, supporting himself on his old staff.

On one side of the road was a row of trees, on the other the town's public garden. The night was darker now and the cold more intense, for the wind was blowing straight along the road and on it there only fell, like frozen snow, the faint light of the morning star. At the end of the garden stood a handsome building of the newest style, and light gleamed through the crevices of its closed doors and windows.

Beholding the wooden arch of this building, the old man was filled with the joy that the pilgrim feels when he first sees the goal of his journey. On the arch hung an old board with the newly painted letters: POST OFFICE.

"The Letter" by (Dhumketu) Gaurishankar Joshi, translated by the author, from TEN TALES FOR INDIAN STUDENTS, by permission of Oxford University Press. Reprinted from *The Literary Review* (Summer 1961, Volume 4, Number 4), published by Fairleigh Dickinson University, Rutherford, New Jersey.
1. *Dhumketu* (dùm kä′tù). 2. *Gujerati*, the language of the people of Gujerat, a region on the west coast of India.

The old man went in quietly and squatted on the veranda. The voices of the two or three people busy at their routine work could be heard faintly through the wall.

"Police Superintendent," a voice inside called sharply. The old man started at the sound, but composed himself again to wait. But for the faith and love that warmed him he could not have borne the bitter cold.

Name after name rang out from within as the clerk read out the English addresses on the letters and flung them to the waiting postmen. From long practice he had acquired great speed in reading out the titles—Commissioner, Superintendent, Diwan Sahib,[3] Librarian—and in flinging out the letters.

In the midst of this procedure a jesting voice from inside called, "Coachman Ali!"

The old man got up, raised his eyes to Heaven in gratitude and, stepping forward, put his hand on the door.

"Godul Bhai!"

"Yes. Who's there?"

"You called out Coachman Ali's name, didn't you? Here I am. I have come for my letter."

"It is a madman, sir, who worries us by calling every day for letters that never come," said the clerk to the postmaster.

The old man went back slowly to the bench on which he had been accustomed to sit for five long years.

Ali had once been a clever shikari.[4] As his skill increased so did his love for the hunt, till at last it was as impossible for him to pass a day without it as it is for the opium eater to forego his daily portion. When Ali sighted the earth-brown partridge, almost invisible to other eyes, the poor bird, they said, was as good as in his bag. His sharp eyes would see the hare crouching in its form. When even the dogs failed to see the creature cunningly hidden in the yellow-brown scrub, Ali's eagle eyes would catch sight of its ears; and in another moment it was dead. Besides this, he would often go with his friends, the fishermen.

But when the evening of his life was drawing in, he left his old ways and suddenly took a new turn. His only child, Miriam, married and left him. She went off with a soldier to his regiment in the Punjab,[5] and for the last five years he had had no news of this daughter for whose sake alone he dragged on a cheerless existence. Now he understood the meaning of love and separation. He could no longer enjoy the sportsman's pleasure and laugh at the bewildered terror of the young partridges bereft of their parents.

Although the hunter's instinct was in his very blood and bones, such a

---

3. *Diwan Sahib*, a high government official. 4. *shikari*, a hunter. 5. *Punjab*, formerly, a province in northwestern India, now divided between India and Pakistan.

loneliness had come into his life since the day Miriam had gone away that now, forgetting his sport, he would become lost in admiration of the green corn fields. He reflected deeply and came to the conclusion that the whole universe is built up through love and that the grief of separation is inescapable. And seeing this, he sat down under a tree and wept bitterly. From that day he had risen each morning at four o'clock to walk to the post office. In his whole life he had never received a letter, but with a devout serenity born of hope and faith he continued and was always the first to arrive.

The post office, one of the most uninteresting buildings in the world, became his place of pilgrimage. He always occupied a particular seat in a particular corner of the building, and when people got to know his habit they laughed at him. The postmen began to make a game of him. Even though there was no letter for him, they would call out his name for the fun of seeing him jump and come to the door. But with boundless faith and infinite patience he came every day—and went away empty-handed.

While Ali waited, peons would come for their firms' letters and he would hear them discussing their masters' scandals. These smart young peons in their spotless turbans and creaking shoes were always eager to express themselves. Meanwhile the door would be thrown open and the postmaster, a man with a head as sad and inexpressive as a pumpkin, would be seen sitting on his chair inside. There was no glimmer of animation in his features; and such men usually prove to be village school-masters, office clerks or postmasters.

One day he was there as usual and did not move from his seat when the door was opened.

"Police Commissioner!" the clerk called out, and a fellow stepped forward briskly for the letters.

"Superintendent!" Another peon came; and so the clerk, like a worshipper of Vishnu,[6] repeated his customary thousand names.

At last they had all gone. Ali too got up and, saluting the post office as though it housed some precious relic, went off, a pitiable figure, a century behind his time.

"That fellow," asked the postmaster, "is he mad?"

"Who, sir? Oh yes," answered the clerk. "No matter what sort of weather, he has been here every day for the last five years. But he doesn't get many letters."

"I can well understand that! Who does he think will have time to write to him every day?"

"But he's a bit touched, sir. In the old days he committed many sins; and maybe he shed blood within some sacred precincts and is paying for it now," the postman added in support to his statement.

---

6. *Vishnu,* in Hinduism, the common religion of India, one of the three chief divinities.

"Madmen are strange people," the postmaster said.

"Yes. Once I saw a madman in Ahmedabad who did absolutely nothing but make little heaps of dust. Another had a habit of going every day to the river in order to pour water on a certain stone!"

"Oh, that's nothing," chimed in another. "I knew one madman who paced up and down all day long, another who never ceased declaiming poetry, and a third who would slap himself on the cheek and then begin to cry out because he was being beaten."

And everyone in the post office began talking of lunacy. All working-class people have a habit of taking periodic rests by joining in general discussion for a few minutes. After listening a little, the postmaster got up and said:

"It seems as though the mad live in a world of their own making. To them, perhaps, we too appear mad. The madman's world is rather like the poet's, I should think!"

He laughed as he spoke the last words, looking at one of the clerks who wrote indifferent verse. Then he went out and the office became still again.

For several days Ali had not come to the post office. There was no one with enough sympathy or understanding to guess the reason, but all were curious to know what had stopped the old man. At last he came again; but it was a struggle for him to breathe, and on his face were clear signs of his approaching end. That day he could not contain his impatience.

"Master Sahib,"[7] he begged the postmaster, "have you a letter from my Miriam?"

The postmaster was in a hurry to get out to the country.

"What a pest you are, brother!" he exclaimed.

"My name is Ali," answered Ali, absent-mindedly.

"I know! I know! But do you think we've got your Miriam's name registered?"

"Then please note it down, brother. It will be useful if a letter should come when I am not here." For how should the villager who had spent three quarters of his life hunting know that Miriam's name was not worth a pice[8] to anyone but her father?

The postmaster was beginning to lose his temper. "Have you no sense?" he cried. "Get away! Do you think we are going to eat your letter when it comes?" And he walked off hastily. Ali came out very slowly, turning after every few steps to gaze at the post office. His eyes were filling with tears of helplessness, for his patience was exhausted, even though he still had faith. Yet how could he still hope to hear from Miriam?

Ali heard one of the clerks coming up behind him and turned to him.

7. *Sahib*, a term of respect used by Hindus and Moslems when addressing people of rank.
8. *pice*, formerly, a bronze coin of British India worth about .0057 of a U.S. cent.

"Brother!" he said.

The clerk was surprised, but being a decent fellow he said, "Well?"

"Here, look at this!" and Ali produced an old tin box and emptied five golden guineas into the surprised clerk's hands. "Do not look so startled," he continued, "they will be useful to you, and they can never be so to me. But will you do one thing?"

"What?"

"What do you see up there?" said Ali, pointing to the sky.

"Heaven."

"Allah is there, and in His presence I am giving you this money. When it comes, you must forward my Miriam's letter to me."

"But where—where am I to send it?" asked the utterly bewildered clerk.

"To my grave."

"What?"

"Yes. It is true. Today is my last day: my very last, alas! And I have not seen Miriam, I have had no letter from her." Tears were in Ali's eyes as the clerk slowly left him and went on his way with the five golden guineas in his pocket.

Ali was never seen again and no one troubled to inquire after him.

One day, however, trouble came to the postmaster. His daughter lay ill in another town and he was anxiously waiting for news from her. The post was brought in and the letters piled on the table. Seeing an envelope of the color and shape he expected, the postmaster eagerly snatched it up. It was addressed to coachman Ali, and he dropped it as though it had given him an electric shock. The haughty temper of the official had quite left him in his sorrow and anxiety and had laid bare his human heart. He knew at once that this was the letter the old man had been waiting for: it must be from his daughter Miriam.

"Lakshmi Das!" called the postmaster, for such was the name of the clerk to whom Ali had given his money.

"Yes, sir?"

"This is for your old coachman Ali. Where is he now?"

"I will find out, sir."

The postmaster did not receive his own letter all that day.

He worried all night and, getting up at three, went to sit in the office. "When Ali comes at four o'clock," he mused, "I will give him the letter myself."

For now the postmaster understood all Ali's heart, and his very soul. After spending but a single night in suspense, anxiously waiting for news of his daughter, his heart was brimming with sympathy for the poor old man who had spent his nights for the last five years in the same suspense. At the stroke of five he heard a soft knock on the door: he felt sure it was

Ali. He rose quickly from his chair, his suffering father's heart recognizing another, and flung the door wide open.

"Come in, brother Ali," he cried, handing the letter to the meek old man, bent double with age, who was standing outside. Ali was leaning on a stick and the tears were wet on his face as they had been when the clerk left him. But his features had been hard then and now they were softened by lines of kindliness. He lifted his eyes and in them was a light so unearthly that the postmaster shrank in fear and astonishment.

Lakshmi Das had heard the postmaster's words as he came towards the office from another quarter. "Who was that, sir? Old Ali?" he asked. But the postmaster took no notice of him. He was staring with wide-open eyes at the doorway from which Ali had disappeared. Where could he have gone? At last he turned to Lakshmi Das. "Yes, I was speaking to Ali," he said.

"Old Ali is dead, sir. But give me his letter."

"What! But when? Are you sure, Lakshmi Das?"

"Yes, it is so," broke in a postman who had just arrived. "Ali died three months ago."

The postmaster was bewildered. Miriam's letter was still lying near the door; Ali's image was still before his eyes. He listened to Lakshmi Das' recital of the last interview, but he could still not doubt the reality of the knock on the door and the tears in Ali's eyes. He was perplexed. Had he really seen Ali? Had his imagination deceived him? Or had it perhaps been Lakshmi Das?

The daily routine began. The clerk read out the addresses—Police Commissioner, Superintendent, Librarian—and flung the letters deftly.

But the postmaster now watched them as though each contained a warm, beating heart. He no longer thought of them in terms of envelopes and postcards. He saw the essential, human worth of a letter.

That evening you might have seen Lakshmi Das and the postmaster walking with slow steps to Ali's grave. They laid the letter on it and turned back.

"Lakshmi Das, were you indeed the first to come to the office this morning?"

"Yes, sir, I was the first."

"Then how . . . No, I don't understand . . ."

"What, sir?"

"Oh, never mind," the postmaster said shortly. At the office he parted from Lakshmi Das and went in. The newly-waked father's heart in him was reproaching him for having failed to understand Ali's anxiety. Tortured by doubt and remorse, he sat down in the glow of the charcoal sigri [9] to wait. ✳

---

9. *sigri*, a small heater made of earthenware or mud. [*Punjabi*]

Achintya Kumar Sen Gupta [1]
(1903-   )

THE BAMBOO TRICK

Translated from the Bengali
by the author

THE ANNUAL GAJAN FAIR was being held in the maidan, or square, at Khorogachi.[2]

This year the fair wasn't much of a success, it hadn't drawn the usual crowds, and the variety of things offered for sale was poor: evil-smelling papadams fried in rancid oil, popcorn and some hail-ridden green mangoes. The scarcity of paper had banished the kites and the fluttering paper toys. Clay toys were there—dogs and cats, horses and elephants—all in one color, with only a dot or a line in black to denote an eye or the end of a tail. Then split-cane and bamboo baskets, small and large. Earthenware pots and pans, cups and plates. But the piles of handwoven towels in gay checks and the glitter of multicolored glass bangles were missing.

Those who had come to the fair looked worn-out and lifeless, as if they had emerged more dead than alive from the bowels of some dark valley of fear. There was no gaiety either in their talk or in their walk. The clothes they wore were drab and shabby—on the verge of turning into rags.

The crowd was thickest under the pakur tree and all the noise and tumult of the fair had concentrated there.

As I went forward, I heard a child wailing, "I'll fall, I'll die!" Eyes blind with streaming tears he sobbed and wailed miserably. A little boy, six or seven years old, with arms and legs like brittle sticks, a strip of rag

GREEN AND GOLD, ed. Humayan Kabir. © 1958 by Government of West Bengal, India. All Rights Reserved. Reprinted by permission of New Directions Publishing Corporation and Asia Publishing House.

1. *Achintya Kumar Sen Gupta* (ä chĕn'tä kù'mär sen gùp'tä). 2. *Gajan Fair . . . Khorogachi*. In India fairs are named after deities or the nearest town. In this case Gajan, a town in southwestern Pakistan, is nearest the village of Khorogachi.

tied tightly below his waist, he looked as helpless as a fledgeling fallen from its nest.

"What is it? Why is he crying?"

A bamboo trick was about to be performed, they informed me.

I didn't understand at first. Were they going to beat up the boy with a bamboo and was that why he sobbed so ceaselessly?

No, the bamboo wasn't going to be used for beating him, they explained. It was to be used for a trick—a trick we were shortly to see.

I knew that orders of attachment decreed by a court were sometimes executed by posting a notice on a bamboo pole near the property to be attached, with a beat of drums. But I was not aware of any other trick that could be performed with a piece of bamboo.

Someone asked, "Will the bamboo be planted in the ground?"

"Oh, no, this isn't an ordinary trick of that sort," someone in the know explained in a tone of authority. "No, the old man will set it on his own tummy and the boy will climb the bamboo pole and go right up to the top. Then the boy will balance himself on the other end and lie on it face downwards. The bamboo pole will then start spinning, and the boy with his hands and legs hanging free will spin on top. I've seen them perform many times before."

"Is that the old man?"

"Yes, that's Mantaj."

The old man's body was shrivelled like a piece of twisted rope, a few grey hairs jutted out from his chin. His chest was arched, moundlike, his stomach a concave hollow, and the little flesh he had hung loose from his bones. His deep-set eyes glittered in the afternoon sunshine. It was his eyes alone that gave evidence of whatever courage and skill he had.

The audience fanned out in a circle. Mantaj went round with an empty old tin mug hoping to collect a few coppers.

Someone scolded him: "The show isn't on yet and here you're asking for money!"

But how was the show to commence? The performer who was to do the act of climbing the pole was busy creating a rumpus with his wailing—"I'll fall, I'll die!"

"What is all this wailing for? If you are so jittery about falling, why come to perform?"

But Mantaj took no notice of the boy's howling. He went round with his tin mug assuring everyone that the show would certainly take place.

"This isn't their first performance, is it? Then why is the boy crying?" I asked the man standing next to me.

"He didn't perform before, he is a novice."

"Then who did it?"

"His elder brother—"

"No, no, this boy too has performed once or twice," someone else protested, "this boy climbed the bamboo when they gave a show during the Saraswati Puja,[3] in the schoolyard at Tentul. He isn't used to it yet, that day his performance consisted of just climbing up the bamboo. His elder brother is the real performer. But whatever you may say, I feel that the real credit for the trick goes to the man who spins the bamboo—Mantaj."

"Where's his brother?"

"I wish I knew!"

Not a solitary tinkle rang in Mantaj's mug. No one was prepared to part with a copper before the show commenced.

Having no other alternative, Mantaj went towards the boy. The boy screamed in fear as if he was facing a blank wall with a wild dog chasing him. "No, no, not I! I'll fall, I'll die—"

The father pulled the boy's hand roughly. He raised his hand to hit the boy.

"Pooh, see how frightened he is. Your father has shown this trick with many a grown-up young man on the bamboo, and now, you think he can't manage you—a stripling of a boy!"

A part of the audience now began to scold the boy on behalf of the father.

Mantaj smiled. Long experience lent a keen edge to his smile.

"Supposing you do slip and fall, won't your father be able to catch you in his arms? Come along, now."

The man who was beating the tom-tom plied his sticks harder.

But the boy refused to budge. The sound of his wailing rose above the din of the fair.

So there was to be no bamboo trick! One, then another, began to slip away.

In exasperation Mantaj craned his neck and looked over the circle of the crowd. A little later, another boy came forward walking on weak, unsteady feet, a half-eaten papadam clutched in his hand.

"That's the brother," some of the audience shouted.

A sickly looking ten-year-old boy with reedy arms and legs, a torn quilt wrapped round his body. All around his lips, on his cheeks and his chin were marks of cuts that had now become sores. A buzzing fly was worrying him as it settled again and again on the tip of his nose. His two big eyes held a blank meaningless look.

He went to his little brother and said, "Don't cry Akku, I'll climb the pole."

Akku quieted down and his tears dried up almost at once.

The crowd drew closer. The beat of the tom-tom became more frenzied. Mantaj gathered and tightened the bit of cloth that hung between his

---

3. *Saraswati Puja.* In Hinduism, the common religion in India, *Saraswati Puja* is a celebration dedicated to Saraswati, the goddess of learning.

waist and knees. He placed the bamboo on his stomach, in the hollow of his navel. He muttered something indistinctly. Perhaps he sent up a prayer to his god. Then he touched the bamboo to his forehead. He now drew it close to his mouth, whispered something to it, then stroked it with his hands.

Nobody had ever seen him behave thus—so lacking in poise, as he was now.

"Come on, Imtaj," he called out to his elder son.

In a moment Imtaj whipped off the torn quilt from his body.

It was as if something had hit me—I gasped in horror. The boy's chest and stomach were covered with sores which ran in long streaks. Scabs had formed on some, others were raw gaping wounds, some had festered and swelled with pus. That wretched fly had fetched a number of buzzing bluebottles to share his feast.

I felt a little relieved when the boy turned his back to me. His back was smooth, spotless.

"How did he get those sores? So many sores?" I asked.

Some of them knew, I learnt. On the festival of spring, while performing at the house of the zamindar [4] at Champali, Imtaj had slipped. The old man had just recovered from a bout of malaria and couldn't keep the bamboo balanced on his stomach. Where Imtaj fell, the ground was covered with gravel and broken tiles, and it had badly cut and bruised his chest and stomach. The boy had been out of sorts ever since.

"Won't you wrap yourself with that rag?" asked Mantaj.

"No." The boy rubbed both hands with dust and jumped up on the bamboo pole which by then rested on his father's stomach. With the suppleness of long practice, he began climbing up swiftly. Mantaj stood motionless, still, the bamboo gripped in both hands and pressed into the pit of his stomach.

"Let him see, let Akkas see, how willingly his brother has come to perform despite his sores."

With his face turned upwards, Akkas or Akku stared at his brother. He had nothing to fear now. He could beat the tom-tom or go round with the mug if he so wished.

On reaching the top of the bamboo, Imtaj paused for a moment, then he gathered his cloth together to fix the pole-end against his stomach. His sores became visible again. The sight was unbearable. I turned to leave.

Somebody stopped me. He said, "When he lies stuck up on the pole like a frog, his arms and legs hanging loose, and starts spinning round and round in space, you won't see those sores any more."

"Does the father turn the bamboo with his hands?"

"He turns the bamboo with his hands a few times, then stuck on his navel, it spins on its own momentum. That's really the trick."

---

4. *zamindar*, an Indian landlord.

Someone else cut in: "To display acrobatics on a bamboo planted in the ground has become out of date now—what's so clever about that?"

The bamboo in the meantime had started spinning in Mantaj's hand. The boy must have become very light after his fall, he was spinning as fast as a paper cartwheel. His arms and legs were spread out and his hideous sores were no longer visible. One could hardly make out whether it was a human being or bat or flying fox that was whirling in space.

My gaze had been fixed skywards, now I turned my eyes to Mantaj when he suddenly placed the revolving pole in his navel and let go his hands. The father's belly, rather than his son's, was a sight worth seeing. The son's stomach was a mass of sores, but the father's stomach was a great big hollow. This pit was not something contrived for the moment to dig in the bamboo. I felt this deep pit must have been there for a long, long time. And who knows what fiery churnstick was churning away inside that pit?

I could hardly believe my eyes when I saw how far back the bamboo-end had pressed into his stomach. I had seen men with bellies flattened to their backs before this. But now I saw a man who seemed to have no belly at all —the bamboo seemed to press straight into his back from the front. His very entrails had shrivelled and disappeared nobody knew where. At each turn the bamboo clattered against his backbone.

What I was apprehending every moment came about, but it was not Imtaj who slipped, it was Mantaj who reeled and crashed to the ground. At the last moment he had held out his hands to catch the falling boy. But however frail the boy was, his father's arms were not strong enough to support him.

"Nowadays the old man seems to be slipping again and again . . ." someone complained.

Mantaj squatted on his haunches with his head pressed into his hands, panting like a hard-run old horse. He was staring blankly at his empty mug.

No wonder he had taken round the mug before starting the performance. He had obtained a few coppers, he could have eaten something—one or two papadams, or perhaps a few of the leathery batter-fried onion and brinjal slices selling nearby. A morsel of food could have made all the difference, it would perhaps have given some strength to his weary old arms. Long habit could train one to bear most things except perhaps to quench the pangs of hunger. The bamboo, the helpless arms, the son, the sores—one could face each in its turn with the courage that practice and experience endows—but hunger—it was unruly, ruthless.

The bamboo had slipped and fallen at a distance, and Imtaj still further away. The din of the crowd drowned his groans. Someone said, "He's finished." Said another: "His heart is still beating!"

There was a charity hospital nearby. Some people carried Imtaj there, doing their best to avoid contact with his sores. The accident had just happened, the hospital could hardly dare turn away the patient. Had Imtaj gone there to have his sores attended to, they would have driven him away because Mantaj couldn't always pay the one-anna [5] bite they demanded for medicine. If half-an-anna or one anna came his way, was Mantaj to spend it on medicine for sores that covered the stomach or to soothe the sores that burned inside!

Mantaj sat grim and silent, but the younger boy began wailing at the top of his voice. I thought he was crying because of his brother.

But no, it was the same lament, in a still more helpless tone: "It's my turn now! I'm sure to fall, I'll die—"

Without a word Mantaj got up, took Akku by the hand and walked towards the hospital.

"I'll fall, I'll die!" What unseen god was being beseeched by a child's piteous wails—for a misery which knew no remedy.

Mantaj remained silent. His stony face looked cruel in its chill detachment. This hard cold silence was the only reply he could give his son. What else could he do? He must eat.   ✕

---

5. *anna*, a former coin of Pakistan, one-sixteenth of a rupee. A rupee is worth about twenty-one cents U.S.

Bhatta Somadeva [1] (12th century)

THE CONFIDENCE MEN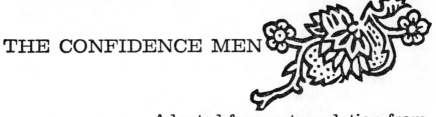

Adapted from a translation from
the Sanskrit by H. H. Wilson

TWO CONFIDENCE MEN named Madhava and Siva had lived in the city of Ratnapura [2] for some time and had fleeced every inhabitant in the place. They thought it high time, therefore, to change the scene of their operations. Now it came to them that a certain Brahman priest [3] named Sankara Swami was a weak, credulous old man, blessed with immense wealth and a beautiful daughter. Since the Brahman served on the staff of the King of Ujjayini, the two confidence men laid their plans, then set out for that city.

Madhava invested a sum of gold in the purchase of stately clothes and in the hire of a large, imposing caravan. He assumed the rank of a Rajput nobleman, [4] traveling with his train to a village a short distance from Ujjayini where he and his attendants set up camp. Siva, meanwhile, entered Ujjayini alone. Having located a deserted temple on the banks of the river Sipra, he took up residence there, posing as a holy man.

By the seeming severity of his penance, Siva soon attracted public attention. Each day at dawn he smeared his body with mud and plunged head first into the river, remaining there under water for many minutes. When the sun had risen well over the horizon, he returned to land to gaze into the sun's bright rays as though lost in prayer and meditation. Towards evening he returned to the temple to offer flowers to the gods.

"The Confidence Men" by Bhatta Somadeva, adapted by Gene Z. Hanrahan from a translation by H. H. Wilson. Copyright © 1963 by Gene Z. Hanrahan. From FIFTY GREAT ORIENTAL STORIES, edited by Gene Z. Hanrahan. Copyright © 1965 by Bantam Books, Inc. All Rights Reserved.
1. *Bhatta Somadeva* (bät'tä sō'mä dä'vä). 2. *Ratnapura,* a city in southern Ceylon. 3. *Brahman priest.* In Hinduism, the common religion in India, adherents are divided into four hereditary castes (classes), with members of one caste having no social intercourse with those of another. The Brahmans belong to the highest caste, which includes priests, scholars, and government officials. 4. *Rajput nobleman,* a member of a warrior clan.

Sometimes Siva assumed the sacred positions of the cult of the Yogi so that it appeared he was fully occupied with abstract devotion. But several times weekly he dressed in the skin of the black deer and, taking up his staff and hollow half of a coconut, journeyed to the city in quest of alms. He pretended to divide the rice so obtained into three parts: one part for the crows, one for the poor and the last part he reserved for himself. Siva spent his nights alone in the temple, for he dared not visit the public houses where he might be recognized.

When Madhava learned that Siva had established himself in his fraudulent role, he judged it time to play his hand. Madhava entered the city and rented a spacious mansion not far from the residence of the wealthy Brahman. Pretending to pay homage at the temple of Sipra, he arranged an accidental encounter with Siva. Madhava promptly feigned extreme veneration for the holy man, informing all gathered there that Siva was a religious ascetic of singular sanctity whom he had previously encountered in his travels. That night Siva repaid the visit, and the two confidence men ate and drank, and made merry together, later agreeing on their next course of action.

The following morning Madhava sent a messenger bearing gifts to Sankara Swami. "A noble of Rajput rank," the messenger stated, "has only recently arrived from the Dakhin and he and his retainers would gladly take service with the King of Ujjayini. As you, Honored Priest, are favored by the good graces of the king, my lord presents these gifts and requests that you make the appeal on his behalf."

The old priest, being greedy and miserly by nature, was much impressed by the seeming value of the gifts and was quick to pledge his assistance. The priest's efforts resulted in the appointment of Madhava and his retainers to the king's court. Hoping to gain even richer rewards from the Rajput noble, the priest insisted that Madhava and his followers take up their residence in his own stately mansion.

The day Madhava appeared at Sankara Swami's home he requested permission to deposit his jewels in the old gentleman's private treasury. As Madhava spread the jewels on the table, Sankara Swami's eyes bulged like two huge balls. Before him lay all manner of beautiful and invaluable gems. As these gems had been fashioned with great skill Sankara Swami had not the slightest notion they were artificial and all but worthless. Thus the greedy priest agreed to have the counterfeit jewels placed in his vaults.

In the weeks that followed Madhava secretly abstained from food. He began to lose weight, and his color turned pale and sickly. Pretending to be dangerously ill, he asked Sankara Swami to seek out some pious holy man. "I fear death is at hand," wailed Madhava, "and it will be my final act to present all my possessions to some worthy ascetic."

The old man knew of many holy men, but none to be entrusted with such a treasure. Acting on earlier instructions, one of Madhava's attendants suggested they send for the holy man living in the temple on the banks of the Sipra. "He is held in high repute," the attendant counseled. "Even my own master speaks well of him."

Sankara Swami accepted the attendant's advice, but having plans of his own for the disposition of the jewels, he decided to see the ascetic before calling him to his mansion. So he went to the temple at Sipra where he bowed before the ascetic, saying:

"A Rajput of high rank is on the verge of death and wishes to present you with his entire estate which includes a valuable collection of jewelry."

"I forgive such a proposal, even though it comes from the lips of a priest," Siva replied with studied solemnity. "It is absurd to offer worldly treasures to an ascetic. Transitory, perishable goods are of no value to one who delights in penance and solitude. I seek divine knowledge, not wealth. Now go back, for I reject your offer."

Siva's apparent indifference only whetted Sankara's zeal, and the priest dwelt eloquently on the pleasures of a rich man's life as contrasted to the privation of an ascetic. He went on to tell of the lofty duties assumed by a landowner, suggesting that the ascetic had discharged his obligations to the gods, but had yet to attend to the betterment of humanity.

At length the old priest's arguments appeared to move the ascetic to a change of heart. Finally Siva sighed. "It is possible that I may be persuaded to resume my connection with society. Still I have no interest in gold or jewels. Now if I could only find a wife whose family is as pure and noble as my own . . ."

Seeing an opportunity for even greater profit, Sankara Swami instantly proposed that his own daughter become the holy man's wife. If Siva would relinquish the Rajput's wealth, signing it over to him, the priest not only would offer his daughter's hand in marriage, but would provide the holy man with a handsome dowry as well.

First affecting reluctance, Siva ultimately consented to wed the daughter of the priest. The matter of the disposition of the Rajput's property, he said, could be left entirely to his new father-in-law's discretion. Sankara Swami, concluding the ascetic was a fool and congratulating himself on his own cunning, lost no time in making the arrangements. He brought Siva to his house and married the holy man to his daughter.

Three days later the priest conducted Siva into the presence of the bed-ridden Madhava. The fake Rajput greeted the fake holy man with practiced reverence, even pleading with Siva to pray over his ashes after his death. Before the meeting ended Madhava presented Siva with his jewels. These the holy man turned over to his father-in-law, all the while professing utter ignorance as to their quality or value. After the holy man bestowed his benediction on the sick man, the two visitors left: Siva with his bride, Sankara Swami with his coveted box of jewelry.

Some days later Madhava pretended to regain his health, his sudden powers of recuperation being credited to the wondrous spell cast by the holy man's benediction. Although Sankara Swami was concerned over the Rajput's quick recovery, he had little time for reflection on this strange turn of events, for his newly-acquired son-in-law was now showing signs of great dissatisfaction with his lot. The holy man had now decided he wanted half of the Rajput's jewelry. In an effort to quiet Siva's clamors Sankara Swami suggested a settlement—he would not part with one jewel, but agreed instead on a considerable amount to be paid in gold and silver. On receiving the first of two payments, Siva took his beautiful bride, left Sankara's Swami's house, and moved into a spacious mansion in another section of the city.

By the time the second and final payment was due, Sankara Swami found he could not raise the full sum. In a state of great agitation he decided to pawn one of the Rajput's jewels. The jewellers examined the stone and, though they openly admired the skill with which it was made, each one pronounced it nothing more than crystal and colored glass set in brass, and of no real value. An apprehensive Sankara then brought out the remaining jewels. Like the first each stone was judged counterfeit. Sankara Swami was struck as if by a thunderbolt, and it was some time before he knew where or who he was.

The priest's first thought after regaining his wits was to force Siva to return his money. But when he visited his son-in-law and proposed to trade the jewels for his first payment of gold and silver—all the while saying nothing of his discovery—the young man smiled and replied, "I have no objection to this offer, but unfortunately I have spent it all."

The terrified priest rushed to the court. After hearing Sankara Swami's tale the king commanded that Madhava and Siva be escorted to his chambers. Within the hour the two men were apprehended and brought to trial.

"I did not seek the bargain," Siva began in response to the charges made by Sankara. "Witnesses will testify that I professed all along my complete ignorance of the nature, quality and value of the Rajput's treasure. I do not understand how the old priest blames me merely because they have no value. Everyone knows I never laid eyes on the jewels, and all will vouch for the fact that I agreed to his proposals only at the insistence of my father-in-law himself."

In a like manner Madhava protested his innocence. "All these jewels," he pleaded, "were inherited from my dear departed father. Not once had I ever had the occasion to have them valued by one skilled in the art of appraisal. And as I gave them freely to the holy man, surely I could not have had any reason for passing off fake gems as genuine pieces. What had I to gain?" Affecting a final look of anguish, Madhava concluded, "It must be evident to Your Majesty that my sudden recovery from a strange and fatal disease is proof enough of my complete innocence."

The defense set up by the two confidence men was so plausible that they were immediately acquitted of fraudulent intent, while Sankara Swami was judged deserving of the consequences of his own greed. He was dismissed with ridicule from the court. In time Sankara Swami lost his official rank, not to mention his daughter and wealth.

On the other hand, Siva and Madhava found themselves praised for their honesty and virtue. The two confidence men reaped a twofold reward: both were introduced into the king's favorite circle and, of course, each enjoyed the wealth he so poorly deserved. ✕

Rabindranath Tagore[1] (1861–1941)

MY LORD, THE BABY

Translated from the Bengali by
C. F. Andrews

RAICHARAN [2] WAS TWELVE YEARS OLD when he came as a servant to his master's house. He belonged to the same caste [3] as his master, and was given his master's little son to nurse. As time went on the boy left Raicharan's arms to go to school. From school he went on to college, and after college he entered the judicial service. Always, until he married, Raicharan was his sole attendant.

But, when a mistress came into the house, Raicharan found two masters instead of one. All his former influence passed to the new mistress. This was compensated for by a fresh arrival. Anukul had a son born to him, and Raicharan by his unsparing attentions soon got a complete hold over the child. He used to toss him up in his arms, call to him in absurd baby language, put his face close to the baby's and draw it away again with a grin.

Presently the child was able to crawl and cross the doorway. When Raicharan went to catch him, he would scream with mischievous laughter and make for safety. Raicharan was amazed at the profound skill and exact judgment the baby showed when pursued. He would say to his mistress with a look of awe and mystery: "Your son will be a judge some day."

New wonders came in their turn. When the baby began to toddle, that was to Raicharan an epoch in human history. When he called his father Ba-ba and his mother Ma-ma and Raicharan Chan-na, then Raicharan's ecstasy knew no bounds. He went out to tell the news to all the world.

After a while Raicharan was asked to show his ingenuity in other ways. He had, for instance, to play the part of a horse, holding the reins between

1. *Rabindranath Tagore* (rə bin′drə nät tə gōr′). 2. *Raicharan* (rī′chä rän). 3. *caste.* Hindu society is divided into four hereditary castes (classes), with members of one having no social intercourse with those of another. The four castes are, in order of rank: (1) *Brahmins*, priests, scholars, and government officials; (2) *Kshatriyas*, warriors and minor officials; (3) *Vaisyas*, merchants and artisans; (4) *Sudras*, unskilled workers. All people outside these groups were called "untouchables" and were considered outcasts. In 1955 the Indian government enacted a law making discrimination against the untouchables a criminal offense.

his teeth and prancing with his feet. He had also to wrestle with his little charge, and if he could not, by a wrestler's trick, fall on his back defeated at the end, a great outcry was certain.

About this time Anukul was transferred to a district on the banks of the Padma. On his way through Calcutta he bought his son a little go-cart. He bought him also a yellow satin waistcoat, a gold-laced cap, and some gold bracelets and anklets. Raicharan was wont to take these out, and put them on his little charge with ceremonial pride, whenever they went for a walk.

Then came the rainy season, and day after day the rain poured down in torrents. The hungry river, like an enormous serpent, swallowed down terraces, villages, cornfields, and covered with its flood the tall grasses and wild casuarinas on the sandbanks. From time to time there was a deep thud, as the river-banks crumbled. The unceasing roar of the main current could be heard from far away. Masses of foam, carried swiftly past, proved to the eye the swiftness of the stream.

One afternoon the rain cleared. It was cloudy, but cool and bright. Raicharan's little despot did not want to stay in on such a fine afternoon. His lordship climbed into the go-cart. Raicharan, between the shafts, dragged him slowly along till he reached the rice-fields on the banks of the river. There was no one in the fields, and no boat on the stream. Across the water, on the farther side, the clouds were rifted in the west. The silent ceremonial of the setting sun was revealed in all its glowing splendor. In the midst of that stillness the child, all of a sudden, pointed with his finger in front of him and cried: "Chan-na! Pitty fow."

Close by on a mud-flat stood a large *Kadamba* tree in full flower. My lord, the baby, looked at it with greedy eyes, and Raicharan knew his meaning. Only a short time before he had made, out of these very flower balls, a small go-cart; and the child had been so entirely happy dragging it about with a string, that for the whole day Raicharan was not made to put on the reins at all. He was promoted from a horse into a groom.

But Raicharan had no wish that evening to go splashing knee-deep through the mud to reach the flowers. So he quickly pointed his finger in the opposite direction, calling out: "Oh, look, baby, look! Look at the bird." And with all sorts of curious noises he pushed the go-cart rapidly away from the tree.

But a child, destined to be a judge, cannot be put off so easily. And besides, there was at the time nothing to attract his eyes. And you cannot keep up for ever the pretense of an imaginary bird.

The little Master's mind was made up, and Raicharan was at his wits' end. "Very well, baby," he said at last, "you sit still in the cart, and I'll go and get you the pretty flower. Only mind you don't go near the water."

As he said this, he made his legs bare to the knee, and waded through the oozing mud toward the tree.

The moment Raicharan had gone, his little Master went off at racing speed to the forbidden water. The baby saw the river rushing by, splashing and gurgling as it went. It seemed as though the disobedient wavelets themselves were running away from some greater Raicharan with the laughter of a thousand children. At the sight of their mischief, the heart of the human child grew excited and restless. He got down stealthily from the go-cart and toddled off toward the river. On his way he picked up a small stick, and leant over the bank of the stream pretending to fish. The mischievous fairies of the river with their mysterious voices seemed inviting him into their play-house.

Raicharan had plucked a handful of flowers from the tree, and was carrying them back in the end of his cloth, with his face wreathed in smiles. But when he reached the go-cart, there was no one there. He looked on all sides and there was no one there. He looked back at the cart and there was no one there.

In that first terrible moment his blood froze within him. Before his eyes the whole universe swam round like a dark mist. From the depth of his broken heart he gave one piercing cry: "Master, Master, little Master." But no voice answered "Chan-na." No child laughed mischievously back; no scream of baby delight welcomed his return. Only the river ran on, with its splashing, gurgling noise as before—as though it knew nothing at all, and had no time to attend to such a tiny human event as the death of a child.

As the evening passed by Raicharan's mistress became very anxious. She sent men out on all sides to search. They went with lanterns in their hands, and reached at last the banks of the Padma. There they found Raicharan rushing up and down the fields, like a stormy wind, shouting the cry of despair: "Master, Master, little Master!"

When they got Raicharan home at last, he fell prostrate at his mistress's feet. They shook him, and questioned him, and asked him repeatedly where he had left the child; but all he could say was, that he knew nothing.

Though everyone held the opinion that the Padma had swallowed the child, there was a lurking doubt left in the mind. For a band of gypsies had been noticed outside the village that afternoon, and some suspicion rested on them. The mother went so far in her wild grief as to think it possible that Raicharan himself had stolen the child. She called him aside with piteous entreaty and said: "Raicharan, give me back my baby. Oh! give me back my child. Take from me any money you ask, but give me back my child!"

Anukul tried to reason his wife out of this wholly unjust suspicion: "Why on earth," he said, "should he commit such a crime as that?"

The mother only replied: "The baby had gold ornaments on his body. Who knows?"

It was impossible to reason with her after that.

Raicharan went back to his own village. Up to this time he had had no son, and there was no hope that any child would now be born to him. But it came about before the end of a year that his wife gave birth to a son and died.

An overwhelming resentment at first grew up in Raicharan's heart at the sight of this new baby. At the back of his mind was resentful suspicion that it had come as a usurper in place of the little Master. He also thought it would be a grave offense to be happy with a son of his own after what had happened to his master's little child. Indeed, if it had not been for a widowed sister, who mothered the new baby, it would not have lived long.

But a change gradually came over Raicharan's mind. A wonderful thing happened. This new baby in turn began to crawl about, and cross the doorway with mischief in its face. It also showed an amusing cleverness in making its escape to safety. Its voice, its sounds of laughter and tears, its gestures, were those of the little Master. On some days, when Raicharan listened to its crying, his heart suddenly began thumping wildly against his ribs, and it seemed to him that his former little Master was crying somewhere in the unknown land of death because he had lost his Chan-na.

Phailna (for that was the name Raicharan's sister gave to the new baby) soon began to talk. It learnt to say Ba-ba and Ma-ma with a baby accent. When Raicharan heard those familiar sounds the mystery suddenly became clear. The little Master could not cast off the spell of his Chan-na, and therefore he had been reborn in his own house.

The arguments in favor of this were, to Raicharan, altogether beyond dispute:

(i.) The new baby was born soon after his little Master's death.

(ii.) His wife could never have accumulated such merit as to give birth to a son in middle age.

(iii.) The new baby walked with a toddle and called out Ba-ba and Ma-ma. There was no sign lacking which marked out the future judge.

Then suddenly Raicharan remembered that terrible accusation of the mother. "Ah," he said to himself with amazement, "the mother's heart was right. She knew I had stolen her child." When once he had come to this conclusion, he was filled with remorse for his past neglect. He now gave himself over, body and soul, to the new baby, and became its devoted attendant. He began to bring it up, as if it were the son of a rich man. He bought a go-cart, a yellow satin waistcoat, and a gold-embroidered cap. He melted down the ornaments of his dead wife, and made gold bangles and anklets. He refused to let the little child play with anyone of the neighborhood, and became himself its sole companion day and night. As the baby grew up to boyhood, he was so petted and spoilt and clad in such finery that the village children would call him "Your Lordship," and jeer at him; and older people regarded Raicharan as unaccountably crazy about the child.

At last the time came for the boy to go to school. Raicharan sold his small piece of land, and went to Calcutta. There he got employment with great difficulty as a servant, and sent Phailna to school. He spared no pains to give him the best education, the best clothes, the best food. Meanwhile he lived himself on a mere handful of rice, and would say in secret: "Ah!

my little Master, my dear little Master, you loved me so much that you came back to my house. You shall never suffer from any neglect of mine."

Twelve years passed away in this manner. The boy was able to read and write well. He was bright and healthy and good-looking. He paid a great deal of attention to his personal appearance, and was specially careful in parting his hair. He was inclined to extravagance and finery, and spent money freely. He could never quite look on Raicharan as a father, because, though fatherly in affection, he had the manner of a servant. A further fault was this, that Raicharan kept secret from everyone that himself was the father of the child.

The students of the hostel, where Phailna was a boarder, were greatly amused by Raicharan's country manners, and I have to confess that behind his father's back Phailna joined in their fun. But, in the bottom of their hearts, all the students loved the innocent and tender-hearted old man, and Phailna was very fond of him also. But, as I have said before, he loved him with a kind of condescension.

Raicharan grew older and older, and his employer was continually finding fault with him for his incompetent work. He had been starving himself for the boy's sake. So he had grown physically weak, and no longer up to his work. He would forget things, and his mind became dull and stupid. But his employer expected a full servant's work out of him, and would not brook excuses. The money that Raicharan had brought with him from the sale of his land was exhausted. The boy was continually grumbling about his clothes, and asking for more money.

Raicharan made up his mind. He gave up the situation where he was working as a servant, and left some money with Phailna and said: "I have some business to do at home in my village, and shall be back soon."

He went off at once to Baraset where Anukul was magistrate. Anukul's wife was still broken down with grief. She had had no other child.

One day Anukul was resting after a long and weary day in court. His wife was buying, at an exorbitant price, an herb from a mendicant quack, which was said to insure the birth of a child. A voice of greeting was heard in the courtyard. Anukul went out to see who was there. It was Raicharan. Anukul's heart was softened when he saw his old servant. He asked him many questions, and offered to take him back into service. Raicharan smiled faintly, and said in reply: "I want to make obeisance to my mistress."

Anukul went with Raicharan into the house, where the mistress did not receive him as warmly as his old master. Raicharan took no notice of this, but folded his hands, and said: "It was not the Padma that stole your baby. It was I."

Anukul exclaimed: "Great God! Eh! What! Where is he?"

Raicharan replied: "He is with me. I will bring him the day after tomorrow."

It was Sunday. There was no magistrate's court sitting. Both husband

and wife were looking expectantly along the road, waiting from early morning for Raicharan's appearance. At ten o'clock he came, leading Phailna by the hand.

Anukul's wife, without question, took the boy into her lap, and was wild with excitement, sometimes laughing, sometimes weeping, touching him, kissing his hair and his forehead, and gazing into his face with hungry, eager eyes. The boy was very good-looking and dressed like a gentleman's son. The heart of Anukul brimmed over with a sudden rush of affection.

Nevertheless the magistrate in him asked: "Have you any proofs?"

Raicharan said: "How could there be any proof of such a deed? God alone knows that I stole your boy, and no one else in the world."

When Anukul saw how eagerly his wife was clinging to the boy, he realized the futility of asking for proofs. It would be wiser to believe. And then—where could an old man like Raicharan get such a boy from? And why should his faithful servant deceive him for nothing?

"But," he added severely, "Raicharan, you must not stay here."

"Where shall I go, Master?" said Raicharan, in a choking voice, folding his hands; "I am old. Who will take an old man as a servant?"

The mistress said: "Let him stay. My child will be pleased. I forgive him."

But Anukul's magisterial conscience would not allow him. "No," he said, "he cannot be forgiven for what he has done."

Raicharan bowed to the ground, and clasped Anukul's feet. "Master," he cried, "let me stay. It was not I who did it. It was God."

Anukul's conscience was worse stricken than ever, when Raicharan tried to put the blame on God's shoulders. "No," he said, "I could not allow it. I cannot trust you any more. You have done an act of treachery."

Raicharan rose to his feet and said: "It was not I who did it."

"Who was it then?" asked Anukul.

Raicharan replied: "It was my fate."

But no educated man could take this for an excuse. Anukul remained obdurate.

When Phailna saw that he was the wealthy magistrate's son, and not Raicharan's, he was angry at first, thinking that he had been cheated all this time of his birthright. But seeing Raicharan in distress, he generously said to his father: "Father, forgive him. Even if you don't let him live with us, let him have a small monthly pension."

After hearing this, Raicharan did not utter another word. He looked for the last time on the face of his son; he made obeisance to his old master and mistress. Then he went out, and was mingled with the numberless people of the world.

At the end of the month Anukul sent him some money to his village. But the money came back. There was no one there of the name of Raicharan. ✕

U Win Pe (1922-   )

PRELUDE TO GLORY

Translated from the Burmese

AT THE STROKE OF FOUR in the morning the cheap alarm clock of ten years ago faithfully clanged its rasping bell. The monk stirred on his low, hard couch. He had been listening for the bell and turning over in his mind the verses he had learned the day before. "Thus was it heard by me. At that time the Buddha, the Blessed One, was staying at Rajagaha, on the Vulture-Peak Hill." He groped for the lighter on the couchside table, clicked it thrice to waken the flame, and lit the long-stemmed kerosene lamp. The smoky glow revealed a faded bookcase with carvings and three missing panes, a small round table with a square shelf between its four legs, leather-bound gold-lettered volumes, oilpaper-wrapped books, dark-green Bandoola exercise books at nine kyats [1] a dozen, an orange robe on a line spanning a corner of the room, and a dim photograph of an elderly monk on the wall.

The monk arose, grasped the lamp, and opened the door of his cubicle. The creak of door leaves shuttled across the main room of the refectory and reverberated above four small figures lying on the floor just outside the door.

Four little boys huddled together with a coverless dirty pillow each, two blankets between the four, and no net to protect them from the savage hordes of mosquitoes that ravaged such places. They were close together to get the warmth of each other's bodies—which they did, along with the musty smell of their long unchanged, unwashed clothes. One of the boys, Tha Nu, had shed his share of the blanket and had a leg thrown over his mate, Khway Ni, who had an arm across Tha Nu's neck.

As the monk crouched to shake Tha Nu's shoulder, a mosquito whined past his face and away.

Reprinted from *Arizona Quarterly*, Winter 1963, Volume 19, Number 4, with permission from the Asia Society, New York, © 1963 by The Asia Society, Inc.
1. *kyat*, a Burmese monetary unit equal to about twenty-one cents U.S.

"Tha Nu. Get up," he said.

Tha Nu was away in yester-afternoon rewinning the three *gon-nyin* from his monastery schoolmates under the jackfruit tree.

"Tha Nu, wake up." The monk shook him vigorously.

Tha Nu sat up. "Yes, your reverence," he murmured.

He disentangled the blanket from a leg and turned to arouse the other boys. Tha Gi, the eldest, awoke easily. Sein Tint jerked up as Tha Nu had heard dead men do when their corpses are possessed by evil spirits, and for a moment a plug of fear choked his throat. Khway Ni refused to get up. Tha Nu got on his feet and dragged Khway Ni awake by a hand.

The monk had lighted another lamp, opened the front door, the upper bolt of which the boys could not reach, and had returned to his cubicle.

Tha Gi and Tha Nu gathered the pillows and blankets and, after opening the other door, put them in a corner of the back room. Sein Tint rolled up the mats. Khway Ni carried the lamp into the back room and placed it near the head of the steps. Then all the four boys ran down towards the back of the monastery.

The latrine was a short distance away, built over a brook which flowed beside the monastery compound. But that was too far for the boys. They stopped beside a clump of bamboo immediately beyond the refectory building where the swollen brook turned inwards and its water lapped the bamboo roots. The air was fresh and cold and there was the rumor of a moon somewhere behind the low-driving wrack of clouds. A gust of wind shook drops from the bamboo leaves. The boys shivered from the touch of the cold drips on bare, thin flesh and from release of tension.

They returned to the building and Tha Nu walked through to the vestibule, in which hung a large hollowed-out log of teak. Tha Nu picked up the stick of *yindaik* wood beside it and beat on the log. The blows boomed out heavily at first, with a long pause between each so that a listener might think they had stopped and would come no more, but then they called out faster and faster like the squawking of an ancient, deep-throated, long-billed bird disturbed in its sleep, anxious and then thoroughly frightened. The sound passed through the confines of the monastery to awaken the monks to prayer and praise and practice, crossed a patch of nursling paddy and into the village to call upon the villagers to arise and cook for alms-food and for the meal they will carry with them into the fields.

With the first few notes of the *on-maung*, one or two of the many dogs in the monastery set up a hesitant howl; as the notes came closer together all the dogs joined to howl in earnest. This daily booming and howling drove to nervousness the ghosts in the compound who would have shifted to somewhere else were not the trees here so broad and cool and the wooden buildings old and comfortable. Moreover, each monastery must have its ghosts, and so they stayed. The noise stopped. Tha Nu put back the beating stick. He could hear in the sudden quiet a passing cloud expend itself with a spatter on the thatch-roofs of the village.

He entered the main refectory room to join the others in prayer which they intoned in their childish voices. Tha Nu was nine come the month of Thadingyut [2] and had been three years in the monastery. He was a spare, brown boy with a thin, serious face but constantly active and falling foul of the monk in charge of the refectory. He came of good stock. His parents were pious, hard working cultivators with a few acres of their own. The head man of the village tract in which the monastery was situated was a maternal uncle and another maternal uncle was a ward headman in the town on the railway. But the real pride of his people was that their members had swelled the company of the Sangha.[3] Tha Nu could count three uncles and cousins who were monks and an aunt was a nun. One of them was abbot of a monastery with forty-three monks and countless novices and schoolboys. And he had heard his relatives speak often of a granduncle, his grandfather's youngest brother who had died as an abbot at thirty-two.

That was a young age for any monk to be an abbot but this granduncle had been exceptional and his practices and learning had been known and commended far and wide, even to Mandalay, it was said. He lived an ascetic life in a small hut with barely enough room for a sleeping mat and a low writing desk. He studied, went the rounds for alms-food, took classes in Abhidhamma and Vinaya,[4] meditated, preached. As his fame grew, more and more monks came to study under him till the existent monastery buildings could hold them no more. People began to see the need for more buildings. A rich devotee from the city visited the monastery and begged permission from the abbot to build a new dormitory.

Now, there are certain things for which some people are not worthy, and the abbot, who was well versed and farseeing in astrology, knew that he was not entitled to the new building and that if it was built he would have to pay for it with his life. And it was not proper for a monk to dissuade anyone from charity. Though he had asked the donor whether it could not be postponed for a season of rains, the donor had been eager and he had had to accept. He died before the buildings were completed.

Tha Nu was born about a year after the abbot had died. It was said that he resembled the abbot, his granduncle, in form and feature. And as he

---

2. *Thadingyut*, the seventh month of the Burmese calendar, approximately October. 3. *Sangha*, any order of Buddhist monks. 4. *Abhidhamma and Vinaya*. The accumulated scriptures of Buddhism (see footnote 2, page 39) were classified into three sections called the *Three Baskets of Learning*: (1) the *Abhidhamma*, the section dealing mainly with psychology and ethics; (2) the *Sûtras*, the most important section, consisting of treatises based on the Buddha's discourses and the *Theragatha*, literally, "verses of elders," a collection of verses composed by monks and nuns; and (3) the *Vinaya*, comprising the 227 rules of discipline binding on the monks of a Buddhist order.

grew up similar mannerisms convinced his parents that he was his grand-uncle reincarnate. After that there was only one vocation for Tha Nu. His grandfather taught him the scriptures with the first few words he could speak. He attended the monastery school as soon as he could walk there by himself and return home at night. At six years of age the monastery became his home. Come Tazaungmon [5] he would enter the Order of the Lord as a novice.

When the boys had finished their prayers Tha Gi and Khway Ni picked up brooms to sweep the refectory rooms. Sein Tint and Tha Nu carried the dishes to the tub at the back to wash them. Halfway through the washing they heard the monk in charge of the refectory come out. They stopped their low conversation about a hussy who had died recently in the village and was said to be haunting her house violently. They stopped because the monk, U Arseinda, had a terrible temper as well as because he was so good at exorcising evil spirits. Perhaps his temper fitted him to be so.

They remembered when one of the boys—who was a novice now—had been possessed by an evil spirit. He had been sent on an errand to the village and had returned at lamp-lighting time. He had come into the refectory where they were doing a chore under the fastidious eyes of U Arseinda and, instead of doing the customary obeisance to the monk, had said in a queer voice: "I want meat."

The boys had heard, but it seemed that U Arseinda had not for he raised his head towards the boy as though to ask him what he wanted.

"I want meat," repeated the boy.

"What are you saying, boy?" the monk asked, not surprised but unbelieving.

"I want meat," said the boy, firmly with a slight tinge of impatience.

The monk caught it this time and he saw into the eyes of the boy and grasped what was wrong.

"Tha Nu, fetch that piece of rope from the storeroom," he ordered.

"Come with me," he told the boy and took him to a post in the middle of the room. "Stand here."

He went into his cubicle and came out with a cane. Tha Nu had returned with the rope. He called Tha Gi and some other boys.

"All right. Tie him to the post," he said. After a short struggle the boy was tied with his face to the post.

The monk took the cane in his hand.

"What do you want? Say it again," he told the boy who was possessed.

"I want meat," the boy repeated in a hard voice of anger.

The monk swung the cane thrice at him. The boy winced at each thwack but kept a tight mouth.

"Do you still want meat?" the monk asked.

---

5. *Tazaungmon*, the eighth month of the Burmese calendar, approximately November.

The boy did not answer.

The monk gave him a few more strokes. This time the boy howled.

"I have been wrong, your reverence. Please release me. I will never do it again," he pleaded.

The monk beat him some more and with each stroke he cried: "Want some more meat. Want some more meat. Ask for more meat. You can get meat in a monastery. Want some more meat."

The evil spirit in the boy howled, pleaded, begged till at last the monk stopped.

"Who are you?" he asked the evil spirit.

"I am from the mango tree on the road to the monastery. I was feeling hungry. The boy came by and I followed him in."

"I told you you could stay if you did not disturb the boys and the people who come to the monastery, and you promised. Now you have broken your word."

"I confess that I have, your reverence. I have committed a great wrong. I promise you I will never do it again."

On that promise the spirit was released with the order to take away with him the marks of the lashes. The boy was untied, weary but unhurt. This the boys remembered, and how they had held U Arseinda in awe ever since.

The monk spoke to the boys at the dishes.

"Has U Po Din arrived?"

U Po Din was a *kappiya*, the layman who did odd jobs in the monastery like boiling the tea water, cooking the rice, carrying water. He dwelt in a *zayat* within the monastery precincts.

The boys looked at the fireplace, dark and cold. They realized that U Po Din had not yet come.

"No, your reverence," replied Tha Nu.

"Go fetch him."

Tha Nu stepped out into the cold, wet air. The rain had blown over but the clouds were still moving after it. The wind still worried the rain-laden branches. The moon was a little brighter now.

As he approached the *zayat* he could see the old man sitting hunched in a far corner, while his huge shadow jumped and leaped above him in the wind-harried candlelight. Tha Nu climbed into the *zayat* and sat on his haunches near the old man. The old man was rummaging in his bedroll.

"What are you looking for?" he asked.

"My cheroot stub," replied the old man feeling his pillow and running his hand inside the pillowcase. Through with the pillow he placed it behind him at the foot of the bedspread. He took the blanket and shook it without unfolding it. He spread it on the floor and pressed it all over, feeling with his hands. He put it aside. Next he took the mosquito net and tried to shake it while sitting, but found the net too long for that. He made as if to rise, and a joint cracked somewhere in his frail, stiff body. He caught his back with a hand and an involuntary cry.

Tha Nu got up. "I'll do it for you," he said.

He took the mosquito net and shook it. A cheroot stub rolled out, together with pieces of its charred stuffing.

"There it is," he said eagerly.

The old man took it and laid it on the floor. He brushed off the cinders but some of the ash smeared his already dirty mosquito net.

Tha Nu helped him fold the net and replace the blanket and pillow. He did not wait to roll up the bed.

"*Upasin* sent me to fetch you," he told the old man. "I'm going back."

He ran back across the wet earth and around the refectory to the back. He climbed the two blocks of tree stumps that served as stairs and wiped his feet perfunctorily on a worn coir doormat.[6] He returned to the dishes. As he sat down he felt that Sein Tint beside him was not working. He glanced towards him and saw in his hands a peeled banana already bitten off at the top.

"What's that?" he asked Sein Tint.

Sein Tint did not reply.

"It's a banana. Where did you get it?"

Sein Tint took another bite.

"Give me a bite, too," he said.

"No," said Sein Tint with his mouth full.

"Come on," said Tha Nu desperately.

"No," said Sein Tint.

"My turn I always share," he said, hurt.

Sein Tint had no reply to that.

Tha Nu looked at the half-eaten banana. In the dim light it looked like a stump of cream with pastry flowering at the base. Sein Tint was beginning to swallow his last bite. There was not much time for argument. Tha Nu's hand darted out, clutched the banana off from its peel and thrust it into his mouth, some of it oozing out between the fingers. Sein Tint made a grab for it but Tha Nu had jumped backwards and was now up and away over the creaking, thumping boards, and swallowing hard. Sein Tint went after him and there was a scuffle against the wall.

"Which boy is that?" They heard the voice of the monk above the sound of struggle and they stopped.

"Which boy is that? Can't you hear me? Come here that boy."

"You go," said Sein Tint.

Tha Nu nodded and as he turned through the door into the main room he saw U Po Din come up the step blocks. He moved reverently towards the monk who was leaning against the doorjamb of his cubicle.

---

6. *coir doormat,* a doormat made out of coconut fiber.

Tha Nu bowed thrice, touching the floor with his forehead. As he bowed he thought of the whack he would receive. Would it be on his knuckles or on his shoulders? He might even be caned. It was true he had not noticed a cane beside the monk, but he could always be asked to fetch one.

"Fetch me the betel box," said the monk.

Tha Nu fetched it and offered it in the prescribed manner, lifting it a little higher and then letting it alight onto the monk's accepting hand.

Now he will ask me to fetch the cane, he thought.

Instead it was, "Has U Po Din come?"

"Yes, your reverend," he replied. So things would be all right this once.

"You may go," the monk said.

Tha Nu bowed thrice and left the room. Released and relieved he went up to U Po Din, who was kindling the fire and said saucily, "You took a long time coming."

Then he went to join Sein Tint at washing the last of the dishes.

"Did you get it?" Sein Tint asked him.

"No," he replied.

Sein Tint took out a dish from the washbasin, let the water drain off, and set it with the others on a low table beside them.

U Po Din's fire flared.

．．．．．

"Pleasant sensation, mendicant brothers, arises in dependence on contact pleasantly felt, and on the cessation of that pleasantly felt contact the pleasant sensation which arose in dependence on that pleasantly felt contact then ceases and subsides.

"For one thus regarding this with right insight as it really is there are no theories of the past; upon the disappearance of theories of the past there are no theories of the future; upon the disappearance of theories of the future there is no obstinate holding on; upon the disappearance of obstinate holding on, his mind becomes without passion for material form, for sensation, for perception, for composite unity, for consciousness, and having ceased to grasp is liberated from the defilements."

Koyin Thila recited the passage from the Sûtras [7] rapidly, his singsong voice rising and dipping like the flight of a greenfinch. He was lying on his stomach on a mat in his part of the dormitory. The light from the open window which reached down to the raised wooden floor burnished the gold lettering on the black leather-bound volume before him. The volume was open at a section of the second of the Three Baskets of Learning [8] but his eyes were not on the text. He was repeating the passage, running it over again and again, trying to memorize it. The rapidity with which he could

---

7. *Sûtras.* See footnote 4. 8. *Three Baskets of Learning.* See footnote 4.

recite it now showed that he had become fluent with it and would soon have it by heart. That night, after evening lessons and prayers, he would go over it again, fixing it once and for all in his memory.

It was midday of the cool season and a light breeze slipped in the fragrance of stubble from the paddy fields and clematis on the monastery fence. The last meal of the day had been eaten an hour ago and for the rest of the day and the night he would partake of no food till the dawn meal at about six. He would take no liquids, except water.

This noon hour was for rest but he had not had any. After the morning meal the abbot had called him to his *kyaung* to dictate a letter to a layman, in the town on the railway, who had sent a gift of cooking oil. But as they had got to the *kyaung* from the refectory building they had found one of the village elders waiting for the abbot. He had come to seek the attendance of the abbot and four other monks three days hence at a feeding of alms-food in commemoration of his wife's death a year ago. This matter had been quickly taken care of but, as always happened, the talk had turned to a fine point of the law and it was another half hour before the elder had gone away satisfied. Fortunately the letter had been dictated, written, sealed, and addressed in another quarter of an hour and had been handed over to the refectory monk for dispatch with a boy to the village headman who would be going up to town next day. At the refectory he had met Koyin Sekkeinda and together they had walked back to the dormitory.

Though ten years had passed, Koyin Thila was still spare and brown and with the same thin face and serious eyes of Tha Nu. His body was lithe and supple but there was no sign in the senior novice of the agitated gestures of the monastery school boy of ten years ago. He walked with a simple grace accentuated by the flowing lines of the robe that dropped from his left shoulder. Youth's rawness shone in his face but at the same time it emphasized the gentleness and calm as of one who has glimpsed the goal and knows that his steps are in the right direction.

Ten years ago a boy had been accepted as a novice in the Order. In lay clothes but with shaved head he had placed a set of robes before the abbot and after making reverence, he had begged of the abbot, in his compassion, to bestow upon him the status of a novice. He had taken refuge in the Buddha, the Dhamma,[9] and the Sangha and had vowed to keep the ten precepts. He had been permitted to don the robes and had been given his new name, Koyin Thila, the novice Thila.

The ten precepts are but a light rein compared to the 227 rules observed by monks, but the donning of the robes and the discarding of the lay name could not change a young boy overnight. Dutifully he had tried to understand the nature of the four articles a novice was permitted to have. That the robes are not to adorn the body but to hide its nakedness, protect it

9. *Dhamma,* the religious laws and teachings of the Buddha.

from heat and cold and the scourge of mosquitoes and gnats; that food is not to beautify the body but to keep away fatigue and illness in the practice of the Buddha's teaching; that the monastery is for protection against inclement weather, scorpions, snakes, mosquitoes, and gnats; that medicine is for the eradication of oppressive disease. Thus knowing their nature it had been expected that he would not become attached to them. Accordingly he had not cared much about robes, the monastery and medicine. With food it had been different. When sometimes he had accompanied the monks and older novices to a feast in the village and had met at table a big dish of pork cut up in large chunks and cooked with much oil and many condiments, he had forgotten that food was merely to keep away fatigue and weakness and had felt for it an engrossing fondness.

There were also those nights when a few young novices had got together secretly to share a few pieces saved from the forenoon meal. It had been exhilarating but he had immediately come to realize that this arose more from the furtive joy of breaking the precept of not eating after noon than from a real love of leftovers. Also it had been an act of heroism to display before the monastery boys. A novice who did not transgress that precept was not worthy to be a man. Invariably he had awakened the following morning sick in his conscience and his restlessness had not been allayed till he had confessed to one of the monks. The monk had then given him the ten precepts again and had made him fetch water from the well or sweep the grounds as a penance.

It was U Arseinda, the refectory monk, who had finally taught him detachment from food. U Arseinda had accidentally overheard him praise curry. It had been the day after the annual robe-offering ceremony in the monastery. He had been helping the men from the village count the dishes and stack them up again in the refectory storeroom. He had said: "That chunk of pork I had yesterday, as big as the cap of my knee, with three layers of fat and meat, so rich and so savory. I was so cloyed from the meal I could neither sit nor stand. Oh, can Bagyi Aw cook." Then he realized that U Arseinda had been standing at the door all the time.

And for the next few months whenever U Arseinda or other monks at their table had brought home pork curry from their begging rounds in the village they had sent a saucer of it to Koyin Thila at the novices' table. A good curry like that, sent down from the monks' table, had had to be shared with the other novices. Since what had been sent down had never been much, there had been little left for him after the others had taken a piece each. He had begrudged them their share but at the same time he could not have kept it all to himself. After a few such occasions he had begun not to care much and had been satisfied with just a taste of it. Then one day U Arseinda had sent the dish down again but this time to Koyin Sekkeinda and not to him. Koyin Sekkeinda had had it passed around to him. He had been piqued and had wanted to decline but finally he had taken a piece. He had eaten it slowly with his head full of hot thoughts. Then while chewing the pork which had tasted as good as ever, he had at last seen it for what it was. The pleasant sensation had arisen in dependence on the contact of the pork on tongue pleasantly felt.

After the meal he had gone to U Arseinda and had recounted his thoughts and feelings. The monk had listened to him calmly and had casually said: "Fetch me the betel box." And Koyin Thila had known.

Then there had been the usual texts to study. He had taken with a will to the "Compendium of the subject matter of the Ultra-doctrine" which was a summarization of the psychological and logical teachings in the Third Basket of Learning. Its dry, terse categories, analytical enumerations, and mnemonic summaries had somehow appealed to him and he had been fascinated by the exposition of the cognitive process. It was held that however swiftly an act of sense perception may be performed, seventeen moments of consciousness took place in every such act, each moment involving the nascent, static, and dissolving time-phases. Koyin Thila had spent many hours working out the cognitive processes for the eighty-nine possible types of consciousness. He had read and studied and memorized the compendium; so also, the various exegetical literature, commentaries, subcommentaries, expositions, and the Little-Finger Manuals. He had memorized the book of verses called "The Footsteps of the Law," the Book of Relations, and had immersed himself in Kaccayana's Pali grammar and the Great Chronicle of the life of the Buddha.

Generally, he had found life pleasant as a novice though it was not for pleasure that he had chosen to continue in this life. He could have returned to lay life at any time had he wished to. He had only to change into lay clothes and take again the five precepts that layfolk were expected to observe. But he had preferred this life where, untouched by the sorrows and selfishness, he could concentrate on learning and practices undisturbed.

He had had his crisis at seventeen, and now that he could look back on it he was glad that it had come early. He had fallen in love with a distant cousin. She had accompanied her parents to the monastery on the sabbath of the full and dark of the moon during the lent of that year. She had been introduced to him as a cousin born of a distant maternal aunt a year after him. She had been brown and pretty with a charm that graced only the brown and not the fair. But it had been the serenity in her face and the quiet tone of her voice that had moved him. Here in the calm glances of a girl was the peace he had been seeking. The shock of the thought and the obvious impossibility had aggravated the pain of longing. He had blackened his thoughts with a burn of passion for her. The robes had been to him a cloak of thorns, the monastery precincts a burning cage, and the food a corrosive as it slid down his throat to fester in his maw. Finally he had decided to tell the abbot that he would discard his robes and return to lay life. That night the monastery had been awakened by the sounds of a fire in the village. The next morning as he went round seeking alms-food he learned that the granary of the girl's parents had been consumed by the fire.

He had hurriedly returned to the monastery and had pleaded illness and absence from classes. He had felt responsible for the tragedy and had deemed that this was the retribution for deviating from the true path. He had wanted to atone for it. His thoughts had turned to the austerities exercised by the Buddha in the six years before the Enlightenment.[10] The Holy One had set the teeth, pressed the tongue to the palate and had tried to restrain, crush, and burn out the mind with the mind. The Holy One had taken food only in small amounts, as much as a hollowed palm would hold. The bones of the spine had become like a row of spindles, the ribs had stuck out like the beams of an old shed, the skin of the head had withered like the bitter gourd that has been cracked and withered through wind and sun. Koyin Thila had thought to expiate his sins by the practice of such severe mortifications. But he had remembered that the Buddha had preached against such self-torture that was painful, ignoble, and useless and had said that happiness could come only to those who had extinguished the fires of passion, illusion, pride, and false views. He could do no good by flagellating the body and mind. Also there was no need for penance nor atonement. The past was to be put aside and the future abandoned. His true vocation was to leave behind him both the pleasant and the unpleasant, to cling to nothing, in all ways, to be independent and without attachment. This realization had brought to him a moment of simple and transparent character. In this manner he had moved another step nearer to the final knowledge.

So here now was Koyin Thila, a senior novice, repeating his lessons in the dormitory and breathing in the smell of the afternoon fields. As a gust of breeze threw in a stronger puff of perfume, the koyin stopped and looked at the fields dancing in the haze. The sunlight was bright on the stubble and the heat was gently pressing to get in through the fence of bamboo and clematis. In his mind's eye, the koyin saw a vision of the fields two moons hence in the fairest month of Tabaung.[11] The heat would have got through the fence by then but it would be lost in the mazes of the mango and the pleasances of the jackfruit trees. That was the month when he would depart on a journey from which there would be no return. He would become a *pabbaji*, a departer, a wayfarer, and he would not need to look back again upon the world.

Thinking of his forthcoming journey brought to mind another journey in another time taken by Buddha in such a month to beat the drum of the

---

10. *the Enlightenment*, in Buddhism the realization of ultimate universal truth. 11. *Tabaung*, the twelfth month in the Burmese calendar, approximately March.

Law before his father, King Suddhodana of Kapilavatthu. The books say that when Suddhodana heard Buddha was preaching at Rajagaha he sent a courtier with a thousand men to invite him. These arrived while he was preaching and as they listened to the Doctrine they attained arahatship.[12] Arahats are indifferent to worldly things, so they never gave Buddha the message. The king sent another courtier and a thousand men with the same result and so on for nine times. Then he sent Kaludayin, the playmate of Buddha, who promised to bring back Buddha. Though like the rest he entered the Order he waited until the full-moon day of Tabaung. Then Kaludayin, seeing that the time was suitable for traveling, uttered his invitation. Koyin Thila softly repeated the verses from the *Theragatha*.[13]

> "Now crimson glow the trees, dear Lord, and cast
> Their aging foliage in quest of fruit.
> Like crests of flame they shine irradiant,
> And rich in hope, great hero, is the hour.
> Verdure and harvest time in every tree,
> Where'er we look, delightful to the eye,
> And every quarter breathing fragrant airs,
> While leaf is falling, yearning comes for fruit.
> It is time, O hero, that we departed.
> Not over hot, not over cold, but sweet,
> O Master, now the season of the year."

In the silence of the pause, the slow beat of the wooden clapper was heard to announce the afternoon classes in the Doctrine. Koyin Thila arose and adjusted his robes. The classes would be on the Visuddhi-Magga, the Path of Purity, taken by the abbot himself; it would not do to be late. He picked up a notebook and pencil and stepped down the dormitory stairs onto the brick path leading to the abbot's *kyaung*. As he walked with unhurried steps he carried in his bearing the unmistakable signs of a scion of the Enlightened One.   ✳

---

12. *arahatship*, the goal of enlightenment attained by a Buddhist monk. 13. *Theragatha.* See footnote 4.

6 ISLAMIC LITERATURE

from *THE KORAN*

Translated from the Arabic by
Mohammed Marmaduke Pickthall[1]

The Koran *is the sacred text of the Moslems. Written in classical Arabic, it is divided into 114 surahs (chapters), containing the revelations of Allah (God) to the Prophet Mohammed. It is regarded by the Moslems as the basis for religious, social, commercial, military, and legal laws of the Islamic World.*

Surah LXXXI: THE OVERTHROWING

REVEALED AT MECCA [2]

In the name of Allah, the Beneficent, the Merciful.

1. When the sun is overthrown,
2. And when the stars fall,
3. And when the hills are moved,
4. And when the camels big with young are abandoned,
5. And when the wild beasts are herded together,
6. And when the seas rise,
7. And when souls are reunited,
8. And when the girl-child that was buried alive [3] is asked

---

"The Overthrowing" from THE MEANING OF THE GLORIOUS KORAN, translated by Mohammed Marmaduke Pickthall. Reprinted by permission of George Allen & Unwin Ltd.
1. *Mohammed Marmaduke Pickthall.* An English convert to Islam, Pickthall was the first scholar to translate *The Koran* into English. **2.** *Mecca.* As the birthplace of Mohammed, Mecca, one of the two capitals of Saudi Arabia, is the chief holy city of the Moslems. **3.** *girl-child . . . alive,* a reference to the custom of pagan Arabs who buried alive the female infants they considered unnecessary.

9. For what sin she was slain,
10. And when the pages are laid open,
11. And when the sky is torn away,
12. And when hell is lighted,
13. And when the garden is brought nigh,
14. (Then) every soul will know what it hath made ready.
15. Oh, but I call to witness the planets,
16. The stars which rise and set,
17. And the close of night,
18. And the breath of morning
19. That this is in truth the word of an honoured messenger,
20. Mighty, established in the presence of the Lord of the Throne,
21. (One) to be obeyed, and trustworthy;
22. And your comrade is not mad.
23. Surely he beheld him on the clear horizon.[4]
24. And he is not avid of the Unseen.
25. Nor is this the utterance of a devil worthy to be stoned.
26. Whither then go ye?
27. This is naught else than a reminder unto creation,
28. Unto whomsoever of you willeth to walk straight.
29. And ye will not, unless (it be) that Allah willeth, the Lord of Creation.

Surah LXXXII: THE CLEAVING

REVEALED AT MECCA

In the name of Allah, the Beneficent, the Merciful.

1. When the heaven is cleft asunder,
2. When the planets are dispersed,
3. When the seas are poured forth,
4. And the sepulchres are overturned,
5. A soul will know what it hath sent before (it) and what left behind.
6. O man! What hath made thee careless concerning thy Lord, the Bountiful,
7. Who created thee, then fashioned, then proportioned thee?

"The Cleaving" from THE MEANING OF THE GLORIOUS KORAN, translated by Mohammed Marmaduke Pickthall. Reprinted by permission of George Allen & Unwin Ltd. THE OVERTHROWING: 4. *he beheld . . . horizon*, a reference to Mohammed's vision at Mt. Hira where an angel descended and spoke to him.

8. Into whatsover form He will, He casteth thee.
9. Nay, but they deny the Judgement.
10. Lo! there are above you guardians,
11. Generous and recording,
12. Who know (all) that ye do.
13. Lo! the righteous verily will be in delight.
14. And lo! the wicked verily will be in hell;
15. They will burn therein on the Day of Judgement,
16. And will not be absent thence.
17. Ah, what will convey unto thee what the Day of Judgment is!
18. Again, what will convey unto thee what the Day of Judgement is!
19. A day on which no soul hath power at all for any (other) soul. The (absolute) command on that day is Allah's.

Surah CXII: THE UNITY

REVEALED AT MECCA

In the name of Allah, the Beneficent, the Merciful.

1. Say: He is Allah, the One!
2. Allah, the eternally Besought of all!
3. He begetteth not nor was begotten.
4. And there is none comparable unto Him.

"The Unity" from THE MEANING OF THE GLORIOUS KORAN, translated by Mohammed Marmaduke Pickthall. Reprinted by permission of George Allen & Unwin Ltd.

Abul-'Ala al-Ma'arri [1] (973–1057)

from *THE MEDITATIONS*

Translated from the Arabic by
Reynold A. Nicholson

V

'Tis sorrow enough for man that after he roamed at will,
The Days beckon him and say, "Begone, enter now a grave!"
How many a time our feet have trodden beneath the dust
A brow of the arrogant, a skull of the debonair!

IX

When I would string the pearls of my desire,
Alas, Life's too short thread denies them room.
Vast folios cannot yet contain entire
Man's hope; his life is a compendium.

XVI

Humanity, in whom the best
Of this world's features are expressed—
The chiefs set over them to reign
Are but as moons that wax and wane.

If ye unto your sons would prove
By act how dearly them ye love,
Then every voice of wisdom joins
To bid you leave them in your loins.

"Meditations V, IX, XVI, XVII, XVIII, XIX, XX" from THE MEDITATIONS OF MA'ARRI, translated by Reynold A. Nicholson. Reprinted by permission of Cambridge University Press.
1. *Abul-'Ala al-Ma'arri* (ä bül' älä' äl mä är rē').

XVII

Two fates still hold us fast,
A future and a past;
Two vessels' vast embrace
Surrounds us—Time and Space.

Whene'er we ask what end
Our Maker did intend,
Some answering voice is heard
That utters no plain word.

XVIII

If criminals are fated,
'Tis wrong to punish crime.
When God the ores created,
He knew that on a time

They should become the sources
Whence sword-blades dripping blood
Flash o'er the manes of horses
Iron-curbed, iron-shod.

XIX

The body, which gives thee during life a form,
Is but thy vase: be not deceived, my soul!
Cheap is the bowl thou storest honey in,
But precious for the contents of the bowl.

XX

We laugh, but inept is our laughter,
We should weep, and weep sore,
Who are shattered like glass and thereafter
Remoulded no more.

Hafiz [1] (1320–1391)

from *THE DIVAN* [2]

Translated from the Persian by
Gertrude Lowthian Bell

ODE I

Wind from the east, oh Lapwing of the day,
I send thee to my Lady, though the way
Is far to Saba,[3] where I bid thee fly;
Lest in the dust thy tameless wings should lie,
Broken with grief, I send thee to thy nest,
    Fidelity.   5

Or far or near there is no halting-place
Upon Love's road—absent, I see thy face,
And in thine ear my wind-blown greetings sound,
North winds and east waft them where they are bound,
Each morn and eve convoys of greeting fair
    I send to thee.   10

Unto mine eyes a stranger, thou that art
A comrade ever-present to my heart,
What whispered prayers and what full meed of praise
    I send to thee.

Poem I from THE DIVAN OF HAFIZ translated by Gertrude Lowthian Bell. Reprinted
by permission of William Heinemann Ltd.
1. *Hafiz* (hä'fəz). 2. *The Divan*, the collected works of an Arabic or Persian poet. 3.
Saba, an ancient kingdom in southwestern Arabia.

Lest Sorrow's army waste thy heart's domain,
I send my life to bring thee peace again,   15
Dear life thy ransom! From thy singers learn
How one that longs for thee may weep and burn;
Sonnets and broken words, sweet notes and songs
    I send to thee.

Give me the cup! a voice rings in mine ears
Crying: "Bear patiently the bitter years!   20
For all thine ills, I send thee heavenly grace.
God the Creator mirrored in thy face
Thine eyes shall see, God's image in the glass
    I send to thee.

"Hafiz, thy praise alone my comrades sing;
Hasten to us, thou that art sorrowing!   25
A robe of honor and a harnessed steed
    I send to thee."

ODE V

I cease not from desire till my desire
Is satisfied; or let my mouth attain
My love's red mouth, or let my soul expire,
Sighed from those lips that sought her lips in vain.
Others may find another love as fair;   5
Upon her threshold I have laid my head:
The dust shall cover me, still lying there,
When from my body life and love have fled.

My soul is on my lips ready to fly,
But grief beats in my heart and will not cease,   10
Because not once, not once before I die,
Will her sweet lips give all my longing peace.
My breath is narrowed down to one long sigh
For a red mouth that burns my thoughts like fire;
When will that mouth draw near and make reply   15
To one whose life is straitened with desire?

Poem V from THE DIVAN OF HAFIZ translated by Gertrude Lowthian Bell. Reprinted
by permission of William Heinemann Ltd.

When I am dead, open my grave and see
The cloud of smoke that rises round thy feet:
In my dead heart the fire still burns for thee;
Yea, the smoke rises from my winding-sheet!　　20
Ah come, Beloved! for the meadows wait
Thy coming, and the thorn bears flowers instead
Of thorns, the cypress fruit, and desolate
Bare winter from before thy steps has fled.

Hoping within some garden ground to find　　25
A red rose soft and sweet as thy soft cheek
Through every meadow blows the western wind,
Through every garden he is fain to seek.
Reveal thy face! that the whole world may be
Bewildered by thy radiant loveliness;　　30
The cry of man and woman comes to thee,
Open thy lips and comfort their distress!

Each curling lock of thy luxuriant hair
Breaks into barbed hooks to catch my heart,
My broken heart is wounded everywhere　　35
With countless wounds from which the red drops start.
Yet when sad lovers meet and tell their sighs,
Not without praise shall Hafiz' name be said,
Not without tears, in those pale companies
Where joy has been forgot and hope has fled.　　40

ODE VIII

From Canaan Joseph shall return,[1] whose face
A little time was hidden: weep no more—
Oh, weep no more! in sorrow's dwelling-place
The roses yet shall spring from the bare floor!
And heart bowed down beneath a secret pain—　　5
Oh stricken heart! joy shall return again,
Peace to the love-tossed brain—oh, weep no more!

Poem VIII from THE DIVAN OF HAFIZ translated by Gertrude Lowthian Bell. Reprinted
by permission of William Heinemann Ltd.
ODE VIII: 1. *From Canaan . . . return.* Joseph, a heroic figure in the Old Testament
and *The Koran,* was born in Canaan, sold into slavery in Egypt, and eventually became
the Pharaoh's prime minister.

Oh, weep no more! for once again Life's Spring
Shall throne her in the meadows green, and o'er
Her head the minstrel of the night shall fling   10
A canopy of rose leaves, score on score.
The secret of the world thou shalt not learn,
And yet behind the veil Love's fire may burn—
Weep'st thou? let hope return and weep no more!

Today may pass, tomorrow pass, before   15
The turning wheel give me my heart's desire;
Heaven's self shall change, and turn not evermore
The universal wheel of Fate in ire.
Oh Pilgrim nearing Mecca's holy fane,[2]
The thorny maghilan [3] wounds thee in vain,   20
The desert blooms again—oh, weep no more!

What though the river of mortality
Round the unstable house of Life doth roar,
Weep not, oh heart, Noah shall pilot thee,
And guide thine ark to the desiréd shore!   25
The goal lies far, and perilous is thy road,
Yet every path leads to that same abode
Where thou shalt drop thy load—oh, weep no more!

Mine enemies have persecuted me,
My love has turned and fled from out my door—   30
God counts our tears and knows our misery;
Ah, weep not! He has heard thy weeping sore.
And chained in poverty and plunged in night,
Oh Hafiz, take thy Koran and recite
Litanies infinite, and weep no more!   35

---

2. *Mecca's holy fane.* Mecca, one of the two capitals of Saudi Arabia, is the chief holy city of the Moslems and the birthplace of Mohammed. *Fane* is an archaic term for temple.
3. *maghilan,* a shrub growing on the outskirts of Mecca, whose presence signalled journey's end to the weary pilgrim.

Tawfiq al-Hakim [1] (1902–   )

THE RIVER OF MADNESS

*(A symbolic play in one act,
based on an Oriental legend)*

Translated from the Arabic

CAST OF CHARACTERS

THE KING
THE VIZIR [2]
THE QUEEN
THE PHYSICIAN
THE GRAND PRIEST

THE KING. What you tell me is terrible!

THE VIZIR. Sire, this is the decree of fate.

THE KING *(astonished)*. And also the Queen?

THE VIZIR *(seriously)*. Unfortunately!

THE KING. Did she also drink the water of this river?

THE VIZIR. As all the other subjects of the kingdom did.

THE KING. Where was the Queen when you saw her?

THE VIZIR. She was strolling in the gardens of the palace.

THE KING. Have we not endured enough without this misfortune!

THE VIZIR. You warned her not to drink the water of this river, and ordered her to drink nothing but wine, but . . . destiny . . .

THE KING. Tell me, how did you discover that she drank the river's water?

THE VIZIR. Her face, her acts, all indicated this.

THE KING. Did she speak to you?

"The River of Madness" by Tawfiq al-Hakim from ISLAMIC LITERATURE, AN INTRO-
DUCTORY HISTORY WITH SELECTIONS by Najib Ullah. Copyright © 1963 by Najib
Ullah. Reprinted by permission of Washington Square Press a division of Simon & Schuster.
1. *Tawfiq al-Hakim* (tṓ′fēk äl hä′kēm). 2. *The Vizir,* a minister of state.

THE VIZIR. No. When I approached she went away in fear. And her escorts shared her emotion and were whispering with each other while glancing furtively at me.

THE KING (talking to himself). Yes, the vision I had predicted this.

THE VIZIR. O heaven, have pity on us!

THE KING. It seems that my eyes have already seen this.

(A silence)

THE VIZIR. When will heaven's malediction spare this river?

THE KING. Who knows?

THE VIZIR. Did not the vision give to his majesty some sign of future liberation?

THE KING (trying to remember). I do not remember.

THE VIZIR. Sire, try to remember.

THE KING (again making an effort to remember). I remember only what I have already told you. . . . The river was turned to the color of dawn. Suddenly a cloud of black snakes fell from the sky, vomiting into the clear water a torrent of poison. In one minute the water became as dark as the night. At the same time a voice told me: "Beware of drinking hereafter from the water of this river. . . ."

THE VIZIR. O gods!

THE KING. But yet, I saw that everyone drank.

THE VIZIR. Save two persons.

THE KING. I and you.

THE VIZIR. What good luck!

THE KING. I do not see here any good luck.

THE VIZIR (conscious of his faux pas). Forgive me, sire. In reality my grief is so great. Ah! I wish to be in the place of the Queen!

THE KING. I hate this sort of talk. I wish you could find her a remedy! I suffer to see one of the most brilliant intellects of the kingdom sinking in the shadows of madness.

THE VIZIR. Yes, she was the sun of this realm!

THE KING. You do not do anything but repeat what I say. Say that the Chief Physician of the court be summoned!

THE VIZIR. The Chief Physician?

THE KING. Yes, perhaps he would cure her.

THE VIZIR. Has his majesty forgotten that the Physician also . . .

THE KING. What?

THE VIZIR. He drank also.

THE KING. Oh, what a misfortune.

THE VIZIR. I saw him near the Queen; everything about him was uncertain. Each time that I encountered him he nodded in a very strange way.

THE KING. Is the Chief Physician mad?

THE VIZIR. Yes.

THE KING. He was the greatest practitioner of his time. What a shame that a man like him becomes mad.

THE VIZIR. And at the moment we are in utmost need of his knowledge.

THE KING. Then there is no one left in the kingdom other than one person to take us out of this dilemma.

THE VIZIR. Who is that, sire?

THE KING. The Grand Priest.

THE VIZIR. O heaven!

THE KING. What?

THE VIZIR. Sire, like all the others.

THE KING. What are you saying? Did he also drink?

THE VIZIR. Yes, like the others.

THE KING. What irreparable misfortune! The Grand Priest also mad. He, of all men the most wise, the most clear-minded, the best man of faith, the most pure and close to heaven!

THE VIZIR. It was predestined, sire. Have I not already said that destiny wanted it this way?

THE KING. Truly, this is a complete misfortune, which was not even known in the legends and stories of bygone times. Suddenly all the subjects of a kingdom affected by madness! A kingdom in which only the King and his Vizir are in their right minds!

THE VIZIR (raising his arms to heaven in supplication). O! Heaven's pity on us!

THE KING. Hear me! This heaven which permitted us to be spared, will it refuse to fulfill our prayers? Let us go to the temple to prostrate ourselves and to pray for the recovery of the Queen and her subjects. This is our last refuge.

THE VIZIR. Yes, our ultimate and best refuge! O heaven!

(They go out. The QUEEN enters through another door, accompanied by the CHIEF PHYSICIAN and the GRAND PRIEST.)

THE QUEEN. It is a fearful misfortune!

THE PHYSICIAN and the GRAND PRIEST (together). Yes, it is a catastrophe!

THE QUEEN (to the PHYSICIAN). There is not any means to treat the minds of these two unfortunates?

THE PHYSICIAN. I suffer, madam, from my ignorance.

THE QUEEN. Do search.

THE PHYSICIAN. I did search very carefully; my science cannot do anything for their illness.

THE QUEEN. Then, should I lose hope for the recovery of my husband?

Al-Hakim 247

THE PHYSICIAN. Do not lose hope, madam. Heaven is full of miracles which go beyond the power of medicine.

THE QUEEN. When do the miracles happen?

THE PHYSICIAN. Who knows, madam?

THE QUEEN. Grand Priest, get a miracle quickly, at once . . . at once.

THE GRAND PRIEST. Get what?

THE QUEEN. One of heaven's miracles.

THE GRAND PRIEST. Who said, madam, that I have the power to get something from heaven?

THE QUEEN. Is not this your business?

THE GRAND PRIEST. Madam, heaven is not like these palm trees, whose fruits one picks at one's wish!

THE QUEEN. Then you cannot do anything? I love my husband. I want to save my man. Save my husband! Oh, save my husband!

THE PHYSICIAN. Patience, madam.

THE GRAND PRIEST. Do not stop the Queen's effusion! She has reason. She cries for an excellent husband, and the subjects, if they knew, would cry also for a just and good King.

THE QUEEN. Be careful that the people do not learn of this misfortune.

THE GRAND PRIEST. We are as mute as a tomb, madam, but I fear the consequences of such an event. We may do our best to keep the secret, but it will be revealed one day or another, and then, what an affair—that the people learn the King and his Vizir—

THE QUEEN. Oh, stop it! It is horrible!

THE GRAND PRIEST. Verily, it is terrible.

THE QUEEN. What shall I do? Do not make it worse. Do something. If it continues, I will also lose my mind.

THE GRAND PRIEST. If I only knew what is passing through his head!

THE QUEEN. He speaks with dread of the river, which he claims to be poisoned.

THE GRAND PRIEST. Then what does he drink?

THE QUEEN. The wine, only wine.

THE PHYSICIAN. It is a matter of fact that he does not drink but wine. I believe that he already abused it, and his mind is disturbed by it.

THE QUEEN. If this were the only disease, its remedy would be easy: to take away his drinks.

THE PHYSICIAN. Then what would he drink?

THE QUEEN. The water of the river.

THE PHYSICIAN. Do you believe that he would permit it?

THE QUEEN. I would know how to convince him.

THE PHYSICIAN *(turning to the sound of someone walking)*. It is the King who comes.

THE QUEEN *(to the* PHYSICIAN *and the* GRAND PRIEST*)*. Leave us two alone.

(They go and the QUEEN *prepares herself to receive the* KING. *The* KING *enters.)*

THE KING *(seeing the* QUEEN, *he suddenly stops)*. You . . . here?

THE QUEEN *(staring at him curiously)*. Yes.

THE KING. Why do you look at me in this way?

THE QUEEN *(she continues to stare, murmuring a prayer)*. Come to my help, O miracles!

THE KING *(looking sadly at her)*. Ah! my heart tears itself into pieces. If you knew how I suffer.

THE QUEEN *(staring)*. Do you suffer? Why?

THE KING. Why? Ah! Yes, you cannot understand. This fair head cannot understand now.

THE QUEEN. What makes you suffer?

THE KING *(looking at her attentively)*. I suffer . . . but can I say it? Ah, I—it is more than I can bear. . . .

THE QUEEN *(seeming astonished)*. So you would feel that—

THE KING. Is there reason to not feel, my friend? And do you ask me about it?

THE QUEEN *(with astonishment)*. It is extraordinary!

THE KING. What a sadness!

THE QUEEN *(looking at him for a while, then drawing him close)*. Come, darling, sit near me on this seat. Don't be so sad. The disease will disappear; the time has come.

THE KING. What are you talking about?

THE QUEEN. Yes, be sure that it will disappear.

THE KING *(looking at her in astonishment)*. Do you feel that—

THE QUEEN. How not to feel it, my friend. It is a sore in my heart.

THE KING *(looking at her in wonder)*. It is extraordinary!

THE QUEEN. Why do you look at me in this way?

THE KING *(with an imploring gesture)*. O heavens!

THE QUEEN. You implore heaven? May heaven answer at last.

THE KING. What is this talk?

THE QUEEN *(joyfully)*. We have found the remedy.

THE KING. Did you find the remedy? When?

THE QUEEN *(enthusiastically)*. Today.

THE KING *(with interest)*. Oh, what good fortune!

THE QUEEN. Yes, what good fortune! But you should hear me and follow my advice: you will cease hereafter to drink wine and you will not drink but the river's water.

THE KING (looking at her, disillusioned). The water of the river!

THE QUEEN (forcefully). Yes!

THE KING (as if speaking to himself). Woe is me! And I believed that heaven had kindly answered my prayers!

THE QUEEN (persuasively). Hear me and follow my advice.

THE KING (with an air of disillusionment). I see that evil is getting worse and worse. Could I predict that she would talk to me some day like this? O gods! However, she must be saved. She must be saved. I will lose my mind. (He goes out quickly, and is heard calling.) The Vizir! Call the Vizir!

THE QUEEN (talking to herself). The Physician is right. It is much more serious. (She sighs and goes out.)

THE VIZIR (entering through the opposite door and looking upset). Sire! Sire!

THE KING (coming back in). Vizir!

THE VIZIR. Do you know what the people say about us?

THE KING. What people?

THE VIZIR. The mad ones.

THE KING. What do they say?

THE VIZIR. They, those mad ones, claim that they are in their right minds, while the King and the Vizir are—

THE KING. Stop it! Who told you such nonsense?

THE VIZIR. Such is their conviction.

THE KING (with a sad, ironic tone). We the mad ones, and they the wise! . . . O! Heaven's pity! They cannot understand that they are mad.

THE VIZIR. You are right.

THE KING. It seems to me that the mad one does not realize his condition.

THE VIZIR. This is also what I think.

THE KING. Oh, what suffering! Just now the Queen was talking to me with an air of understanding. And more than that, she seemed to want to give me her advice and to pity my fate!

THE VIZIR. It is exactly the same with the persons who met me in the streets of the town or inside the palace.

THE KING. O heaven, have pity on them.

THE VIZIR (with hesitation). And on us.

THE KING. And on us?

THE VIZIR. Sire, I . . . I wanted to speak.

THE KING (afraid). What do you want to say?

THE VIZIR. That they are—

THE KING. Who are they?

THE VIZIR. The people, the mad ones; they accuse us of being mad. Already they murmur and conspire. Whatever may be the weakness of their minds, they are the majority, and thus they have logic on their side. More than that, they alone have the right to judge madness or wisdom. They are the ocean, while we, we are not more than two grains of sand. Do you want advice, sire?

THE KING. I know what you want to do.

THE VIZIR. Let us do like them. Let us drink the water of the river!

THE KING (looking attentively at the VIZIR). O unfortunate! Did you also drink the water? I see in your eyes a gleam of madness.

THE VIZIR. No, sire, I did not drink.

THE KING. Speak frankly.

THE VIZIR (forcefully). I tell you in all frankness, I will drink. I have decided to be crazy like all the others. I do not know what to do with my reason.

THE KING. Then, do you want to extinguish with your own hands the flame of your spirit?

THE VIZIR. Oh, the flame of the spirit! What value can it have in a kingdom of the mad? Believe me, we are in danger of being overthrown by the people if we follow our own judgment. Already revolt shines in their eyes. It would not be too long before we would hear in the streets the people shouting: "The King and his Vizir are mad. Down with the madmen."

THE KING. Woe to you! Are you talking seriously?

THE VIZIR. Sire, you have just said that the mad ones do not realize their condition.

THE KING (shouting). But I am in my right mind, and these people are crazy!

THE VIZIR. They also claim the same thing.

THE KING. And you? Do you not think that I am in my right mind?

THE VIZIR. My opinion alone—of what use will it be? The word of a mad one in the favor of another has no weight!

THE KING. But you know very well that I did not drink the water of the river.

THE VIZIR. I know it.

THE KING. Therefore, I am not mad, because I did not drink, while the others are crazy because they did drink.

THE VIZIR. They say the contrary: They are not mad, because they drank the water, and you are mad because you did not!

THE KING. What stupidity!

THE VIZIR. This is what they say, and they are believed, while you cannot find a soul to hear what you say!

THE KING. Then is this the way to interpret the truth?

THE VIZIR. The truth? *(He covers his laugh.)*

THE KING. Do you laugh?

THE VIZIR. Now those words seem strange on our lips.

THE KING *(shivering)*. Why?

THE VIZIR. Truth, reason, virtue, and all the words which are the exclusive property of those persons. They, alone, are their possessors.

THE KING. And I?

THE VIZIR. You, alone, you possess nothing.

(A silence. The KING *meditates.)*

THE KING *(raising his head)*. You are right. It is impossible to continue such a life.

THE VIZIR. Yes, sire, it is in your interest to live in perfect harmony with the Queen and your subjects. Do it, even if it requires you to offer your reason as a sacrifice!

THE KING *(reflecting)*. Yes, this is in my interest. Madness guarantees my happy life with the Queen and among my subjects. What you said is right. And about wisdom—what does that wisdom offer me?

THE VIZIR. Nothing, sire! On the contrary, you may be banished by the others; you will be branded by your own subjects with folly. In one word, you will be considered mad.

THE KING. Therefore, it would be madness not to choose madness!

THE VIZIR. That is what I wanted to say.

THE KING. And it is wiser to prefer madness to any other thing?

THE VIZIR. I do not doubt this.

THE KING. Then, in that case, what difference exists between wisdom and madness?

THE VIZIR. Please wait. *(He reflects.)* I do not see any!

THE KING *(with insistence)*. Let there be brought to me a cup of the river's water!

Al-Jahiz[1] (?-869)

FLIES AND MOSQUITOES
from *The Book of Animals*

Translated from the Arabic by
Reynold A. Nicholson

IN THE FLY there are two good qualities. One of these is the facility with which it may be prevented from causing annoyance and discomfort. For if any person wish to make the flies quit his house and secure himself from being troubled by them without diminishing the amount of light in the house, he has only to shut the door, and they will hurry forth as fast as they can and try to outstrip each other in seeking the light and fleeing from the darkness. Then no sooner is the curtain let down and the door opened than the light will return and the people of the house will no longer be harassed by flies. If there be a slit in the door, or if, when it is shut, one of the two folding leaves does not quite close on the other, that will serve them as a means of exit; and the flies often go out through the gap between the bottom of the door and the lintel. Thus it is easy to get rid of them and escape from their annoyance. With the mosquito it is otherwise, for just as the fly has greater power (for mischief) in the light, so the mosquito is more tormenting and mischievous and bloodthirsty after dark; and it is not possible for people to let into their houses sufficient light to stop the activity of the mosquito, because for this purpose they would have to admit the beams of the sun, and there are no mosquitoes except in summer when the sun is unendurable. All light that is derived from the sun partakes of heat, and light is never devoid of heat, though heat is sometimes devoid of light. Hence, while it is easily possible to contrive a remedy against flies, this is difficult in the case of mosquitoes.

"Flies and Mosquitoes" from KITAB AL-HAYAWAN (*The Book of Animals*), translated by Reynold A. Nicholson. Reprinted by permission of Cambridge University Press.
1. *Al-Jahiz* (äl jä′həz).

The second merit of the fly is that unless it ate the mosquito, which it pursues and seeks after on the walls and in the corners of rooms, people would be unable to stay in their houses. I am informed by a trustworthy authority that Muhammad son of Jahm said one day to some of his acquaintance, "Do you know the lesson which we have learned with regard to the fly?" They said, "No." "But the fact is," he replied, "that it eats mosquitoes and chases them and picks them up and destroys them. I will tell you how I learned this. Formerly, when I wanted to take the siesta, I used to give orders that the flies should be cleared out and the curtain drawn and the door shut an hour before noon. On the disappearance of the flies, the mosquitoes would collect in the house and become exceedingly strong and powerful and bite me violently as soon as I began to rest. Now on a certain day I came in and found the room open and the curtain up. And when I lay down to sleep, there were no mosquitoes and I slept soundly, although I was very angry with the slaves. Next day they cleared out the flies and shut the door as usual, and on my coming to take the siesta I saw a multitude of mosquitoes. Then on another day they forgot to shut the door, and when I perceived that it was open I reviled them. However, when I came for the siesta, I did not find a single mosquito and I said to myself, 'Methinks I have slept on the two days on which my precautions were neglected, and have been hindered from sleeping whenever they were carefully observed. Why should not I try today the effect of leaving the door open? If I sleep three days with the door open and suffer no annoyance from the mosquitoes, I shall know that the right way is to have the flies and the mosquitoes together, because the flies destroy them, and that our remedy lies in keeping near us what we used to keep at a distance.' I made the experiment, and now the end of the matter is that whether we desire to remove the flies or destroy the mosquitoes, we can do it with very little trouble."

Jibran Khalil Jibran [1] (1883–1931)

Song of Man

Translated from the Arabic by
Anthony Rizeallah Ferris

I was here from the moment of the
Beginning, and here I am still. And
I shall remain here until the end
Of the world, for there is no
Ending to my grief-stricken being.   5

I roamed the infinite sky, and
Soared in the ideal world, and
Floated through the firmament. But
Here I am, prisoner of measurement.

I heard the teachings of Confucius;   10
I listened to Brahma's wisdom;
I sat by Buddha under the Tree of Knowledge.

Yet here I am, existing with ignorance and heresy.
I was on Sinai when Jehovah approached Moses;
I saw the Nazarene's miracles at the Jordan;   15
I was in Medina when Mohammed visited.
Yet here I am, prisoner of bewilderment.

"Song of Man" by Jibran Khalil Jibran, translated by Anthony Rizeallah Ferris from THE
TREASURY OF JIBRAN KHALIL JIBRAN. Copyright 1951 by The Citadel Press, Inc.
Reprinted by permission of the Philosophical Library.
1. *Jibran Khalil Jibran* (jĕ′brän Hä lēl′ jĕ′brän).

Then I witnessed the might of Babylon;
I learned of the glory of Egypt;
I viewed the warring greatness of Rome.   20
Yet my earlier teachings showed the
Weakness and sorrow of those achievements.

I conversed with the magicians of Ain Dour [2];
I debated with the priests of Assyria;
I gleaned depth from the prophets of Palestine.   25
Yet I am still seeking the truth.

I gathered wisdom from quiet India;
I probed the antiquity of Arabia;
I heard all that can be heard.
Yet my heart is deaf and blind.   30

I suffered at the hands of despotic rulers;
I suffered slavery under insane invaders;
I suffered hunger imposed by tyranny;
Yet I still possess some inner power
With which I struggle to greet each day.   35

My mind is filled, but my heart is empty;
My body is old, but my heart is an infant.
Perhaps in youth my heart will grow, but I
Pray to grow old and reach the moment of
My return to God. Only then will my heart fill!   40

I was here from the moment of the
Beginning, and here I am still. And
I shall remain here until the end
Of the world, for there is no
Ending to my grief-stricken being.   45

---

2. *Ain Dour*, a village in Palestine (now Israel) famous in Biblical times for its sooth-sayers.

Omar Khayyám (d. 1123)

from *THE RUBÁIYÁT*[1] *OF OMAR KHAYYÁM*

Translated from the Persian by
Edward Fitzgerald

Wake! For the Sun, who scattered into flight
The Stars before him from the Field of Night,
   Drives Night along with them from Heav'n and strikes
The Sultàn's Turret with a Shaft of Light.

Come, fill the Cup, and in the fire of Spring   5
Your Winter garment of Repentance fling;
   The Bird of Time has but a little way
To flutter—and the Bird is on the Wing.

A Book of Verses underneath the Bough,
A Jug of Wine, a Loaf of Bread—and Thou   10
   Beside me singing in the Wilderness—
Oh, Wilderness were Paradise enow!

Some for the Glories of This World, and some
Sigh for the Prophet's [2] Paradise to come;
   Ah, take the Cash, and let the Credit go,   15
Nor heed the rumble of a distant Drum!

Look to the blowing Rose [3] about us—"Lo,
Laughing," she says, "into the world I blow,
   At once the silken tassel of my Purse
Tear, and its Treasure on the Garden throw."   20

---

1. *Rubáiyát*, the feminine plural of *rubā'iy*, quatrain. [*Persian*] 2. *the Prophet*, Mohammed. 3. *blowing Rose*, blossoming rose.

And those who husbanded the Golden Grain,
And those who flung it to the winds like Rain,
    Alike to no such aureate Earth are turned
As, buried once, Men want dug up again.

The Worldly Hope men set their Hearts upon   25
Turns Ashes—or it prospers; and anon,
    Like Snow upon the Desert's dusty Face,
Lighting a little hour or two—is gone.

Think, in this battered Caravanserai [4]
Whose Portals are alternate Night and Day,   30
    How Sultàn after Sultàn with his Pomp
Abode his destined Hour, and went his way.

I sometimes think that never blows so red
The Rose as where some buried Caesar bled;
    That every Hyacinth the Garden wears   35
Dropped in her lap from some once lovely Head. [5]

And this reviving Herb whose tender Green
Fledges the River-Lip on which we lean—
    Ah, lean upon it lightly! for who knows
From what once lovely Lip it springs unseen!   40

Ah, my Belovèd, fill the Cup that clears
TODAY of past Regrets and future Fears:
    TOMORROW!—Why, Tomorrow I may be
Myself with Yesterday's Sev'n Thousand Years. [6]

For some we loved, the loveliest and the best   45
That from his Vintage rolling Time hath prest,
    Have drunk their Cup a Round or two before,
And one by one crept silently to rest.

Ah, make the most of what we yet may spend,
Before we too into the Dust descend;   50
    Dust into Dust, and under Dust, to lie,
Sans [7] Wine, sans Song, sans Singer, and—sans End!

---

4. *Caravanserai*, a large inn where caravans put up for the night. 5. *Hyacinth . . . Head.*
In Greek mythology Hyacinthus, a beautiful youth, was accidently slain by the god Apollo
who caused a flower (the hyacinth) to grow from his blood. 6. *Sev'n Thousand Years.*
Ancient astronomers believed the world was seven thousand years old. 7. *Sans*, without.
[*French*]

Myself when young did eagerly frequent
Doctor and Saint,[8] and heard great argument
    About it [9] and about; but evermore   55
Came out by the same door where in I went.

With them the seed of Wisdom did I sow,
And with mine own hand wrought to make it grow;
    And this was all the Harvest that I reaped—
"I came like Water, and like Wind I go."   60

And if the Wine you drink, the Lip you press,
End in what All begins and ends in—Yes;
    Think that you are TODAY what YESTERDAY
You were—TOMORROW you shall not be less.

So when that Angel of the darker Drink   65
At last shall find you by the river brink,
    And offering his Cup, invite your Soul
Forth to your Lips to quaff—you shall not shrink.

Oh threats of Hell and Hopes of Paradise!
One thing at least is certain—*This* Life flies;   70
    One thing is certain and the rest is Lies—
The Flower that once has blown forever dies.

Strange, is it not? that of the myriads who
Before us passed the door of Darkness through,
    Not one returns to tell us of the Road,   75
Which to discover we must travel too.

The Revelations of Devout and Learned
Who rose before us, and as Prophets burned,
    Are all but Stories, which, awoke from Sleep,
They told their comrades, and to Sleep returned.   80

I sent my Soul through the Invisible,
Some letter of that Afterlife to spell;
    And by and by my Soul returned to me,
And answered, "I Myself am Heav'n and Hell"—

---

8. *Doctor and Saint*, philosopher and religious teacher. 9. *About it*, about life and death.

Heav'n but the Vision of fulfilled Desire,   85
And Hell the Shadow from a Soul on fire
   Cast on the Darkness into which Ourselves,
So late emerged from, shall so soon expire.

We are no other than a moving row
Of Magic Shadow-shapes that come and go   90
   Round with the Sun-illumined Lantern [10] held
In Midnight by the Master of the Show;

But helpless Pieces of the Game He plays
Upon this Checkerboard of Nights and Days;
   Hither and thither moves, and checks, and slays,   95
And one by one back in the Closet lays.

The Moving Finger writes, and, having writ,
Moves on; nor all your Piety nor Wit
   Shall lure it back to cancel half a line,
Nor all your Tears wash out a Word of it.   100

And this I know: whether the one True Light
Kindle to Love, or Wrath—consume me quite,
   One Flash of It within the Tavern caught
Better than in the Temple lost outright.

What! out of senseless Nothing to provoke   105
A conscious Something to resent the yoke
   Of unpermitted Pleasure, under pain
Of Everlasting Penalties, if broke!

What! from his helpless Creature be repaid
Pure Gold for what he lent him dross-allayed—   110
   Sue for a Debt he never did contract,
And cannot answer—Oh, the sorry trade!

O Thou, who didst with pitfall and with gin [11]
Beset the Road I was to wander in,
   Thou wilt not with Predestined Evil round   115
Enmesh, and then impute my Fall to Sin!

---

10. *Lantern*, the globe. 11. *gin*, a snare.

Oh Thou, who Man of Baser Earth didst make,
And ev'n with Paradise devise the Snake,
    For all the Sin wherewith the Face of Man
Is blackened—Man's forgiveness give—and take!   120

Yet, Ah, that Spring should vanish with the Rose!
That Youth's sweet-scented manuscript should close!
    The Nightingale that in the branches sang,
Ah whence, and whither flown again, who knows!

Would but the Desert of the Fountain yield   125
One glimpse—if dimly, yet indeed, revealed,
    To which the fainting Traveler might spring,
As springs the trampled herbage of the field!

Would but some wingèd Angel ere too late
Arrest the yet unfolded Roll of Fate,   130
    And make the stern Recorder otherwise
Enregister, or quite obliterate!

Ah, Love! could you and I with Him conspire
To grasp this sorry Scheme of Things entire,
    Would not we shatter it to bits—and then   135
Remold it nearer to the Heart's Desire!

Khalil Matran [1] (1872–1949)

Childhood in Zahla

Translated from the Arabic

Do you remember when we both were children,
Those happy days in Zahla
When our shadows met, exchanging laughter,
Amidst the grapevines' secrecy.

Do you remember how we rushed,   5
Drunk with joy, to pick the best of the grapes,
And paid for them with our smiles?

Do you remember that morning when two angels
Took us both to the replenishing heaven
Of the highest and lowest, and to the Pleiades? [2]   10

And that river?
Is it still flowing as it did
When it was haunted by us?
Do you remember it?
It nursed the gardens   15
With its sweet, refreshing water,
And its love assured their splendor.

---

1. *Khalil Matran* (hä′lēl mät′rän). 2. *Pleiades*, in Greek mythology the seven daughters
of Atlas who were transformed into a group of stars.

Mikha'il Nu'ayma[1] (1889-   )

O Brother

Translated from the Arabic

O Brother!
If after the war the Western soldier boasts about his exploits,
And venerates the memory of those who died,
And glorifies his heroes,
You, do not praise the victors and do not blame the vanquished,   5
But kneel in silence like me,
With a humble bleeding heart,
To cry upon the fate of our dead ones.

O Brother!
When the soldier returns after the war to his home,   10
He throws himself in the arms of his loved ones;
But you, when you return to your home,
Do not ask about your loved ones,
Because hunger did not leave us the companions to welcome us
Save the ghosts of our dead ones.   15

O Brother!
When the farmer returns to his land, he wants to plow
And sow again, and to build anew, after a long exile,
His home, destroyed by cannons.
But our water wheels are dried up,   20
And our hearths are wrecked,
And our enemies have not left us any seedling
Other than the moldering of our dead ones.

"O Brother" by Mikha'il Nu'ayma from ISLAMIC LITERATURE, AN INTRODUCTORY
HISTORY WITH SELECTIONS by Najib Ullah. Copyright © 1963 by Najib Ullah. Reprinted by permission of Washington Square Press a division of Simon & Schuster.
1. *Mikha'il Nu'ayma* (mēH hä ēl′ nù ī′mä).

O Brother!
All this happened because we wanted it to happen,   25
And catastrophe dominates everywhere,
Because we wanted it to spread;
Do not lament, O brother;
No one else will hear our complaints;
But come with me, with pick and shovel,   30
To dig a trench to hide our dead ones.

O Brother! What are we?
We have no kin, no home and no neighbor;
If we sleep, if we stand, we are covered with shame;
The world is corrupted with our stench   35
As our dead ones stank.
Come, and follow me with a shovel
To dig another trench
And to hide in it our living selves.

Rumi (1207-1273)

Translated from the Persian by
Reynold A. Nicholson

Remembered Music

'Tis said, the pipe and lute that charm our ears
Derive their melody from rolling spheres [1];
But Faith, o'erpassing speculation's bound,
Can see what sweetens every jangled sound.

We, who are parts of Adam, heard with him   5
The song of angels and of seraphim.
Our memory, though dull and sad, retains
Some echo still of those unearthly strains.

Oh, music is the meat of all who love,
Music uplifts the soul to realms above.   10
The ashes glow, the latent fires increase:
We listen and are fed with joy and peace.

"Remembered Music" from RUMI POET AND MYSTIC by Rumi, translated by Reynold A. Nicholson. Reprinted by permission of George Allen & Unwin Ltd.
1. *rolling spheres.* In Moslem philosophy it is believed that the celestial bodies create heavenly music as they turn.

The Truth Within Us

'Twas a fair orchard, full of trees and fruit
And vines and greenery. A Sūfī [1] there
Sat with eyes closed, his head upon his knee,
Sunk deep in meditation mystical.
"Why," asked another, "dost thou not behold   5
These Signs of God the Merciful displayed
Around thee, which He bids us contemplate?"
"The signs," he answered, "I behold within;
Without is naught but symbols of the Signs."

What is all beauty in the world? The image,   10
Like quivering boughs reflected in a stream,
Of that eternal Orchard which abides
Unwithered in the hearts of Perfect Men.

The Evil in Ourselves

The lion took the Hare with him: they ran together to the well and
    looked in.
The Lion saw his own image: from the water appeared the form of a
    lion with a plump hare beside him.
No sooner did he espy his enemy than he left the Hare and sprang into
    the well.
He fell into the pit which he had dug: his iniquity recoiled on his own
    head.

"The Truth Within Us" and "The Evil in Ourselves" from RUMI POET AND MYSTIC by Rumi, translated by Reynold A. Nicholson. Reprinted by permission of George Allen & Unwin Ltd.
THE TRUTH WITHIN US: 1. Sūfī (sü'fē), a member of a Moslem mystic order which believes that communion with God can be achieved by meditation and ecstasy.

O Reader, how many an evil that you see in others is but your own
    nature reflected in them!   5
In them appears all that *you* are—your hypocrisy, iniquity, and inso-
    lence.
You do not see clearly the evil in yourself, else you would hate yourself
    with all your soul.
Like the Lion who sprang at his image in the water, you are only
    hurting yourself, O foolish man.
When you reach the bottom of the well of your own nature, then you
    will know that the wickedness is in *you.*

The Soul of Goodness in Things Evil

Fools take false coins because they are like the true.
If in the world no genuine minted coin
Were current, how would forgers pass the false?
Falsehood were nothing unless truth were there,
To make it specious. 'Tis the love of right   5
Lures men to wrong. Let poison but be mixed
With sugar, they will cram it into their mouths.
Oh, cry not that all creeds are vain! Some scent
Of truth they have, else they would not beguile.
Say not, "How utterly fantastical!"   10
No fancy in the world is all untrue.
Amidst the crowd of dervishes hides one,
One true fakir. Search well and thou wilt find!

"The Soul of Goodness in Things Evil" from RUMI POET AND MYSTIC by Rumi, translated by Reynold A. Nicholson. Reprinted by permission of George Allen & Unwin Ltd.

The Progress of Man

First he appeared in the realm inanimate;
Thence came into the world of plants and lived
The plant life many a year, nor called to mind
What he had been; then took the onward way
To animal existence, and once more   5
Remembers naught of that life vegetive.
Save when he feels himself moved with desire
Towards it in the season of sweet flowers,
As babes that seek the breast and know not why.

Again the wise Creator whom thou knowest   10
Uplifted him from animality
To Man's estate; and so from realm to realm
Advancing, he became intelligent,
Cunning and keen of wit, as he is now.
No memory of his past abides with him,   15
And from his present soul he shall be changed.

Though he is fallen asleep, God will not leave him
In this forgetfulness. Awakened, he
Will laugh to think what troublous dreams he had,
And wonder how his happy state of being   20
He could forget and not perceive that all
Those pains and sorrows were the effect of sleep
And guile and vain illusion. So this world
Seems lasting, though 'tis but the sleeper's dream;
Who, when the appointed Day shall dawn, escapes   25
From dark imaginings that haunted him,
And turns with laughter on his phantom griefs
When he beholds his everlasting home.

"The Progress of Man" from RUMI POET AND MYSTIC by Rumi, translated by Reynold
A. Nicholson. Reprinted by permission of George Allen & Unwin Ltd.

Jamil Sidqi al-Zahawi [1] (1863–1936)

To My Wife

Translated from the Arabic

O Buthayna, if the foe quickens the hour of my departure
By a bullet or a sword,
Remain firm in that misfortune,
Believing I will always be your companion in dreams.
Patience in adversity is the patrimony of   5
A noble woman of high birth. . . .

I will not be the first one who dies for his country,
Nor the first one among those
Who hope for the progress of their people
With the other nations.   10
Rejecting fanaticism and striving to save the people from prejudice,
I wish them life, and they wish me death.
Oh, what a difference between their wish and mine! . . .

"To My Wife" by Jamil Sidqi al-Zahawi from ISLAMIC LITERATURE, AN INTRODUC-
TORY HISTORY WITH SELECTIONS by Najib Ullah. Copyright © 1963 by Najib
Ullah. Reprinted by permission of Washington Square Press a division of Simon & Schuster.
1. *Jamil Sidqi al-Zahawi* (jä′mēl sid′kē äl zä′hə wē).

Poetry/Tanka

Translated from the Japanese by
Kenneth Rexroth

For a thousand years the most popular form of Japanese poetry was the tanka. *By the time the* Manyōshū, *the oldest and most important Japanese anthology, was compiled in the eighth century, the* tanka *had already existed for several hundred years. It remained in this prime position until the development of the* haiku *(see page 278) in the sixteenth century.*

The tanka *is a poem of thirty-one syllables arranged in five lines (5–7–5–7–7). Through the strict limits of its form,* tanka *intensifies; it reduces a universal experience to the compressed essence of one mood or event or image or idea.*

Akahito [1] (d.736)

V

The mists rise over
The still pools at Asuka. [2]
Memory does not
Pass away so easily.

Asuka gawa
Kawa yodo sarazu
Tatsu kiri no
Omoi sugu beki
Koi ni aranaku ni [3]

AKAHITO

Kenneth Rexroth, ONE HUNDRED POEMS FROM THE JAPANESE. All Rights Reserved. Reprinted by permission of New Directions Publishing Corporation.
1. *Akahito* (ä kä hē tô). 2. *Asuka,* a former Imperial Palace site. 3. *Asuka . . . ni.* In italics is the transliteration into Roman (i.e. European) characters of the original Japanese verse. *Transliteration* means putting the letters of one alphabet into another. Below is the full name of the poet, Yamabe no Akahito, in Chinese-Japanese characters.

Hitómaro [1] (c.680–c.710)

XVII

In the empty mountains
The leaves of the bamboo grass
Rustle in the wind.
I think of a girl
Who is not here.

XXI

Your hair has turned white
While your heart stayed
Knotted against me.
I shall never
Loosen it now.

XXII

A strange old man
Stops me,
Looking out of my deep mirror.

XXIII

The colored leaves
Have hidden the paths
On the autumn mountain.
How can I find my girl,
Wandering on ways I do not know?

---

1. *Hitómaro* (hē tô mä rô).

Lady Horikawa[1] (12th century)

XXX

Will he always love me?
I cannot read his heart.
This morning my thoughts
Are as disordered
As my black hair.

Narihira[1] (9th century)

LVI

I have always known
That at last I would
Take this road, but yesterday
I did not know that it would be today.

xxx: 1. *Horikawa* (hô rē kä wä).
LVI: 1. *Narihira* (nä rē hē rä).

Tsurayuki[1] (882-946)

LXXXV

No, the human heart
Is unknowable.
But in my birthplace
The flowers still smell
The same as always.

Yakamochi[1] (718-785)

LXXXIX

When I see the first
New moon, faint in the twilight,
I think of the moth eyebrows
Of a girl I saw only once.

Kenneth Rexroth, ONE HUNDRED POEMS FROM THE JAPANESE. All Rights Reserved. Reprinted by permission of New Directions Publishing Corporation.
LXXXV: 1. *Tsurayuki* (tsù rä yù kē).
LXXXIX: 1. *Yakamochi* (yä kä mô chē).

Translated from the Japanese by

Kenneth Rexroth

The two poems by Hitómaro printed below are naga uta or "long poems." Such "long" poems, which are comparatively rare in Japanese poetry, are usually elegies or reveries. Like the tanka, they represent the classical period in Japanese poetry.

Hitómaro (c.680–c.710)

CIV

The Bay of Tsunu
In the sea of Iwami
Has no fine beaches
And is not considered beautiful.
Perhaps it is not,   5
But we used to walk
By the sea of the whale fishers
Over the rocky shingle of Watazu
Where the wind blows
The green jewelled seaweed   10
Like wings quivering in the morning,
And the waves rock the kelp beds [1]
Like wings quivering in the evening.

1. *kelp beds*, beds of seaweed.

Just as the sea tangle sways and floats
At one with the waves, 15
So my girl clung to me
As she lay by my side.
Now I have left her,
To fade like the hoarfrost.
I looked back ten thousand times. 20
At every turn of the road.
Our village fell away,
Farther and farther away.
The mountains rose between us,
Steeper and steeper. 25
I know she thinks of me, far off,
And wilts with longing, like summer grass,
Maybe if the mountains would bow down
I could see her again,
Standing in our doorway. 80

CV

When she was still alive
We would go out, arm in arm,
And look at the elm trees
Growing on the embankment
In front of our house.   5
Their branches were interlaced.
Their crowns were dense with spring leaves.
They were like our love.
Love and trust were not enough to turn back
The wheels of life and death.   10
She faded like a mirage over the desert.
One morning like a bird she was gone
In the white scarves of death.
Now when the child
Whom she left in her memory   15
Cries and begs for her,
All I can do is pick him up
And hug him clumsily.
I have nothing to give him.
In our bedroom our pillows   20
Still lie side by side,
As we lay once.
I sit there by myself
And let the days grow dark.
I lie awake at night, sighing till daylight.   25
No matter how much I mourn
I shall never see her again.
They tell me her spirit
May haunt Mount Hagai
Under the eagle's wings.   80
I struggle over the ridges
And climb to the summit.
I know all the time
That I shall never see her,
Not even so much as a faint quiver in the air.   85
All my longing, all my love
Will never make any difference.

Poetry/Haiku

Translated from the Japanese by
Harold G. Henderson

The haiku *is far better known in the United States than the older* tanka. *It is even shorter than the* tanka, *being composed of three lines made up of seventeen syllables (5–7–5). Although it may look like a truncated* tanka, *it is a complete form in itself.*

Matsuo Bashō[1] (1644–1694)

Persistence

Did it yell
till it became *all* voice?
   Cicada-shell!

Clouds

Clouds come from time to time—
   and bring to men a chance to rest
      from looking at the moon.

From AN INTRODUCTION TO HAIKU, by Harold G. Henderson. Copyright © 1958 by Harold G. Henderson. Reprinted by permission of Doubleday & Company, Inc.
1. *Matsuo Bashō* (mät sù ō bä shô).

In a Wide Wasteland

On the moor: from things
    detached completely—
        how the skylark sings!

The Poor Man's Son

Poverty's child—
    he starts to grind the rice,
        and gazes at the moon.

The Sun Path

The sun's way:
    hollyhocks turn toward it
        through all the rain of May.

Summer Voices

So soon to die,
    and no sign of it showing—
        locust-cry.

Lightning at Night

A lightning gleam:
    into darkness travels
        a night heron's scream.

From AN INTRODUCTION TO HAIKU, by Harold G. Henderson. Copyright © 1958 by Harold G. Henderson. Reprinted by permission of Doubleday & Company, Inc.

Bashō 279

Taniguchi Buson [1] (1715–1783)

The Sound

Here . . . there . . .
  the sound of waterfalls is heard—
    young leaves, everywhere.

Symphony in White

Blossoms on the pear—
  and a woman in the moonlight
    reads a letter there.

Spring Breeze

These morning airs—
  one can see them stirring
    caterpillar hairs!

Summer Garments

Upon the golden screens
  gauze clothes are painted—whose?
    The autumn winds . . .

From AN INTRODUCTION TO HAIKU, by Harold G. Henderson. Copyright © 1958
by Harold G. Henderson. Reprinted by permission of Doubleday & Company, Inc.
1. *Taniguchi Buson* (tä nē gủ chē bủ sôn).

Issa [1] (1762–1826)

Contentment in Poverty

A one-foot waterfall—
   it too makes noises,
      and the night is cool.

The Great Buddha at Nara

Out from the hollow
   of Great Buddha's nose—
      comes a swallow!

Conscience

Somehow it seems wrong:
   to take one's noonday nap and hear
      a rice-planting song.

A Wish

My grumbling wife—
   if only she were here!
      This moon tonight . . .

From AN INTRODUCTION TO HAIKU, by Harold G. Henderson. Copyright © 1958
by Harold G. Henderson. Reprinted by permission of Doubleday & Company, Inc.
1. *Issa* (ē sä).

Masaoka Shiki[1] (1867–1902)

The Apprentice Priestling

A boy not ten years old
   they are giving to the temple!
      Oh, it's cold!

The New and the Old

Railroad tracks; a flight
   of wild geese close above them
      in the moonlit night.

Treasure Trove

A long-forgotten thing:
   a pot where now a flower blooms—
      this day of spring!

In the Moonlight

They look like men
   on moonlight nights—and scarecrows
      draw one's pity then.

From AN INTRODUCTION TO HAIKU, by Harold G. Henderson. Copyright © 1958
by Harold G. Henderson. Reprinted by permission of Doubleday & Company, Inc.
1. *Masaoka Shiki* (mä sä ô kä shē kē).

The Nō Play

In Japanese theater the Nō play, of which The Damask Drum *is an example, has endured for centuries. The Nō drama is as much a dance as it is a play, and the music (drums and flute) make up important elements. The acting is extremely stylized; all performances are by male actors who use masks to portray women, evil spirits, old men, and other characters. The chorus not only comments on the action and helps tell the story, but also takes over the speeches of specific characters as they pantomime or dance. By tradition the Nō stage is bare and only simple properties are used; but the characters are costumed in splendid traditional Japanese dress.*

In Japan today the old Nō plays by Seami and others are produced as originally conceived, and new Nō plays are being written. There is a loyal following of fans who take scripts along to the theater and follow the text as the play progresses, much as an opera fan might follow along with a libretto. In the early part of the twentieth century the Nō drama attracted the attention of American and English authors, including Ezra Pound and William Butler Yeats, and influenced their own poetry and plays.

Included here are two versions of The Damask Drum, *Seami's (?) original drama and a modern version by Yukio Mishima.*

Seami[1] ? (1363–1443)

THE DAMASK DRUM

Translated from the Japanese by
Arthur Waley

PERSONS

A COURTIER   AN OLD GARDENER
THE PRINCESS

COURTIER. I am a courtier at the Palace of Kinomaru in the country of
Chikuzen. You must know that in this place there is a famous pond called
the Laurel Pond, where the royal ones often take their walks; so it happened that one day the old man who sweeps the garden here caught sight
of the Princess. And from that time he has loved her with a love that
gives his heart no rest.

Someone told her of this, and she said, "Love's equal realm knows no
divisions," and in her pity she said, "By that pond there stands a laurel
tree, and on its branches there hangs a drum. Let him beat the drum, and
if the sound is heard in the Palace, he shall see my face again."

I must tell him of this.

Listen, old Gardener! The worshipful lady has heard of your love and
sends you this message: "Go and beat the drum that hangs on the tree
by the pond, and if the sound is heard in the Palace, you shall see my
face again." Go quickly now and beat the drum!

GARDENER. With trembling I receive her words. I will go and beat the
drum.

COURTIER. Look, here is the drum she spoke of. Make haste and beat it!

"Aya No Tsuzumi" from THE NŌ PLAYS OF JAPAN translated by Arthur Waley. Reprinted by permission of Grove Press, Inc. and George Allen & Unwin Ltd. All Rights
Reserved.
1. *Seami* (se ä mē).

(He leaves the GARDENER *standing by the tree and seats himself at the foot of the "Waki's pillar."* [2]*)*

GARDENER. They talk of the moon-tree, the laurel that grows in the Garden of the Moon. . . . But for me there is but one true tree, this laurel by the lake. Oh, may the drum that hangs on its branches give forth a mighty note, a music to bind up my bursting heart.

Listen! the evening bell to help me chimes;

But then tolls in

A heavy tale of day linked on to day,

CHORUS *(speaking for the* GARDENER*).* And hope stretched out from dusk to dusk

But now, a watchman of the hours, I beat

The longed-for stroke.

GARDENER. I was old, I shunned the daylight,

I was gaunt as an aged crane;

And upon all that misery

Suddenly a sorrow was heaped,

The new sorrow of love.

The days had left their marks,

Coming and coming, like waves that beat on a sandy shore . . .

CHORUS. Oh, with a thunder of white waves

The echo of the drum shall roll.

GARDENER. The afterworld draws near me,

Yet even now I wake not

From this autumn of love that closes

In sadness the sequence of my years.

CHORUS. And slow as the autumn dew

Tears gather in my eyes, to fall

Scattered like dewdrops from a shaken flower

On my coarse-woven dress.

See here the marks, imprint of tangled love,

That all the world will read.

GARDENER. I said "I will forget,"

CHORUS. And got worse torment so

Than by remembrance. But all in this world

Is as the horse of the aged man of the land of Sai [3];

---

2. *"Waki's pillar,"* a support on stage used in *Nō* plays. **3.** *the horse . . . Sai.* According to a Japanese tale a man's horse bolted and consequently was saved from being requisitioned by the government during a revolutionary period. After the revolution the man found his horse. The moral is as follows: what appears to be bad luck is sometimes good luck and vice versa.

And as a white colt flashes
Past a gap in the hedge, even so our days pass.
And though the time be come,
Yet can none know the road that he at last must tread,
Goal of his dewdrop life.
All this I knew; yet knowing,
Was blind with folly.

GARDENER. "Wake, wake," he cries,—

CHORUS. The watchman of the hours,—
"Wake from the sleep of dawn!"
And batters on the drum.
For if its sound be heard, soon shall he see
Her face, the damask of her dress . . .
Aye, damask! He does not know
That on a damask drum he beats,
Beats with all the strength of his hands, his aged hands,
But hears no sound.
"Am I grown deaf?" he cries, and listens, listens:
Rain on the windows, lapping of waves on the pool—
Both these he hears, and silent only
The drum, strange damask drum.
Oh, will it never sound?
I thought to beat the sorrow from my heart,
Wake music in a damask drum; an echo of love
From the voiceless fabric of pride!

GARDENER. Longed for as the moon that hides
In the obstinate clouds of a rainy night
Is the sound of the watchman's drum,
To roll the darkness from my heart.

CHORUS. I beat the drum. The days pass and the hours.
It was yesterday, and it is to-day.

GARDENER. But she for whom I wait

CHORUS. Comes not even in dream. At dawn and dusk

GARDENER. No drum sounds.

CHORUS. She has not come. Is it not sung that those
Whom love has joined
Not even the God of Thunder can divide?
Of lovers, I alone
Am guideless, comfortless.
Then weary of himself and calling her to witness of his woe,
"Why should I endure," he cried,

"Such life as this?" and in the waters of the pond
He cast himself and died.

(GARDENER leaves the stage.)

(Enter the PRINCESS.)

COURTIER. I would speak with you, madam.

    The drum made no sound, and the aged Gardener in despair has flung himself into the pond by the laurel tree, and died. The soul of such a one may cling to you and do you injury. Go out and look upon him.

PRINCESS (<i>speaking wildly, already possessed by the</i> GARDENER'<i>s</i> angry <i>ghost, which speaks through her</i>). Listen, people, listen!
In the noise of the beating waves
I hear the rolling of a drum.
Oh, joyful sound, oh joyful!
The music of a drum.

COURTIER. Strange, strange!
This lady speaks as one
By phantasy possessed.
What is amiss, what ails her?

PRINCESS. Truly, by phantasy I am possessed.
Can a damask drum give sound?
When I bade him beat what could not ring,
Then tottered first my wits.

COURTIER. She spoke, and on the face of the evening pool
A wave stirred.

PRINCESS. And out of the wave

COURTIER. A voice spoke.

    (<i>The voice of the</i> GARDENER <i>is heard; as he gradually advances along the hashigakari ⁴ it is seen that he wears a "demon mask," leans on a staff and carries the "demon mallet" at his girdle.</i>)

GARDENER'S GHOST. I was driftwood in the pool, but the waves of bitterness

CHORUS. Have washed me back to the shore.

GHOST. Anger clings to my heart,
Clings even now when neither wrath nor weeping
Are aught but folly.

CHORUS. One thought consumes me,
The anger of lust denied
Covers me like darkness.
I am become a demon dwelling

---

4. <i>hashigakari</i>, runway. [<i>Japanese</i>]

In the hell of my dark thoughts,
Storm cloud of my desires.
GHOST. "Though the waters parch in the fields
Though the brooks run dry,
Never shall the place be shown
Of the spring that feeds my heart."
So I had resolved. Oh, why so cruelly
Set they me to win
Voice from a voiceless drum,
Spending my heart in vain?
And I spent my heart on the glimpse of a moon that slipped
Through the boughs of an autumn tree.
CHORUS. This damask drum that hangs on the laurel tree
GHOST. Will it sound, will it sound?

    (He seizes the PRINCESS *and drags her towards the drum.)*
Try! Strike it!
CHORUS. "Strike!" he cries;
  "The quick beat, the battle-charge!
Loud, loud! Strike, strike," he rails,
And brandishing his demon stick
Gives her no rest.
"Oh woe!" the lady weeps,
"No sound, no sound. Oh misery!" she wails.
And he, at the mallet stroke, "Repent, repent!"
Such torments in the world of night
Abōrasetsu, chief of demons, wields,
Who on the Wheel of Fire
Sears sinful flesh and shatters bones to dust.
Not less her torture now!
"Oh, agony!" she cries, "What have I done,
By what dire seed this harvest sown?"
GHOST. Clear stands the cause before you.
CHORUS. Clear stands the cause before my eyes;
                         I know it now.
By the pool's white waters, upon the laurel's bough
The drum was hung.
He did not know his hour, but struck and struck
Till all the will had ebbed from his heart's core;
Then leapt into the lake and died.
And while his body rocked
Like driftwood on the waves,

His soul, an angry ghost,
Possessed the lady's wits, haunted her heart with woe.
The mallet lashed, as these waves lash the shore,
Lash on the ice of the eastern shore.
The wind passes; the rain falls
On the Red Lotus, the Lesser and the Greater.[5]
The hair stands up on my head.
"The fish that leaps the falls
To a fell snake is turned," [6]
I have learned to know them;
Such, such are the demons of the World of Night.
"O hateful lady, hateful!" he cried, and sank again
Into the whirlpool of desire.

---

5. *the rain . . . Greater.* In Buddhism the *Red Lotus* is an emblem of paradise, whereas *the Lesser and the Greater* are the names of two cold hells. Accordingly the rain falls on both the virtuous and the evil. 6. *"The fish . . . turned."* According to a legend the fish which successfully cleared a certain waterfall became a dragon. Thus, the Gardener's efforts to attain equality with the Princess have turned him into an evil spirit.

Yukio Mishima[1] (1925–1970)

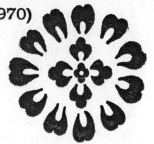

THE DAMASK DRUM

Translated from the Japanese by
Donald Keene

CHARACTERS

IWAKICHI (ē wä kē chē), *an old janitor*
KAYOKO (kä yô kô), *a girl of about 20, a clerk*
SHUNNOSUKE FUJIMA (shùn nô sù ke fù jē mä), *a teacher of Japanese dance*
TOYAMA (tô yä mä), *a young man*
KANEKO (kä ne kô), *a member of the Ministry of Foreign Affairs*
MADAME, *owner of a fashionable dressmaking establishment*
SHOP ASSISTANT, *a girl*
HANAKO TSUKIOKA (hä nä kô tsù kē ô kä)

The center of the stage is a street between buildings. Windows and signboards face each other on the third floors of the buildings on either side.

Stage-right is a third-floor law office. A musty-looking room. A room in good faith, a forthright room. There is a potted laurel tree.

Stage-left is a third-floor couturière. A room in the most modern style A room in bad faith, a deceitful room. There is a large mirror.

Spring. Evening.

(In the room to the right)

IWAKICHI *(He is sweeping the room with a broom. He sweeps up to the window).* Out of the way, out of the way. You act as if you're trying to protect the dirt around your feet.

1. *Yukio Mishima* (yù kē ô mē shē mä).

KAYOKO (*She takes a mirror from her cheap handbag and stands in the light applying a fresh coating of lipstick*). Just a minute. I'll be finished in just one minute now. (IWAKICHI *pushes up* KAYOKO's *skirt from behind with his broom.*) Oh-h-h—you're dreadful. Really. The old men these days are getting to be horrible lechers. (*She finally moves aside.*)

IWAKICHI (*sweeping*). And what about the young ladies? A girl of nineteen or twenty looks better when her lips aren't covered with all the paint. I'll bet your boy friend thinks so too.

KAYOKO (*glancing at her watch*). I can't afford expensive clothes. Lipstick's the best I can do. (*She looks at her watch again.*) Oh, I'm really sick of it. I wonder why he and I can't both get off from work at the same time. Heaven help me if I tried to kill time waiting for him anywhere outside the office. The first thing you know it'd cost money.

IWAKICHI. I've never once set foot in any of those fashionable drinking places. But they know my face in all the counter restaurants. If you want to know where the bean soup is good, just ask me. (*Pointing at the desk*) Once I invited the boss and he said it was first rate. I couldn't have been more pleased if he'd praised the bean soup in my own house.

KAYOKO. Business has not been good for the boss lately.

IWAKICHI. There're too many laws. That's why there're more lawyers than anybody knows what to do with.

KAYOKO. I wonder—when he's got such a stylish place for an office.

IWAKICHI. The boss hates anything crooked. I'm sure of that. (*Looking at a picture on the wall*) It bothers him even if that picture frame is a quarter of an inch crooked. That's why I've decided to spend the rest of my days working for him.

KAYOKO (*opening the window*). The wind's died down since evening.

IWAKICHI (*approaching the window*). I can't stand that dusty wind that blows at the beginning of spring. . . . The calm of evening. Oh, there's a good smell coming from somewhere.

KAYOKO. It's from the Chinese restaurant on the ground floor.

IWAKICHI. The prices are too high for me.

KAYOKO. Look at the beautiful sunset. It's reflected in the windows of all the buildings.

IWAKICHI. Those are pigeons from the newspaper office. Look at them scatter. Now they've formed a circle again. . . .

KAYOKO. I'm glad you're in love too. It's made you young again.

IWAKICHI. Don't be silly. My love is a one-sided affair, not like yours.

KAYOKO. You're in love with a great lady whose name you don't even know.

IWAKICHI. She's the princess of the laurel, the tree that grows in the garden of the moon.

KAYOKO *(pointing at the potted tree)*. That's the tree you mean, isn't it? There's nothing so wonderful about a laurel.

IWAKICHI. Oh! I've forgotten to water my precious laurel.   *(Exits)*

KAYOKO. Isn't he the sly one? Running off to cover his embarrassment.

IWAKICHI *(enters with a watering can)*. Laurel, I'm sorry I forgot to water you. One more effort now and you'll be covered with glossy leaves. *(As he waters the plant he strokes the leaves fondly.)* Poets often talk about hair glossy as leaves. . . .

KAYOKO. You still haven't got any answer?

IWAKICHI. Mmmm.

KAYOKO. I call that disgusting. It makes me sick. Not to have the decency to send you an answer. Nobody else but me would go on being your messenger. How many letters has it been? Thirty, isn't it? Today makes exactly thirty.

IWAKICHI. If you count in all the love letters I wrote without sending them, it'd make seventy more. For seventy days—every day I wrote her one and every day I burned it. That's what it was like before you were kind enough to take pity on me and become my postman. Let's see, that makes a total of . . . *(Thinks)*

KAYOKO. A hundred, of course. Can't you count any more?

IWAKICHI. Unrequited love is a bitter thing.

KAYOKO. You haven't the sense to give up.

IWAKICHI. Sometimes I think I'll try to forget. But I know now that trying to forget is worse than being unable to. I mean, even if being unable to forget is painful in the same way, it's still better.

KAYOKO. How did you ever get into such a state, I wonder.

(As she speaks a light is lit in the room to the left.)

IWAKICHI. They've switched on the light. Every day at the same time . . . when this room dies that one comes to life again. And in the morning when this room returns to life, that one dies. . . . It was three months ago. I'd finished sweeping and I just happened to look at the room over there, with nothing particular on my mind. . . . Then I saw her for the first time. She came into the room with her maid. The Madame was showing her the way. . . . She was wearing a coat of some kind of golden fur, and when she took it off, her dress was all black. Her hat was black too. And her hair, of course, it was black, black as the night sky. If I tried to describe to you how beautiful her face was— It was like the moon, and everything around it was shining. . . . She said a few words, then she smiled. I trembled all over. . . . She smiled. . . . I stood behind the window staring at her until she went into the fitting-room. . . . That's when it began.

KAYOKO. But she's not all that beautiful. It's her clothes—they're exquisite.

IWAKICHI. Love's not that sort of thing. It's something that shines on the one you love from the mirror of your own ugliness.

KAYOKO. In that case, even I qualify.

IWAKICHI. There's nothing for you to worry about! You look like a great beauty to your boy friend.

KAYOKO. Does that mean there's a moon for every woman in the world?

IWAKICHI. Some women are fat, and some are thin. . . . That's why there's both a full moon and a crescent.

(*Three men appear in the room to the left.* FUJIMA, TOYAMA, KANEKO.)

IWAKICHI. It'll be time soon. I've got to finish the rest of today's love letter.

KAYOKO. Hurry, won't you? I'll read a book while I wait.

(IWAKICHI *goes to the desk and finishes his letter.* KAYOKO *sits and begins to read.*)

(In the room to the left)

FUJIMA (*He carries a parcel wrapped in a purple square of cloth*). I am Shunnosuke Fujima. Very pleased to meet you.

TOYAMA. How do you do? My name is Toyama. And this is Mr. Kaneko from the Ministry of Foreign Affairs. (*Introduces the men*) Mr. Fujima.

KANEKO. How do you do?

FUJIMA. You and Mr. Kaneko seem to be old friends.

TOYAMA. Yes. He was at the same school, but ahead of me.

FUJIMA. Oh, really? . . . My pupils are about to put on a dance-play. (*Hands them leaflets*) Please take these. . . . Mrs. Tsukioka said she would buy a hundred tickets.

TOYAMA (*jealously*). Mrs. Tsukioka wouldn't do that unless she were sure of making a profit.

KANEKO. No, she's not like you. She's the kind who makes losses, never a profit.

FUJIMA. Yes, that's the kind of person she really is.

KANEKO (*firmly*). I am perfectly well aware what kind of person she is.

FUJIMA (*changing the subject*). The plot of the dance-play is charming, if I must say so myself.

TOYAMA (*looking at his watch*). She's late, isn't she? Summoning people here like that. . . . It's bad taste to keep a man waiting in a dress shop.

KANEKO. In the reign of Louis XIV they used to receive men in their boudoirs. And when a man wanted to compliment a woman he'd say something like "Who does the shading under your eyes?" *(He says it in French.)*

FUJIMA. Excuse me? What was that?

(KANEKO translates word for word. TOYAMA looks the other way.)

FUJIMA. Shading under a woman's eyes is a lovely thing, isn't it? Like clouds hovering under the moon, you might say.

KANEKO *(interested only in what he himself has to say)*. That's the secret of all diplomacy. To ask who did the shading under a woman's eyes when you know perfectly well she did it herself.

TOYAMA. Mr. Kaneko is about to become an ambassador.

FUJIMA *(bowing)*. Congratulations.

(In the room to the right)

IWAKICHI. I've written it. It's done. And very good this time.

KAYOKO. It must be a terrific strain always thinking up new things to say.

IWAKICHI. This is one of the more agreeable hardships of love.

KAYOKO. I'll leave it on my way home.

IWAKICHI. Sorry to bother you, Kayoko. Please don't lose it.

KAYOKO. You talk as if it wasn't just across the street. I couldn't lose it even if I wanted to. . . . Good night.

IWAKICHI. Good night, Kayoko.

KAYOKO *(waving the letter as she stands in the door)*. Maybe I will forget about the letter after all. I'm in a big hurry myself, you know.

IWAKICHI. You mustn't tease an old man like that.

(In the room to the left)

KANEKO. She certainly is late.

TOYAMA *(He stands in front of the mirror and fiddles with his necktie)*. Mrs. Tsukioka's taste in neckties always runs to something like this. I really hate loud ties.

FUJIMA. This is a tobacco case Mrs. Tsukioka gave me when I succeeded as head of the company. The *netsuké* [2] is more valuable than the case itself. Just have a look at it. *(He holds it up to the light.)* You'd never think it was made entirely of wood, would you? It's exactly like ivory, isn't it?

KANEKO. We civil servants must refuse all presents. There's always the suspicion of bribery. I envy artists.

---

2. *netsuké* (net sù ke), a small piece of sculpture fastened onto a pouch or case. [*Japanese*]

FUJIMA. Everybody says that.

TOYAMA (in a tearful voice). Damned old woman! Why should she have invited everybody except me?

KAYOKO (out of breath). Oh, excuse me. Is the Madame here?

TOYAMA. She went to the shop a couple of minutes ago. I think she had some business to do.

KAYOKO. Now what am I going to do?

TOYAMA. Is it something urgent?

KAYOKO. Yes. It's a letter. I give one to Madame every day, at somebody's request. . . .

KANEKO (haughtily). I'll take care of it.

KAYOKO (hesitantly). It's very kind of you. . . .

KANEKO. I'll accept responsibility.

KAYOKO. I'm much obliged. Please. (Exits)

TOYAMA. What a terrific hurry that girl is in!

KANEKO (He reads the address on the envelope). Well, I never! It says "To the princess of the laurel of the moon."

FUJIMA. Very romantic, isn't it?

KANEKO. You didn't write it yourself, by any chance?

FUJIMA. You're joking. When a dancing teacher has the time to write love letters, he holds hands instead.

KANEKO. The sender is one Iwakichi.

FUJIMA. He writes a very good hand, whoever he is.

TOYAMA. Just imagine—calling the Madame a "princess of the laurel of the moon"! I don't think I've ever seen a laurel. Is it a very big tree?

FUJIMA. Only around the middle, I think.

KANEKO. There's no accounting for tastes, is there? Let's see—there's a French expression something like that—

MADAME (Enters. She is unusually tall). It's so good to find you all here.

TOYAMA. A love letter's come for you.

MADAME. I wonder who it can be from. There are five or six gentlemen who might be sending me one.

KANEKO. Your affairs are touch-and-go, I take it?

MADAME. Yes, that's right. I never forget my defenses.

TOYAMA. Your armor must take a lot of material.

MADAME. Darling boy! You always say such amusing things.

FUJIMA (dramatically). "The princess of the laurel of the moon," I presume?

MADAME. Oh, is that the love letter you're talking about? In that case, it's not for me.

KANEKO. Don't try to fool us.

MADAME. You're quite mistaken. It's for Mrs. Tsukioka.

ALL. What?

MADAME (sitting). These letters are driving me simply frantic. They're from the janitor who works in the building across the street. An old man almost seventy. He's fallen in love with Mrs. Tsukioka, from having seen her through the window.

KANEKO. That doesn't surprise me. They say that the aged tend to be far-sighted. (He laughs, amused at his own joke.) I can't wait to grow old. It must be very convenient being far-sighted.

MADAME. The old man has sent her dozens—no, hundreds—of letters.

TOYAMA. If he sent out all his letters to different women, one of them might have been successful.

KANEKO. There's something in what you say. But if, after all, love were a question of probability, the probability for one woman might be the same as the probability for innumerable women.

FUJIMA. Have you shown her the letters? Mrs. Tsukioka, I mean.

MADAME. How could I possibly show them to her? I've used them all as comb wipers.

TOYAMA. Do combs get as dirty as all that?

MADAME. They're for my dogs' combs. I have five wire-haired fox terriers. They shut their eyes in positive rapture when I comb them.

KANEKO. Which runs faster—love or a dog?

FUJIMA. Which gets dirty faster?

MADAME. It makes me quite giddy to talk with such enchanting men.

KANEKO. Sidetracked again. What's happened to the love letters?

MADAME. This is what has happened. The one who's been delivering the letters is that sweet girl from the office across the way.

TOYAMA. The girl who was just here? What's sweet about her?

MADAME. She's a well-behaved, good girl, and I've become so fond of her that I've been accepting the letters every day. But I've never dreamed of giving one to Mrs. Tsukioka.

KANEKO. If the girl knew that, she'd never give you another one.

MADAME. You'll have to excuse me. Just put yourself in my place. If Mrs. Tsukioka should read them and get upset—

(Knock at the door)

MADAME. Now what shall I do? It's Mrs. Tsukioka.

KANEKO. Attention. (HANAKO enters.) Salute!

TOYAMA (clutching her). It's cruel of you. To be late again.

FUJIMA. We were expecting you at any minute.

MADAME. You always look lovely, no matter how often I see you.

(HANAKO does not answer. She smilingly removes her gloves.)

MADAME *(trying to take the initiative).* Everybody's been waiting so impatiently I don't want to waste another minute. We'll start the fitting at once. *(She examines* HANAKO *from the front and from behind.)* A dressy model really suits your naturally elegant line best, Mrs. Tsukioka. But in a spring suit, you know, I think we should try for a different effect. With your figure you can carry off something sporty. This time I've been really daring in the cut. The lines are simple, divinely simple. Just the barest of pleats on the sides of the waist, as you suggested. Very effective in bringing out the accents. . . . And now, would you mind stepping into the fitting-room? We can have a leisurely cup of coffee afterward.

KANEKO. A love letter came for you, Mrs. Tsukioka. Guess how old the man is who sent it. Twenty? Thirty? Older?

(HANAKO holds up one finger.)

TOYAMA. No, no. He's not a high-school student.

(HANAKO with a smile holds up two fingers. The others shake their heads. She holds up one more finger each time until finally, with a look of incredulity on her face, she holds up seven.)

KANEKO. You've guessed it, at last. A blushing seventy. I'm told he's the janitor in the building across the street.

(The MADAME, *flustered, lowers the blinds.* IWAKICHI, *in the room to the right, stares fixedly at the shut window. During the interval* KANEKO *hands the letter to* HANAKO. *She opens it. The others stand behind her and read over her shoulder.)*

TOYAMA *(reads).* "Please read this thirtieth expression of my love, and take it to your heart," it says. Madame's been lying again. She said there were hundreds of letters. You know, Mrs. Tsukioka, the Madame has embezzled all the previous letters.

KANEKO *(reads).* "My love grows only the stronger as the days go by. To heal the scars of the whip of love which torments my aged body from morn to night, I ask for one, for just one kiss." Isn't that touching? All he wants is one little kiss.

(They all burst into laughter.)

TOYAMA. Just one kiss? He's very modest in his demands.

FUJIMA. It really surprises me. The old men nowadays are younger at heart than we are.

MADAME. Is that the sort of thing he's been writing? I confess I haven't read any of his other efforts. *(The letter is passed to her.)* Oh, dear. *(Reads)* "That which we call love is an eternal, unending sorrow." Trite, isn't it? He might just as well say: "That which we call vinegar, unlike honey, is an unending source of bitterness."

KANEKO. This old man thinks he's the only one who's suffering. Such conceit is detestable. All of us are suffering in exactly the same way. The only difference is that some people talk about it and others don't.

FUJIMA. That's because we have self-respect, isn't it?

TOYAMA. Even I can understand that much. I can't bear that tone which implies that he's the only one who knows real love, and the rest of us are all frivolous and fickle.

KANEKO. I'd be glad to show anyone who's willing to be shown how much repeated suffering we have to endure just in order to fool ourselves, all of us who are living in these depraved times.

FUJIMA. There's nothing you can do about people who are set in their ways. He must think there are special reserved seats for love.

TOYAMA. A romanticist.

MADAME. Little boys should not interfere in the conversation of grown-ups. The argument has become serious. *(She rings a bell.)* Isn't it enchanting, Mrs. Tsukioka, how heated men get over an argument?

KANEKO *(as if he were delivering a speech)*. I believe I may state without fear of contradiction that we are convinced that entities like this old man are abhorrent, and that such entities cannot further be tolerated by us— entities, that is, who believe in genuine feelings. There is not a village, no matter how remote, where the genuine and original Nagasaki sponge cake is not sold. I despise any shopkeeper who would really believe such nonsense and fatuously sell the cake as the genuine article. It is far better to sell it knowing all along that it is fake. That makes the sale a cheat and a fraud, the splendid product of a conscious human mind. We have tongues to recognize the taste of the sponge cake. Our loves begin from the tongue.

MADAME. How erotic!

KANEKO. The tongue admits the existence of no "genuine," of no "original." What it depends on is the sense of taste common to all men. The tongue can say: "This tastes good." Its natural modesty forbids it to say more. The "genuine and original" is merely a label people paste on the wrapping. The tongue confines itself to determining whether or not the sponge cake tastes good.

SHOP ASSISTANT *(enters)*. Did you ring?

MADAME. It wasn't for sponge cake. What was it? Oh yes, please bring five cups of coffee immediately.

ASSISTANT. Yes, Madame.

KANEKO. All questions are relative. Love is the architecture of the emotion of disbelief in genuine articles. That old man, on the other hand, is impure, polluted—he's making fools of us. He is delighted with himself, inflated with pride.

FUJIMA. I'm afraid what you say is much too difficult for someone like myself, who's never had an education, to follow, but I was told by my teacher that all disputes about who was the senior member of a company or which was the oldest tradition in a dance have nothing whatsoever to do with art. He said that the only true atmosphere for the dance is one where the gesture to the front and the gesture to the rear can be performed in absolute freedom. . . . That old man is so anxious to found a school for himself that he *(mimes dance action)* . . . one and two and over to the side . . . neglects the free, unconfined realms of the ecstasy of love.

TOYAMA. And what do you think about all this, Mrs. Tsukioka? It isn't very nice of you to keep so silent. But I suppose it isn't entirely distasteful to receive love letters even from such an old man. Isn't that the case? Say something, laurel of the moon.

MADAME. Mrs. Tsukioka had a refined upbringing, and I'm sure she dislikes arguments.

TOYAMA. But she's very fond of tormenting people all the same.

MADAME. That's a taste common to all beautiful women.

FUJIMA. And one which only becomes beautiful women, they say.

MADAME. When it comes to colors, the ones which suit her best are the difficult ones like green.

KANEKO. Those, of course, are the colors she doesn't wear in public. She saves them for her nightgowns, and pretends she doesn't know they become her.

TOYAMA. I can testify that Mrs. Tsukioka never wears green nightgowns.

KANEKO. You've become increasingly cheeky of late.

MADAME. Come, come.

(THE ASSISTANT *enters with the coffee. They all drink unhurriedly.)*

(In the room to the right)

IWAKICHI. I wonder what's the matter. Why don't they open the curtains? Oh, the suspense. All I could get was just the barest glimpse of her. . . . And I was so sure that tonight she would take pity on me and at least stand at the window and smile at me, like a picture in a frame. . . . But I'm still not giving up hope. . . . No, I won't give up hope.

(In the room to the left)

KANEKO. Well, now.

FUJIMA. Oops. *(He spills coffee on his lap and wipes it.)*

KANEKO. What is it?

FUJIMA. Just now as I was drinking my coffee, a fine idea came to me.

KANEKO. I have also been considering what we might do to teach that old man a little lesson. What do you say, Mrs. Tsukioka? In general . . .

FUJIMA. My plan was . . .

KANEKO (paying him no attention). In general, such entities are incapable of seeing the light unless they have once been administered a sound thrashing. We need show him no pity simply because he's an old man. It is essential to make him realize that where he lives is a little room nobody will enter.

TOYAMA. You mean, human beings won't go in a dog's house?

KANEKO (recovering his good mood). Yes, exactly.

FUJIMA. My plan is this. (He unfolds the parcel wrapped in purple silk, revealing a small hand drum.) Do you see this?

MADAME. It's a drum, isn't it?

FUJIMA. It's a prop for my forthcoming dance-play. Oh, since I mentioned the play, I must thank you, Mrs. Tsukioka . . . the tickets. . . . At any rate, about the drum. Shall I beat it for you? (He beats it.) You see, it doesn't make the least sound. It looks exactly like a real drum, but instead of a skin, which is essential of course, it's covered with damask.

TOYAMA. You mean they've invented a drum that doesn't make any noise?

FUJIMA. No, as I was saying, it's a prop.

KANEKO. And what do you propose to do with it?

FUJIMA. To attach a note to this drum and throw it into the old man's room. I've had the most wonderful idea about what to write in the note.

MADAME. That sounds fascinating. Tell us.

FUJIMA. In the note we should write: "Please beat this drum." Do you follow me? "Please beat this drum. If the sound of your drum can be heard in this room above the street noises, I will grant your wish." That's all.

TOYAMA. Excellent idea! That will take the old man down a peg or two.

KANEKO. Don't you think you ought to add: "If the sound doesn't reach me, your wish will not be granted"?

FUJIMA. There's such a thing as an implied meaning.

KANEKO. In diplomatic correspondence you can't be too careful.

FUJIMA (excitedly). Don't you think it's a good plan, Mrs. Tsukioka? I'll be glad to sacrifice this prop to protect you.

TOYAMA. For a customer who buys a hundred tickets, what's one drum?

FUJIMA. I'll thank you not to interpret it in that way. Mrs. Tsukioka, you do agree, don't you? (HANAKO nods smilingly.)

MADAME. It will be a great relief to me too. This will probably be the last day the old man will bother us.

FUJIMA. Let's have some paper and a pen.

(They set about their preparations with animation. FUJIMA *writes a note to attach to the drum. The* MADAME *draws the curtains.* HANAKO *is led to the window, which* KANEKO *opens.)*

KANEKO. His room is pitch dark. Are you sure the old man is there?

MADAME. The girl who comes as his messenger says that he stares at this window until Mrs. Tsukioka leaves.

KANEKO. Still, I wonder if our voices will reach him.

TOYAMA. That'll be my responsibility. Oh, doesn't it look pretty up here to see the neon lights everywhere?

FUJIMA. Who will throw the drum?

KANEKO. I will. I was quite a renowned pitcher in my high-school days. *(He limbers his arm by way of preparation.)*

TOYAMA. Hey! Iwakichi! Open your window!

(The window opens. IWAKICHI *timidly shows himself.)*

TOYAMA. Can you hear me? We're going to throw you something. Be sure to catch it.

*(*IWAKICHI *nods.* KANEKO *throws the drum.* IWAKICHI *barely gets it. He takes the drum to the desk.)*

IWAKICHI. What can this mean? She's sent me a drum. She's standing at the window looking at me. It's strange, when she looks straight this way it's all I can do to keep from hiding myself. I wonder if she's always hidden herself from me because I stared too much. . . . Oh, there's a note attached. *(Reads)* At last my wish will be granted! What carries better than the sound of a drum, even above the traffic noise? It must be her elegant way of saying things—she can't pronounce a simple yes, but has to say it in some roundabout manner. . . . Oh, my heart hurts. It's never known such joy before. It's weak, like the stomach of a poor man's child before a feast. It hurts because it's been struck by happiness. . . . They're all waiting in the window over there. It must be for the fun of it. They think it will be amusing to hear an old man play the drum for the first time. . . . Ah, I've a good idea. I'll hang the drum on my laurel tree and beat it there. *(He kneels before the tree.)* Laurel, lovely, dear laurel, forgive me. I'm going to hang the drum in your green hair. Heavy, is it? Just be patient for a while. It becomes you. It becomes you very well, like a big beautiful ornament that has fallen from heaven into your hair. . . . It's all right, isn't it? Even when I begin to beat the drum, I won't shake your leaves. I've never before been so happy before you. Whenever I've seen you I've thought: My unhappiness has made you more beautiful, has made you put forth your leaves more abundantly. And it's true, my laurel, it's true.

TOYAMA. Hurry up and beat the drum. We're standing in the cold waiting for you.

IWAKICHI. All right! I'm going to beat it now, so listen! *(He strikes the drum. It makes no sound. He strikes the other side. It is also silent. He strikes frantically but to no avail.)* It doesn't make a noise. They've given me a drum that doesn't make a noise! I've been made a fool of. I've been played with. *(He sinks to the floor and weeps.)* What shall I do? What shall I do? A refined lady like that—to play such a low trick on me. It's something that should never have happened. It couldn't have happened. *(The people at the window to the left laugh. The window is slammed shut.)* Laugh! Go ahead and laugh! Laugh all you like! . . . You'll still be laughing when you die. You'll be laughing when you rot away. That won't happen to me. People who are laughed at don't die just like that. . . . People who are laughed at don't rot away. *(He opens the window at the back. Climbs out on the window sill. He sits there motionlessly for a minute, sadly staring below. Then he pushes himself over the edge in a crumbling gesture. Shouts from below. Inarticulate cries from the crowd continue awhile.)*

(In the room to the left they are all chatting and laughing. They cannot see the window from which the old man committed suicide, and they are unaware what has happened. Suddenly the door opens.)

ASSISTANT. The janitor from the building across the way has just jumped out of the window and killed himself.

(They get up with confused outcries. Some rush to the window, others run toward the stairs. HANAKO stands alone rigidly in the center of the stage.)

(Late at night. The sky between the two buildings is now full of stars. A clock on a shelf in the room to the left gives forth two delicate chimes. The room is pitch dark. Presently there is a scratching sound of a key in the door. The door opens. A flashlight beam shines in. HANAKO enters. She wears a half-length coat thrown over the shoulders of her evening gown. In one hand she holds a key, in the other a flashlight. She puts the key in her handbag. She goes to the window, opens it, and stares motionlessly at the window on the right.)

HANAKO *(Her voice is low. She talks as if to someone present)*. I've come. You told me to come and I've come. I slipped out of a party, even though it was the middle of the night. . . . Answer me, please. Aren't you there?

(The window at the back of the room to the right opens. The ghost of IWAKICHI *climbs in the window from which he jumped. He walks to the left. The window facing left gradually opens as he approaches it.)*

HANAKO. You've come. . . . You've really come.

IWAKICHI. I've been going back and forth between your dreams and this room.

HANAKO. You summoned me and I am here. But you still do not know me. You don't know how I was able to come.

IWAKICHI. Because I drew you here.

HANAKO. No. Without human strength no door opens for human beings to pass through.

IWAKICHI. Do you intend to deceive even a ghost?

HANAKO. Where would I get the strength? My strength was enough only to kill a pitiful old man. And even in that all I did was to nod. I did nothing else. *(*IWAKICHI *does not answer.)* Can you hear me? *(*IWAKICHI *nods.)* My voice carries even when I speak as low as this. But when I talk to people they can't hear me unless I shout. . . . It would have been better if voices had not carried between this room and yours.

IWAKICHI. The sky is full of stars. You can't see the moon. The moon has become covered with mud and fallen to earth. I was following the moon when I jumped. You might say that the moon and I committed suicide together.

HANAKO *(looking down at the street).* Can you see the corpse of the moon anywhere? I can't. Only the all-night taxis cruising in the streets. There's a policeman walking there. He's stopped. But I don't think that means he's found a corpse. The policeman won't meet anything except the policeman who comes from the opposite direction. Is he a mirror, I wonder?

IWAKICHI. Do you think that ghosts meet only ghosts, and the moon meets only the moon?

HANAKO. In the middle of the night that's true of everything. *(She lights a cigarette.)*

IWAKICHI. I'm not a phantom any more. While I was alive I was a phantom. Now all that remains is what I used to dream about. Nobody can disappoint me any more.

HANAKO. From what I can see, however, you still aren't precisely the incarnation of love. I don't mean to criticize your growth of beard or your janitor's uniform or your sweaty undershirt— There's something lacking, something your love needs before it can assume a form. There's insufficient proof that your love in this world was real, if that was the only reason why you died.

IWAKICHI. Do you want proof from a ghost? *(He empties his pockets.)*

Ghosts don't own anything. I've lost every possession which might have served as proof.

HANAKO. I am teeming with proofs. A woman simply crawls with proofs of love. When she has produced the last one, she is full of proofs that the love is gone. It's because women have the proofs that men can make love empty-handed.

IWAKICHI. Please don't show me such things.

HANAKO. A little while ago I opened the door and came in, didn't I? Where do you suppose I got the key to the door?

IWAKICHI. Please don't ask me such things.

HANAKO. I stole the key from Madame's pocket. My fingers are very nimble, you know. It gave me great pleasure to discover my skill at pickpocketing has still not left me.

IWAKICHI. I understand now. You're afraid of my tenacity, and you're trying to make me hate you. That must be it.

HANAKO. Then shall I show you? You gave me a very appropriate name, princess of the moon. I used otherwise to be known by the nickname of Crescent, from a tattoo on my belly. The tattoo of a crescent.

IWAKICHI. Ah-h-h.

HANAKO. It wasn't that I asked to have it tattooed myself. A man did it, violently. When I drink the crescent turns a bright red, but usually it is pale as a dead man's face.

IWAKICHI. Whore! You've made a fool of me twice. Once wasn't enough.

HANAKO. Once wasn't enough. Yes, that's right, it wasn't. For our love to be fulfilled, or for it to be destroyed.

IWAKICHI. You were poisoned by men who were untrue.

HANAKO. That's not so. Men who were untrue molded me.

IWAKICHI. I was made a fool of because I was true.

HANAKO. That's not so. You were made a fool of because you were old.

(*The room to the right becomes red with the wrath of the ghost. The laurel tree on which the drum had been hung appears in the glow.*)

IWAKICHI. Don't you feel ashamed of yourself? I'll place a curse on you.

HANAKO. That doesn't frighten me in the least. I'm strong now. It's because I've been loved.

IWAKICHI. By whom?

HANAKO. By you.

IWAKICHI. Was it the strength of my love that made you tell the truth?

HANAKO. Look at me. It's not the real me you love. (*She laughs.*) You tried to place a curse on me. Clumsy men are all like that.

IWAKICHI. No, no. I am in love with you, passionately. Everybody in the world of the dead knows it.

HANAKO. Nobody knows it in this world.

IWAKICHI. Because the drum didn't sound?

HANAKO. Yes, because I couldn't hear it.

IWAKICHI. It was the fault of the drum. A damask drum makes no noise.

HANAKO. It wasn't the fault of the drum that it didn't sound.

IWAKICHI. I yearn for you, even now.

HANAKO. Even now! You've been dead all of a week.

IWAKICHI. I yearn for you. I shall try to make the drum sound.

HANAKO. Make it sound. I have come to hear it.

IWAKICHI. I will. My love will make a damask drum thunder. *(The ghost of* IWAKICHI *strikes the drum. It gives forth a full sound.)* It sounded! It sounded! You heard it, didn't you?

HANAKO *(smiling slyly)*. I can't hear a thing.

IWAKICHI. You can't hear this? It's not possible. Look. I'll strike it once for every letter I wrote you. Once, twice, you can hear it, I know, three, four, the drum has sounded. *(The drum sounds.)*

HANAKO. I can't hear it. Where is a drum sounding?

IWAKICHI. You can't hear it? You're lying. You can't hear this? Ten, eleven. You can't hear this?

HANAKO. I can't. I can't hear any drum.

IWAKICHI. It's a lie! *(In a fury)* I won't let you say it—that you can't hear what I can. Twenty, twenty-one. It's sounded.

HANAKO. I can't hear it. I can't hear it.

IWAKICHI. Thirty, thirty-one, thirty-two. . . . You can't say you don't hear it. The drum is beating. A drum that never should have sounded is sounding.

HANAKO. Ah, hurry and sound it. My ears are longing to hear the drum.

IWAKICHI. Sixty-six, sixty-seven. . . . Could it possibly be that only my ears can hear the drum?

HANAKO *(in despair, to herself)*. Ah, he's just the same as living men.

IWAKICHI *(in despair, to himself)*. Who can prove it—that she hears the drum?

HANAKO. I can't hear it. I still can't hear it.

IWAKICHI *(weakly)*. Eighty-nine, ninety, ninety-one. . . . It will soon be over. Have I only imagined I heard the sound of the drum? *(The drum goes on sounding.)* It's useless. A waste of time. The drum won't sound at all, will it? Beat it and beat it as I may, it's a damask drum.

HANAKO. Hurry, strike it so I can hear. Don't give up. Hurry, so it strikes my ears. *(She stretches her hand from the window.)* Don't give up!

IWAKICHI. Ninety-four, ninety-five. . . . Completely useless. The drum doesn't make a sound. What's the use of beating a drum that is silent?

. . . Ninety-six, ninety-seven. . . . Farewell, my laurel princess, fare-well. . . . Ninety-eight, ninety-nine. . . . Farewell, I've ended the hundred strokes. . . . Farewell.

(The ghost disappears. The beating stops. HANAKO *stands alone, an empty look on her face.* TOYAMA *rushes in excitedly.)*

TOYAMA. Is that where you've been? Oh, I'm so relieved. . . . We've all been out searching for you. What happened to you? Running off like that in the middle of the night. What happened to you? *(He shakes her.)* Get a hold on yourself.

HANAKO *(as in a dream).* I would have heard if he had only struck it once more.

CURTAIN

Prose

Akutagawa Ryūnosuké[1] (1892-1927)

HELL SCREEN

Translated from the Japanese by
W. H. H. Norman

1

I DOUBT WHETHER there will ever be another man like the Lord of
Horikawa. Certainly there has been no one like him till now. Some say that
a Guardian King appeared to her ladyship his mother in a dream before he
was born; at least it is true that from the day he was born he was a most
extraordinary person. Nothing he did was commonplace; he was constantly
startling people. You have only to glance at a plan of Horikawa to perceive
its grandeur. No ordinary person would ever have dreamt of the boldness
and daring with which it was conceived.

But it certainly was not his lordship's intention merely to glorify himself; he was generous, he did not forget the lower classes; he wanted the
whole country to enjoy itself when he did.

There is the story about the famous Kawara Palace at Higashi Sanjō. It
was said that the ghost of Tōru, Minister of the Left, appeared there night
after night until his lordship exorcised it by rebuking it. Such was his
prestige in the capital that everyone, man, woman, and child, regarded
him, with good reason, as a god incarnate. Once, as he was returning in his

---

"Hell Screen" by Akutagawa Ryūnosuké, translated by W. H. H. Norman from MODERN
JAPANESE LITERATURE, edited by Donald Keene. Published by Grove Press, Inc. Reprinted by permission of W. H. H. Norman.
1. *Akutagawa Ryūnosuké* (ă kù tä gä wä ryù nô sù ke). In naming the authors of these
selections, the Japanese practice of placing the surname before the first name has been observed except in the case of Junichiro Tanizaki and Yukio Mishima.

carriage from the Feast of the Plum Blossoms, his ox got loose and injured an old man who happened to be passing. But the latter, they say, put his hands together in reverence and was actually grateful that he had been knocked over by an ox of his lordship.

Thus, there are the makings of many good stories in the life of his lordship. At a certain banquet he made a presentation of thirty white horses; another time he gave a favorite boy to be the human pillar of Nagara Bridge. There would be no end if I started to tell them all. Numerous as these anecdotes are, I doubt if there are any that match in horror the story of the making of the Hell Screen, one of the most valuable treasures in the house. His lordship is not easily upset, but that time he seemed to be startled. How much more terrified, then, were we who served him; we feared for our very souls. As for me, I had served him for twenty years, but when I witnessed that dreadful spectacle I felt that such a thing could never have happened before. But in order to tell this story, I must first tell about Yoshihide,[2] who painted the Hell Screen.

2

YOSHIHIDE is, I expect, remembered by many even today. In his time he was a famous painter surpassed by no contemporary. He would be about fifty then, I imagine. He was cross-grained, and not much to look at: short of stature, a bag of skin and bones, and his youthful red lips made him seem even more evil, as though he were some sort of animal. Some said it was because he put his reddened paint brush to his lips, but I doubt this. Others, more unkind, said that his appearance and movements suggested a monkey. And that reminds me of this story. Yoshihide's only daughter, Yūzuki, a charming girl of fifteen, quite unlike her father, was at that time a maid in Horikawa. Probably owing to the fact that her mother had died while she was still very small, Yūzuki was sympathetic and intelligent beyond her years, and greatly petted by her ladyship and her attendants in consequence.

About that time it happened that someone presented a tame monkey from Tamba. The mischievous young lord called it Yoshihide. The monkey was a comical-looking beast, anyway; with this name, nobody in the mansion could resist laughing at him. But they did more than that. If he climbed the pine tree in the garden, or soiled the mats, whatever he did they teased him, shouting, "Yoshihide, Yoshihide."

One day Yūzuki was passing along one of the long halls with a note in a twig of red winter-plum blossom when the monkey appeared from behind a sliding door, fleeing as fast as he could. Apparently he had dislocated a leg,

---

2. *Yoshihide* (yô shē hē de).

for he limped, unable, it seemed, to climb a post with his usual agility. After him came the young lord, waving a switch, shouting, "Stop thief! Orange thief!" Yūzuki hesitated a moment, but it gave the fleeing monkey a chance to climb to her skirt, crying most piteously. Suddenly she felt she could not restrain her pity. With one hand she still held the plum branch, with the other, the sleeve of her mauve kimono sweeping in a half-circle, she picked the monkey up gently. Then bending before the young lord, she said sweetly, "I crave your pardon. He is only an animal. Be kind enough to pardon him, my lord."

But he had come running with his temper up; he frowned and stamped his foot two or three times. "Why do you protect him? He has stolen some oranges."

"But he is only an animal." She repeated it; then after a little, smiling sadly, "And since you call him Yoshihide, it is as if my father were being punished. I couldn't bear to see it," she said boldly. This defeated the young lord.

"Well, if you're pleading for your father's skin, I'll pardon him," he said reluctantly, "against my better judgment." Dropping the switch, he turned and went back through the sliding door through which he had come.

3

Yūzuki and the monkey were devoted to each other from that day. She hung a golden bell that she had received from the Princess by a bright red cord around the monkey's neck, and the monkey would hardly let her out of his sight. Once, for instance, when she caught cold and took to her bed, the monkey, apparently much depressed, sat immovable by her pillow, gnawing his nails.

Another strange thing was that from that time the monkey was not teased as badly as before. On the contrary, they began to pet him and even the young lord would occasionally toss him a persimmon or a chestnut. Once he got quite angry when he caught a samurai [3] kicking the monkey. As for his lordship, they say that when he heard his son was protecting the monkey from abuse, he had Yūzuki appear before him with the monkey in her arms. On that occasion he must have heard why she had made a pet of the monkey.

"You're a filial girl. I'll reward you for it," he said, and gave her a crimson ceremonial kimono. Whereupon the monkey with the greatest deference mimicked her acceptance of the kimono. That greatly tickled his lordship. Thus the girl who befriended the monkey became a favorite of his

---

3. *samurai*, a member of a hereditary military class in feudal Japan.

lordship, because he admired her filial piety—not, as rumor had it, because he was too fond of her. There may have been some grounds for this rumor, but of that I shall tell later. It should be enough to say that the Lord of Horikawa was not the sort of person to fall in love with an artist's daughter, no matter how beautiful she was.

Thus honored, Yoshihide's daughter withdrew from his presence. Since she was wise and good, the other maids were not jealous of her. Rather she and her monkey became more popular than ever, particularly, they say, with the Princess, from whom she was hardly ever separated. She invariably accompanied her in her pleasure carriage.

However, we must leave the daughter awhile and turn to the father. Though the monkey was soon being petted by everybody, they all disliked the great Yoshihide. This was not limited to the mansion folk only. The Abbot of Yokogawa hated him, and if Yoshihide were mentioned would change color as though he had encountered a devil. (That was after Yoshihide had drawn a caricature of the Abbot, according to the gossip of the domestics, which, after all, may have been nothing more than gossip.) Anyhow, the man was unpopular with anyone you met. If there were some who did not speak badly of him, they were but two or three fellow-artists, or people who knew his pictures, but not the man.

Yoshihide was not only very repellent in appearance: people disliked him more because of his habits. No one was to blame for his unpopularity except himself.

4

HE WAS STINGY, he was bad-tempered, he was shameless, he was lazy, he was greedy, but worst of all, he was arrogant and contemptuous, certain that he was the greatest artist in the country.

If he had been proud only of his work it would not have been so bad, but he despised everything, even the customs and amenities of society.

It was in character, therefore, that when he was making a picture of the Goddess of Beauty he should paint the face of a common harlot, and that for Fudō [4] he should paint a villainous ex-convict. The models he chose were shocking. When he was taken to task for it, he said coolly, "It would be strange if the gods and buddhas I have given life with my brush should punish me."

His apprentices were appalled when they thought of the dreadful fate in store for him, and many left his studio. It was pride—he imagined himself to be the greatest man in Japan.

---

4. *Fudō*, in Japanese Buddhism (see footnote 2, page 39) a god of righteousness and subduer of demons.

In short, though exceptionally gifted, he behaved much above his station. Among artists who were not on good terms with him, many maintained that he was a charlatan, because his brushwork and coloring were so unusual. Look at the door paintings of the famous artists of the past! You can almost smell the perfume of the plum blossom on a moonlit night; you can almost hear some courtier on a screen playing his flute. That is how they gained their reputation for surpassing beauty. Yoshihide's pictures were reputed to be always weird or unpleasant. For instance, he painted the "Five Aspects of Life and Death" on Ryugai Temple gate, and they say if you pass the gate at night you can hear the sighing and sobbing of the divinities he depicted there. Others say you can smell rotting corpses. Or when, at the command of his lordship, he painted the portraits of some of his household women, within three years everyone of them sickened as though her spirit had left her, and died. Those who spoke ill of Yoshihide regarded this as certain proof that his pictures were done by means of the black art.

Yoshihide delighted in his reputation for perversity. Once, when his lordship said to him jokingly, "You seem to like the ugly," Yoshihide's unnaturally red lips curled in an evil laugh. "I do. Daubers usually cannot understand the beauty of ugly things," he said contemptuously.

But Yoshihide, the unspeakably unscrupulous Yoshihide, had one tender human trait.

5

And that was his affection for his only child, whom he loved passionately. As I said before, Yūzuki was gentle, and deeply devoted to her father, but his love for her was not inferior to her devotion to him. Does it not seem incredible that the man who never gave a donation to a temple could have provided such kimono and hairpins for his daughter with reckless disregard of cost?

But Yoshihide's affection for Yūzuki was nothing more than the emotion. He gave no thought, for instance, to finding her a good husband. Yet he certainly would have hired roughs to assassinate anyone who made improper advances to her. Therefore, when she became a maid at Horikawa, at the command of his lordship, Yoshihide took it very badly; and even when he appeared before the daimyo,[5] he sulked for awhile. The rumor that, attracted by her beauty, his lordship had tasted her delights in spite of her father, was largely the guess of those who noted Yoshihide's displeasure.

Of course, even if the rumor were false it was clear that the intensity of his affection made Yoshihide long to have his daughter come down from

---

5. *the daimyo* (dī myô), the feudal lord (Horikawa).

among his lordship's women. When Yoshihide was commanded to paint Monju, the God of Wisdom, he took as his model his lordship's favorite page, and the Lord of Horikawa, highly pleased—for it was a beautiful thing—said graciously, "I will give you whatever you wish as a reward. Now what would you like?" Yoshihide acknowledged the tribute; but what do you think was the bold request that he made? That his daughter should leave his lordship's service! It would be presumptuous to ask that one's daughter be taken in; who but Yoshihide would have asked for his daughter's release, no matter how much he loved her! At this even the genial daimyo seemed ruffled, and he silently watched Yoshihide's face for a long moment.

"No," he spat out, and stood up suddenly. This happened again on four or five different occasions, and as I recall it now, with each repetition, the eye with which his lordship regarded Yoshihide grew colder. Possibly it was on account of this that Yūzuki was concerned for her father's safety, for often, biting her sleeves, she sobbed when she was in her room. Without doubt it was this that made the rumors that his lordship had fallen in love with Yoshihide's daughter become widely current. One of them had it that the very existence of the Hell Screen was owing to the fact that she would not comply with his wishes, but of course this could not have been true.

We believe his lordship did not dismiss her simply because he pitied her. He felt sorry for her situation, and rather than leave her with her hardened father he wanted her in the mansion where there would be no inconvenience for her. It was nothing but kindness on his part. It was quite obvious that the girl received his favors, but it would have been an exaggeration to say that she was his mistress. No, that would have been a completely unfounded lie.

Be that as it may, owing to his request about his daughter, Yoshihide came to be disliked by his lordship. Then suddenly the Lord of Horikawa summoned Yoshihide, whatever may have been his reason, and bade him paint a screen of the circles of hell.

6

WHEN I SAY screen of the circles of hell, the scenes of those frightful paintings seem to come floating before my very eyes. Other painters have done Hell Screens, but from the first sketch Yoshihide's was different. In one corner of the first leaf he painted the Ten Kings [6] and their households in small scale, the rest was an awful whirlpool of fire around the Forest of Swords which likewise seemed ready to burst into flames. In fact, except

---

6. *Ten Kings*, in Japanese mythology the judges of the underworld.

for the robes of the hellish officials, which were dotted yellows and blues, all was a flame color, and in the center leapt and danced pitch-black smoke and sparks like flying charcoal.

The brushwork of this alone was enough to astonish one, but the treatment of the sinners rolling over and over in the avenging fire was unlike that of any ordinary picture of hell. From the highest noble to the lowest beggar every conceivable sort of person was to be seen there. Courtiers in formal attire, alluring young maidens of the court in palace robes, priests droning over their prayer beads, scholars on high wooden clogs, little girls in white shifts, diviners flourishing their papered wands —I won't name them all. There they all were, enveloped in flame and smoke, tormented by bull- and horse-headed jailers: blown and scattered in all directions like fallen leaves in a gale, they fled hither and yon. There were female fortunetellers, their hair caught in forks, their limbs trussed tighter than spiders' legs. Young princes hung inverted like bats, their breasts pierced with javelins. They were beaten with iron whips, they were crushed with mighty weights of adamant, they were pecked by weird birds, they were devoured by poisonous dragons. I don't know how many sinners were depicted, nor can I list all their torments.

But I must mention one dreadful scene that stood out from the rest. Grazing the tops of the sword trees, that were as sharp as an animal's fangs—there were several souls on them, spitted two or three deep—came falling through space an ox-carriage. Its blinds were blown open by the winds of hell and in it an emperor's favorite, gorgeously attired, her long black hair fluttering in the flames, bent her white neck and writhed in agony. Nothing made the fiery torments of hell more realistic than the appearance of that woman in her burning carriage. The horror of the whole picture was concentrated in this one scene. So inspired an accomplishment was it that those who looked at her thought they heard dreadful cries in their ears.

Ah, it was for this, it was for this picture that that dreadful event occurred! Without it how could even Yoshihide have expressed so vividly the agonies of hell? It was to finish this screen that Yoshihide met a destiny so cruel that he took his own life. For this hell he pictured was the hell that he, the greatest painter in the country, was one day to fall into. . . .

I may be telling the strange story of the Hell Screen too hastily; I may have told the wrong end of the story first. Let me return to Yoshihide, bidden by his lordship to paint a picture of hell.

7

FOR FIVE OR SIX MONTHS Yoshihide was so busy working on the screen that he was not seen at the mansion at all. Was it not remarkable that with all his affection, when he became absorbed in his painting, he did not even want to see his daughter? The apprentice to whom I have already referred said that when Yoshihide was engaged on a piece of work it was as though he had been bewitched by a fox.[7] According to the stories that circulated at that time Yoshihide had achieved fame with the assistance of the black art because of a vow he had made to some great god of fortune. And the proof of it was that if you went to his studio and peered at him unbeknownst you could see the ghostly foxes swarming all around him. Thus it was that when once he had taken up his brushes everything was forgotten till he had finished the picture. Day and night he would shut himself up in one room, scarcely seeing the light of day. And when he painted the Hell Screen this absorption was complete.

The shutters were kept down during the day and he mixed his secret colors by the light of a tripod lamp. He had his apprentices dress in all sorts of finery, and painted each with great care. It did not take the Hell Screen to make him behave like that: he demanded it for every picture he painted. At the time he was painting the "Five Aspects of Life and Death" at Ryugaiji, he chanced to see a corpse lying beside the road. Any ordinary person would have averted his face, but Yoshihide stepped out of the crowd, squatted down, and at his leisure painted the half-decayed face and limbs exactly as they looked.

How can I convey his violent concentration? Some of you will still fail to grasp it. Since I cannot tell it in detail, I shall relate it broadly.

The apprentice, then, was one day mixing paints. Suddenly Yoshihide appeared. "I'd like to take a short nap," he said. "But I've been bothered a lot by bad dreams recently."

Since this was not extraordinary the apprentice answered briefly but politely, "Indeed, sir," without lifting his hand from his work. Whereupon the artist said, with a loneliness and diffidence that were strange to him, "I mean I would like to have you sit by my pillow while I rest." The apprentice thought it unusual that he should be troubled so badly by dreams, but the request was a simple one and he assented readily. Yoshihide, still anxious, asked him to come back in at once. "And if another apprentice comes, don't let him enter the room while I am sleeping," he said hesitantly. By "room" he meant the room where he was painting the screen. In that room the doors were shut fast as if it were night, and a light was usually left burning. The screen stood around the sides of the room; only the charcoal sketch of the design was completed. Yoshihide put his elbow on the pillow like a man completely exhausted and quietly fell asleep. But before an hour was out an indescribably unpleasant voice began to sound in the apprentice's ears.

---

7. *fox*. In Japanese folklore the fox is believed to be able to bewitch people and assume human form.

AT FIRST it was nothing more than a voice, but presently there were clear words, as of a drowning man moaning in the water. "What . . . you are calling me? Where? Where to . . . to hell? To the hell of fire . . . Who is it? Who is your honor? Who is your honor? If I knew who . . ."

Unconsciously the apprentice stopped mixing the colors; feeling that he was intruding on privacy he looked at the artist's face. That wrinkled face was pale; great drops of sweat stood out on it, the lips were dry, and the mouth with its scanty teeth was wide open, as though it gasped for air. And that thing that moved so dizzily as if on a thread, was that his tongue!

"If I knew who . . . Oh, it is your honor, is it? I thought it was. What! You have come to meet me. So I am to come. I am to go to hell! My daughter awaits me in hell!"

At that moment a strange, hazy shadow seemed to descend over the face of the screen, so uncanny did the apprentice feel. Immediately, of course, he shook the master with all his might, but Yoshihide, still in the clutch of the nightmare, continued his monologue, unable, apparently, to wake out of it. Thereupon the apprentice boldly took the water that stood at hand for his brushes and poured it over Yoshihide's face.

"It is waiting: get in this carriage. Get in this carriage and go down to hell." As he said these words Yoshihide's voice changed, he sounded like a man being strangled, and at length he opened his eyes. Terrified, he leapt up like one pierced with needles: the weird things of his dream must still have been with him. His expression was dreadful, his mouth gaped, he stared into space. Presently he seemed to have recovered himself. "It's all right now. You may leave," he said curtly.

As the apprentice would have been badly scolded had he disobeyed, he promptly left the room. When he saw the good light of day, he sighed with relief like one awakening from a bad dream.

But this was not the worst. A month later another apprentice was called into the back room. As usual Yoshihide was gnawing his brushes in the dim light of the oil lamp. Suddenly he turned to the apprentice. "I want you to strip again."

Since he had been asked to do this several times before, the apprentice obeyed immediately. But when that unspeakable man saw him stark naked before him, his face became strangely distorted. "I want to see a man bound with a chain. I want you to do as I tell you for a little while," he said coldly and unsympathetically. The apprentice was a sturdy fellow who had formerly thought that swinging a sword was better than handling a brush, but this request astonished him. As he often said afterwards, "I began to wonder if the master hadn't gone crazy and wasn't going to kill me." Yoshihide, however, growing impatient with the other's hesitation, produced from somewhere a light iron chain a-rattle in his hand; and without giving him the opportunity of obeying or refusing, sprang on the apprentice, sat on his back, twisted up his arms and bound him around and around. The pain was almost intolerable, for he pulled the end of the chain brutally, so that the apprentice fell loudly sideways and lay there extended.

9

He said that he lay there like a wine jar rolled over on its side. Because his hands and feet were cruelly bent and twisted he could move only his head. He was fat, and with his circulation impeded, the blood gathered not only in his trunk and face but everywhere under his skin. This, however, did not trouble Yoshihide at all; he walked all around him, "a wine jar," making sketch after sketch. I do not need to elaborate on the apprentice's sufferings.

Had nothing occurred, doubtless the torture would have been protracted longer. Fortunately—or maybe unfortunately—something like black oil, a thin streak, came flowing sinuously from behind a jar in the corner of the room. At first it moved slowly like a sticky substance, but then it slid more smoothly until, as he watched it, it moved gleaming up to his nose. He drew in his breath involuntarily. "A snake! A snake!" he screamed. It seemed that all the blood in his body would freeze at once, nor was it surprising. A little more and the snake would actually have touched with its cold tongue his head into which the chains were biting. Even the unscrupulous Yoshihide must have been startled at this. He dropped his brush, bent down like a flash, deftly caught the snake by its tail and lifted it up, head downward. The snake raised its head, coiled itself in circles, twisted its body, but could not reach Yoshihide's hand.

"You have made me botch a stroke." Complaining offensively, Yoshihide dropped the snake into the jar in the corner of the room and reluctantly loosed the chain that bound the apprentice. All he did was to loose him; not a word of thanks did the long-suffering fellow get. Obviously Yoshihide was vexed that he had botched a stroke instead of letting his apprentice be bitten by the snake. Afterwards they heard that he kept the snake there as a model.

This story should give you some idea of Yoshihide's madness, his sinister absorption. However, I should like to describe one more dreadful experience that almost cost a young apprentice his life. He was thirteen or fourteen at the time, a girlish, fair-complexioned lad. One night he was suddenly called to his master's room. In the lamplight he saw Yoshihide feeding a strange bird, about the size of an ordinary cat, with a bloody piece of meat which he held in his hand. It had large, round, amber-colored eyes and feather-like ears that stuck out on either side of its head. It was extraordinarily like a cat.

YOSHIHIDE always disliked anyone sticking his nose into what he was doing. As was the case with the snake, his apprentices never knew what he had in his room. Therefore sometimes silver bowls, sometimes a skull, or one-stemmed lacquer stands—various odd things, models for what he was painting—would be set out on his table. But nobody knew where he kept these things. The rumor that some great god of fortune lent him divine help certainly arose from these circumstances.

Then the apprentice, seeing the strange bird on the table and imagining it to be something needed for the Hell Screen, bowed to the artist and said respectfully, "What do you wish, sir?" Yoshihide, as if he had not heard him, licked his red lips and jerked his chin towards the bird. "Isn't it tame!"

While he was saying this the apprentice was staring with an uncanny feeling at that catlike bird with ears. Yoshihide answered with his sneer, "What! Never seen a bird like this? That's the trouble with people who live in the capital. It's a horned owl. A hunter gave it to me two or three days ago. But I'll warrant there aren't many as tame as this."

As he said this he slowly raised his hand and stroked the back of the bird, which had just finished eating the meat, the wrong way. The owl let out a short piercing screech, flew up from the table, extended its claws, and pounced at the face of the apprentice. Panic-stricken, the latter raised his sleeve to shield his face. Had he not done so he undoubtedly would have been badly slashed.

As he cried out he shook his sleeve to drive off the owl, but it screeched and, taking advantage of his weakness, attacked again. Forgetting the master's presence, the lad fled distracted up and down the narrow room; standing, he tried to ward it off, sitting, to drive it away. The sinister bird wheeled high and low after its prey, darting at his eyes, watching for an opening.

The noisy threshing of its wings seemed to evoke something uncanny like the smell of dead leaves, or the spray of a waterfall. It was dreadful, revolting. The apprentice had the feeling that the dim oil lamp was the vague light of the moon, and the room a valley shut in the ill-omened air of some remote mountain.

But the apprentice's horror was due not so much to the attack of the horned owl. What made his hair stand on end was the sight of the artist Yoshihide.

The latter watched the commotion coolly, unrolled his paper deliberately, and began to paint the fantastic picture of a girlish boy being mangled by a horrible bird. When the apprentice saw this out of the corner of his eye, he was overwhelmed with an inexpressible horror, for he thought that he really was going to be killed for the artist.

YOU COULD NOT say that this was impossible to believe. Yoshihide had called the apprentice deliberately that night in order to set the owl after him and paint him trying to escape. Therefore the apprentice, when he saw what the master was up to, involuntarily hid his head in his sleeves, began screaming he knew not what, and huddled down in the corner of the room by the sliding door. Then Yoshihide shouted as though he were a little flustered and got to his feet, but immediately the beating of the owl's wings became louder and there was the startling noise of things being torn or knocked down. Though he was badly shaken, the apprentice involuntarily lifted his head to see. The room had become as black as night, and out of it came Yoshihide's voice harshly calling for his apprentices.

Presently one of them answered from a distance, and in a minute came running in with a light. By its sooty illumination he saw the tripod lamp overturned and the owl fluttering painfully with one wing on mats that were swimming in oil. Yoshihide was in a half-sitting position beyond the table. He seemed aghast and was muttering words unintelligible to mortals. This is no exaggeration. A snake as black as the pit was coiling itself rapidly around the owl, encircling its neck and one wing. Apparently in crouching down the apprentice had knocked over the jar, the snake had crawled out, and the owl had made a feeble attempt to pounce on it. It was this which had caused the clatter and commotion. The two apprentices exchanged glances and simply stood dumbfounded, eying that remarkable spectacle. Then without a word they bowed to Yoshihide and withdrew. Nobody discovered what happened to the owl and the snake.

This sort of thing was matched by many other incidents. I forgot to say that it was in the early autumn that Yoshihide received orders to paint the screen. From then until the end of the winter his apprentices were in a constant state of terror because of his weird behavior. But towards the end of the winter something about the picture seemed to trouble Yoshihide; he became even more saturnine than usual and spoke more harshly. The sketch of the screen, eight-tenths completed, did not progress. In fact, there did not seem to be any chance that the outlines would ever be painted in and finished.

Nobody knew what it was that hindered the work on the screen and nobody tried to find out. Hitherto the apprentices had been fascinated by everything that happened. They had felt that they were caged with a wolf or a tiger, but from this time they contrived to keep away from their master as much as possible.

ACCORDINGLY, there is not much that is worth telling about this period. But if one had to say something, it would be that the stubborn old man was, for some strange reason, easily moved to tears, and was often found weeping, they say, when he thought no one was by. One day, for instance, an apprentice went into the garden on an errand. Yoshihide was standing absently in the corridor, gazing at the sky with its promise of spring, his eyes full of tears. The apprentice felt embarrassed and withdrew stealthily without saying a word. Was it not remarkable that the arrogant man who had used a decaying corpse as model for the "Five Aspects of Life and Death" should weep so childishly?

While Yoshihide painted the screen in a frenzy incomprehensible to the sane, it began to be noticed that his daughter was very despondent and often appeared to be holding back tears. When this happens to a girl with a pale modest face, her eyelashes become heavy, shadows appear around her eyes, and her face grows still sadder. At first they said that she was suffering from a love affair, or blamed her father, but soon it got around that the Lord of Horikawa wanted to have his way with her. Then suddenly all talk about the girl ceased as if everybody had forgotten her.

It was about that time that late one night I happened to be passing along a corridor. Suddenly the monkey Yoshihide sprang out from somewhere and began pulling the hem of my skirt insistently. As I remember it, the night was warm, there was a pale moon shining, and the plum blossoms were already fragrant. The monkey bared his white teeth, wrinkled the tip of his nose, and shrieked wildly in the moonlight as though he were demented. I felt upset and very angry that my new skirts should be pulled about. Kicking the monkey loose, I was about to walk on when I recalled that a samurai had earned the young lord's displeasure by chastising the monkey. Besides his behavior did seem most unusual. So at last I walked a dozen yards in the direction he was pulling me.

There the corridor turned, showing the water of the pond, pale white in the night light, beyond a pine tree with gently bending branches. At that point what sounded like people quarreling fell on my ears, weird and startling, from a room nearby. Except for this everything around was sunk in silence. In the half-light that was neither haze nor moonlight I heard no other voices. There was nothing but the sound of the fish jumping in the pond. With that din in my ears, I stopped instinctively. My first thought was "Some ruffians," and I approached the sliding door quietly, holding my breath, ready to show them my mettle.

BUT THE MONKEY must have thought me too hesitant. He ran around me two or three times, impatiently, crying out as though he were being strangled, then leapt straight up from the floor to my shoulder. I jerked back my head so as not to be clawed, but he clung to my sleeve to keep from falling to the floor. Staggering back two or three steps, I banged heavily into the sliding door. After that there was no cause for hesitation. I opened the door immediately and was about to advance into the inner part of the room where the moonlight did not fall. But just then something passed before my eyes—what was this?—a girl came running out from the back of the room as though released from a spring. She barely missed running into me, passed me, and half fell outside the room, where she knelt gasping, looking up at my face, and shuddering as though she still saw some horror.

Do I need to say she was Yūzuki? That night she appeared vivid, she seemed to be a different person. Her big eyes shone, her cheeks flamed red. Her disordered kimono and skirt gave her a fascination she did not ordinarily possess. Was this really that shrinking daughter of Yoshihide's? I leaned against the sliding door and stared at her beautiful figure in the moonlight. Then, indicating the direction where the alarmed footsteps had died away, "What was it?" I asked with my eyes.

But she only bit her lips, shook her head, and said nothing. She seemed unusually mortified. Then I bent over her, put my mouth to her ear, and asked, "Who was it?" in a whisper. But the girl still shook her head; tears filled her eyes and hung on her long lashes; she bit her lips harder than ever.

I have always been a stupid person and unless something is absolutely plain I cannot grasp it. I did not know what to say and stood motionless for a moment, as though listening to the beating of her heart. But this was because I felt I ought not to question her too closely.

I don't know how long it lasted. At length I closed the door I had left open and, looking back at the girl, who seemed to have recovered from her agitation, said as gently as possible, "You had better go back to your room." Then, troubled with the uncomfortable feeling that I had seen something I should not have, embarrassed though no one was near, I quietly returned to where I had come from. But before I had gone ten steps, something again plucked the hem of my skirt, timidly this time. Astonished, I stopped and turned around. What do you think it was? The monkey Yoshihide, his gold bell jingling, his hands together like a human, was bowing most politely to me, again and again.

ABOUT TWO WEEKS LATER Yoshihide came to the mansion and asked for an immediate audience with the Lord of Horikawa. He belonged to the lower classes but he had always been in favor, and his lordship, ordinarily difficult of access, granted Yoshihide an audience at once. The latter prostrated himself before the daimyo deferentially and presently began to speak in his hoarse voice.

"Some time ago, my lord, you ordered a Hell Screen. Day and night have I labored, taking great pains, and now the result can be seen: the design has almost been completed."

"Congratulations. I am content." But in his lordship's voice there was a strange lack of conviction, of interest.

"No, congratulations are not in order." With his eyes firmly lowered Yoshihide answered almost as if he were becoming angry. "It is nearly finished, but there is just one part I cannot paint—now."

"What! You cannot paint part of it!"

"No, my lord. I cannot paint anything for which a model is lacking. Even if I try, the pictures lack conviction. And isn't that the same as being unable to paint it?"

When he heard this a sneering sort of smile passed over his lordship's face. "Then in order to paint this Hell Screen, you must see hell, eh?"

"Yes, my lord. Some years ago in a great fire I saw flames close up that resembled the raging fires of hell. The flames in my painting are what I then saw. Your lordship is acquainted with that picture, I believe."

"What about criminals? You haven't seen jailers, have you?" He spoke as though he had not heard Yoshihide, his words following the artist's without pause.

"I have seen men bound in iron chains. I have copied in detail men attacked by strange birds. So I cannot say I have not seen the sufferings of criminals under torture. As for jailers—" Yoshihide smiled repulsively, "I have seen them before me many times in my dreams. Cows' heads, horses' heads, three-faced six-armed demons, clapping hands that make no noise, voiceless mouths agape—they all come to torment me. I am not exaggerating when I say that I see them every day and every night. What I wish to paint and cannot are not things like that."

His lordship must have been thoroughly astonished. For a long moment he stared at Yoshihide irritably; then he arched his eyebrows sharply. "What is it you cannot paint?"

"IN THE MIDDLE of the screen I want to paint a carriage falling down through the sky," said Yoshihide, and for the first time he looked sharply at his lordship's face. When Yoshihide spoke of pictures I have heard that he looked insane. He certainly seemed insane when he said this. "In the carriage an exquisite court lady, her hair disordered in the raging fire, writhes in agony. Her face is contorted with smoke, her eyebrows are drawn; she looks up at the roof of the carriage. As she plucks at the bamboo blinds she tries to ward off the sparks that shower down. And strange birds of prey, ten or twenty, fly around the carriage with shrill cries. Ah, that beauty in the carriage. I cannot possibly paint her."

"Well, what else?"

For some reason his lordship took strange pleasure in urging Yoshihide on. But the artist's red lips moved feverishly, and when he spoke it was like a man in a dream. "No," he repeated, "I cannot paint it." Then suddenly he almost snarled, "Burn a carriage for me. If only you could . . ."

His lordship's face darkened, then he burst out laughing with startling abruptness. "I'll do entirely as you wish," he said, almost choking with the violence of his laughter. "And all discussion as to whether it is possible or not is beside the point."

When I heard this I felt a strange thrill of horror. Maybe it was a premonition. His lordship, as though infected with Yoshihide's madness, changed, foam gathered white on his lips, and like lightning the terror flashed in the corners of his eyes. He stopped abruptly, and then a great laugh burst from his throat. "I'll fire a carriage for you. And there'll be an exquisite beauty in the robes of a fine lady in it. Attacked by flames and black smoke the woman will die in agony. The man who thought of painting that must be the greatest artist in Japan. I'll praise him. Oh, I'll praise him!"

When he heard his lordship's words, Yoshihide became pale and moved his lips as though he were gasping. But soon his body relaxed, and placing both hands on the mats, he bowed politely. "How kind a destiny," he said, so low that he could scarcely be heard. Probably this was because the daimyo's words had brought the frightfulness of his plan vividly before his eyes. That was the only time in my life that I pitied Yoshihide.

16

TWO OR THREE DAYS after this his lordship told Yoshihide that he was ready to fulfill his promise. Of course the carriage was not to be burned at Horikawa, but rather at a country house outside the capital, which the common people called Yukige. Though it had formerly been the residence of his lordship's younger sister, no one had occupied Yukige for many years. It had a large garden that had been allowed to run wild. People attributed its neglect to many causes: for instance, they said that on moonless nights the daimyo's dead sister, wearing a strange scarlet skirt, still walked along the corridors without touching the floor. The mansion was desolate enough by day, but at night, with the splashing sounds of the invisible brook and the monstrous shapes of the night herons flying through the starlight, it was entirely eerie.

As it happened, that night was moonless and pitch black. The light of the oil lamps shone on his lordship, clad in pale yellow robes and a dark purple skirt embroidered with crests, sitting on the veranda on a plaited straw cushion with a white silk embroidered hem. I need not add that before and behind, to the left and to the right of him, five or six attendants stood respectfully. The choice of one was significant—he was a powerful samurai who had eaten human flesh to stay his hunger at the Battle of Michinoku, and since then, they say, he has been able to tear apart the horns of a live deer. His long sword sticking out behind like a gull's tail, he stood, a forbidding figure, beneath the veranda. The flickering light of the lamps, now bright, now dark, shone on the scene. So dreadful a horror was on us that we scarcely knew whether we dreamed or waked.

They had drawn the carriage into the garden. There it stood, its heavy roof weighing down the darkness. There were no oxen harnessed to it, and the end of its black tongue rested on a stand. When we saw its gold metalwork glittering like stars, we felt chilly in spite of the spring night. The carriage was heavily closed with blue blinds edged with embroidery, so that we could not know what was inside. Around it stood attendants with torches in their hands, worrying over the smoke that drifted towards the veranda and waiting significantly.

Yoshihide knelt facing the veranda, a little distance off. He seemed smaller and shabbier than usual, the starry sky seemed to oppress him. The man who squatted behind him was doubtless an apprentice. The two of them were at some distance from me and below the veranda so that I could not be sure of the color of their clothes.

17

IT MUST HAVE BEEN near midnight. The darkness that enveloped the brook seemed to watch our very breathing. In it was only the faint stir of the night wind that carried the sooty smell of the pine torches to us. For some time his lordship watched the scene in silence, motionless. Presently he moved forward a little and called sharply, "Yoshihide."

The latter must have made some sort of reply, though what I heard sounded more like a groan.

"Yoshihide, tonight in accordance with your request I am going to burn this carriage for you."

His lordship glanced sidelong at those around him and seemed to exchange a meaningful smile with one or two, though I may have only imagined it. Yoshihide raised his head fearfully and looked up at the veranda, but said nothing and did not move from where he squatted.

"Look. That is the carriage I have always used. You recognize it, don't you? I am going to burn it and show you blazing hell itself."

Again his lordship paused and winked at his attendants. Suddenly his tone became unpleasant. "In that carriage, by my command, is a female malefactor. Therefore, when it is fired her flesh will be roasted, her bones burnt, she will die in extreme agony. Never again will you find such a model for the completion of your screen. Do not flinch from looking at snow-white skin inflamed with fire. Look well at her black hair dancing up in sparks."

His lordship ceased speaking for the third time. I don't know what thoughts were in his mind, but his shoulders shook with silent laughter. "Posterity will never see anything like it. I'll watch it from here. Come, come, lift up the blinds and show Yoshihide the woman inside."

At the daimyo's word one of the attendants, holding high his pine torch in one hand, walked up to the carriage without more ado, stretched out his free hand, and raised the blind. The flickering torch burned with a sharp crackling noise. It brightly lit up the narrow interior of the carriage, showing a woman on its couch, cruelly bound with chains. Who was she? Ah, it could not be! She was clad in a gorgeously embroidered cherry-patterned mantle; her black hair, alluringly loosened, hung straight down; the golden hairpins set at different angles gleamed beautifully, but there was a gag over her mouth tied behind her neck. The small slight body, the modest profile—the attire only was different—it was Yūzuki. I nearly cried aloud.

At that moment the samurai opposite me got to his feet hastily and put his hand on his sword. It must have been Yoshihide that he glared at. Startled I glanced at the artist. He seemed half-stunned by what he now saw.

Suddenly he leapt up, stretched out both his arms before him, and forgetting everything else, began to run toward the carriage. Unfortunately, as I have already said, he was at some distance in the shadow, and I could not see the expression on his face. But that was momentary, for now I saw that it was absolutely colorless. His whole form cleaving the darkness appeared vividly before our eyes in the half-light—he was held in space, it seemed, by some invisible power that lifted him from the ground. Then, at his lordship's command, "Set fire," the carriage with its passenger, bathed in the light of the torches that were tossed on to it, burst into flames.

AS WE WATCHED, the flames enveloped the carriage. The purple tassels that hung from the roof corners swung as though in a wind, while from below them the smoke swirled white against the blackness of the night. So frightful was it that the bamboo blinds, the hangings, the metal ornaments in the roof, seemed to be flying in the leaping shower of sparks. The tongues of flame that licked up from beneath the blinds, those serried flames that shot up into the sky, seemed to be celestial flames of the sun fallen to the earth. I had almost shouted before, but now I felt completely overwhelmed and dumbfounded; mouth agape, I could do nothing but watch the dreadful spectacle. But the father—Yoshihide. . . .

I still remember the expression on his face. He had started involuntarily toward the carriage, but when the fire blazed up he stopped, arms outstretched, and with piercing eyes watched the smoke and fire that enveloped the carriage as though he would be drawn into it. The blaze lit his wrinkled face so clearly that even the hairs of his head could be seen distinctly: in the depths of his wide staring eyes, in his drawn distorted lips, in his twitching cheeks, the grief, dread, and bewilderment that passed through his soul were clearly inscribed. A robber, guilty of unspeakable crimes and about to be beheaded, or dragged before the court of the Ten Kings, could hardly have looked more agonized. Even that gigantic samurai changed color and looked fearfully at the Lord of Horikawa.

But the latter, without taking his eyes off the carriage, merely bit his lips or laughed unpleasantly from time to time. As for the carriage and its passenger, that girl—I am not brave enough to tell you all that I saw. Her white face, choking in the smoke, looked upward; her long loosened hair fluttered in the smoke, her cherry-patterned mantle—how beautiful it all was! What a terrible spectacle! But when the night wind dropped and the smoke was drawn away to the other side, where gold dust seemed to be scattered above the red flames, when the girl gnawed her gag, writhing so that it seemed the chains must burst, I, and even the gigantic samurai, wondered whether we were not spectators of the torments of hell itself, and our flesh crept.

Then once more we thought the night wind stirred in the treetops of the garden. As that sound passed over the sky, something black that neither touched ground nor flew through the sky, dancing like a ball, leaped from the roof of the house into the blazing carriage. Into the crumbling blinds, cinnabar-stained, he fell, and putting his arms around the straining girl, he cried shrill and long into the smoke, a cry that sounded like tearing silk. He repeated it two or three times, then we forgot ourselves and shouted out together. Against the transparent curtain of flames, clinging to the girl's shoulder, was Yoshihide, Yoshihide the monkey, that had been left tied at the mansion.

BUT WE SAW HIM only for a moment. Like gold leaf on a brown screen the sparks climbed into the sky. The monkey and Yūzuki were hidden in black smoke while the carriage blazed away with a dreadful noise in the garden. It was a pillar of fire—those awful flames stabbed the very sky.

In front of that pillar Yoshihide stood rooted. Then, wonderful to say, over the wrinkled face of this Yoshihide, who had seemed to suffer on a previous occasion the tortures of hell, over his face the light of an inexpressible ecstasy passed, and forgetful even of his lordship's presence he folded his arms and stood watching. It was almost as if he did not see his daughter dying in agony. Rather he seemed to delight in the beautiful color of the flames and the form of a woman in torment.

What was most remarkable was not that he was joyfully watching the death of his daughter. It was rather that in him seemed to be a sternness not human, like the wrath of a kingly lion seen in a dream. Surprised by the fire, flocks of night birds that cried and clamored seemed thicker—though it may have been my imagination—around Yoshihide's cap. Maybe those soulless birds seemed to see a weird glory like a halo around that man's head.

If the birds were attracted, how much more were we, the servants, filled with a strange feeling of worship as we watched Yoshihide. We quaked within, we held our breath, we watched him like a Buddha unveiled. The roaring of the fire that filled the air, and Yoshihide, his soul taken captive by it, standing there motionless—what awe we felt, what intense pleasure at this spectacle. Only his lordship sat on the veranda as though he were a different sort of being. He grew pale, foam gathered on his lips, he clutched his purple-skirted knee with both hands, he panted like some thirsty animal. . . .

IT GOT AROUND that his lordship had burnt a carriage at Yukige that night —though of course nobody said anything—and a great variety of opinions were expressed. The first and most prevalent rumor was that he had burnt Yoshihide's daughter to death in resentment over thwarted love. But there was no doubt that it was the daimyo's purpose to punish the perversity of the artist, who was painting the Hell Screen, even if he had to kill someone to do so. In fact, his lordship himself told me this.

Then there was much talk about the stony-heartedness of Yoshihide, who saw his daughter die in flames before his eyes and yet wanted to paint the screen. Some called him a beast of prey in human form, rendered incapable of human love by a picture. The Abbot of Yokogawa often said,

"A man's genius may be very great, great his art, but only an understanding of the Five Virtues [8] will save him from hell."

However, about a month later the Hell Screen was completed. Yoshihide immediately took it to the mansion and showed it with great deference to the Lord of Horikawa. The Abbot happened to be visiting his lordship at the time, and when he looked at it he must have been properly startled by the storm of fire that rages across the firmament on one of the leaves. He pulled a wry face, stared hard at Yoshihide, but said, "Well done," in spite of himself. I still remember the forced laugh with which his lordship greeted this.

From that time on, there was none that spoke badly of Yoshihide, at least in the mansion. And anyone who saw the screen, even if he had hated the artist before, was struck solemn, because he felt that he was experiencing hell's most exquisite tortures.

But by that time Yoshihide was no longer among the living. The night after the screen was finished he hanged himself from a beam in his studio. With his only daughter preceding him he felt, no doubt, that he could not bear to live on in idleness. His remains still lie within the ruins of his house. The rains and winds of many decades have bleached the little stone that marked his grave, and the moss has covered it in oblivion.   ✕

8. *the Five Virtues.* In Confucianism the ethical teachings, formulated by the Chinese sage and founder Confucius (551–478 B.C.), are based on five cardinal virtues: Humanity, Justice, Propriety, Wisdom, and Fidelity.

Anonymous (9th century)

THE BAMBOO CUTTER
AND THE MOON CHILD

Adapted from a

translation from the Japanese by

F. B. Harris

IN ANCIENT TIMES a poor bamboo cutter named Takétori [1] went one day
into the mountain forests. While entering a stand of bamboo, he was
startled by brilliant rays of light coming from a tree in the middle of the
grove. He cut down the tree and was amazed to see a lovely creature,
barely three inches tall, emerge from the shining bamboo.

"If I had not cut down the cane, you would never have gotten out," the
old man announced. "By rights you belong to me." So he placed the tiny
being in the palm of his hand and carried her home to his wife. The old
woman put the child in a small box for safe keeping and, in the days that
followed, she fed and cared for it without thought of weariness.

The fairy child was not to be the only blessing to come to the old
bamboo cutter and his wife. Not long afterwards, Takétori cut down a
second bamboo tree, discovering inside gold and all manner of precious
gems. Once poor, the bamboo cutter suddenly found himself very rich, and
soon his life was filled with an abundance of comforts and luxuries.

The fairy child grew quickly and it was not long before the box cradling
her became too small. The old man and his wife released her in their newly
built mansion, being very careful to keep the girl safely within doors. The
fairy's beauty kept pace with her growth until it was without its match in
all the world, and the glory radiating from her filled the house, lighting the
dwelling even in the dark of night, so that if the old couple chanced to fall

1. *Takétori* (tä ke tô rē).

ill they soon forgot their aches and pains in its cheering rays; nor could anger or evil thoughts torment them while they gazed upon the fairy child.

During this time the old man and his wife gave the child a fitting name, calling her Kakuya Himé,[2] or Graceful Bamboo, Night-Illuminating Princess.

As Kakuya Himé grew into womanhood, her loveliness flowered until the fame of it became known through the length and breadth of the land. All young men who chanced to look upon her beauty longed to win her as their bride, but even a passing glimpse was not to be had easily, for the maiden was closely sheltered in the inner apartments of the mansion. Because of this her suitors were in a lamentable state, scarcely sleeping for dwelling on the charms and loveliness they were not allowed to see. In time the young men of the region went to ruin, becoming unmindful of their duties and wasting their time foolishly—all from their love of Kakuya Himé.

Eventually, however, most of the young men tired of the futile pursuit until only five noble suitors stayed on, lingering about the mansion, hoping for an opportunity to show their love. These suitors were the feudal lords (daimyo): Ishidzukuri [3]; Kuramochi [4]; Abé no Mimuraji,[5] second in rank only to the emperor himself; Otsu no Miyuki [6]; and Lord Morotaka,[7] of the province of Iso.

Finally one of their number succeeded in getting Takétori's attention. Throwing himself at the old man's feet with the utmost respect, he cried out imploringly, "I beg you, listen to my plea and give me your lovely daughter in marriage."

"The maiden is not my daughter," Takétori replied, "and I have no right to compel her obedience." So saying he went away.

Though month after month passed, still the five suitors remained outside the mansion, begging—whenever they found an opportunity—for Takétori to listen to their requests. But the old man always put them off, while the fairy maiden, undecided as to which among them was the noblest, would have none of them for a husband.

Seeing he could not stop their constant coming to his house, Takétori finally advised Kakuya Himé. "Although you are immortal," he began, "you have taken the form of a woman. While there is nothing wrong with you remaining a maiden during my lifetime, what will become of you when I die? Daily these five young men come to seek your hand. I beg that you fix your heart on one of them."

"I am not so beautiful that five suitors should come wooing me," Kakuya Himé answered modestly, "and if I become the bride of one

---

2. *Kakuya Himé* (kä kù yä hē me). 3. *Ishidzukuri* (ē shēd zù kù rē). 4. *Kuramochi* (kù-rä mô chē). 5. *Abé no Mimuraji* (ä be nô mē mù rä jē). 6. *Otsu no Miyuki* (ôt sù nô mē-yù kē). 7. *Morotaka* (mô rô tä kä).

without first proving his heart, I may regret my choice. I cannot marry without testing my future husband first."

"But all are men of rank and accomplishment. You could easily choose from among them now."

"It is not enough that they come here day after day. Each must show me some noble deed, some brilliant accomplishment, so that I can choose the man who excels for my husband. Please give this message to them."

At sunset that same evening the five lovers gathered before the mansion prepared to demonstrate their talents. One played the flute, a second danced, another was a gifted singer, still another was skilled in the art of whistling, while the last could use the fan as a harmonious accompaniment to music.

When all had finished, Takétori came to the gate. "Welcome to my humble dwelling," he greeted them. "I thank you warmly for the fine entertainment. As I am more than seventy years of age, I may die at any time—perhaps today, or it may be tomorrow—so I have pleaded with my daughter to choose a husband from among such a brilliant circle of young men. But as you are all equally accomplished, my daughter feels that any choice is impossible. I ask you, therefore, to grant her one more demand. Her words are these: 'He who fulfills my request shall claim me as a bride.'"

"Since she cannot judge from among us, the maiden's words are reasonable," all cried eagerly as with one voice. "We will do whatever she asks."

The old man then announced Kakuya Himé's test: "Let Prince Ishidzukuri find the famous stone jar held in the hands of the gods; let Prince Kuramochi travel the eastern seas in search of Mt. Horai, where springs that priceless tree with roots of silver, a trunk of gold, and boughs laden with lustrous white gems. Make it his task to bring me one of its branches. Let Abé no Mimuraji find the red fire rat of China, bringing back its glistening fur; let Otsu no Miyuki seek the five-tinted jewel that sparkles in the dragon's head; while, as for Morotaka, Lord of Iso, I ask that he return with the shell which the swallow is said to own."

When he had first heard these requests, the old man was quite distressed, and only reluctantly did he inform the young men of the tasks laid upon them by Kakuya Himé. Yet none of the noble lords showed even the slightest concern over the mission given them. However, in their hearts there was irritation and all returned home full of resentment. Nonetheless, all knew they would surely die from sheer despair should they not be allowed to look upon the wondrous Kakuya Himé, and each resolved that, even if obliged to journey to distant India to fulfill her wishes, he would make the attempt.

It happened that the first suitor, Prince Ishidzukuri, was a man given to deep-laid schemes. The more he pondered the matter, the more clearly he saw that he might travel one hundred times ten million miles and still not be certain of finding the stone jar held by the gods. There was probably only one of its kind in all the world. So he sent a message to the maiden's home, falsely declaring that he was about to start for India that very day in search of the jar. Instead Prince Ishidzukuri traveled into the Yamato district and there remained for three years. In a mountain temple he found a black jar suited to his purpose. Placing the jar in a brocade bag along with a branch laden with artificial blossoms, he returned with the gifts to Kakuya Himé's home. The maiden was very surprised, for she never believed that such a jar could be found. But a close examination of the jar revealed a poem inside which, in quaint meter, disclosed that the jar came from the forest temple of Mount Ogura in the Yamato region. Sure now of the fraud, the princess wrote a second poem, placed it in the jar, and ordered the jar returned to the prince. The prince returned to his house where he read Kakuya Himé's poem. With his trick exposed, he threw the jar out of the gate, swearing on holy vows to remain in seclusion until he could forget the maiden of his dreams.

Prince Kuramochi, the second suitor, being a very shrewd man, let it be known that he was setting out in search of Mt. Horai. Having deceived everyone as to his real intentions, he secretly returned home. Calling together six skilled carpenters, the prince ordered them to build a house in a secluded area with a furnace hidden by three arches of earth so that no one might see the smoke. As soon as the house was completed, the prince moved in, sending for artisans skilled in delicate work. These he commanded to fashion counterfeit gems of pure white to be fastened on a branch. So carefully was his order carried out that the jeweled branch, when finished, was the exact likeness of the one described by Kakuya Himé.

As soon as the branch was ready, the prince took a ship from Osaka—that he might deceive the maiden by returning from the sea—later landing at the place of his departure. Prince Kuramochi's retainers flocked to Osaka to welcome him. They escorted the prince, along with a chest covered with beautiful drapery and holding the supposed branch, to his residence. Before long news of Prince Kuramochi's treasure spread throughout the region, causing people everywhere to talk about the branch of gems rare as *udongé*, the fabled flower said to blossom but once in a thousand years.

Once she learned of Prince Kuramochi's return, Kakuya Himé was troubled, saying sorrowfully to herself: "I will have to yield to this prince," and even while these words were on her lips, a servant came with word that he was just then knocking at the gate.

"I have not held even life itself precious in my search for the jeweled branch," the prince said on greeting the old man. "Here, I give this treasure to you, asking only that you show it to your daughter."

Takétori immediately carried the branch of jeweled flowers along with a poem from the prince to the maiden. "Without a doubt," he said, "the noble prince has brought this branch all the way from Mt. Horai." When Kakuya Himé appeared reluctant to accept the offering, the old man asked, "What more can you want? He has even rushed to our home in traveling clothes. I beg you, agree to marry Prince Kuramochi."

As the maiden was too upset to reply, Takétori wrongly concluded that her silence meant consent, and he hurried to tell her waiting lover of the good news. While servants made preparations for the marriage feast, it occurred to the old man to ask the prince where he had come across the jeweled tree.

Prince Kuramochi replied, "The year before last, on the tenth day of the second month, I set sail on the great deep, not knowing my destination. We were blown along at the will of the wind, and I thought I would never live to return, but that while life lasted I would cross the seas in search of Mt. Horai. After we left the Sea of Japan, the waves at times rolled high enough to sink our ship, while fierce winds often drove us to unknown coasts inhabited by demons waiting to destroy us. Sometimes we roamed the seas not knowing in what direction we were going, and then again we lost everything and had to live off roots of sea grass or shellfish. I find it impossible to describe the fearful monsters which came upon us. And there were times beneath the skies of our journeyings when we fell sick and suffered terribly with no one to help.

"After we had wandered over the seas for the space of five hundred days, one day at the hour of the Hare—about dawn—I saw what looked like a small mountain rising from the waters. I quickly woke the ship's company. As we drew nearer, it seemed to grow wonderfully large, and from its beautiful outline, I knew it must be the object of my quest. It was like a miracle.

"For three days we sailed around the coast until we saw a woman looking like a goddess drawing water with a silver cup. Before she finished her work, we landed and went over to her. I asked the name of the mountain rising before us. She answered that it was called Mt. Horai.

"We rejoiced. But when I questioned this beautiful creature, she would say nothing else than her name, 'I am called Hakaruru,' then she suddenly vanished in the recesses of the mountain. As it looked impossible to scale the heights of the mountain, I contented myself with a walk around its base. I saw flowers unlike those anywhere else on earth, and streams— gold, silver and emerald in color, and spanned by jeweled bridges—flowing down from the mountain. I came across row upon row of trees, glittering with precious gems, but the branch of the tree I brought back was the poorest of all. Since the maiden ordered one like this—with jeweled fruit— I obeyed her command. Though the enchanting scenes of this mountain were beyond imagination, I grew uneasy and hurried back to my ship. After a voyage of four hundred days and more we finally returned to

Japan. After landing at Osaka, I journeyed with all speed to the capital, and have even come here in traveling clothes still drenched with the salt spray of the sea."

The old man listened to the marvelous tale with compassion and admiration. At that moment, however, several artisans entered the courtyard and, bowing humbly, begged to be allowed to present a petition. "For more than a thousand days," stated their leader, "we have not spared our strength and skill in fashioning the jeweled branch. But so far we have received nothing in payment for our work. Give us our wages, we beg of you, so that we may feed our families at home."

The artisans presented a written scroll of their complaints to the shocked maiden, Kakuya Himé, whereupon Prince Kuramochi was so struck with shame that he lost his mind.

The fairy princess, on the other hand, seemed pleased. She called to her father. "I really thought this branch came from Mt. Horai. But since I have been deceived by so shallow a hoax, I ask you to return the gift at once."

The prince by this time was so chagrined that he could neither stand nor sit, but wandered about the courtyard until the sun had set, then, under cover of darkness, fled into the night.

With a light heart, Kakuya Himé called the petitioning artisans and gave each more than enough to compensate him for his work. But on their way home, the artisans were set upon by the retainers of Prince Kuramochi. Their money was taken from them and all were left half dead by the road. As to the prince—his knights and retainers searched the mountains for days, but he was never seen in that land again.

The third suitor, Abé no Mimuraji, held office as chief minister of state and was a man of great wealth and influence. To accomplish his task, Abé sent a messenger to a friend in China with a letter and a huge sum of money, commissioning the friend to obtain the skin of the famous fire rat. In due course, he received a reply declaring that the skin was not to be found in China. "However," his friend wrote, "if it is to be found in the world, someone is surely to bring it to China." Not long after, a courier arrived from China. A robe made from the desired fur had been brought as treasure in ancient times from India to China. The courier presented Abé with the robe, saying that it was to be returned if the price could not be paid. Abé happily gave the courier the required sum and, in gratitude, prostrated himself in respect towards the kingdom of China.

The box containing the skin was fashioned of a beautiful emerald tint, while the robe itself was a rich blue, the tip of each hair glistening in a glorious manner. It was a treasure of unrivaled beauty and, aside from its rarity, valuable for its color alone.

Attired in handsome dress, the noble suitor and his retainers arrived at Takétori's mansion, where they waited at the entrance until the old man came to greet them and receive the gift.

"Truly a beautiful fur robe," Kakuya Himé said when she first saw it, "but whether real or fake I do not know. Let the flames be the test!"

"Well spoken," answered her father.

"Such suspicion is groundless," Abé no Mimuraji objected, "but give it the test if you must." So they cast the robe into the flames where it immediately took fire and was consumed. At the sight of the burning fur, the noble's face took on the hue of leaves of grass. The amused Kakuya Himé then returned the emerald-tinted box to Abé no Mimuraji.

The fourth suitor, Otsu no Miyuki, devised a more straightforward plan for winning the maiden's hand. Calling together his warriors, he said: "In the dragon's head is a gem glittering with five colors. He who brings me this gem shall have whatever his heart desires." Even though the warriors quickly agreed, the nobleman laughed scornfully, chiding, "Since you are part of my household, you have no choice but to agree. Now set about with your task at once." After outfitting his troops with vast stocks of silk, cotton, food and money, Otsu no Miyuki ordered them to the port of Osaka. "Let no one return until the five-colored jewel has been found," he said, "and I vow to fast and pay homage to the gods in your absence."

While waiting for their ships at Osaka, the warriors gathered to discuss the venture. All considered Otsu no Miyuki to be haughty and selfish, and they decided that their master should have led the quest himself. So they ended up by dividing the supplies and money between themselves and going their separate ways.

Lord Otsu meanwhile began building a magnificent mansion for the bride he was sure would soon be his. The mansion was fashioned bright with lacquer, red and golden and a dozen other colors; its roof was suspended from vari-colored strands of silken thread, while in the many apartments delicate paintings hung on rich brocades.

Once the mansion was completed, Lord Otsu watched anxiously each day for the coming of his warriors. But when a year had gone by without their return, he disguised himself as a commoner and, accompanied by two servants, started out in search of his men. On reaching the port of Osaka, Lord Otsu asked of news of the mission. But the seamen he questioned responded with laughter and scorn.

"Yours is the talk of fools. No one would ever go on such a mission," they all answered.

In desperation, Lord Otsu finally said: "By the might of my bow, were the dragon here I would kill him and take his head. No, I will not wait for the return of those rascals. The three of us will board ship and set out together."

That day Otsu hired a ship and sailed out into the sea. As the ship approached a land far from the shores of Japan, a storm arose. Soon the skies grew black and a mighty gale arose, driving the ship off course. The gale blew as though it would drive the ship beneath the sea, while angry waves beat upon her and tossed her about as though she were caught in a whirlpool, and so powerful were the flashes of lightning that the crew expected momentarily that one of the great thunderbolts would strike and sink the ship.

"What will become of us?" the terrified Otsu asked the captain.

"I have sailed the oceans far and wide," replied the captain, "but never have I encountered perils like these. If we are not swallowed by the sea the thunder will strike us. And even if the gods favor us, the force of the gale may carry the ship far off to the southern oceans." Shedding a torrent of tears, the captain added, "We face disaster from following a merciless master like you."

"Why accuse me so bitterly?" cried out Lord Otsu. He was now dismally seasick. "One commits himself on the oceans to the care of the captain, as though he were putting his trust in the majesty of a lofty mountain."

"I am not a god," replied the captain, "and I can't control everything. A great gale is blowing, the waves are raging, and a thunderbolt is about to fall on our heads—all because you wanted to slay a dragon. I am sure this must be his work. I beg you—pray for our salvation."

Lord Otsu prayed, vowing a thousand times that he would give up his plan to steal even a single hair from the dragon's head. Before long there were signs that the gods had heard, for though the wind blew even more fiercely, the thunder had ceased and the flashes of lightning became less frequent. The wind proved favorable and in four days the ship managed to return to the coast of Japan.

Once back on land, Lord Otsu found himself exhausted and sick with cold, and his eyes had become so swollen that they looked like two large red plums. Soon all his warriors returned to him, saying: "Now you yourself know just how difficult it is to steal the jewel from the dragon's head."

"You are right," Lord Otsu agreed, "and I welcome you back into my service. Certainly the dragon belongs to the family of thunder gods, and he who seeks his jewel must come to an evil end. You were right in not going after it. This Kakuya Himé is nothing more than a fiend which tries to destroy men. I forbid anyone to go near her again."

And so crows and fish hawks carried away the strands of silken thread from the roof of the new mansion, while people jeered behind Lord Otsu's back, pointing at his still-swollen eyes.

> "The gem from the dragon's head,"
>   HAI! they said
> "He brought back two red plums instead!"

Now the fifth suitor was Lord Morotaka of the province of Iso, whose task it was to secure the rare shell found in the swallow's nest. Lord Morotaka learned that a large number of swallows had built their nests on the roof of a certain government building, so he had a scaffolding erected, stationing twenty men there to watch the birds. However, the swallows became frightened at the sight of so many men and soon left the roof.

On the advice of a sage, Lord Morotaka dismissed all his servants but one, and with that servant he set out and searched day and night for the shell. It was a weary time of waiting, for Lord Morotaka had been told that the magic shell could be found only when the swallow deposits its eggs in the nest. Finally, one evening at sunset, Morotaka saw a swallow whirling about the top of her nest. Hurriedly, he raised his servant to the roof in a basket. But the servant frightened the bird and returned empty-handed, causing his master to fly into a rage: "You are too awkward," he cried. "I'll do it myself."

After Lord Morotaka was raised to the roof, he put his hand in the nest and, feeling something flat, grasped it tightly, then called out to the servant to lower him to the ground. The servant hurriedly seized the rope, making it snap, and plunging Morotaka into a large water jar that had been sacred to one of the gods. Recovering from the shock, Lord Morotaka found that he could not stand up. Despite his injuries, Morotaka was exalted at finding the treasure. Then the servant struck a light. In the glare of the flame, Lord Morotaka discovered that his treasure was not the rare shell, but a common rock. Lord Morotaka tried his best to hide the mishap from the people, but failed, and soon the story traveled throughout the land. What with his injuries and mental distress, the physical condition of Morotaka grew worse and, finally, he died from complications of sickness and humiliation.

The story of Kakuya Himé and her five suitors soon reached the ears of the emperor himself. The fascinated emperor ordered one of his courtiers to visit the maiden and report back on what manner of woman it was who forced men to suffer yet would not give her hand in marriage. The bamboo cutter's daughter refused the imperial representative an audience. At first the emperor was furious, but in time he decided her refusal was an indication of the maiden's wish to test him. Accordingly, one day while out hunting, the emperor took the opportunity of stopping at the bamboo cutter's mansion.

He peered into the house, where he saw a woman resplendent with light seated in a room. Sure that this could be none other than the fabled Kakuya Himé, he hurried in. The emperor took hold of the sleeve of her gown. Even though the startled maiden turned to hide her face, he caught a glimpse of its radiant loveliness. The emperor immediately demanded that she accompany him to the palace. But the maiden suddenly vanished. The emperor was grief-stricken, realizing then that Kakuya Himé was no mortal.

"Oh, Kakuya Himé, reappear. I beg you. Let me look upon your beauty once more, then I will return to my palace."

The emperor was overjoyed when the maiden again took human form. Words would be exhausted in depicting the raptures of the man as he gazed upon the maiden. After the courtiers had prepared a great feast of rejoicing, the emperor regretfully returned to his palace, leaving his heart in the mansion of the old bamboo cutter.

Three years passed. In the spring of the fourth year, servants noticed that Kakuya Himé was watching the moon with troubled eyes. One pleaded with her to stop, for it was clear that the maiden was becoming daily more saddened with its brightness. But Kakuya Himé would not stop staring up at the moon. The handmaidens then told the old bamboo cutter. He immediately asked the maiden why she was unhappy.

"I cannot tell you," she answered. "It is enough to say that my heart grows sad whenever I gaze upon the moon."

On moonless nights Kakuya Himé did not cry, but with the return of the moon, her grief was at once apparent. Then, as the fifteenth day of the eighth month drew near, Kakuya Himé grew so unhappy she no longer made even the slightest effort to hide her tears. Once more Takétori begged the maiden to tell him of the reason for her distress.

At last she agreed. "Long ago," she began, "I thought about telling you the truth. But I didn't want to hurt you." Tears filled the maiden's eyes. "I do not belong to your world. I am of the Moon world, and the time approaches when I shall have to return. On the fifteenth day of this month, messengers will descend to carry me home."

"Surely this is beyond all reason," the old man cried in wrath and anguish. "When you were no bigger than a ripe seed I found you in the hollow of a bamboo cane, and I have reared you with bone-breaking care. I will die if you are taken from me."

"It is not what I want. The lord of the Moon world commands it. And I must obey."

News of Kakuya Himé's plight soon reached the emperor, and he sent a page to the bamboo cutter's home. Excessive grief had doubled the old bamboo cutter's years: his beard had grown snow white, his body was bent and his eyes were red from constant weeping. Between tears and wails, Takétori asked the page to have the emperor send warriors so that, on the fifteenth day of the month, the celestial envoys might be taken captive.

On the dawn of the fifteenth day, the emperor dispatched a general with two thousand warriors. Half of these were stationed on a hill next to the mansion; the rest took up their positions on the roof of the house itself. Takétori ordered his many servants to arm themselves with bows and arrows and join in the defense. Kakuya Himé, meanwhile, was placed in a strong storehouse where serving women held her arms. Outside the door, the old bamboo cutter took up guard.

"If so much as a dewdrop descends from the heavens, destroy it," cried Takétori to the warriors, whereupon they all answered bravely. But Kakuya Himé said, "The bolted doors of a storehouse and two thousand warriors will not protect me. Bows and arrows are useless against heavenly armies. At their coming the stoutest of my defenders will lose courage."

"Let them beware," Takétori shouted in reply. "I will tear out their eyes, pull out their hair, rip off their clothing, and humiliate them before the people."

But Kakuya Himé answered, "It is best that none of the others should hear your boastful words. You have shown me much love and kindness and I long to be with you and my foster mother in your final years. I do not want to return to the Moon world, though sorrow never enters that land, and though all its subjects, fair of face and body, live in immortal youth."

"Don't trouble yourself," Takétori said boldly. "I'll have nothing to do with these heavenly messengers, however fair."

As nightfall deepened the moon became full, then grew ten times its normal size, so that the light from its rays filled the bamboo cutter's house. Finally the skies were filled by a host of mighty warriors riding atop great clouds. Soon they descended, where they stood rank upon rank five feet off the ground.

At the sight of them the maiden's defenders lost courage. Some later rallied and tried to give battle, but each found his hand too numb to take aim. There was one among them—a stalwart soul—who managed to shoot off all his arrows. But each missed its mark. And so all stood helpless, gazing like fools at the celestial array. So beautiful was the dress of the envoys from the moon that there is nothing on earth to which it could be compared, and the chariot brought to convey Kakuya Himé to her home was covered with a magnificent canopy.

One who seemed to be their leader started towards the door to the storehouse. Immediately Takétori staggered about like a man drunk with saké [8] and, as a sleeper might fall, so he stumbled and fell to the ground.

"For some slight merit on your part," the leader said, "Kakuya Himé was permitted to bless your home. In years past she sinned in heaven. As the penalty for her sin she was exiled for a brief moment in eternity to your humble dwelling. The end of her punishment is at hand and your pleas are of no use. I order you to produce her at once."

Ignoring Takétori's protests, the celestial officer ordered the chariot brought and called out, "Come quickly!" At once the door to the storehouse flew open and some unseen, irresistible force pulled Kakuya Himé from the arms of the handmaidens. Going up to her heartbroken father, she said: "I do not want to return to the moon. But since I must, please look at me as I go."

---

8. *saké*, a Japanese fermented alcoholic beverage made from rice.

"Take me with you," the old man pleaded, weeping. The maiden shook her head, handing him a note she had written to comfort him after she had gone.

A feather robe such as celestial beings wear was brought to Kakuya Himé as well as a cup holding the elixir of immortality. Though commanded to drink, the maiden only sipped from the cup, determined to leave enough elixir for the old man and the emperor. The celestial officer gave his reluctant consent, at the same time drawing the winged robe about the body of Kakuya Himé.

No sooner did the cloth of the immortals touch the maiden than the sadness in her heart vanished. No longer did she regret her departure from the world of man. She willingly mounted the chariot and, while the old man wailed and watched, the maiden and a thousand celestial warriors ascended into the skies.

When Kakuya Himé was gone the old bamboo cutter lost all interest in life. Not even the maiden's note would lighten his spirits, nor did he want to taste of the elixir of immortality. Before long, languishing in sickness and remorse, he lay down on his bed, never to rise again.

The general reported all these events to the emperor upon his return to the palace. He brought with him Kakuya Himé's note and the cup containing the wine of immortality. The emperor's heart was heavy. After long moments of suffering, the emperor called one of his advisors, questioning the sage as to which mountain in the empire rose nearest to the moon.

"In Surga province is a sounding mountain [9] which reaches far up into the skies. Surely that must be the highest and the mountain nearest to the moon," the advisor replied.

The emperor then commanded that the letter and the elixir of immortality be brought to the top of that mountain and cast in where it would be consumed by the flames. . .

> Because the *fushi* [elixir] was burned
> Upon the crest of the great yama [mountain]
> It was thus called ever after
> *Fushi no Yama.*
> And even to this day, it is said
> Smoke rising from the still-burning elixir
> Can be seen ascending from the depths
> Of the great sounding mountain
> And that mountain
> Is Fujiyama.

9. *sounding mountain,* a volcanic mountain.

Anonymous (18th century)

HŌICHI[1] THE EARLESS
from *Hyaku Monogatari*

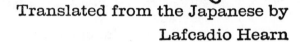

Translated from the Japanese by
Lafcadio Hearn

The Hyaku Monogatari *(hundred tales) was written during an era of peace in Japanese history. A greater literacy among the people, the emergence of new writers who were no longer court nobles, and the development of cheap printing helped to bring books to a much wider public.*

SOME CENTURIES AGO there lived at Akamagaséki a blind man named Hōichi, who was famed for his skill in recitation and in playing upon the *biwa*.[2] From childhood he had been trained to recite and to play; and while yet a lad he had surpassed his teachers. As a professional *biwa hoshi*[3] he became famous chiefly by his recitations of the history of the Heiké and the Genji; and it is said that when he sang the song of the battle of Dan-no-ura[4] "even the goblins [kijin] could not refrain from tears."

At the outset of his career, Hōichi was very poor; but he found a good friend to help him. The priest of the Amidaji[5] was fond of poetry and music; and he often invited Hōichi to the temple to play and recite. Afterwards, being much impressed by the wonderful skill of the lad, the priest proposed that Hōichi should make the temple his home; and this offer was gratefully accepted. Hōichi was given a room in the temple building; and, in return for food and lodging, he was required only to gratify the priest with a musical performance on certain evenings, when otherwise disengaged.

"Hōichi the Earless" from *Hyaku Monogatari*, translated by Lafcadio Hearn.
1. *Hōichi* (hoi chē). **2.** *biwa* (bē wä), a lute. [*Japanese*] **3.** *biwa hoshi*, a lute-playing priest. [*Japanese*] **4.** *Dan-no-ura*, the scene of a famous sea battle in 1185, in which the Genji clan defeated the Heiké who perished with their families. **5.** *Amidaji*, a Buddhist temple near Akamagaséki, the site of the battle. It was built to pacify the spirits of the Heiké dead who, it was believed, haunted the sea and beaches of Dan-no-ura.

One summer night the priest was called away, to perform a Buddhist service at the house of a dead parishioner; and he went there with his acolyte, leaving Hōichi alone in the temple. It was a hot night; and the blind man sought to cool himself on the verandah before his sleeping room. The verandah overlooked a small garden in the rear of the Amidaji. There Hōichi waited for the priest's return, and tried to relieve his solitude by practicing upon his *biwa*. Midnight passed; and the priest did not appear. But the atmosphere was still too warm for comfort within doors; and Hōichi remained outside. At last he heard steps approaching from the back gate. Somebody crossed the garden, advanced to the verandah, and halted directly in front of him—but it was not the priest. A deep voice called the blind man's name—abruptly and unceremoniously, in the manner of samurai [6] summoning an inferior:

"Hōichi!"

Hōichi was too much startled, for the moment, to respond; and the voice called again, in a tone of harsh command.

"Hōichi!"

"*Hai!*" answered the blind man, frightened by the menace in the voice. "I am blind!—I cannot know who calls!"

"There is nothing to fear," the stranger exclaimed, speaking more gently. "I am stopping near this temple, and have been sent to you with a message. My present lord, a person of exceedingly high rank, is now staying in Akamagaséki, with many noble attendants. He wished to view the scene of the battle of Dan-no-ura; and today he visited that place. Having heard of your skill in reciting the story of the battle, he now desires to hear your performance: so you will take your *biwa* and come with me at once to the house where the august assembly is waiting."

In those times, the order of a samurai was not to be lightly disobeyed. Hōichi donned his sandals, took his *biwa*, and went away with the stranger, who guided him deftly, but obliged him to walk very fast. The hand that guided was iron; and the clank of the warrior's stride proved him fully armed—probably some palace guard on duty. Hōichi's first alarm was over: he began to imagine himself in good luck; for, remembering the retainer's assurance about a "person of exceedingly high rank," he thought that the lord who wished to hear the recitation could not be less than a lord of the first class. Presently the samurai halted; and Hōichi became aware that they had arrived at a large gateway; and he wondered, for he could not remember any large gate in that part of the town, except the main gate of the Amidaji. "Kaimon!" [7] the samurai called, and there was a sound of unbarring; and the twain passed on. They traversed a space of garden, and halted again before some entrance; and the retainer cried in a loud voice,

---

6. *samurai*, a member of a hereditary military class in feudal Japan. 7. "*Kaimon!*" A polite term used to request admission from a guard on duty. [*Japanese*]

"Within there! I have brought Hōichi." Then came sounds of feet hurrying, and screens sliding, and rain-doors opening, and voices of women in converse. By the language of the women Hōichi knew them to be domestics in some noble household; but he could not imagine to what place he had been conducted. Little time was allowed him for conjecture. After he had been helped to mount several stone steps, upon the last of which he was told to leave his sandals, a woman's hand guided him along interminable reaches of polished planking, and round pillared angles too many to remember, and over amazing widths of matted floor, into the middle of some vast apartment. There he thought that many great people were assembled: the sound of the rustling of silk was like the sound of leaves in a forest. He heard also a great humming of voices, talking in undertones; and the speech was the speech of courts.

Hōichi was told to put himself at ease, and he found a kneeling-cushion ready for him. After having taken his place upon it, and tuned his instrument, the voice of a woman—whom he divined to be the *Rōjo*, or matron in charge of the female service—addressed him, saying,

"It is now required that the history of the Heiké be recited, to the accompaniment of the *biwa*."

Now the entire recital would have required a time of many nights: therefore Hōichi ventured a question:

"As the whole of the story is not soon told, what portion is it augustly desired that I now recite?"

The woman's voice made answer:

"Recite the story of the battle at Dan-no-ura, for the pathos is most deep."

Then Hōichi lifted up his voice, and chanted the chant of the fight on the bitter sea, wonderfully making his *biwa* to sound like the straining of oars and the rushing of ships, the whirr and the hissing of arrows, the shouting and trampling of men, the crashing of steel upon helmets, the plunging of slain in the flood. And to left and right of him, in the pauses of his playing, he could hear voices murmuring praise: "How marvelous an artist!" "Never in our own province was playing heard like this!" "Not in all the empire is there another singer like Hōichi!" Then fresh courage came to him, and he played and sang yet better than before; and a hush of wonder deepened about him. But when at last he came to tell the fate of the fair and helpless, the piteous perishing of the women and children, and the death-leap of Nii-no-Ama, with the imperial infant in her arms, then all the listeners uttered together one long, long shuddering cry of anguish; and thereafter they wept and wailed so loudly and so wildly that the blind man was frightened by the violence of the grief that he had caused. For some time the sobbing and the wailing continued. But gradually the sounds of lamentation died away; and again, in the great stillness that followed, Hōichi heard the voice of the woman whom he supposed to be the Rōjo.

She said:

"Although we had been assured that you were a very skillful player upon the *biwa*, and without an equal in recitation, we did not know that anyone could be so skillful as you have proved yourself tonight. Our lord has been pleased to say that he intends to bestow upon you a fitting reward. But he desires that you shall perform before him once every night for the next six nights—after which time he will probably make his august return journey. Tomorrow night, therefore, you are to come here at the same hour. The retainer who tonight conducted you will be sent for you. . . . There is another matter about which I have been ordered to inform you. It is required that you shall speak to no one of your visits here, during the time of our lord's sojourn at Akamagaséki. As he is traveling incognito, he commands that no mention of these things be made. . . . You are now free to go back to your temple."

After Hōichi had duly expressed his thanks, a woman's hand conducted him to the entrance of the house, where the same retainer, who had guided him before, was waiting to take him home. The retainer led him to the verandah at the rear of the temple, and there bade him farewell.

It was almost dawn when Hōichi returned; but his absence from the temple had not been observed, as the priest, coming back at a very late hour, had supposed him asleep. During the day Hōichi was able to take some rest; and he said nothing about his strange adventure. In the middle of the following night the samurai again came for him, and led him to the august assembly, where he gave another recitation with the same success that had attended his previous performance. But during this second visit his absence from the temple was accidentally discovered; and after his return in the morning he was summoned to the presence of the priest who said to him, in a tone of kindly reproach:

"We have been very anxious about you, friend Hōichi. To go out, blind and alone, at so late an hour, is dangerous. Why did you go without telling us? I could have ordered a servant to accompany you. And where have you been?"

Hōichi answered, evasively,

"Pardon me, kind friend! I had to attend to some private business; and I could not arrange the matter at any other hour."

The priest was surprised, rather than pained, by Hōichi's reticence: he felt it to be unnatural, and suspected something wrong. He feared that the blind lad had been bewitched or deluded by some evil spirits. He did not ask any more questions; but he privately instructed the men servants of the temple to keep watch upon Hōichi's movements, and to follow him in case that he should again leave the temple after dark.

On the very next night, Hōichi was seen to leave the temple; and the servants immediately lighted their lanterns, and followed after him. But it was a rainy night, and very dark; and before the temple-folks could get to the roadway, Hōichi had disappeared. Evidently he had walked very fast, a strange thing, considering his blindness; for the road was in a bad condition. The men hurried through the streets, making inquiries at every house which Hōichi was accustomed to visit; but nobody could give them any news of him. At last, as they were returning to the temple by way of the shore, they were startled by the sound of a *biwa*, furiously played, in the cemetery of the Amidaji. Except for some ghostly fires—such as usually flitted there on dark nights—all was blackness in that direction. But the men at once hastened to the cemetery; and there, by the help of their lanterns, they discovered Hōichi, sitting alone in the rain before the memorial tomb of Antoku Tennō,[8] making his *biwa* resound, and loudly chanting the chant of the battle of Dan-no-ura. And behind him, and about him, and everywhere above the tombs, the fires of the dead were burning, like candles. Never before had so great a host of *Oni-bi*[9] appeared in the sight of mortal man. . . .

"Hōichi San![10] Hōichi San!" the servants cried, "you are bewitched! . . . Hōichi San!"

But the blind man did not seem to hear. Strenuously he made his *biwa* to rattle and ring and clang; more and more wildly he chanted the chant of the battle of Dan-no-ura. They caught hold of him; they shouted into his ear:

"Hōichi San! Hōichi San!—come home with us at once!"

Reprovingly he spoke to them:

"To interrupt me in such a manner, before this august assembly, will not be tolerated."

Whereat, in spite of the weirdness of the thing, the servants could not help laughing. Sure that he had been bewitched, they now seized him, and pulled him up on his feet, and by main force hurried him back to the temple, where he was immediately relieved of his wet clothes, by order of the priest, and reclad, and made to eat and drink. Then the priest insisted upon a full explanation of his friend's astonishing behavior.

Hōichi long hesitated to speak. But at last, finding that his conduct had really alarmed and angered the good priest, he decided to abandon his reserve; and he related everything that had happened from the time of the first visit of the samurai.

The priest said:

"Hōichi, my poor friend, you are now in great danger! How unfortunate that you did not tell me all this before! Your wonderful skill in music has indeed brought you into strange trouble. By this time you must be aware that you have not been visiting any house whatever, but have been passing

---

8. *Antoku Tennō*, the infant emperor of the Heiké who drowned at the battle of Dan-no-ura. 9. *Oni-bi*, demon fires, so-called by the fishermen who claimed that the sea and beaches of Dan-no-ura were covered by ghostly fires. [*Japanese*] 10. *San*, a Japanese term of respect used in addressing a male or female.

your nights in the cemetery, among the tombs of the Heiké; and it was before the memorial tomb of Antoku Tennō that our people tonight found you, sitting in the rain. All that you have been imagining was illusion—except the calling of the dead. By once obeying them, you have put yourself in their power. If you obey them again, after what has already occurred, they will tear you in pieces. But they would have destroyed you, sooner or later, in any event. . . . Now I shall not be able to remain with you tonight: I am called away to perform another service. But, before I go, it will be necessary to protect your body by writing holy texts upon it."

Before sundown the priest and his acolyte stripped Hōichi: then, with their writing-brushes, they traced upon his breast and back, head and face and neck, limbs and hands and feet—even upon the soles of his feet, and upon all parts of his body—the text of the holy sûtra [11] called Hannya-Shin-Kyō. When this had been done, the priest instructed Hōichi, saying:

"Tonight, as soon as I go away, you must seat yourself on the verandah, and wait. You will be called. But, whatever may happen, do not answer, and do not move. Say nothing, and sit still—as if meditating. If you stir, or make any noise, you will be torn asunder. Do not get frightened; and do not think of calling for help—because no help could save you. If you do exactly as I tell you, the danger will pass, and you will have nothing more to fear."

After dark the priest and the acolyte went away; and Hōichi seated himself on the verandah, according to the instructions given him. He laid his *biwa* on the planking beside him, and, assuming the attitude of meditation, remained quite still, taking care not to cough, or to breathe audibly. For hours he stayed thus.

Then, from the roadway, he heard the steps coming. They passed the gate, crossed the garden, approached the verandah, stopped—directly in front of him.

"Hōichi!" the deep voice called. But the blind man held his breath, and sat motionless.

"Hōichi!" grimly called the voice a second time. Then a third time—savagely:

"Hōichi!"

Hōichi remained as still as a stone, and the voice grumbled:

"No answer!—that won't do! . . . Must see where that fellow is."

There was a noise of heavy feet mounting upon the verandah. The feet approached deliberately, halted beside him. Then, for long minutes, during which Hōichi felt his whole body shake to the beating of his heart, there was dead silence.

At last the gruff voice muttered close to him:

---

11. *holy sûtra.* In Buddhism (see footnote 2, page 39) the sûtras are treatises, often in verse, based on the religious and philosophical discourses of the Buddha.

"Here is the *biwa;* but of the *biwa* player I see—only two ears! . . . So that explains why he did not answer: he had no mouth to answer with—there is nothing left of him but his ears. . . . Now to my lord those ears I will take—in proof that the august commands have been obeyed, so far as was possible."

At that instant Hōichi felt his ears gripped by fingers of iron, and torn off! Great as the pain was, he gave no cry. The heavy footfalls receded along the verandah, descended into the garden, passed out to the roadway, ceased. From either side of his head, the blind man felt a thick warm trickling; but he dared not lift his hands.

Before sunrise the priest came back. He hastened at once to the verandah in the rear, stepped and slipped upon something clammy, and uttered a cry of horror; for he saw, by the light of his lantern, that the clamminess was blood. But he perceived Hōichi sitting there, in the attitude of meditation—with the blood still oozing from his wounds.

"My poor Hōichi!" cried the startled priest, "what is this? . . . You have been hurt?"

At the sound of his friend's voice, the blind man felt safe. He burst out sobbing, and tearfully told his adventure of the night.

"Poor, poor Hōichi!" the priest exclaimed, "all my fault!—my very grievous fault! . . . Everywhere upon your body the holy texts had been written—except upon your ears! I trusted my acolyte to do that part of the work; and it was very, very wrong of me not to have made sure that he had done it! . . . Well, the matter cannot now be helped; we can only try to heal your hurts as soon as possible. . . . Cheer up, friend!—the danger is now well over. You will never again be troubled by those visitors."

With the aid of a good doctor, Hōichi soon recovered from his injuries. The story of his strange adventure spread far and wide, and soon made him famous. Many noble persons went to Akamagaséki to hear him recite; and large presents of money were given to him, so that he became a wealthy man. . . . But from the time of his adventure, he was known only by the appellation of *Mimi-nashi-Hōichi:* "Hōichi-the-Earless." ✕

Ibusé Masuji[1] (1898–   )

THE CHARCOAL BUS

Translated from the Japanese by
Ivan Morris

ON A RECENT TRIP to the country, I rode once again on the Binan-line bus.
I hadn't been on this bus for some time—not since the war,[2] in fact.
However, I remembered it well.

During the war, all the country buses were pretty decrepit, but the bus
on the Binan route was in a class of its own. It rarely got through a run
without a series of mishaps: first there would be a puncture, then the
engine would break down, and when this had finally been repaired the gear
box would give trouble. Almost all the windows were broken; some of the
openings were covered with cellophane, others with wooden boards.

Now, five years after the war, the bus still ran on charcoal, though the
body had been painted over and most of the windows repaired. The driver
was a young fellow whom I recognized from the war days, when he had
been the conductor. Apparently he had changed places with the mustachioed man who had previously occupied the driver's seat. I wondered
whether this had any particular significance.

"Haven't the driver and the conductor switched round?" I said to a
woman in the seat next to mine. "Surely this conductor used to be the
driver. Has he had an accident or something so that he can't drive any
longer?"

"No," put in the woman's companion, "he became unpopular during the
war and had to be demoted. He was too strict with the passengers, you
see. As soon as the war was over, people began to write the company
complaining about his behavior and saying he should be purged. . . .
Well, this is where we get off."

The couple nodded to me and left the bus. An old man in a peasant's

"The Charcoal Bus" by Ibusé Masuji, translated by Ivan Morris from MODERN JAPA-
NESE SHORT STORIES. Reprinted by permission of Charles E. Tuttle Co., Inc.
1. *Ibusé Masuji* (ē bù se mä sù jē). 2. *the war*, World War II.

smock, who had been listening to the conversation, took the woman's place beside me.

"That's all very well," he said as soon as he had sat down, "but the conductor will soon be back where he was before, mark my words. Of course, he was so unpopular after the war that they couldn't help purging him; they lowered his salary and made him a conductor. But nowadays the purgees are all coming back into favor. It's people like him who are going to get ahead now." The old man nodded his head and murmured, as if to himself: "Yes, that's how things are moving these days."

I glanced at the conductor. How well I remembered that little mustache! He was standing now at the back of the bus looking out the window. We crossed a bridge over a dried-up river; beyond the rice fields I could see the slopes of a barren-looking mountain. As we passed a Shinto shrine [3] by the side of the road, the conductor removed his cap and wiped the perspiration from his forehead. As he did so, he bowed his head slightly, and I wondered whether this was intended as a mark of respect for the shrine. Such reverence had been unfashionable for some time after the war but was now gradually coming back into favor. The conductor's gesture seemed deliberately ambiguous.

My memories of the man were far from favorable. During his long term of duty as driver for the Binan-line bus, he had never missed an opportunity to hector the young man who was then conductor. The burden of his abuse was usually the alleged misdemeanors of the passengers, and among his favorite points of attack were rucksacks.

"No rucksacks inside the bus!" he used to roar at the conductor. "Kindly tell that passenger to remove his rucksack. You know perfectly well they aren't allowed. What are you waiting for anyhow? Make him get off!"

There was indeed a rule that each piece of luggage, including rucksacks, had to be checked, paid for, and piled on top of the bus. Occasionally the police would stop the bus at a crossroads and examine the luggage for black-market articles, such as rice or firewood, the discovery of which meant confiscation and a fine. Under the circumstances we preferred to take our baggage with us and push it under the seats, but such attempts were almost invariably frustrated by the mustachioed driver. He, on the other hand, did not scruple to transport large quantities of carrots, peas, and other contraband in the tool box next to his seat.

Not only did I and the other regular passengers regard the driver as a disagreeable bully, but we also despised him for his inefficiency in handling the bus. The constant delays and breakdowns used to leave him quite unperturbed. As soon as the engine failed, he would announce in a sten-

---

3. *Shinto shrine*, a shrine of Shinto, the native religion of Japan, primarily a form of nature and ancestor worship.

torian tone: "All passengers out! Start pushing!" When we had pushed for fifty or sixty yards, the engine usually started and he would order us aboard.

Toward the end of the war, however, these periodic breakdowns became more serious and the last time I had taken the bus (shortly before the destruction of Hiroshima) I had helped push it almost four miles. I had gone fishing in a mountain stream and after spending the night at an inn, had gone early next morning to the Otaki Bridge bus stop. About forty people were already waiting. The time for departure came but there was no sign of the bus. A few people gave up at once and left; others vented their annoyance by reviling the driver, a luxury that they certainly would not have permitted themselves had he been within earshot. Only about half of us remained when the bus finally arrived, over two hours late.

I gave the conductor my return ticket and luggage check, passed him my rucksack, and stepped aboard. There were seats for all of us. When the conductor had finished stoking the burner with charcoal, the driver pressed the starting button. Nothing happened. He pressed it again several times, but still the engine would not fire. This, of course, was a fairly normal occurrence and, without waiting to be told, we all got out of the bus—all, that is, except for a young couple who remained unconcernedly in their seats. They were obviously not familiar with the Binan-line bus.

With one accord we started to push. As the burner, which stuck out in the back, was extremely hot, we split into groups on each side. One enterprising passenger found a long board and used it to push the burner. The conductor also jumped down and began pushing. The road here was at a slight incline and the bus moved along without too much effort on our part. The driver sat calmly in his seat, hands on the steering wheel.

We had pushed the bus three or four hundred yards without the engine once firing, when suddenly we heard a hysterical voice from inside the bus. It was the driver, who evidently had just noticed the young couple.

"Hey, you two back there!" he roared. "What do you think you're doing? Can't you see that everyone else is pushing? Get out and lend a hand! Don't just sit there!"

A man's voice answered calmly: "Would you mind not shouting at me? I may not be much of a traveler, but I always thought that buses ran on their engines."

"I see," said the driver. "So that's your attitude! You're too good to push like everyone else, eh? Well, let me tell you something: I don't care if you're honeymooners or not, if you don't get out this minute and start pushing, you'll damned well wish you had!"

"If you want to continue this conversation," answered the man, "you'd better address me politely."

There was a pause. A little later, as the road passed through a quiet grove, the driver's voice again broke the silence.

"Hey, you two back there! Don't be so damned stubborn. How can you go on sitting there in comfort when all the others are sweating away on the road? We're beginning to go uphill now. Get out and help!"

"Why don't you pay attention to the engine?" said the young man loudly. "You're the one that's stubborn! You're so interested in making us get out and push that you aren't even trying to start the engine. Concentrate on your job like other drivers! You're a disgrace to the public-transport system!"

"Shut up!" said the driver. Then in a milder tone he added: "See here, young man, we're going up Sampun Hill now. You don't want to let the others do all the work, do you? Look at them back there sweating away!"

Sampun Hill was a steep cutting; both sides of the road were clay cliffs. It took all our strength to move the bus. From the top of the cutting the road went steeply downward, and if the engine didn't fire there, it was hard to see when it would. We all stopped at the summit and watched the bus gathering speed as it ran downhill. It passed a large irrigation tank on one side of the road and disappeared behind a clump of trees. We pricked up our ears for the sound of the engine, while the conductor ran down the hill after the bus.

A man in an open-neck shirt, a peaked cap, and a pair of khaki plus-fours [4] stained with paint came up to me. "Can you hear if it's started?" he said.

"I believe it's started," replied a girl in slacks who was standing next to me. "I think I can hear the engine. . . . But maybe it's just my imagination."

"I can't hear a thing," said the man in plus-fours. "How many more miles is it to town?"

"About four and a half," said the girl. "But in just over two miles we come to Three Corners Crossing, where we can catch a decent bus."

"And I'm taking that bus for the rest of the way," declared the man in plus-fours. "I'm fed up with this charcoal contraption!"

Just then the conductor appeared at the bottom of the hill. He stood there waving his arms and shaking his head, before disappearing again in a clump of trees.

"We've never had to push this far before," said the girl in slacks as we started disconsolately down the hill. "That couple has annoyed the driver. He's taking it out on the rest of us."

"Yes, I bet he'll have us pushing the bus all the way to the end of the line," said the man in plus-fours angrily. "There's only one thing for us to do—look exhausted. We must make him think we're on our last legs; then maybe he'll change his mind." He pulled his shirt out of his trousers to give himself a disheveled appearance.

---

4. *plus-fours*, baggy trousers gathered by a band below the knees.

Finally we caught sight of the bus parked by a farmhouse near the trees. The driver was standing beside it with arms folded, while the conductor was busily turning the handle to stoke the burner. I could see a girl in a green dress drawing water from a well.

"Isn't that the girl who was in the bus?" I suggested.

"That's right," said a horse-faced man in an old army uniform with a mourning band. "I've got a feeling something's gone wrong. Look, the girl's carrying a bucket into the bus. Hey, what's got into you?" he called out to the driver. "What are you doing, just standing there looking up at the sky? Have you decided to give up driving or what?"

"That's right," said the driver, fingering his mustache. "I've resigned."

"What do you mean, you've resigned?" said the horse-faced man.

"That stubborn fool in there wouldn't get out and push when I told him. So I had to give him a good beating. But first I resigned, because employees aren't allowed to hit the passengers. Once I'd resigned, I was a private citizen and could give him the beating he deserved."

"Look here," said the horse-faced man, "you've gone too far this time. And who do you think is going to drive if you don't?"

The driver shrugged his shoulders. He glanced disdainfully at the passengers assembled beside the bus. "I can't drive any more," he repeated stubbornly. "I tell you I've resigned."

At this point a tall old man stalked out of the farmhouse.

"I've had about enough of this!" he shouted to the driver. "I've seen everything that's gone on. I saw you attacking that peaceful couple. What do you mean by behaving like that in front of my house?"

"I'm a private citizen," said the driver. "I've got a perfect right to strike anyone I want to."

"Don't talk like a fool," said the old farmer. "And kindly get your bus away from my house. I'll help push the damned thing in place of the honeymoon couple if that's what's bothering you. My old woman can give a hand too. You get in and steer!"

We all followed the old couple to the back of the bus, and as I passed one of the windows, I glanced inside. The young man was lying back pale in his seat. He had some tissue paper stuffed in his nostrils and one of his eyes was red and swollen. The girl in the green dress had apparently just finished swabbing his face; she took the bucket to the back of the bus and handed it to one of the passengers, who returned it to the well.

The driver stood with his arms folded and refused to get into his seat. The old couple began pushing the bus with all their might. It would not budge.

"Hey, all you others," shouted the old man, "give us a hand!"

"Right you are," said the horse-faced man and ran to the back of the bus. "Come on, all of you," he shouted, "push away! Yo-heave-ho!"

We all pushed. The bus began to move. The driver opened his eyes wide in amazement. "Hey, wait a minute!" he shouted. "Don't be crazy! Wait till I get hold of the wheel."

He ran after the bus, jumped on to the driver's platform, and grasped the steering wheel before even sitting down. We all pushed now with redoubled vigor, spurred on by the feeling that we had taken matters into our own hands, at least temporarily. The road was fairly straight and the bus ran along at a steady speed.

"Hey, driver," shouted the horse-faced man, "can't you get the engine started? Are you sure you aren't doing it on purpose?"

"Don't be so suspicious," answered the driver. "It's not my fault it won't start. The engine's worn out. The battery isn't charging right either. But of course you people wouldn't know about such things."

"That's right," said a man who was wearing a light yellow shirt and a surplice inscribed with a Buddhist prayer. "We laymen are only good for pushing. 'Push and don't ask questions!' That seems to be the motto of this bus company."

"Yes, it's going a little too far," said the horse-faced man. "We've got to push whether we want to or not, and no one even bothers to tell us what's wrong with the damned bus. I'm exhausted!"

The driver turned round with a cigarette in his mouth.

"Hey there, you two," he shouted to the honeymoon couple, "did you hear what that passenger said just now? He's exhausted. They're all exhausted because of your damned selfishness! Aren't you ashamed of yourselves? Listen to the voice of the people back there! Get out this minute and push—both of you!"

"Are you still worrying about us, you poor fool?" said the young man. "I've told you already—leave us alone and concentrate on the engine or the battery or whatever it is. First you charge us high fares and then you try to make us do a lot of useless pushing. I'll have something to say about all this when we arrive, I warn you!"

"What's that, you bastard?" roared the conductor. "Do you want another beating?"

"You tell me to listen to the voice of the people," answered the young man calmly. "Well, by protesting like this, I'm trying to make it penetrate your ears too."

"So you still think you're pretty smart, do you?" cried the driver, shaking with fury. "You still think you're better than everyone else? All right, I'll show you! You've asked for it!" He got to his feet.

"Sit down, sit down!" shouted the horse-faced man, who had now become our spokesman. "Don't let go of the steering wheel!" Then turning to us, he said: "Come on, push harder! Don't let the driver leave the steering wheel. Push away!"

We pushed harder than ever and the bus moved rapidly along the straight, narrow road. On the left was a low stone wall beyond which was a steep drop to the paddyfields; on the right was a shallow river. The driver could ill afford to let the bus swerve in either direction. In the distance I noticed a car approaching.

"Stop a minute!" cried the driver. "I've got to give that fool another beating."

"Oh no, you don't!" said the horse-faced man. "Come on, everyone, push away! Let's really get this old crate moving!"

We pushed—in fact we almost hurled ourselves at the back of the bus. In our excitement we had forgotten that the driver could stop the bus whenever he wanted simply by applying the brakes. We were all out of breath by now, but this did not deter us.

"Hey, what's wrong with you all?" shouted the driver. "Why do you stand up for that insolent bastard anyway? It's his fault you're all worn out."

"Don't worry about us!" said the horse-faced man. "Just keep steering! If you let go of that wheel, you'll really have something to worry about."

"That's right," added the man with the surplice. "You'll be with your ancestors before you know it."

Just then a large van approached from the opposite direction. The bus jerked to a sudden stop which almost knocked us off balance; it was a moment before I realized that the driver had applied the brakes. We exchanged disappointed, frustrated looks.

"Well, at least we've arrived at the crossroads," remarked the horse-faced man. "We've pushed it four miles already. Quite an achievement, I must say! But I've had enough. I'm taking the proper bus from here on."

He gave his luggage check to the conductor, loaded his rucksack on his back, and started walking toward Three Corners Crossing. I also decided to take the other bus; so did the man in plus-fours, the girl in slacks, and a few others. The rest said they would continue pushing—some because they were convinced the bus was about to start, others to prevent the driver from attacking the honeymoon couple, still others because they did not want to lose their fares. The refractory couple decided to remain in the bus. The man in plus-fours went to fetch his luggage and joined us at the crossroads. "They're sitting in there having lunch," he reported. "They've taken out a tin of dried beef."

"What about the driver?"

"It looks as if he's going to leave them in peace to enjoy their meal. They've got a bottle of whisky too."

I looked back at the charcoal bus. The driver had opened the hood and was tinkering at the engine with a wrench more for form's sake than anything, I imagined. The conductor put some charcoal in the burner and began turning the blower furiously. He seemed to have unbounded confidence in the engine. I noticed that the old farmer and his wife were trudging back toward their home.   ✳

Kikuchi Kan[1] (1888–1948)

THE MADMAN ON THE ROOF

Translated from the Japanese
by Yozan T. Iwasaki
and Glenn Hughes

CHARACTERS

KATSUSHIMA YOSHITARO (kät sù shē mä   yô shē tä rô), *the madman, twenty-four years of age*

KATSUSHIMA SUEJIRO (kät sù shē mä   sù e jē rô), *his brother, a seventeen-year-old high school student*

KATSUSHIMA GISUKE (kät sù shē mä gē sù ke), *their father*

KATSUSHIMA OYOSHI (kät sù shē mä   ô yô shē), *their mother*

TOSAKU (tô sä kù), *a neighbor*

KICHIJI (kē chē jē), *a manservant, twenty years of age*

A PRIESTESS, *about fifty years of age*

PLACE: *A small island in the Inland Sea*

TIME: *1900*

The stage setting represents the backyard of the Katsushimas, who are the richest family on the island. A bamboo fence prevents one from seeing more of the house than the high roof, which stands out sharply against the rich greenish sky of the southern island summer. At the left of the stage one can catch a glimpse of the sea shining in the sunlight.

YOSHITARO, *the elder son of the family, is sitting astride the ridge of the roof, and is looking out over the sea.*

"The Madman on the Roof" by Kikuchi Kan, translated by Yozan T. Iwasaki and Glenn Hughes. Reprinted by permission of The National Bank of Commerce of Seattle as executor of the estate of Glenn Hughes.
1. *Kikuchi Kan* (kē kù chē kän).

GISUKE *(speaking from within the house).* Yoshi is sitting on the roof again. He'll get a sunstroke—the sun's so terribly hot. *(Coming out)* Kichiji!— Where is Kichiji?

KICHIJI *(appearing from the right).* Yes! What do you want?

GISUKE. Bring Yoshitaro down. He has no hat on, up there in the hot sun. He'll get a sunstroke. How did he get up there, anyway? From the barn? Didn't you put wires around the barn roof as I told you to the other day?

KICHIJI. Yes, I did exactly as you told me.

GISUKE *(coming through the gate to the center of the stage, and looking up to the roof).* I don't see how he can stand it, sitting on that hot slate roof. *(He calls.)* Yoshitaro! You'd better come down. If you stay up there you'll get a sunstroke, and maybe die.

KICHIJI. Young master! Come on down. You'll get sick if you stay there.

GISUKE. Yoshi! Come down quick! What are you doing up there, anyway? Come down, I say! *(He calls loudly.)* Yoshi!

YOSHITARO *(indifferently).* Wha-a-at?

GISUKE. No "whats"! Come down right away. If you don't come down, I'll get after you with a stick.

YOSHITARO *(protesting like a spoiled child).* No, I don't want to. There's something wonderful. The priest of the god Kompira [2] is dancing in the clouds. Dancing with an angel in pink robes. They're calling to me to come. *(Crying out ecstatically)* Wait! I'm coming!

GISUKE. If you talk like that you'll fall, just as you did once before. You're already crippled and insane—what will you do next to worry your parents? Come down, you fool!

KICHIJI. Master, don't get so angry. The young master will not obey you. You should get some fried bean cake; when he sees it he will come down, because he likes it.

GISUKE. No, you had better get the stick after him. Don't be afraid to give him a good shaking-up.

KICHIJI. That's too cruel. The young master doesn't understand anything. He's under the influence of evil spirits.

GISUKE. We may have to put bamboo guards on the roof to keep him down from there.

KICHIJI. Whatever you do won't keep him down. Why, he climbed the roof of the Honzen Temple without even a ladder; a low roof like this one is the easiest thing in the world for him. I tell you, it's the evil spirits that make him climb. Nothing can stop him.

_____

2. *Kompira,* a demon converted to Buddhism (see footnote 2, page 39) who became a god of happiness and the patron saint of sailors.

GISUKE. You may be right, but he worries me to death. If we could only keep him in the house it wouldn't be so bad, even though he is crazy; but he's always climbing up to high places. Suejiro says that everybody as far as Takamatsu knows about Yoshitaro the Madman.

KICHIJI. People on the island all say he's under the influence of a fox-spirit,[3] but I don't believe that. I never heard of a fox climbing trees.

GISUKE. You're right. I think I know the real reason. About the time Yoshitaro was born, I bought a very expensive imported rifle, and I shot every monkey on the island. I believe a monkey-spirit is now working in him.

KICHIJI. That's just what I think. Otherwise, how could he climb trees so well? He can climb anything without a ladder. Even Saku, who's a professional climber, admits that he's no match for Yoshitaro.

GISUKE (with a bitter laugh). Don't joke about it! It's no laughing matter, having a son who is always climbing on the roof. (Calling again) Yoshitaro, come down! Yoshitaro!—When he's up there on the roof, he doesn't hear me at all—he's so engrossed. I cut down all the trees around the house so he couldn't climb them, but there's nothing I can do about the roof.

KICHIJI. When I was a boy I remember there was a gingko tree in front of the gate.

GISUKE. Yes, that was one of the biggest trees on the island. One day Yoshitaro climbed clear to the top. He sat out on a branch, at least ninety feet above the ground, dreaming away as usual. My wife and I never expected him to get down alive, but after a while, down he slid. We were all too astonished to speak.

KICHIJI. That was certainly a miracle.

GISUKE. That's why I say it's a monkey-spirit that's working in him. (He calls again.) Yoshi! Come down! (Dropping his voice) Kichiji, you'd better go up and fetch him.

KICHIJI. But when anyone else climbs up there, the young master gets angry.

GISUKE. Never mind his getting angry. Pull him down.

KICHIJI. Yes, master.

(KICHIJI goes out after the ladder. TOSAKU, the neighbor, enters.)

TOSAKU. Good day, sir.

GISUKE. Good day. Fine weather. Catch anything with the nets you put out yesterday?

TOSAKU. No, not much. The season's over.

---

3. *fox-spirit.* In Japanese folklore the fox is believed to be able to bewitch people and assume human form.

GISUKE. Maybe it *is* too late now.

TOSAKU *(looking up at* YOSHITARO*).* Your son's on the roof again.

GISUKE. Yes, as usual. I don't like it, but when I keep him locked in a room he's like a fish out of water. Then, when I take pity on him and let him out, back he goes up on the roof.

TOSAKU. But after all, he doesn't bother anybody.

GISUKE. He bothers us. We feel so ashamed when he climbs up there and shouts.

TOSAKU. But your younger son, Suejiro, has a fine record at school. That must be some consolation for you.

GISUKE. Yes, he's a good student, and that is a consolation to me. If both of them were crazy, I don't know how I could go on living.

TOSAKU. By the way, a Priestess has just come to the island. How would you like to have her pray for your son?—That's really what I came to see you about.

GISUKE. We've tried prayers before, but it's never done any good.

TOSAKU. This Priestess believes in the god Kompira. She works all kinds of miracles. People say the god inspires her, and that's why her prayers have more effect than those of ordinary priests. Why don't you try her once?

GISUKE. Well, we might. How much does she charge?

TOSAKU. She won't take any money unless the patient is cured. If he is cured, you pay her whatever you feel like.

GISUKE. Suejiro says he doesn't believe in prayers. . . . But there's no harm in letting her try.

(KICHIJI *enters carrying the ladder and disappears behind the fence.)*

TOSAKU. I'll go and bring her here. In the meantime you get your son down off the roof.

GISUKE. Thanks for your trouble. *(After seeing that* TOSAKU *has gone, he calls again.)* Yoshi! Be a good boy and come down.

KICHIJI *(who is up on the roof by this time).* Now then, young master, come down with me. If you stay up here any longer you'll have a fever tonight.

YOSHITARO *(drawing away from* KICHIJI *as a Buddhist* [4] *might from a heathen).* Don't touch me! The angels are beckoning to me. You're not supposed to come here. What do you want?

KICHIJI. Don't talk nonsense! Please come down.

YOSHITARO. If you touch me the demons will tear you apart.

(KICHIJI *hurriedly catches* YOSHITARO *by the shoulder and pulls him to the ladder.* YOSHITARO *suddenly becomes submissive.)*

---

4. *Buddhist.* See footnote 2, page 39.

KICHIJI. Don't make any trouble now. If you do you'll fall and hurt yourself.

GISUKE. Be careful!

(YOSHITARO *comes down to the center of the stage, followed by*
KICHIJI. YOSHITARO *is lame in his right leg.*)

GISUKE *(calling)*. Oyoshi! Come out here a minute.

OYOSHI *(from within)*. What is it?

GISUKE. I've sent for a Priestess.

OYOSHI *(coming out)*. That may help. You never can tell what will.

GISUKE. Yoshitaro says he talks with the god Kompira. Well, this Priestess
is a follower of Kompira, so she ought to be able to help him.

YOSHITARO *(looking uneasy)*. Father! Why did you bring me down? There
was a beautiful cloud of five colors rolling down to fetch me.

GISUKE. Idiot! Once before you said there was a five-colored cloud, and you
jumped off the roof. That's the way you became a cripple. A Priestess
of the god Kompira is coming here today to drive the evil spirit out of
you, so don't you go back up on the roof.

(TOSAKU *enters, leading the* PRIESTESS. *She has a crafty face.*)

TOSAKU. This is the Priestess I spoke to you about.

GISUKE. Ah, good afternoon. I'm glad you've come—this boy is really a disgrace to the whole family.

PRIESTESS *(casually)*. You needn't worry any more about him. I'll cure him
at once with the god's help. *(Looking at* YOSHITARO*)* This is the one?

GISUKE. Yes. He's twenty-four years old, and the only thing he can do is
climb up to high places.

PRIESTESS. How long has he been this way?

GISUKE. Ever since he was born. Even when he was a baby, he wanted to
be climbing. When he was four or five years old, he climbed onto the
low shrine, then onto the high shrine of Buddha, and finally onto a very
high shelf. When he was seven he began climbing trees. At fifteen he
climbed to the tops of mountains and stayed there all day long. He says
he talks with demons and with the gods. What do you think is the matter
with him?

PRIESTESS. There's no doubt but that it's a fox-spirit. I will pray for him.
(Looking at YOSHITARO*)* Listen now! I am the messenger of the god
Kompira. All that I say comes from the god.

YOSHITARO *(uneasily)*. You say the god Kompira? Have you ever seen him?

PRIESTESS *(staring at him)*. Don't say such sacrilegious things! The god
cannot be seen.

YOSHITARO *(exultantly)*. I have seen him many times! He's an old man with
white robes and a golden crown. He's my best friend.

PRIESTESS *(taken aback at this assertion, and speaking to* GISUKE*)*. This is a fox-spirit, all right, and a very extreme case. I will address the god. *(She chants a prayer in a weird manner.* YOSHITARO, *held fast by* KICHIJI, *watches the* PRIESTESS *blankly. She works herself into a frenzy, and falls to the ground in a faint. Presently she rises to her feet and looks about her strangely.)*

PRIESTESS *(in a changed voice)*. I am the god Kompira!
(All except YOSHITARO *fall to their knees with exclamations of reverence.)*

PRIESTESS *(with affected dignity)*. The elder son of this family is under the influence of a fox-spirit. Hang him up on the branch of a tree and purify him with the smoke of green pine needles. If you fail to do what I say, you will all be punished!
(She faints again. There are more exclamations of astonishment.)

PRIESTESS *(rising and looking about her as though unconscious of what has taken place)*. What has happened? Did the god speak?

GISUKE. It was a miracle.

PRIESTESS. You must do at once whatever the god told you, or you'll be punished. I warn you for your own sake.

GISUKE *(hesitating somewhat)*. Kichiji, go and get some green pine needles.

OYOSHI. No! It's too cruel, even if it is the god's command.

PRIESTESS. He will not suffer, only the fox-spirit within him. The boy himself will not suffer at all. Hurry! *(Looking fixedly at* YOSHITARO*)* Did you hear the god's command? He told the spirit to leave your body before it hurt.

YOSHITARO. That was not Kompira's voice. He wouldn't talk to a priestess like you.

PRIESTESS *(insulted)*. I'll get even with you. Just wait! Don't talk back to the god like that, you horrid fox!
*(*KICHIJI *enters with an armful of green pine boughs.* OYOSHI *is frightened.)*

PRIESTESS. Respect the god or be punished!
*(*GISUKE *and* KICHIJI *reluctantly set fire to the pine needles, then bring* YOSHITARO *to the fire. He struggles against being held in the smoke.)*

YOSHITARO. Father! What are you doing to me? I don't like it! I don't like it!

PRIESTESS. That's not his own voice speaking. It's the fox within him. Only the fox is suffering.

OYOSHI. But it's cruel!
*(*GISUKE *and* KICHIJI *attempt to press* YOSHITARO'S *face into the*

smoke. Suddenly SUEJIRO's *voice is heard calling within the house, and presently he appears. He stands amazed at the scene before him.)*

SUEJIRO. What's happening here? What's the smoke for?

YOSHITARO *(coughing from the smoke, and looking at his brother as at a savior)*. Father and Kichiji are putting me in the smoke.

SUEJIRO *(angrily)*. Father! What foolish thing are you doing now? Haven't I told you time and time again about this sort of business?

GISUKE. But the god inspired the miraculous Priestess . . .

SUEJIRO *(interrupting)*. What nonsense is that? You do these insane things merely because he is so helpless.

(With a contemptuous look at the PRIESTESS *he stamps the fire out.)*

PRIESTESS. Wait! That fire was made at the command of the god!

*(*SUEJIRO *sneeringly puts out the last spark.)*

GISUKE *(more courageously)*. Suejiro, I have no education, and you have, so I am always willing to listen to you. But this fire was made at the god's command, and you shouldn't have stamped on it.

SUEJIRO. Smoke won't cure him. People will laugh at you if they hear you've been trying to drive out a fox. All the gods in the country together couldn't even cure a cold. This Priestess is a fraud. All she wants is the money.

GISUKE. But the doctors can't cure him.

SUEJIRO. If the doctors can't, nobody can. I've told you before that he doesn't suffer. If he did, we'd have to do something for him. But as long as he can climb up on the roof, he is happy. Nobody in the whole country is as happy as he is—perhaps nobody in the world. Besides, if you cure him now, what can he do? He's twenty-four years old and he knows nothing, not even the alphabet. He's had no practical experience. If he were cured, he would be conscious of being crippled, and he'd be the most miserable man alive. Is that what you want to see? It's all because you want to make him normal. But wouldn't it be foolish to become normal merely to suffer? *(Looking sidewise at the* PRIESTESS*)* Tosaku, if you brought her here, you had better take her away.

PRIESTESS *(angry and insulted)*. You disbelieve the oracle of the god. You will be punished! *(She starts her chant as before. She faints, rises, and speaks in a changed voice.)* I am the great god Kompira! What the brother of the patient says springs from his own selfishness. He knows if his sick brother is cured, he'll get the family estate. Doubt not this oracle!

SUEJIRO *(excitedly knocking the* PRIESTESS *down)*. That's a damned lie, you old fool.

(He kicks her.)

PRIESTESS (getting to her feet and resuming her ordinary voice). You've hurt me! You savage!

SUEJIRO. You fraud! You swindler!

TOSAKU (coming between them). Wait, young man! Don't get in such a frenzy.

SUEJIRO (still excited). You liar! A woman like you can't understand brotherly love!

TOSAKU. We'll leave now. It was my mistake to have brought her.

GISUKE (giving TOSAKU some money). I hope you'll excuse him. He's young and has such a temper.

PRIESTESS. You kicked me when I was inspired by the god. You'll be lucky to survive until tonight.

SUEJIRO. Liar!

OYOSHI (soothing SUEJIRO). Be still now. (To the PRIESTESS) I'm sorry this has happened.

PRIESTESS (leaving with TOSAKU). The foot you kicked me with will rot off!

(The PRIESTESS and TOSAKU go out.)

GISUKE (to SUEJIRO). Aren't you afraid of being punished for what you've done?

SUEJIRO. A god never inspires a woman like that old swindler. She lies about everything.

OYOSHI. I suspected her from the very first. She wouldn't do such cruel things if a real god inspired her.

GISUKE (without any insistence). Maybe so. But, Suejiro, your brother will be a burden to you all your life.

SUEJIRO. It will be no burden at all. When I become successful, I'll build a tower for him on top of a mountain.

GISUKE (suddenly). But where's Yoshitaro gone?

KICHIJI (pointing at the roof). He's up there.

GISUKE (having to smile). As usual.

(During the preceding excitement, YOSHITARO has slipped away and climbed back up on the roof. The four persons below look at each other and smile.)

SUEJIRO. A normal person would be angry with you for having put him in the smoke, but you see, he's forgotten everything. (He calls.) Yoshitaro!

YOSHITARO (for all his madness there is affection for his brother). Suejiro! I asked Kompira and he says he doesn't know her!

SUEJIRO (smiling). You're right. The god will inspire you, not a priestess like her.

(Through a rift in the clouds, the golden light of the sunset strikes the roof.)

SUEJIRO *(exclaiming).* What a beautiful sunset!

YOSHITARO *(his face lighted by the sun's reflection).* Suejiro, look! Can't you see a golden palace in that cloud over there? There! Can't you see? Just look! How beautiful!

SUEJIRO *(as he feels the sorrow of sanity).* Yes, I see. I see it, too. Wonderful.

YOSHITARO *(filled with joy).* There! I hear music coming from the palace. Flutes, what I love best of all. Isn't it beautiful?

(The parents have gone into the house. The mad brother on the roof and the sane brother on the ground remain looking at the golden sunset.)

Shiga Naoya[1] (1883–1971)

SEIBEI'S GOURDS[2]

Translated from the Japanese by
Ivan Morris

THIS IS THE STORY of a young boy called Seibei, and of his gourds. Later on Seibei gave up gourds, but he soon found something to take their place: he started painting pictures. It was not long before Seibei was as absorbed in his paintings as he once had been in his gourds.

• • • • •

Seibei's parents knew that he often went out to buy himself gourds. He got them for a few sen[3] and soon had a sizable collection. When he came home, he would first bore a neat hole in the top of the gourd and extract the seeds. Next he applied tea leaves to get rid of the unpleasant gourd smell. He then fetched the saké[4] which he had saved up from the dregs in his father's cup and carefully polished the surface.

Seibei was passionately interested in gourds. One day as he was strolling along the beach, absorbed in his favorite subject, he was startled by an unusual sight: he caught a glimpse of the bald, elongated head of an old man hurrying out of one of the huts by the beach. "What a splendid gourd!" thought Seibei. The old man disappeared from sight, wagging his bald pink pate. Only then did Seibei realize his mistake and he stood there laughing loudly to himself. He laughed all the way home.

Whenever he passed a grocery, a curio shop, a confectioner's, or in fact any place that sold gourds, he stood for minutes on end, his eyes glued to the window, appraising the precious fruit.

"Seibei's Gourds" (original title: "The Artist") by Shiga Naoya, translated by Ivan Morris from JAPAN QUARTERLY. Reprinted by permission of Charles E. Tuttle Co., Inc.

1. *Shiga Naoya* (shē gä nä ô yä). 2. *Seibei's* (sä yē bä yē) *Gourds*. In Japan the cultivation and collection of gourds, the hard-shelled fruit of certain vines, is a popular practice. The dried shells are used as bottles. 3. *sen*, a Japanese coin of little value. About 360 sen equal in value one U.S. cent. 4. *saké*, a Japanese fermented alcoholic beverage made from rice.

Seibei was twelve years old and still at primary school. After class, instead of playing with the other children, he usually wandered about the town looking for gourds. Then in the evening he would sit cross-legged in the corner of the living room working on his newly acquired fruit. When he had finished treating it, he poured in a little saké, inserted a cork stopper which he had fashioned himself, wrapped it in a towel, put this in a tin especially kept for the purpose and finally placed the whole thing on the charcoal footwarmer. Then he went to bed.

As soon as he woke the next morning, he would open the tin and examine the gourd. The skin would be thoroughly damp from the overnight treatment. Seibei would gaze adoringly at his treasure before tying a string round the middle and hanging it in the sun to dry. Then he set out for school.

Seibei lived in a harbor town. Although it was officially a city, one could walk from one end to the other in a matter of twenty minutes. Seibei was always wandering about the streets and had soon come to know every place that sold gourds and to recognize almost every gourd on the market.

He did not care much about the old, gnarled, peculiarly formed gourds usually favored by collectors. The type that appealed to Seibei was even and symmetrical.

"That youngster of yours only seems to like the ordinary looking ones," said a friend of his father's who had come to call. He pointed at the boy, who was sitting in the corner busily polishing a plain, round gourd.

"Fancy a lad spending his time playing around like that with gourds!" said his father, giving Seibei a disgusted look.

"See here, Seibei my lad," said the friend, "there's no use just collecting lots of those things. It's not the quantity that counts, you know. What you want to do is to find one or two really unusual ones."

"I prefer this kind," said Seibei and let the matter drop.

Seibei's father and his friend started talking about gourds.

"Remember that Bakin gourd they had at the agricultural show last spring?" said his father. "It was a real beauty, wasn't it?"

"Yes, I remember. That big, long one. . . ."

As Seibei listened to their conversation, he was laughing inwardly. The Bakin gourd had made quite a stir at the time, but when he had gone to see it (having no idea, of course, who the great poet Bakin might be) he had found it rather a stupid-looking object and had walked out of the show.

"I didn't think so much of it," interrupted Seibei. "It's just a clumsy great thing."

His father opened his eyes wide in surprise and anger.

"What's that?" he shouted. "When you don't know what you're talking about, you'd better shut up!"

Seibei did not say another word.

One day when he was walking along an unfamiliar back street he came upon an old woman with a fruit stall. She was selling dried persimmons and oranges; on the shutters of the house behind the stall she had hung a large cluster of gourds.

"Can I have a look?" said Seibei and immediately ran behind the stall and began examining the gourds. Suddenly he caught sight of one which was about five inches long and at first sight looked quite commonplace. Something about it made Seibei's heart beat faster.

"How much is this one?" he asked, panting out the words.

"Well," said the old woman, "since you're just a lad, I'll let you have it for ten sen."

"In that case," said Seibei urgently, "please hold it for me, won't you? I'll be right back with the money."

He dashed home and in no time at all was back at the stall. He bought the gourd and took it home.

From that time on, he was never separated from his new gourd. He even took it along to school and used to polish it under his desk during class time. It was not long before he was caught at this by one of the teachers, who was particularly incensed because it happened to take place in an ethics class.

This teacher came from another part of Japan and found it most offensive that children should indulge in such effeminate pastimes as collecting gourds. He was forever expounding the classical code of the samurai,[5] and when Kumoemon, the famous Naniwabushi performer,[6] came on tour and recited brave deeds of ancient times, he would attend every single performance, though normally he would not deign to set foot in the disreputable amusement area. He never minded having his students sing Naniwabushi ballads, however raucously. Now, when he found Seibei silently polishing his gourd, his voice trembled with fury.

"You're an idiot!" he shouted. "There's absolutely no future for a boy like you." Then and there he confiscated the gourd on which Seibei had spent so many long hours of work. Seibei stared straight ahead and did not cry.

When he got home, Seibei's face was pale. Without a word, he put his feet on the warmer and sat looking blankly at the wall.

After a while the teacher arrived. As Seibei's father was not yet home from the carpenter's shop where he worked, the teacher directed his attack at Seibei's mother.

"This sort of thing is the responsibility of the family," he said in a stern voice. "It is the duty of you parents to see that such things don't happen." In an agony of embarrassment, Seibei's mother muttered some apology.

---

5. *samurai*, a member of a hereditary military class in feudal Japan. 6. *Naniwabushi performer*, a balladeer who performs in a small theater and accompanies himself on a samisen (a guitarlike instrument).

Meanwhile, Seibei was trying to make himself as inconspicuous as possible in the corner. Terrified, he glanced up at his vindictive teacher and at the wall directly behind where a whole row of fully prepared gourds was hanging. What would happen if the teacher caught sight of them?

Trembling inside, he awaited the worst, but at length the man exhausted his rhetoric and stamped angrily out of the house. Seibei heaved a sigh of relief.

Seibei's mother was sobbing softly. In a querulous whine she began to scold him, and in the midst of this, Seibei's father returned from his shop. As soon as he heard what had happened, he grabbed his son by the collar and gave him a sound beating. "You're no good!" he bawled at him. "You'll never get anywhere in the world the way you're carrying on. I've a good mind to throw you out into the street where you belong!" The gourds on the wall caught his attention. Without a word, he fetched his hammer and systematically smashed them to pieces one after another. Seibei turned pale but said nothing.

The next day the teacher gave Seibei's confiscated gourd to an old porter who worked in the school. "Here, take this," he said, as if handing over some unclean object. The porter took the gourd home with him and hung it on the wall of his small, sooty room.

About two months later the porter, finding himself even more hard pressed for money than usual, decided to take the gourd to a local curio shop to see if he could get a few coppers for it. The curio dealer examined the gourd carefully; then, assuming an uninterested tone, he handed it back to the porter saying: "I might give you five yen [7] for it."

The porter was astounded, but being quite an astute old man, he replied coolly: "I certainly wouldn't part with it for that." The dealer immediately raised his offer to ten yen, but the porter was still adamant.

In the end the curio dealer had to pay fifty yen for the gourd. The porter left the shop, delighted at his luck. It wasn't often that the teachers gave one a free gift equivalent to a year's wages! He was so clever as not to mention the matter to anyone, and neither Seibei nor the teacher ever heard what had happened to the gourd. Yes, the porter was clever, but he was not clever enough: little did he imagine that this same gourd would be passed on by the curio dealer to a wealthy collector in the district for six hundred yen.

. . . . .

Seibei is now engrossed in his pictures. He no longer feels any bitterness either toward the teacher, or toward his father who smashed all his precious gourds to pieces.

Yet gradually his father has begun to scold him for painting pictures. ✕

---

7. *yen*, a Japanese monetary unit, worth about one quarter of a U.S. cent.

Junichiro Tanizaki[1] (1886–1965)

THE THIEF

Translated from the Japanese by
Howard Hibbett

IT WAS YEARS AGO, at the school where I was preparing for Tokyo
Imperial University.

My dormitory roommates and I used to spend a lot of time at what we
called "candlelight study" (there was very little studying to it), and one
night, long after lights-out, the four of us were doing just that, huddled
around a candle talking on and on.

I recall that we were having one of our confused, heated arguments
about love—a problem of great concern to us in those days. Then, by a
natural course of development, the conversation turned to the subject of
crime: we found ourselves talking about such things as swindling, theft,
and murder.

"Of all crimes, the one we're most likely to commit is murder." It was
Higuchi,[2] the son of a well-known professor, who declared this. "But I
don't believe I'd ever steal—I just couldn't do it. I think I could be friends
with any other kind of person, but a thief seems to belong to a different
species." A shadow of distaste darkened his handsome features. Somehow
that frown emphasized his good looks.

"I hear there's been a rash of stealing in the dormitory lately." This
time it was Hirata[3] who spoke. "Isn't that so?" he asked, turning to
Nakamura,[4] our other roommate.

"Yes, and they say it's one of the students."

"How do they know?" I asked.

"Well, I haven't heard all the details—" Nakamura dropped his voice to
a confidential whisper. "But it's happened so often it must be an inside
job."

---

1. *Junichiro Tanizaki* (jù nē chē rô   tä nē zä kē). 2. *Higuchi* (hē gù chē). 3. *Hirata*
(hē rä tä). 4. *Nakamura* (nä kä mù rä).

"Not only that," Higuchi put in, "one of the fellows in the north wing was just going into his room the other day when somebody pushed the door open from the inside, caught him with a hard slap in the face, and ran away down the hall. He chased after him, but by the time he got to the bottom of the stairs the other one was out of sight. Back in his room, he found his trunk and bookshelves in a mess, which proves it was the thief."

"Did he see his face?"

"No, it all happened too fast, but he says he looked like one of us, the way he was dressed. Apparently he ran down the hall with his coat pulled up over his head—the one thing sure is that his coat had a wisteria crest."

"A wisteria crest?" said Hirata. "You can't prove anything by that." Maybe it was only my imagination, but I thought he flashed a suspicious look at me. At the same moment I felt that I instinctively made a wry face, since my own family crest is a wisteria design. It was only by chance that I wasn't wearing my crested coat that night.

"If he's one of us it won't be easy to catch him. Nobody wants to believe there's a thief among us." I was trying to get over my embarrassment because of that moment of weakness.

"No, they'll get him in a couple of days," Higuchi said emphatically. His eyes were sparkling. "This is a secret, but they say he usually steals things in the dressing room of the bathhouse, and for two or three days now the proctors have been keeping watch. They hide overhead and look down through a little hole."

"Oh? Who told you that?" Nakamura asked.

"One of the proctors. But don't go around talking about it."

"If *you* know so much, the thief probably knows it too!" said Hirata, looking disgusted.

Here I must explain that Hirata and I were not on very good terms. In fact, by that time we barely tolerated each other. I say "we," but it was Hirata who had taken a strong dislike to me. According to a friend of mine, he once remarked scornfully that I wasn't what everyone seemed to think I was, that he'd had a chance to see through me. And again: "I'm sick of him. He'll never be a friend of mine. It's only out of pity that I have anything to do with him."

He only said such things behind my back; I never heard them from him directly, though it was obvious that he loathed me. But it wasn't in my nature to demand an explanation. "If there's something wrong with me he ought to say so," I told myself. "If he doesn't have the kindness to tell me what it is, or if he thinks I'm not worth bothering with, then I won't think of *him* as a friend either." I felt a little lonely when I thought of his contempt for me, but I didn't really worry about it.

Hirata had an admirable physique and was the very type of masculinity that our school prides itself on, while I was skinny and pale and high-strung. There was something basically incompatible about us: I had to resign myself to the fact that we lived in separate worlds. Furthermore, Hirata was a judo expert of high rank, and displayed his muscles as if to say: "Watch out, or I'll give you a thrashing!" Perhaps it seemed cowardly of me to take such a meek attitude toward him, and no doubt I *was* afraid of his physical strength; but fortunately I was quite indifferent to matters of trivial pride or prestige. "I don't care how contemptuous the other fellow is; as long as I can go on believing in myself I don't need to feel bitter toward him." That was how I made up my mind, and so I was able to match Hirata's arrogance with my own cool magnanimity. I even told one of the other boys: "I can't help it if Hirata doesn't understand me, but I appreciate his good points anyway." And I actually believed it. I never considered myself a coward. I was even rather conceited, thinking I must be a person of noble character to be able to praise Hirata from the bottom of my heart.

"A wisteria crest?" That night, when Hirata cast his sudden glance at me, the malicious look in his eyes set my nerves on edge. What could that look possibly mean? Did he know that my family crest was wisteria? Or did I take it that way simply because of my own private feelings? If Hirata suspected *me*, how was I to handle the situation? Perhaps I should laugh good-naturedly and say: "Then I'm under suspicion too, because I have the same crest." If the others laughed along with me, I'd be all right. But suppose one of them, say Hirata, only began looking grimmer and grimmer—what then? When I visualized that scene I couldn't very well speak out impulsively.

It sounds foolish to worry about such a thing, but during that brief silence all sorts of thoughts raced through my mind. "In this kind of situation what difference is there, really, between an innocent man and an actual criminal?" By then I felt that I was experiencing a criminal's anxiety and isolation. Until a moment ago I had been one of their friends, one of the elite of our famous school. But now, if only in my own mind, I was an outcast. It was absurd, but I suffered from my inability to confide in them. I was uneasy about Hirata's slightest mood—Hirata who was supposed to be my equal.

"A thief seems to belong to a different species." Higuchi had probably said this casually enough, but now his words echoed ominously in my mind.

"A thief belongs to a different species. . . ." A thief! What a detestable name to be called! I suppose what makes a thief different from other men is not so much his criminal act itself as his effort to hide it at all costs, the strain of trying to put it out of his mind, the dark fears that he can never confess. And now I was becoming enshrouded by that darkness. I was trying not to believe that I was under suspicion; I was worrying about fears that I could not admit to my closest friend. Of course it must have been because Higuchi trusted me that he told us what he'd heard from the proctor. "Don't go around talking about it," he had said, and I was glad. But why should I feel glad? I thought. After all, Higuchi has never suspected me. Somehow I began to wonder about his motive for telling us.

It also struck me that if even the most virtuous person has criminal tendencies, maybe I wasn't the only one who imagined the possibility of being a thief. Maybe the others were experiencing a little of the same discomfort, the same elation. If so, then Higuchi, who had been singled out by the proctor to share his secret, must have felt very proud. Among the four of us it was he who was most trusted, he who was thought least likely to belong to that "other species." And if he won that trust because he came from a wealthy family and was the son of a famous professor, then I could hardly avoid envying him. Just as his social status improved his moral character, so my own background—I was acutely conscious of being a scholarship student, the son of a poor farmer—debased mine. For me to feel a kind of awe in his presence had nothing to do with whether or not I was a thief. We *did* belong to different species. I felt that the more he trusted me, with his frank, open attitude, the more the gulf between us deepened. The more friendly we tried to be, joking with each other in apparent intimacy, gossiping and laughing together, the more the distance between us increased. There was nothing I could do about it.

For a long time afterward I worried about whether or not I ought to wear that coat of mine with the "wisteria crest." Perhaps if I wore it around nonchalantly no one would pay any attention. But suppose they looked at me as much as to say: "Ah, he's wearing it!" Some would suspect me, or try to suppress their doubts of me, or feel sorry for me because I was under suspicion. If I became embarrassed and uneasy not only with Hirata and Higuchi but with all the students, and if I then felt obliged to put my coat away, that would seem even more sinister. What I dreaded was not the bare fact of being suspect, but all the unpleasant emotions that would be stirred up in others. If I were to cause doubt in other people's minds I would create a barrier between myself and those who had always been my friends. Even theft itself was not as ugly as the suspicions that would be aroused by it. No one would want to think of me as a thief: as long as it hadn't been proved, they'd want to go on associating with me as freely as ever, forcing themselves to trust me. Otherwise, what would friendship mean? Thief or not, I might be guilty of a worse sin than stealing from a friend: the sin of spoiling a friendship. Sowing seeds of doubt about myself was criminal. It *was* worse than stealing. If I were a prudent, clever thief—no, I mustn't put it that way—if I were a thief with the least bit of conscience and consideration for other people, I'd try to keep my friendships untarnished, try to be open with my friends, treat them with a sincerity and warmth that I need never be ashamed of, while carrying out my thefts in secrecy. Perhaps I'd be what people call "a brazen thief," but if you look at it from the thief's point of view, it's the most honest attitude to take. "It's true that I steal, but it's equally true that I value my friends," such a man would say. "That is typical of a thief, that's why he belongs to a different species." Anyhow, when I started thinking that way, I couldn't help becoming more and more aware of the distance between me and my friends. Before I knew it I felt like a full-fledged thief.

One day I mustered up my courage and wore the crested coat out on the school grounds. I happened to meet Nakamura, and we began walking along together.

"By the way," I remarked, "I hear they haven't caught the thief yet."

"That's right," Nakamura answered, looking away.

"Why not? Couldn't they trap him at the bathhouse?"

"He didn't show up there again, but you still hear about lots of things being stolen in other places. They say the proctors called Higuchi in the other day and gave him the devil for letting their plan leak out."

"Higuchi?" I felt the color drain from my face.

"Yes. . . ." He sighed painfully, and a tear rolled down his cheek. "You've got to forgive me! I've kept it from you till now, but I think you ought to know the truth. You won't like this, but you're the one the proctors suspect. I hate to talk about it—I've never suspected you for a minute. I believe in you. And because I believe in you, I just had to tell you. I hope you won't hold it against me."

"Thanks for telling me. I'm grateful to you." I was almost in tears myself, but at the same time I thought: "It's come at last!" As much as I dreaded it, I'd been expecting this day to arrive.

"Let's drop the subject," said Nakamura, to comfort me. "I feel better now that I've told you."

"But we can't put it out of our minds just because we hate to talk about it. I appreciate your kindness, but I'm not the only one who's been humiliated—I've brought shame on you too, as my friend. The mere fact that I'm under suspicion makes me unworthy of friendship. Any way you look at it, my reputation is ruined. Isn't that so? I imagine you'll turn your back on me too."

"I swear I never will—and I don't think you've brought any shame on me." Nakamura seemed alarmed by my reproachful tone. "Neither does Higuchi. They say he did his best to defend you in front of the proctors. He told them he'd doubt himself before he doubted you."

"But they still suspect me, don't they? There's no use trying to spare my feelings. Tell me everything you know. I'd rather have it that way."

Then Nakamura hesitantly explained: "Well, it seems the proctors get all kinds of tips. Ever since Higuchi talked too much that night there haven't been any more thefts at the bathhouse, and that's why they suspect you."

"But I wasn't the only one who heard him!"—I didn't say this, but the thought occurred to me immediately. It made me feel even more lonely and wretched.

"But how did they know Higuchi told us? There were only the four of us that night, so if nobody else knew it, and if you and Higuchi trust me—"

"You'll have to draw your own conclusions," Nakamura said, with an imploring look. "You know who it is. He's misjudged you, but I don't want to criticize him."

A sudden chill came over me. I felt as if Hirata's eyes were glaring into mine.

"Did you talk to him about me?"

"Yes. . . . But I hope you realize that it isn't easy, since I'm his friend as well as yours. In fact, Higuchi and I had a long argument with him last night, and he says he's leaving the dormitory. So I have to lose one friend on account of another."

I took Nakamura's hand and gripped it hard. "I'm grateful for friends like you and Higuchi," I said, tears streaming from my eyes. Nakamura cried too. For the first time in my life I felt that I was really experiencing the warmth of human compassion. This was what I had been searching for while I was tormented by my sense of helpless isolation. No matter how vicious a thief I might be, I could never steal anything from Nakamura.

After a while I said: "To tell you the truth, I'm not worth the trouble I'm causing you. I can't stand by in silence and see you two lose such a good friend because of someone like me. Even though he doesn't trust me, I still respect him. He's a far better man than I am. I recognize his value as well as anyone. So why don't I move out instead, if it's come to that? Please —let *me* go, and you three can keep on living together. Even if I'm alone I'll feel better about it."

"But there's no reason for you to leave," said Nakamura, his voice charged with emotion. "I recognize his good points too, but you're the one that's being persecuted. I won't side with him when it's so unfair. If *you* leave, *we* ought to leave too. You know how stubborn he is—once he's made up his mind to go he's not apt to change it. Why not let him do as he pleases? We might as well wait for him to come to his senses and apologize. That shouldn't take very long anyway."

"But he'll never come back to apologize. He'll go on hating me forever."

Nakamura seemed to assume that I felt resentful toward Hirata. "Oh, I don't think so," he said quickly. "He'll stick to his word—that's both his strength and his weakness—but once he knows he's wrong he'll come and apologize, and make a clean breast of it. That's one of the likable things about him."

"It would be fine if he did . . . ," I said thoughtfully. "He may come back to you, but I don't believe he'll ever make friends with me again. . . . But you're right, he's really likable. I only wish he liked me too."

Nakamura put his hand on my shoulder as if to protect his poor friend, as we plodded listlessly along on the grass. It was evening and a light mist hung over the school grounds: we seemed to be on an island surrounded by endless gray seas. Now and then a few students walking the other way would glance at me and go on. They already know, I thought; they're ostracizing me. I felt an overwhelming loneliness.

That night Hirata seemed to have changed his mind; he showed no intention of moving. But he refused to speak to us—even to Higuchi and Nakamura. Yet for me to leave at this stage was impossible, I decided. Not only would I be disregarding the kindness of my friends, I would be making myself seem all the more guilty. I ought to wait a little longer.

"Don't worry," my two friends were forever telling me. "As soon as they catch him the whole business will clear up." But even after another week had gone by, the criminal was still at large and the thefts were as frequent as ever. At last even Nakamura and Higuchi lost some money and a few books.

"Well, you two finally got it, didn't you? But I have a feeling the rest of us won't be touched." I remember Hirata's taunting look as he made this sarcastic remark.

After supper Nakamura and Higuchi usually went to the library, and Hirata and I were left to confront each other. I found this so uncomfortable that I began spending my evenings away from the dormitory too, either going to the library or taking long walks. One night around nine-thirty I came back from a walk and looked into our study. Oddly enough, Hirata wasn't there, nor did the others seem to be back yet. I went to look in our bedroom, but it was empty too. Then I went back to the study and over to Hirata's desk. Quietly I opened his drawer and ferreted out the registered letter that had come to him from his home a few days ago. Inside the letter were three ten-yen [5] money orders, one of which I leisurely removed and put in my pocket. I pushed the drawer shut again and sauntered out into the hall. Then I went down to the yard, cut across the tennis court, and headed for the dark weedy hollow where I always buried the things I stole. But at that moment someone yelled: "Thief!" and flew at me from behind, knocking me down with a blow to my head. It was Hirata.

"Come on, let's have it! Let's see what you stuck in your pocket!"

"All right, all right, you don't have to shout like that," I answered calmly, smiling at him. "I admit I stole your money order. If you ask for it I'll give it back to you, and if you tell me to come with you I'll go anywhere you say. So we understand each other, don't we? What more do you want?"

Hirata seemed to hesitate, but soon began furiously raining blows on my face. Somehow the pain was not wholly unpleasant. I felt suddenly relieved of the staggering burden I had been carrying.

---

5. *yen,* a Japanese monetary unit, worth about one quarter of a U.S. cent.

"There's no use beating me up like this, when I fell right into your trap for you. I made that mistake because you were so sure of yourself—I thought: 'Why the devil can't I steal from *him*?' But now you've found me out, so that's all there is to it. Later on we'll laugh about it together."

I tried to shake Hirata's hand good-naturedly, but he grabbed me by the collar and dragged me off toward our room. That was the only time Hirata seemed contemptible in my eyes.

"Hey, you fellows, I've caught the thief! You can't say I was taken in by him!" Hirata swaggered into our room and shoved me down in front of Nakamura and Higuchi, who were back from the library. Hearing the commotion, the other boys in the dormitory came swarming around our doorway.

"Hirata's right!" I told my two friends, picking myself up from the floor. "I'm the thief." I tried to speak in my normal tone, as casually as ever, but I realized that my face had gone pale.

"I suppose you hate me," I said to them. "Or else you're ashamed of me. . . . You're both honest, but you're certainly gullible. Haven't I been telling you the truth over and over again? I even said: 'I'm not the person you think I am. Hirata's the man to trust. He'll never be taken in.' But you didn't understand. I told you: 'Even if you become friendly with Hirata again, he'll never make friends with *me!*' I went as far as to say: 'I know better than anyone what a fine fellow Hirata is!' Isn't that so? I've never lied to you, have I? You may ask why I didn't come out and tell you the whole truth. You probably think I was deceiving you after all. But try looking at it from my position. I'm sorry, but stealing is one thing I can't control. Still, I didn't like to deceive you, so I told you the truth in a roundabout way. I couldn't be any more honest than that—it's your fault for not taking my hints. Maybe you think I'm just being perverse, but I've never been more serious. You'll probably ask why I don't quit stealing, if I'm so anxious to be honest. But that's not a fair question. You see, I was born a thief. I tried to be as sincere as I could with you under the circumstances. There was nothing else I could do. Even then my conscience bothered me—didn't I ask you to let *me* move out, instead of Hirata? I wasn't trying to fool you, I really wanted to do it for your sake. It's true that I stole from you, but it's also true that I'm your friend. I appeal to your friendship: I want you to understand that even a thief has feelings."

Nakamura and Higuchi stood there in silence, blinking with astonishment.

"Well, I can see you think I've got a lot of nerve. You just don't understand me. I guess it can't be helped, since you're of a different species." I smiled to conceal my bitterness, and added: "But since I'm your friend I'll warn you that this isn't the last time a thing like this will happen. So be on your guard! You two made friends with a thief because of your gullibility. You're likely to run into trouble when you go out in the world. Maybe you get better grades in school, but Hirata is a better man. You can't fool Hirata!"

When I singled him out for praise, Hirata made a wry face and looked away. At that moment he seemed strangely ill at ease.

Many years have passed since then. I became a professional thief and have been often behind bars; yet I cannot forget those memories—especially my memories of Hirata. Whenever I am about to commit a crime I see his face before me. I see him swaggering about as haughtily as ever, sneering at me: "Just as I suspected!" Yes, he was a man of character with great promise. But the world is mysterious. My prediction that the naïve Higuchi would "run into trouble" was wrong: partly through his father's influence, he has had a brilliant career—traveling abroad, earning a doctoral degree, and today holding a high position in the Ministry of Railways. Meanwhile nobody knows what has become of Hirata. It's no wonder we think life is unpredictable.

I assure my reader that this account is true. I have not written a single dishonest word here. And, as I hoped Nakamura and Higuchi would, I hope you will believe that delicate moral scruples can exist in the heart of a thief like me.

But perhaps you won't believe me either. Unless of course (if I may be pardoned for suggesting it) you happen to belong to my own species.   ✕

Tayama Katai[1] (1871-1930)

ONE SOLDIER

Translated from the Japanese by
G. W. Sargent

HE STARTED WALKING AGAIN.

The rifle was heavy, the pack was heavy, his legs were heavy. His aluminum canteen clanked noisily against his bayonet. The sound jarred horribly on his strained nerves, and he tried first one, and then another and another way of silencing it; but the clanking went on and on. He gave up.

The sickness had not really gone, and he breathed with difficulty. Shivering fits, spasms of heat and icy cold, passed incessantly through his frame. His head burned like fire, and his temples throbbed. What had made him leave the hospital, he wondered? Why—when the army doctor had asked him to stay—why had he left the hospital? He asked the question, but he felt no regrets over his decision. There had been fifteen of them there, sick and wounded, lying on bare boards in a small room, part of a dilapidated house which the retreating enemy had abandoned. For twenty days he had endured the decay and the dirt, the moaning, the oppressive closeness, and the swarms of frightening flies. For food they had had rice-bran porridge with the merest pinch of salt, and he had often known the pangs of hunger. He felt sick even now as he recalled the latrine at the rear of the hospital. The pits were shallow, dug in haste, and the stench struck forcibly at your eyes and nostrils. Flies zoomed around you. Dirty, and black as coal.

Anything was better than that. It was better to be here on this broad open plain. You could not imagine how much better. The plains of Manchuria were vast and deserted, endless fields of tall, ripening cane. But the air was fresh and clean. There was sunshine, there were clouds, there were mountains—he became suddenly aware of a dreadful clamor, and he

"One Soldier" by Tayama Katai, translated by G. W. Sargent from MODERN JAPANESE LITERATURE, edited by Donald Keene. Reprinted by permission of the translator.
1. *Tayama Katai* (tä yä mä kä tä I).

stopped and turned in its direction. It was the same train that he had seen before, still over there on the track. Hundreds of Chinese coolies swarmed about the long, boiler-less, funnel-less monster, pushing frantically, like ants returning home with some gigantic prey.

The rays of the evening sun slanted across the scene, giving it the unreal clarity of a painting.

The noncommissioned officer he had noticed before was still riding on the train. There he was, the one standing aloft on the freight car with the tallest load of rice bales. He shouted to him.

"I'm sick. I can't walk. Can you give me a lift as far as Anshan?"

The fellow was laughing at him. "This train's not for soldiers. I don't know any regulation which says the infantry should ride on trains."

"I'm sick. Can't you see I'm sick? It's beriberi.[2] If I can get to Anshan my unit will be there, I'm certain. Soldiers should help each other, you know. Give me a lift, please!"

He was imploring him, but the fellow would not listen. He only mocked. "Still a private, eh? Time you got yourself some stripes!"

The battles at Chin Chou and Têli-ssu had been won by common soldiers, hadn't they? Blockhead! Brute!

Suddenly a different train—the train in which he had set out for the war[3] from the barracks at Toyohashi—passed before his mind's eye. The station was a mass of flags. Cheers resounded—banzai![4] banzai! Then, without warning, he was gazing into his wife's face. It was not the tear-stained face which had bade him good-bye at the gate, but a beautiful, smiling face from some moment—he could not remember the time or place exactly—when he had wondered at its loveliness with all his heart. His mother was shaking him by the shoulder now. It was time to get up, she was saying. He would be late for school. Somehow his mind had slipped back to his school days. And now the evening sun was glistening on the bald pate of a ship's captain, in the bay at the back of the house. The captain was scolding a group of children, and one of those children was himself.

These shadows from the past and the painful, unpleasant realities of the present were clearly differentiated in his mind, but only a hairsbreadth separated them. The rifle was heavy, the pack was heavy, his legs were heavy. From the waist down he might have been another man, and he hardly knew whether it was he or someone else walking. The brown road —its parched mud surface deeply pocked and rutted by the boots, straw sandals, and gun-carriage wheels which had once sunk into it—stretched on and on before him. He had little love left for these Manchurian roads. How

---

2. *beriberi,* a disease prevalent in Asian countries, caused by a deficiency of vitamin B₁ and characterized by extreme weakness and wasting away. 3. *the war,* the Russo-Japanese war of 1904 to 1905. 4. *banzai!* A Japanese patriotic cheer.

far must he go before the road came to an end? How far before he need walk no farther along it? The pebbled roads of his home district, the sandy roads along the seashore, wet after rain . . . how he longed for those smooth pleasant surfaces. This was a big broad highway, but there was not a smooth level patch to be seen. After a day's rain it would be as sticky as wet wall-plaster, and your boots, perhaps even the calves of your legs, would sink halfway into the mud. On the night before the battle at Ta-shih-ch'iao he had trudged in darkness through ten miles of oozy mire. Flecks of it had caked the back of his blouse and even the hair at the back of his head. That was the time when they were detailed to convoy the gun carriages. The carriages had sunk into the mud and wouldn't budge an inch, and they had shoved and shoved to get them moving again. If the Third Regiment's artillery failed to move on ahead and take up their positions there could be no attack. And after working the night through there was that battle the next day. Endless streams of shells, theirs and the enemy's, passing overhead with a nasty, whining rush. The hot midday sun scorching down from directly above. Past four o'clock they came to close quarters with the enemy infantry. There was the sharp crackle of rifle fire, like beans popping in a frying pan. Now and again a shot had zipped close by his ear. Someone nearby in the line had gasped. He had looked around, startled, and seen the soldier topple forward, blood oozing slowly from a bullet wound in his stomach, glistening red in the warm evening sun. That soldier had been a good sort: cheerful, a nondrinker, at home in any company. After the landing they had gone out together on foraging duties, and they had rounded up pigs together. But that man was gone from the world of the living. It was somehow impossible to think it, but impossible to deny it.

Overtaking him, along the brown road, came a line of wagons loaded with army provisions. Some were drawn by donkeys, some by mules, and he listened to the strident shouts of their Chinese drivers—whoa, whoa, whee!—and to the cracking of the long whips as they flashed in the evening sun. The road was so deeply pitted that the carts moved forward in a series of uneasy lurches, like ships crashing into waves. He felt weak. His breathing was as difficult as ever. He could go no farther like this. He started running after the wagons to ask for a lift.

The canteen went clank-clank. It jarred horribly. The odds and ends in his pack and the rounds in his ammunition pouches clattered noisily up and down. At times the butt of his rifle struck against his thigh, and he almost leapt in agony.

"Hi! Hi!"

They could not hear him.

"Hi! Hi!"

He put his body's whole strength behind his shouts. They had heard, of course, but not one of them turned to look. They must have guessed that there was no money in it. Momentarily he slackened his pace, but he ran forward again, and this time managed to draw level with the last wagon in the line.

The load of rice bales towered above him like a mountain. He saw the Chinaman glance behind. It was a plump, unpleasant face—but he gave the man no chance to say yes or no. He jumped on, and gasping painfully for breath, settled himself among the bales. The Chinaman urged on his mules, seemingly resigned to suffer the intrusion. The wagon bumped and lurched on its way.

His head reeled, and heaven and earth seemed to revolve about him. His chest was aching, his forehead throbbing. He was going to be sick. A sense of uneasiness and foreboding invaded every corner of his being with fearful insistence. And at the same time, while the dreadful lurching started again, all kinds of voices whispered inside his head and close around his ears. He had experienced similar bouts before, but none of them had been as bad as this.

They must have left the open plain and entered a village. A greenness of thick shady willows waved above him. The rays of the evening sun, piercing the greenness, clearly revealed each tiny leaf. He saw low shapeless roofs, and as he passed they seemed to be quivering as though shaken by a violent earthquake. Suddenly he realized that the cart had stopped.

They were on a stretch of road shaded by willows. He counted five carts, drawn up close one behind the other.

Someone grasped him by the shoulder.

It was a Japanese, a corporal.

"You there, what are you up to?"

He raised his aching body.

"What are you doing, riding on this cart?"

It was too much trouble to explain things. He had even lost the will to speak.

"You can't ride up there. Even if it was allowed, the load's already too heavy. You're from the Eighteenth Regiment, aren't you?"

He nodded in agreement.

"What's the matter?"

"I was in the hospital until yesterday."

"Are you better now?"

He nodded again, but without any particular meaning.

"It's hard luck your being sick, but you've got to get off this cart. We're in a hurry. The fighting's started at Liaoyang.[5] "

"Liaoyang!" The single word was enough to set his nerves on edge again. "Has it started already?"

---

5. *Liaoyang.* The Battle of Liaoyang, named after a town in northeast China, lasted nine days and resulted in a significant victory for the Japanese forces.

"Can't you hear those guns?"

Some time back he had imagined that a kind of rumbling noise had begun over beyond the horizon, but he had told himself it could hardly be Liaoyang yet.

"Has Anshan fallen?"

"We took it the day before yesterday. Looks as if they'll put up some resistance this side of Liaoyang. It started at six this evening they say."

Yes, there was a faint, distant rumbling, and if you listened carefully there could be no mistake. They were guns. The old disagreeable noises moved through the air above his head. The infantry was attacking, weaving through the thick of it. Blood was flowing. As the thoughts flashed through his mind he experienced a strange mixture of panic and attraction. His comrades were in that battle. They were shedding their blood for the Japanese Empire.

He pictured the horrors of the battlefield and the scenes of triumph. But here, twenty miles away, here on the Manchurian plain all was at peace, only a sad autumn breeze blowing beneath the evening sun. The tide of great armies had swept over these villages, and their peace was as if it had never been disturbed.

"It'll be a big battle, I suppose?"

"Certainly will."

"Not over in a day?"

"Of course not."

The corporal was speaking eagerly to him now, as one soldier to another, while the distant booming of the guns sounded in their ears. The drivers of the five heavily loaded wagons and the foremen of the Chinese coolies were squatting in a circle, jabbering noisily among themselves. The rays of the evening sun shone aslant the donkeys' long ears, and at times the air was rent with piercing brays. Over among the willows stood a row of five or six white-walled Chinese country houses, and in their gardens he could see tall pagoda trees. There were wells, too, and sheds. An old woman with bound feet hobbled by laboriously. Behind, visible through the leaves of the willows, was the vast empty plain. The corporal was pointing to a chain of brown hills. Beyond them rose a purple-tinged mountain. That was where the guns were firing.

The five wagons moved off.

He was left behind, alone again. He had been told that the next army supply depot was at Hsin-t'ai-tzu. That was another three miles, but there was nowhere to stay the night unless he reached there.

He made up his mind to go on, and he started walking again.

He moved with the utmost difficulty, he was so dog-tired, but somehow even walking was a relief after that wagon. The pain in his stomach was no better, but there was no sense in worrying about that now.

Again the same brown road ahead, the same fields of cane on either side, the same evening sunshine. The same train, even, was passing by on the track. This time it was returning, on the downgrade, and traveling at considerable speed. A train with a locomotive could not have traveled faster, and it made him giddy to watch the cars flashing in and out of the cuttings. The Japanese flag was fluttering on the last car, and he watched it appear and disappear a hundred times amid the cane fields. When it disappeared for a last time, only the noise of the train was left, and mingled with it, the insistent rumble of distant gunfire.

On the road itself there was not a village in sight, but to the west, discernible among gloomy clusters of willow trees, were the occasional brown or white shapes of cottages. There was no sign of inhabitants, but from the cottages rose thin threads of bluish smoke, lonely and cheerless.

The evening shadows had grown to great lengths. Those of the tall canes were darkening the whole breadth of the road, and had already begun to climb the canes opposite. Even the shadows of small weeds by the roadside were stretching enormous distances. In contrast, the hills to the east were now so sharply illuminated that they seemed to float in the air. With its indescribable strength of shadows the loneliness of evening came pressing in upon him.

He came to a break in the canes. Suddenly he saw his own shadow before him, amazingly long. The rifle on his shoulder was moving across the grass far out in the fields. He was stricken with a sense of his isolation.

Insects were singing in the grass. Their cries were strangely unlike those to which he had listened in the fields around his home. This foreignness, coupled with the immensity of the plain, sent a stab of pain through him. The flow of recollections, checked for more than an hour, came suddenly flooding in again.

The face of his mother, his wife, his brother, the faces of women he had known, passed before him in rapid succession as though they were pictures on a revolving paper lantern. The old house in the village, the warm security of his life at home, a fleeting image of himself—so very young he looked—setting out for Tokyo to earn his living.

Tokyo. He saw the busy streets at night, the flower-shops, the magazine booths, the rows of newly published books, and—around the corner— the crowded vaudeville theatres and the reception houses: he heard the strumming of samisens,[6] and the forced laughter of the women. Those were good times. The girl he liked best was in a house in Naka-chō, and he had gone there often. She had a round, winsome face, and even now he remembered her with affection. As the eldest son of a prosperous country household he had never known the lack of money, and life had been a series of pleasant experiences. His friends of those days had all gone out into the world now. Only a little while back he had run across one of them,

---

6. *samisen,* a Japanese guitarlike instrument.

an army captain of the Sixth Division. The fellow had a very high opinion of himself now.

Nothing was more cruel, he thought, than the narrow discipline of army life. But today, oddly enough, the thought roused in him none of the usual spirit of rebellion, not even a sense of martyrdom. He was gripped with fear. When he set out for the war he had dedicated himself body and soul to the service of his country and the Emperor. He had made a fine speech on the theme at his old school in the village. "I have no wish to return alive," he had said. He was in the prime of spirits and health, at that time. He had made that speech, but, of course, he had never expected to die. Beneath it all had been nothing but dreams of victory and glory. Now, for the first time, he was experiencing an uneasiness on the score of death. He really felt that it was possible that he might not, after all, return alive, and the thought filled him with terror. There was this sickness, this beriberi—and even if he recovered, the war itself was nothing but a vast prison from which, no matter how he struggled and craved for freedom, there was no escape. He recalled some words which his comrade who had been killed had once used to him.

"There's no way out of this hole. We have to be ready to die, and we have to put a good face on it."

And how on earth could he—a prey to fatigue, sickness, and fear—expect to escape from this dreadful inferno? Desertion? He would try even that if it were any good. The undying disgrace to his name would be bad enough, of course, but on top of that, on the dawn after his recapture, there was still the firing squad. The end was death again. But what were his prospects if he pressed on? He must become a man of the battlefields. A man of the battlefields must be resigned to annihilation. For the first time he marveled at his stupidity in leaving the hospital. It would have been so easy to have had himself invalided to the rear. . . .

It was too late now, he was trapped, there was no road of escape. Negative despair invaded his whole being, pressing upon him with irresistible strength. The will to walk was gone. Tears flowed uncontrollably. If there are any gods in this life, help me, help me! Show me a way out! I shall bear every trial with patience after this! I shall do any amount of fine deeds! If I promise you anything I shall never go back on it!

He raised his voice, shouting and sobbing.

His breast heaved. He cried like a baby, the tears streaming down his cheeks. The thought that his body might perish was agonizing. In his breast, until this moment, passions of patriotism had often blazed. On the deck of the transport ship, joining with the others in the military songs, his imagination had been fired by notions of heroic death. If an enemy warship were to appear, he had thought, and sink their ship with a shot . . . if he were destined to be a corpse drifting among the weeds on the sea bottom, he would be proud to die in such a way. At the battle of Chin Chou, crouching low amid the death-dealing rattle of machine guns, he had gone bravely forward. Though there were times when he had been horrified at the bloodshed, the suffering of his comrades, he had felt that it was all for the motherland, all for honor. But the blood of his comrades was not his blood. Face to face with his own death the bravest soldier panicked.

His legs were heavy and weary. He felt sick. The thirty-mile journey—two days on the road, and a bitterly cold night in the open—had certainly played havoc with his already disordered system. The dysentery was gone, but the mild beriberi had become acute. He knew what that might mean . . . paralysis of the heart. He shuddered at the thought. Was there no way of escape at all? He wept aloud as he walked, his nerves on edge, his body shaking, his legs racked with cramp.

The plain was at peace. Now that the huge red sun was about to sink beneath the horizon one half of the sky was gold, the other a dark, deep blue. A speck of cloud, like a bird whose wings were tipped with gold, drifted across the sky. The shadows of the cane merged with the general shadow, and across the vast plain blew the autumn wind. Only a few minutes ago the guns from Liaoyang had been rumbling steadily and distinctly, but now they too had dwindled imperceptibly to silence.

Two privates were running up behind him.

They continued past for a dozen yards or so. Then one turned and started back.

He pulled himself together. He was ashamed to be seen like this, weeping aloud.

"Hi! What's the trouble?"

"Beriberi."

"That's hard luck. Is it bad?"

"It's pretty painful."

"You *are* in a mess. If beriberi affects your heart it's no joke. How far are you going?"

"My unit's over beyond Anshan, I think."

"You can't get that far today."

"I suppose not."

"Come along with us as far as Hsin-t'ai-tzu. We'll get a doctor to look at you."

"Is it a long way?"

"Just over there. You see that hill? This side of it there's the railroad. Where you see the flag flying, that's the Hsin-t'ai-tzu depot."

His spirits revived. He walked along behind the two of them. They were sorry for him, and they carried his rifle and pack. As they walked in front they talked of the day's fighting at Liaoyang.

"Plenty of reserves moving up, aren't there?"

"We're too few to attack. The enemy positions are pretty strong, I'm told."

"Do you think we'll win?"

"We're in for it if we lose."

"If only we could cut behind them for once."

"We'll do it properly this time. You'll see."

He listened intently to what they said. The guns opened up again in the distance.

The supply depot at Hsin-t'ai-tzu was a scene of tremendous activity and confusion. A regiment of the reserve had arrived, and in the shadow of the buildings above the railroad, alongside the stacks of provisions, were rows and rows of soldiers' caps, rifles, and swords. Five barrack buildings, formerly occupied by the enemy railway guard, flanked the rails. A flag fluttered above the building which now served as the supply-depot head-quarters, and there the confusion was at its worst. Soldiers were gathered outside it in a dense throng, and in and out, in endless succession, hurried officers with long swords hanging at their sides. Fires were lit beneath the depot's three large rice caldrons, and clouds of smoke curled upwards into the evening sky. In one the rice was already cooked, and the mess sergeant, bellowing commands at his subordinates, was supervising a hasty distribution of rations to the assembled soldiers. But since these three caldrons were obviously insufficient to meet the requirements of a whole regiment, the majority had been issued with a ration of hulled rice in their mess kits and were scattering to various parts of the field to prepare their suppers for themselves. The neighborhood was soon dotted with the flames of hundreds of cane fires.

Near one of the barrack buildings men were settling down to the nightlong labor of loading ammunition boxes on to freight trains bound for the front. Infantrymen and railway troops moved to and fro among the freight cars in feverish, ceaseless activity. A single noncommissioned officer directed their movements, issuing rapid words of command from a perch high on the load of a car.

The day was over, but the war went on. From beyond the dark saddle-shaped mountain of Anshan the sound of guns persisted.

Now that he had arrived he made inquiries about a doctor. But there was something incongruous about asking for a doctor here. This was no time or place for people to stop and concern themselves over the life or death of a single soldier.

He managed, thanks to the efforts of his two friends, to get himself a small portion of boiled rice. That was all. We can't do much more now. Just wait a little longer. As soon as this regiment moves on we'll find the doctor and bring him to you. Take things easy and get a rest. If you go straight along the road from here, three or four hundred yards at most, you'll see a big house. You'll recognize it without any trouble—there's a saké stall [7] in the entrance. Go right inside and get some sleep . . . that was all they could suggest.

He was sick to death of walking. He took back his rifle and pack, but when he placed them across his shoulders he almost collapsed beneath the weight. But it was impossible to give up here. If he were going to die, he must die in privacy. Yes, privacy . . . anywhere would do. He longed to enter some quiet place and sleep, and rest.

The dark road went on and on. Here and there he passed groups of soldiers. His mind returned suddenly to the barracks at Toyohashi. He had slipped away to a quiet bar and had drunk solidly. In his drunkenness he had struck a sergeant. They gave him a spell in detention. This really was a long road. There was no sign of anything resembling the house they had described. Three or four hundred yards, they had said. He must have come a thousand yards already. Perhaps he'd missed it. He turned and looked back—in the supply depot he could see the gleam of lamps and watchfires, and dark groups of soldiers moving uncertainly, as though they had lost their way. The shouts of the men at work on the ammunition trains reached him through the night air with startling clarity.

It was secluded here. Not a soul around. Suddenly he felt horribly sick. Even if there was no house to hide himself in, he thought, this was a good place to die; and he sank to the ground in exhaustion. Strangely enough he no longer felt as dejected and miserable as before. No memories came back from the past. The shimmering light of the stars shone into his eyes. He raised his head and glanced casually around.

He was surprised to see that a little way before him, somehow unnoticed till now, was a solitary Western-style house. Inside a lamp was burning, and he could see a round, red, paper lantern hanging in the doorway. He heard voices.

Sure enough, in the entrance was something which might well be a saké stall. It was difficult to be certain in the dark, but in one corner of the entrance there appeared to be an object like a stove, with embers glowing red beneath it. A straggle of smoke curled up, lightly enfolding the lantern. He could read the writing on the lantern: "Sweet Bean Soup. 5 Sen." [8]

He moved forward to see better. In the darkness at one side of the entrance he could make out a low stone step. This is the place, he thought. His first reaction, on realizing that now he might rest, was a feeling of unutterable content. Silently and stealthily he mounted the stone step. It was dark inside. He could not be sure, but he seemed to have entered a corridor. He pushed at what he thought was the first door, but it would not

---

7. *saké stall*, a stall for the sale of saké, a Japanese fermented alcoholic beverage made of rice. **8.** *Sen*, a Japanese coin of little value. About 360 sen equal in value one U.S. cent.

open. Two or three steps farther on was another door. He pushed, but again it would not open.

He went farther inside.

The corridor came to an end. There was no turning. Not knowing what to do next he pressed against the wall on his right, and suddenly the darkness was broken. A door swung back. He could see nothing inside the room, but stars were shining at him, and he knew that in front was a glass window.

He set down his rifle, unhitched his pack, and dropped, suddenly, full length to the floor. He drew a deep, laborious breath. He had reached his haven of peace.

Beneath the feeling of satisfaction a new uneasiness was advancing and taking possession of him. Something akin to fatigue, mental exhaustion, and despair pressed heavily upon his whole being like a weight of lead. Recollections came in disjointed fragments, sometimes flashing at lightning speed, sometimes growing slowly upon his consciousness with the ponderous insistence of a bullock's breathing.

There were throbbing pains in his calves like those of cramp. He writhed on the floor. His body was nearing the limit of its endurance. He tossed and turned, without knowing what he did.

The pain advanced on him like the tide. It raged with the ferocity of a great wind. He raised his legs and banged them on the hard wooden boards. He rolled his body to this side and to that. "This pain . . . !" Not thinking or knowing what he said he cried aloud.

In reality the pain did not yet seem unbearable. It was severe, but he told himself constantly that he must reserve his strength for the next great pain, and that helped, if only a little, to lessen the suffering of the moment.

He did not think so much how sad it was to die, but rather how best to conquer this pain. The weak, tearful, spiritless despair which gripped him was more than matched by this positive will to resist, which stemmed from his conviction, as a human being, that he had a right to live.

He was beyond knowing how much time had passed. He wished the doctor would come, but he had little leisure to dwell on the thought. New pains gripped him.

Nearby, beneath the floor boards, a cricket was singing. Even as he struggled in agony he said to himself that a cricket was singing. The insect's monotonous note of melancholy sank deep into him.

The cramp was returning. He writhed on the boards.

"This pain, this pain, this pain!"

He screamed the words at the top of his voice.

"This pain! Somebody . . . is there no one here?"

The powerful instinct to resist, to live, had fast dwindled, and he was not consciously calling for assistance. He was almost in a stupor. His outbursts were the rustling of leaves disturbed by forces of nature, the voices of waves, the cries of tragic humanity.

"This pain, this pain!"

His voice echoed startlingly in the silence of the room. In this room, until a month ago, officers of the Russian railway guard had lived and slept. When Japanese soldiers first entered it they had found a soot-stained image of Christ nailed to the wall. Last winter those officers had looked out through this window at the incessant snowstorms sweeping across the Manchurian plain, and they had drunk vodka. Outside had stood sentries, muffled in furs. They had joked among themselves about the shortcomings of the Japanese army, and they had bragged. In this room, now, sounded the agonized cries of a dying soldier.

He lay still a moment. The cricket was singing the same melancholy, pleasing song. A late moon had risen over the broad Manchurian plain, the surroundings had grown clearer, and the moonlight already illuminated the ground outside the window.

He cried again. Moaning, despairing, he writhed on the floor. The buttons of his blouse were torn away, the flesh on his neck and chest was scratched and bloody, his army cap was crushed, the strap still about his chin, and one side of his face was smeared with vomit.

Suddenly a light shone into the room. In the doorway, like some statue in its niche, he saw a man, a candle in one hand. The man came silently into the room and held the candle above the sick soldier, where he lay twisting and turning on the floor. The soldier's face was colorless, like that of a dead man.

"What's the matter?"

"This pain, this pain!"

The man hesitated to touch the soldier. He stood by his side a while, looking down; then he placed the candle on the table, fixing it firmly in drops of molten wax, and hurried out of the room. Every object in the room stood clearly revealed in the candlelight. He saw that the untidy bundle in the corner of which he had been dimly aware was his own rifle and pack.

The flame on the candle flickered. The wax rolled down like tears.

After a while the man returned, bringing a soldier with him. He had roused one of a unit lodged for the night in a house across the way. The soldier looked at the sick man's face, and glanced around the room. Then he peered closely at the regimental markings on his shoulder.

The sick man could hear everything they said.

"He's from the Eighteenth Regiment."

"Is that so?"

"When did he come in here?"

"I've no idea. I woke about ten to hear someone screaming in pain. I couldn't make it out—there shouldn't have been anyone in the rest of the house. After I'd listened for a while I heard the cries again, getting louder, and I came here to see what was wrong. It's beriberi . . . a heart attack, too. There's nothing anyone can do about it."

"I suppose there's a doctor at the depot?"

"There is, but I doubt whether he'd come so late as this."

The two stood in silence.

The pain came flooding back again. He groaned. Cry followed cry, in unbearable crescendo.

"He's suffering terribly. Where's he from, I wonder?"

He felt the soldier searching in his breast pocket, removing his regimental paybook. He saw the man's dark, strong features, and he watched him walk close to the candle on the table to examine what he had found, his form dark against the light.

He heard the soldier read, every word reaching him distinctly. . . . Private Katō Heisuke, Fukue Village, Atsumi District, Province of Mikawa. Again images of home floated before his eyes. His mother's face, his wife's face, the great house standing amid camphor trees, the slippery rocks on the beach, the blue sea, the faces of the fishermen he had known so well.

The two watchers stood in silence. Their faces were white. From time to time they muttered words of sympathy. He knew now that he was going to die, but the knowledge did not carry with it any particular terror or sadness. He felt that the object which those two were regarding with such anxiety was not himself, but some inanimate thing in which he had no part. If only he could escape from this pain, this intolerable pain!

The candle flickered. The cricket sang on.

At dawn, when the doctor arrived from the depot, the soldier had been dead an hour. He died at about the time that loud cheering from the depot workers announced the departure of the first ammunition train for Anshan, while the morning moon, pale and wan, hung in the sky.

Soon the steady rumble of the guns was heard again. It was the morning of the first of September, and the attack on Liaoyang had begun.   ✕

Asian Languages

THE CHINESE LANGUAGE

中
國
話

The Chinese language, which is spoken by more people than any other language in the world, is quite unlike our own. An alphabet does not exist. Instead, the language consists of written characters, each one representing a complete idea, thing, or sound. Many of the characters were originally pictures. Later, two or more simple pictures were combined to represent new ideas.

There are thousands of Chinese characters, and a Chinese schoolboy has to learn to recognize at least two thousand of them. This is not as difficult as it sounds; for once he has mastered a few hundred basic characters, it becomes merely a question of forming the combinations. The characters are arranged in columns, written from top to bottom, right to left.

An old Chinese proverb makes the exaggerated claim that there are as many Chinese dialects as days of the year. There is, however, a variety of dialects, and by far the most important is Mandarin, now considered the official language and taught in all the schools.

The inauguration of mass literacy campaigns by the Chinese Communist government, after it assumed power in 1949, has been accompanied by efforts to simplify the written language. Hundreds of characters have been radically changed, and attempts to introduce a romanized alphabet have made gradual progress.

THE JAPANESE LANGUAGE

日
本
語

Nothing is known with certainty as to the origins of the Japanese language. Research has shown certain similarities between Japanese and Polynesian languages; but there is insufficient evidence to conclude that Japanese is of Polynesian origin.

During the third century A.D. Chinese philosophy and literature were introduced into Japan. (Before this time native legends, tales, and poems had been handed down orally from generation to generation.) After Japanese scholars had learned to read and write in Chinese, they began experimenting with Chinese characters, using them for their sound value to represent words in their own language. Gradually it was possible, though by no means easy, to develop a Japanese system of writing based on Chinese characters. As the Chinese had a much longer history of culture than the Japanese, the latter could hardly fail to adopt many Chinese words into their own vocabulary.

The characters of the Japanese language are either arranged in columns, like those of the Chinese, and written from top to bottom, right to left, or horizontally, like English letters, and written from left to right. A movement to simplify the writing system finally succeeded in 1947 when the Japanese Ministry of Education decreed important changes. Many of the characters were simplified, and their number was reduced from over four thousand to under two thousand for use in newspapers and magazines.

ISLAMIC LANGUAGES

العربية

Arabic. Of all the Semitic languages, Arabic is the most important and is spoken throughout the Middle East and northern Africa. In addition, as the language of the Koran and the prayers of Islam, it is the liturgical language of all Moslems except the Turks.

In its development, Arabic borrowed freely from other languages. In structure its alphabet is completely different from the Roman, consisting of twenty-eight letters, all consonants. Vowels are indicated by diacritical marks above or below the letters. As it reads from right to left, an Arabic book begins where an English one ends.

Turkish. Of Central Asiatic origin, the Turkish language, during the mass conversion of Turks to Islam in the tenth century, adopted the Arabic alphabet. Moreover, the Turkish vocabulary borrowed heavily from the Arabic and the Persian.

When Turkey became a republic in 1923, the language did not escape the radical reforms undertaken by President Mustafa Kemal. The Arabic alphabet was replaced by the Roman on the justifiable ground that it was better adapted to the sound of Turkish. Furthermore, many Arabic and Persian terms were eliminated.

Persian. Of Indo-European origin, Persian is the official language of Iran (formerly Persia). After the Arab conquest of the seventh century, many Persians converted to Islam, and the Persian vocabulary was enriched by borrowings from Arabic.

The Persians make use of the Arabic alphabet, to the twenty-eight letters of which they have added four new characters to express sounds not represented in Classical Arabic. Like Arabic, Persian is written from right to left.

HINDUSTANI LANGUAGES

With an immense population of various races which came from outside the country, India is naturally a land of many languages. In earlier times diversity of language was not a grave problem, as the masses were content with their dialects, and the ruling classes used Sanskrit, the classical and religious language of India. Under British rule, English served as the official language of successive administrations and of educated Indians.

About 179 languages plus many more dialects are spoken in India. Of these languages 116 can be dismissed as tribal languages spoken by less than one percent of the population. Of the rest, fifteen are recognized as major languages for literature, education, and public life. The most frequently spoken language is Hindi.

Prior to India's obtaining her full independence in 1949, the problem arose of choosing an official language for the whole country as a symbol of national unity. While deciding that Hindi should become the official language, the parliament voted that the transition from English to Hindi should not take place until 1965. At that time, however, attempts to implement the official use of Hindi precipitated violent and bloody riots. As a result of this language crisis, English has been retained for those who desire it, but all official documents must be issued in both languages.

THE HEBREW LANGUAGE

עִבְרִית Widely used in Biblical times, Hebrew underwent an eclipse after the dispersal by the Romans of the Jewish people. The Jews and their descendants spoke the vernaculars of their adopted countries, and Hebrew was generally restricted to religious observance and scholarship. When large-scale immigration to Palestine began at the end of the nineteenth century, immigrants were encouraged to use Hebrew as normal everyday speech; Hebrew is now the tongue of the Israeli Jews.

A Semitic language, Hebrew is written from right to left, has twenty-two letters, all consonants. Vowel sounds are indicated by diacritical marks placed above or below the letters. Since Hebrew lacked many modern terms, especially in the sciences and technology, such terms have been borrowed from Western languages and Hebraicized.

DISCUSSION QUESTIONS
Chinese Literature

Poetry

Anonymous: WOMAN (*page 17*)

1. One would guess from reading this little tirade that man's image of woman hasn't changed much through the centuries. List the faults the poet finds in women and defend or refute each charge.

2. The sincerity of the writer's rage is incontestable—what might have inspired it?

Fu Hsüan: WOMAN (*page 18*)

A traditional Chinese family was founded on two unwritten but well-defined rules: the superiority of the older over the younger generation and the superiority of men over women. In cases of conflict, the first rule prevailed over the second; this made the role of the young female in any household unenviable at best.

1. This cry from ages long past still has great poignancy. Why? Surely it is not because the situation of women has remained unchanged, even in China. What, then, is it that gives the poem its great appeal?

2. Compare this poem to the anonymous poem entitled "Woman" (page 17).

Anonymous: SOUTH OF THE GREAT SEA (*page 19*)

1. There is a before and an after in this poem; explain what happens in each. Is there anything in the speaker's tone to indicate the change?

2. The girl's embarrassment is human and understandable. But what seems to upset her more, the humiliation or the hurt?

General Su Wu: TO HIS WIFE (*page 20*)

1. What portrait of the general emerges from this brief poem?

2. Compare the general's sentiments with those expressed by the Cavalier poet Richard Lovelace in "To Lucasta, On Going to the Wars." Which sentiments are more frequently voiced in poetry written on such occasions?

Yüan Chi: REGRET (*page 21*)

1. Why is the poem entitled "Regret"?

2. Account for the difference in tone between the first and second stanzas.

Anonymous: PLUCKING THE RUSHES (*page 22*)

1. There is much use of nature's colors here. Analyze their effect upon you; their possible effect on the boy and girl.

2. Is there a note of regret in the last line, or do the two seem entirely pleased with themselves?

Li Po
A Bitter Love and A Sigh from a Staircase of Jade (*page 23*)

1. In these poems Li Po sketches for us two unhappy women—or perhaps the same woman—and leaves us to speculate on the reasons for their feelings. Why, do you think, has the love of the woman in the first poem grown bitter? Try to answer the question posed in the last two lines of the second.

2. Discuss the beauty-in-pain theme that dominates both poems. What devices does the poet use to create his tone? How does the conjunction of beauty and pain

affect the speaker? Does the beauty-in-pain idea seem to you aesthetically perfect, or is there something morbid in it?

3. "A Sigh from a Staircase of Jade" was originally written to music—what kind of music do you see best suited to it?

On Hearing Chün the Buddhist Monk from Shu Play His Lute (page 24)

1. What happens to the speaker as he hears the Buddhist monk play his lute?

2. The lute was to ancient China what the guitar is to modern America. Does the guitar—not the guitar of hard rock, but the one of soft and plaintive songs—make you feel anything similar to the experience Li Po records here?

A Song of Ch'ang-kan (page 24)

1. This tender, haunting little poem, a capsule summary of how a love grew, says little but implies much. Talk about the marriage—how it came about, what it has come to mean to both man and wife. Explore the reasons for the girl's changing feelings, her love, her fears, her yearnings. Is she any different from a young American wife whose husband goes off to war or leaves her to conduct his business?

2. Ezra Pound is one of several other English poets who translated this beautiful love lyric. He calls his version "The River Merchant's Wife." Find a copy and compare Pound's performance with this.

Parting at a Wine Shop in Nan-king (page 25)

1. Although this is a poem about parting, would you characterize it as a sad poem? Explain.

Tu Fu

On Meeting Li Kuêi-nien down the River (page 26)

1. Li Kuêi-nien was a musician, a favorite performer of Emperor Hsuan-tsung. What words or phrases suggest the passing of time and changing fortune?

Remembering My Brothers on a Moonlight Night (page 26)

1. What is the message here? Is it pessimistic, or resigned, or is it a simple statement of things as they are?

2. Discuss: ". . . How much brighter the moonlight is at home!"

3. In what ways do the season and hour in which the poet writes reinforce what he has to say?

A Night Abroad and On the Gate-Tower at Yo-chou (page 27)

Tu Fu, like many gentlemen of his time, was a civil servant sent from post to post, often away from his family for as long as a year at a time.

1. What attitude toward his office does the poet express in these poems? To what does he compare himself? What are his complaints? What are his wishes?

2. Metaphor is unusual in Chinese poetry—these poets seldom went beyond the strict bonds of reality—but Tu Fu employs some here. Find some metaphors and explore their meanings. What do they add to the poems?

A Hearty Welcome and To My Retired Friend Wêi (page 28)

1. What do these two poems tell you about the importance of friendship and hospitality to the ancient Chinese? Compare the attitudes expressed here with those of the modern Western world.

Night in the Watch-Tower (page 29)

1. What are the reflections of the speaker as he watches in the night? How do the details from nature strengthen his mood?

2. The last line of the poem—"Hush for a moment, O tumult of the world"—is not in the original. Why do you think the translator added it? What did he probably feel he gained by doing so? Do you like the poem better with or without this line?

A Drawing of a Horse by General Ts'ao at Secretary Wêi Fêng's House (*page 30*)

1. In this poem Tu Fu pours forth a profusion of praise; what do his compliments tell you about his feelings for art? About its place in the ancient Oriental world?

2. The line, "The high clear glance, the deep firm breath" is still used by the Chinese to describe superior art and literature. Discuss its meanings.

3. For another look at artistic perfection, this time carried to an extreme, read Akutagawa's "Hell Screen" (page 307), a story filled with Poe-like horrors.

A Song of War-Chariots (*page 31*)

Were you surprised to find an anti-war poem among so many lyrics concerned with love and friendship and nature? Actually, the social-protest poem was born in China; it was, during Tu Fu's time, a very popular theme.

Discuss, in terms of the modern world, these lines:

1. "Father, mother, son, wife, stare at you going . . ."

2. "And every time a bystander asks you a question,/You can only say to him that you have to go."

3. "The mayor wound their turbans for them when they started out."

4. "At the border where the blood of men spills like the sea—/And still the heart of Emperor Wu is beating for war."

5. ". . . We have learned that to have a son is bad luck—/It is very much better to have a daughter/Who can marry and live in the house of a neighbour,/While under the sod we bury our boys."

Po Chü-i

Golden Bells and Remembering Golden Bells (*page 33*)

1. The first poem is humorous; the speaker a kind of Chinese Spencer Tracy in *Father of the Bride*. Are his concerns universal ones, or is he more callous than he should be?

2. In the second poem, also, the speaker seems a bit brusque. Justify his brusqueness. Is his grief real?

Chu-ch'ēn Village (*page 34*)

1. The speaker sees Chu-ch'ēn Village as a kind of Utopia embodying all that is simple and good in the world. What are some of the things he finds so admirable?

2. How has the life of the speaker differed from the life of the people of Chu-Ch'ēn Village?

3. The concluding line of the poem is: "Long I have envied the people of Ch'ēn Village." Do you think the speaker could really be happy there? Or is he, in a manner typical of human nature, indulging in an edifying but purely romantic dream?

4. Compare the speaker's attitude here with that of the speaker in "A Night Abroad" (page 27). Which seems more sincere?

The Philosophers and The Red Cockatoo (*page 36*)

1. What are the objects of satire in these two poems? Which attack do you consider more valid, and why?

Wang Chien: HEARING THAT HIS FRIEND WAS COMING BACK FROM THE WAR (*page 37*)

1. What two emotions would you say make up the speaker's feelings? What conflict do they set up in him?

2. Read the poem aloud; what does its rhythm make you feel?

3. Why are the last two lines an appropriate conclusion to the poem?

Su Tung-p'o: ON THE BIRTH OF HIS SON (*page 38*)

1. Is the poem the type the title leads you to expect? How would you describe the poem?

2. What changes, if any, would be necessary to make this poem relevant to today's world?

Han-shan: THE COLD MOUNTAIN POEMS OF HAN-SHAN (*page 39*)

The essence of "The Cold Mountain Poems," as of much Oriental philosophy and religion (Japanese Zen, for example), is paradox. The poems may be apprehended more quickly by intuitive feeling than by rational understanding.

1. In Poem 1, why is the path to Han-shan's place laughable?

2. Frequently in these poems, the images stand alone or are juxtaposed to ideas without clear connection with them. Take Poem 11 for example: there is, at the beginning, mention of clear spring-water and white moonlight, followed by the two lines:

> Silent knowledge—the spirit is enlightened of itself
> Contemplate the void: this world exceeds stillness.

What is the meaning of: "this world exceeds stillness"? Explore the relationship of imagery to idea in these lines.

3. In Poem 12, what does the concluding line mean: "I'll sleep by the creek and purify my ears"?

4. The last six lines of Poem 23 seem to hover closest to the heart of the poet's meaning. Explore these lines in depth and discuss their meaning or suggestion.

5. Explain the last line of Poem 24: "Try and make it to Cold Mountain." Compare it with one of the closing lines of Walt Whitman's "Song of Myself": "If you want me again look for me under your boot soles."

6. In the essay "A Humanized World," Ling Chung writes: "When a Chinese hermit-poet finds himself alone in nature—he is utterly at peace with his environment because he believes that man and nature are one" (page 12). What evidence of the truth of this statement do you find in "The Cold Mountain Poems"?

7. In his preface to the poems the governor of T'ai prefecture gives a vivid picture of Han-shan. Does the individual described by the governor seem to be the same person who writes the poems? Explain your answer.

Prose

Anonymous: THE LADY WHO WAS A BEGGAR (*page 50*)

Unlike the ancient Chinese poets who said what they had to say, simply, straightforwardly, and then were done with it, the storytellers loved to embroider. In telling this story of the lady who was a beggar, for example, the anonymous storyteller first tells us of a woodcutter who becomes a Prefect . . .

1. What, if anything, is the connection between the two tales?

2. What human faults does the first of the two tales attack? the second? Would you say that the primary function of the tales is to point a moral?

3. Aside from the coincidental meetings on which both stories hinge, are they believable? Are the situations true to life, or does the triumph of the meek and the good move the stories into the realm of fairy tales and wishful thinking? Are the characters properly motivated; do they behave as real people would in similar circumstances?

4. How did you feel about the snatches of poetry introduced periodically? These stories were, of course, told orally long before they were written down. What might have been the value of these poetic refrains to an audience *hearing* the tales?

5. Choose a European fairy tale that was one of your childhood favorites and compare it with these tales for content, tone, and message.

Lao Shê: THE LAST TRAIN (*page 65*)

1. In this story Lao Shê creates his characters through the repetition of a few key traits. How does he characterize Mr. Chiao, Mr. K'ou, Little Tsui, and the "boy" who is over forty? In general are the characters sympathetic or unattractive? What reasons might Lao Shê have for picturing them as he does?

2. Trace the events leading to the fire. Was it inevitable or could it have been avoided? Do you attribute it to fate or to human stupidity and cowardice?

3. Analyze and discuss the possible reasons for the narrator's attitude toward the fire, paying special attention to such lines as: "The whole carriage was transparent with light, and tongues of fire streamed away like streamers, a thousand torches burning brightly in the wind" (page 75, line 8); "It [the fire] was mad with joy" (page 75, paragraph 3); "It was a lovely cremation" (page 76, line 6); and "From them [the carriages] a plume of blue smoke curled up—languidly and leisurely" (page 76, paragraph 1).

4. Despite the horror of what happens, there are touches of broad humor here. Find and discuss.

5. The following information emerges from the investigation of the fire: "No station reported the sale of second-class tickets; it followed that the second class must have been empty, and therefore the fire could not have started in the second-class carriage" (page 76, paragraph 4). What is the reason for this conclusion? Comment on the irony of the situation.

6. What is the tone of the last two paragraphs: bitter, remorseful, matter-of-fact? What purpose does this short conversation between the waiter and his wife serve the story? Is this the ending you expected? Is it a good ending?

Lusin: THE WIDOW (*page 77*)

1. What is the essential position of women in nineteenth-century China? Use specific details to make your answer concrete.

2. Who is the narrator? What effect does use of this point of view have on the story?

3. What is the importance of the questions Sister Hsiang-lin asks the narrator? Why does he answer as he does? Do you regard his answer as a contributory cause of Sister Hsiang-lin's death?

4. What is the purpose of the long introduction before the story of Sister Hsiang-lin begins?

5. What is the effect of the abrupt break between Hsiang-lin's story and the final description of the New Year's celebration?

6. The story of Sister Hsiang-lin is told as a flashback in a narrative that begins and ends with the New Year's celebrations. What do you see as the reason for placing the story of the widow in this setting? Does the tone of the narrator reflect the joyousness of the holiday, the unhappiness of Hsiang-lin's story, or is it withdrawn and neutral?

7. For comparison read Gustave Flaubert's long short story "A Simple Heart." Then write a short essay in which you examine the place of each protagonist in her society, the attitude of the narrator in each story, and the outcome of two similar lives spent in different cultures.

Mao Tun: SPRING SILKWORMS (*page 90*)

This narrative is interesting as exposition; and since so much of the detail concerns the raising of silkworms, analysis is necessary to determine what makes "Spring Silkworms" a short story.

1. What is the primary plot? What forces are in conflict? What does the secondary plot, concerning Lotus and Ah Dou, contribute to the development of the primary plot?

2. Who, probably, are the foreigners? What is Tung Pao's attitude toward them? Do you sympathize with this attitude? Judging from details in the story itself, what do you think the author's attitude toward the foreigners is?

3. Many of the rites by which man has safeguarded his ways of making a living are superstitions—that is, man has forgotten the reason, doubtless at one time a practical measure, behind the ceremony. What processes in the raising of silkworms seem to belong in this category?

4. How would you characterize the tone of the last paragraph: bitter, restrained, matter-of-fact? What does this paragraph add to all that has gone before?

Tuan-mu Hung-liang: THE SORROWS OF THE LAKE OF EGRETS (*page 103*)

1. The author's imagery is almost lyrical, but it is a somber, brooding lyricism that echoes the misery of the situation it describes. Find examples to support this statement.

2. The young girl and the old man feel no guilt, ask no mercy, display only anger and annoyance when caught stealing. Is this a reflection on their characters or a comment on the circumstances of their lives? Discuss.

3. The narrator tells us "Mah-nao never knew why his voice suddenly became kind." In what way might the earlier encounter with his father have influenced his behavior with the girl? What of his own frustrations and desires might have been brought to this moment in the field?

4. The narrator avoids commenting on the action, leaving us with the feeling that this is the way of poor men, this is the way they must live. What does Mah-nao's small but heroic action at the end of the story add to that feeling?

Babylonian Literature

Anonymous: THE ADVENTURES OF GILGAMESH (*page 111*)

When a nation or ethnic group begins to grow conscious of its identity and seeks to perpetuate its ideals through pride in a great hero of the past, the epic arises; and it embodies much of what the people who created it believe.

1. What is the subject matter of this epic? What beliefs about man and the world underlie it? Does the story seem concerned with proving a point, or is it just a good tale?

2. What picture of Gilgamesh emerges from the first paragraph? How does this characterization change as the epic progresses? How do you account for this change?

3. Gilgamesh is part god, part man, a fairly usual ancestry for folk heroes. In his case, which traits are dominant, the divine or the human? What does this dominance tell you about the people who created the epic?

4. One of the truly exciting things about studying folk literature is the discovery that stories told in one place are often told in another. Perhaps migration or diffusion is responsible; perhaps it is only that people at the same level of culture think the same way. Choose one of the subjects on the following page and investigate it. Then report on it or write a short comparative study.

(*a*) Compare this story of the flood with the Biblical version, or the version to be found in the Koran.

(*b*) Compare the garden of delights and the Biblical Eden. (*Eden* is, incidentally, the Hebrew word for *delight*.)

(*c*) Compare the land of the dead and the classical Hades.

(*d*) Compare Humbaba with the creatures of Greek myth.

(*e*) Compare the behavior of the gods, particularly that of "the heavenly queen Ninsun" and the Lady Ishtar, with that of their Greek counterparts.

(*f*) The significance of dreams. Compare the function of dreams in *Gilgamesh* particularly with the place of dreams in the story of Joseph (Genesis).

(*g*) The search for restored youth.

Hebrew Literature

The Bible

The Story of Samson (*Judges 13–16*) (*page 125*)

1. The Bible is an exemplary book, written to teach, instruct, and guide. Samson is certainly not the usual figure of the saintly man. Why, then, is his story probably included?

2. Is Samson's story tragic in the classical sense? Does he bring the anger of God upon himself? What is his tragic flaw, the characteristic most responsible for his fate?

3. There are interesting parallels between the Biblical Samson and Enkidu in *The Adventures of Gilgamesh* (page 111). What makes each a hero to his people? Compare their strength, their charismatic powers, their temperaments, their ways with women, and the part prophecy plays in their lives.

4. Milton's *Samson Agonistes* treats of the last phase of Samson's life, when, blinded, he is a prisoner of the Philistines. Comparing the character of Samson as Milton develops it with Samson as he appears in the Biblical account would make an interesting study.

FROM THE *Psalms* (*page 132*)

1. It has been said: "God made man in His own image, but man also makes God in his own image." What is the image of God presented in these poems? From this picture of God as the Israelites saw him, what do you learn of the Israelites themselves? What do you learn of how they lived?

2. Note examples of figurative language, imagery, repetition and rhythm in these poems. What do these various devices add to their effectiveness?

3. What is there about the Psalms that has made them appeal to man throughout the ages?

4. In Act II, Scene 2 of *Hamlet*, Hamlet says: "What a piece of work is a man! how noble in reason! how infinite in faculty! in form and moving how express and admirable! in action how like an angel! in apprehension how like a god! the beauty of the world! the paragon of animals!" What echoes of Psalm 8 may be traced in this passage?

Ecclesiastes 3 (*page 136*)

1. What is the purpose, the moral function, of this melodic piece of writing?

2. Explain the philosophy behind the statement, "To every thing there is a season, and a time to every purpose under the heaven."

3. Compare the ideas expressed in this chapter with the ancient Greek belief that man must live in moderation lest he incur the wrath of the gods.

4. Select one verse and illustrate it with references to current events.

Amir: NOTHINGNESS (*page 138*)

1. Amir has made for us a man robbed of the ability to speak, even to think, his mind reduced to an amorphous mass of fear. Study the way in which he makes us share that man's terror by:

(*a*) discussing the effect of the starkness, simplicity, directness of the opening line;

(*b*) analyzing the use of explicit statement (the experiences to which the speaker compares his fear, for example);

(*c*) exploring the possible reasons for omitting punctuation and capitalization, and discussing what their omission adds to the nightmarish effect.

2. What is the poet saying about man and his language, about man's need to communicate? Considering Amir's theme, why is the last line an appropriate conclusion?

Avidan: PRELIMINARY CHALLENGE (*page 139*)

1. What is the point of lines 1–4?

2. What is the speaker's one hope of escaping death? Comment on lines 15–35. What impression do they produce?

3. Is the speaker being ironic, mocking, or straightforward about his feelings?

Ben-Itzhak: POEMS (*page 141*)

1. In form "Blessing" echoes the Beatitudes (Matthew 5:3–12). Read these verses from the Bible and compare the spirit of Christ's statements with the feeling of this Hebrew writer. What is the force of the word *unremembrance* (line 12)?

2. What is the impression created by "Avenue in Ellul"? Does the arrangement of the poem on the page add anything to this impression, or is it simply a device to catch the eye?

Bernstein: BIRDS HAVE THOUGHTS (*page 143*)

1. Explain the title—what are the birds' thoughts?—and relate it to the last two lines of the poem.

2. Note the complex but unobtrusive rhyme scheme. What makes it unnoticeable?

3. This is, of course, a poem about birds. Can you apply any of the things the poet has to say about them to men, also?

Bialik: POEMS (*page 144*)

1. In the first poem explore the connection between "Summer is dying" (line 1) and "The heart is orphaned" (line 9). What is the poet implying?

2. Relate the last two lines of "Summer Is Dying" to the rest of the poem. Why might Bialik have chosen to italicize them? Notice they are in quotation marks. Who do you think is speaking them?

3. Sometimes we get so caught up in a poet's use of imagery that we fail to think about what he is really saying. Try paraphrasing the first stanza of "Summer Is Dying" in very literal statements. Are there any images you cannot reduce to literal statements? If so, is it because the stanza is ambiguous or unclear?

4. The poem entitled "On My Return" gives no indication where the speaker is returning from. From where might it be—or is that information nonessential? Explain.

5. Is the return a pleasant one? Why or why not?

6. Who are the friends the speaker addresses in line 19 of "On My Return"? In your opinion do the last two lines weaken or strengthen the poem?

Ghilan: ARS PO (*page 146*)

The poet has given his poem the title *Ars Po*, suggesting that he regards it, at least in one sense, as literary theory; that is, as an expression of the nature of poetic art and of its relationship to human life. He has presented his literary theory in the form of a series of images relating to the act of dying. The poem is balanced about the image "The soft/Cry in the night," expressive of the moment of death. The lines preceding describe details of the sick room, while those that follow suggest acts performed for the dead.

1. The poem is a series of metaphors relating to death, which the poet has equated to poetry. Point out and explain some of these metaphors. What quality does the phrase "grass-grained" (line 11) convey?

2. Compare and contrast this poem with Archibald MacLeish's "Ars Poetica."

Ka-Tzetnik 135633: *from* THE CLOCK OVERHEAD (*page 147*)

1. You who do not remember World War II—with what feeling do these excerpts leave you? Do you suppose these are the feelings the poet hoped to inspire?

2. How does the poet risk sentimentality? How does he avoid it?

3. What qualifies this poem as poetry?

Karni: EVENING IN JERUSALEM (*page 157*)

1. Does the poem fulfill the expectations set up by the title? What common poetic concepts of night does Karni repudiate?

2. What is it that evening "seizes, fetters," and "Hands on to the night"?

3. Do you think this "Evening in Jerusalem" describes natural phenomena, human tensions, or both? Explain.

Megged: THE NAME (*page 158*)

Of central concern to this story is not the generation gap but the survival of Jewish tradition in Israel.

1. Grandfather Zisskind sees the unborn child as heir to a great tradition, and tradition is all that remains of his previous life. Why does it mean so much to him that that tradition survive? Are his demands unreasonable? Are his motives selfish? Just how important is tradition anyway?

2. To Raya and her husband tradition has become alien, irrelevant, or at least profoundly ambiguous. They want to lead their own lives, not merely serve as a continuance for their ancestors. Is this bad? Isn't it the same thinking upon which the United States is founded?

3. What rôle does Rachel play in the conflict between the old ways and the new ones? Why is she necessarily so ineffective?

4. Discuss the symbolism the "key to the clock" takes on in the third paragraph from the end, the irony of the events that follow.

5. Rôle play (dramatize) the conflict expressed in the story, using the same situation or a comparable one. Explain the thinking of Grandfather Zisskind, Raya, Yehuda, and Rachel.

Paggis: EPILOGUE TO ROBINSON CRUSOE (*page 170*)

1. Who is Robinson Crusoe? What does the title of the poem mean?

2. Summarize the picture of the returned Robinson Crusoe the poet gives. Cite lines that lead you to this summary and explain the meaning of these lines.

3. What does Paggis' Crusoe have in common with Irving's Rip Van Winkle after the latter's return to civilization?

Shalom
The Dance of the Torches (page 171)
1. Visualize the feat described in the quotation from the Sukkah. What devices does the poet use to capture in language the same impression the act must have had on the audience? (Reading the poem aloud may help you answer this question.)
2. The poem contains many paradoxes. Cite some of them. Why is paradox appropriate to a poem of this nature?
3. How do you understand the meaning of "Love" in the last line? Comment on the force of this line.
The Cat (page 173)
1. Reread lines 7–9 and lines 16–18, noting carefully the difference between them. What seems to be the reason for this difference?
2. Restate as simply as you can what the poet is saying in this poem.

Shteinberg: THE BLIND GIRL (page 174)
1. Which one word in this story is the key to all its mysteries? What is it that Chana discovers in that last terrible moment of the narrative?
2. In an unusual and sensitive manner, the reader is made to "see" through Chana's senses and intelligence as she explores object after object. Select examples that illustrate Chana's use of the different senses.
3. Does Chana's mother love her daughter? Why does she deceive her? What social forces underlie the human tragedy of this story?
4. A student critic called the ending of this story "weak." Why might he have considered it so? Is there any justification for this criticism?

Hindustani Literature

Anand: THE GOLD WATCH (page 181)
1. From what point of view is the story told? What effect does the point of view have on the opinion you form of Acton Sahib, Miss Violet Dixon, and Sharma?
2. Sharma is described as having "nobility of soul and fundamental innocence." What does this mean? Does his history bear out this characterization?
3. What seems to be the author's attitude toward the English in India? Give evidence to support your answer. Suppose the story is propaganda or biased—does this make Sharma less poignant or his problem less important?

Anonymous: from the *Mahabharata*, SAVITRI'S LOVE (page 189)
To enjoy this story one must employ Coleridge's willing suspension of disbelief, that principle that maintains that all characters and situations are acceptable in literature so long as their development is coherent and consistent.
1. Assuming an acceptance of the initial fantasies on which this tale is based, how believable is it?
2. This was originally a poem; its first prose version was set down in the nineteenth century. Can you find any vestiges of the original poetry in the language of this translation?
3. Critics call the *Mahabharata*, from which "Savitri's Love" is taken, didactic or instructional in nature. If the didactic purpose of this particular tale is to set forth Savitri as an ideal of Indian womanhood, what qualities do the Indians apparently desire in their women? How well does Savitri fill your conception of the ideal woman?

Chauras: *from* BLACK MARIGOLDS (*page 194*)

1. The language of this love lament is profuse, vivid, ecstatic. Discuss the effect of the sheer quantity of words upon you.

2. Underneath the rich coating of language is a rather simple story. Trace the details of the story from bits of information dropped into various stanzas. Where is the lover as he writes? From what point in time does he write?

3. What does the poet gain with the "Even now" that begins each stanza? Does his phrase, for example, have the same force as the magnificently gloomy "Nevermore" that Poe repeats in "The Raven"?

4. With the seventh stanza the poem makes an abrupt rise from earth, becoming more than a song of worldly love. Discuss.

5. Compare the depth of emotion here with that in Li Po's "A Song of Ch'ang-kan" (page 24).

Dhumketu: THE LETTER (*page 201*)

1. Do you think the postmaster *really* saw Ali's ghost? If not, what did he see?

2. What is the lesson the postmaster learns?

3. Discuss the author's attitude toward Ali and explain the ways in which he reveals it.

4. Does the message of this simple little tale ring true to you, or does the whole story seem weighted down by sentimentality? Explain.

Sen Gupta: THE BAMBOO TRICK (*page 207*)

1. How does the description of this year's Gajan fair prepare the reader for the story, condition him to a mood?

2. What is the function of the narrator?

3. In a starving audience such as the one at the fair, would you expect sympathy with the performers or anger at a poor performance? Explain. Why do you think the narrator's reactions differ from those of the other spectators?

4. In the hard, unpleasant, realistic description of Imtaj's scarred, festering body and the statement that one does not notice the poor little body when it is whirling, what statement about life in general is being made?

Somadeva: THE CONFIDENCE MEN (*page 213*)

The Sanskrit tale, a type of narrative that might be called the "courtly folk tale," emerged in India centuries before Boccaccio in Italy wrote his *Decameron*. The scene of these picaresque, moralistic tales is the court; and courtiers or highborn clerics are often the actors and victims.

1. One of the standard devices of comedy is the reversal, as in the trickster tricked. Who is the trickster tricked in this tale?

2. Are the characters in this tale individuals or stereotypes?

3. With whom are your sympathies in this tale—with the victim or the confidence men? Why?

4. Analyze the legitimacy of the defense Siva pleads at his trial. Comment on Madhava's defense.

5. Is there a moral lesson given or implied in this tale?

Tagore: MY LORD, THE BABY (*page 218*)

1. How do you explain Raicharan's behavior at the death of the little Master? Does his conduct throughout the balance of the story seem eccentric to your Western understandings?

2. Mysticism, transmigration of souls, and abnegation of self are three concepts we associate with Indian culture. Find examples of these ideas in Tagore's narrative.

3. Explain this passage: "Then suddenly Raicharan remembered that terrible accusation of the mother. 'Ah,' he said to himself with amazement, 'the mother's heart was right. She knew I had stolen her child'" (page 221, paragraph 8).

4. Anukul is a judge; the child is "destined to be a judge." Judging from the story, what is the attitude of the common people toward the judicial service? What is Tagore's attitude?

5. How can Raicharan insist on "fate" as the cause of his conduct (page 223)?

Burmese Literature

U Win Pe: PRELUDE TO GLORY (*page 224*)

1. The English poet Wordsworth wrote, "The Child is father of the Man. . . ." To what extent is Tha Mu the father of Koyin Thila? What insights into the training of a Buddhist monk are provided by showing the boy at nine and at nineteen?

2. What is the essential conflict of this work?

3. Is the intention of the story to (a) describe a way of life, (b) create atmosphere for its own sake, (c) develop a character, or (d) serve as a moral example? If more than one of these applies, describe the narrative in each aspect that you believe should be included.

4. How is the passage about the "cognitive" process (page 233, paragraph 2) related to the quotation from the Sutras (page 230, paragraphs 14–15)? What connection is there between understanding the cognitive process and becoming a *pabbaji?*

Islamic Literature

from THE KORAN (*page 236*)

1. Briefly summarize the messages set forth in these three *surahs* and compare them to Judaic-Christian teachings.

2. As scripture, the Koran demands respect; millions of peoples consider it the word of God. Does it, also, have any literary values that merit its inclusion in a book such as this one? Discuss.

Abul-'Ala al-Ma'arri: *from* THE MEDITATIONS (*page 239*)

1. Discuss Ma'arri's feelings about life, death, propagation, religion, the afterlife, and God.

2. Are there any traces of hope for mankind evident in these aphorisms?

3. Compare these poems to some of the maxims of France's LaRochefoucauld, who shares, if not Ma'arri's depth, at least his punch.

Hafiz: *from* THE DIVAN (*page 241*)

There is argument over whether Hafiz deserves the label *mystic*, but his poems do have what one expert calls a "pleasing ambiguity," a lyrical/mystical double level of meaning. One thing that simplifies the reading of Islamic mystical literature for the Western reader is the knowledge that at its base there is a pattern, almost a formula, to which most mystical writers adhere, in varying degrees. The lyrical terms of profane (worldly) love are used symbolically to express exalted emotions of divine love. For the mystics the beloved is God; the cupbearer a spiritual leader; wine the truth or mystical experience. In the writing of the mystics, drunkenness is ecstasy, unconsciousness the point at which man becomes one with God.

1. In Ode I to whom does Hafiz send his message? What is the message he sends? What word does he receive in return?

2. Is Ode V addressed to a woman or to God? Support your answer with lines from the poem.

3. In Ode VIII we have a series of variations on a theme, a common convention in Islamic literature. What idea or conviction underlies each of the five stanzas? Is this a happy poem, a sad one, a hopeful one, a prayerful one?

4. Why do you think these poems are considered odes?

5. In English poetry the metaphysical writers of the seventeenth century perhaps came closest in their use of symbols and devices to the Islamic mystics. For examples sample some poems by John Donne, George Herbert, Richard Crashaw, and Henry Vaughan.

Al-Hakim: THE RIVER OF MADNESS (*page 245*)

1. Who *is* sane, who insane? Is sanity merely a question of what the majority considers normal or correct or acceptable?

2. Is the King right to give up what he calls his wisdom so that he can live a happy life with his queen and his subjects? Does wisdom offer nothing, as the Vizir claims? Is the King's decision to drink from the river a cowardly one or a supremely brave one?

3. The subhead calls this play symbolic. Explain the symbolism you find in the play.

4. The Japanese play "The Madman on the Roof" (page 354) also considers the question of sanity and madness. Read and compare these plays.

Al-Jahiz: FLIES AND MOSQUITOES (*page 253*)

1. This essay written to glorify the fly is reminiscent of those fables and tales in which some insignificant creature proves its worth (Aesop's "The Lion and the Mouse," for instance). Usually, such stories have a moral, either stated or implied. Does this essay have a moral?

2. Do flies really eat mosquitoes?

Jibran: SONG OF MAN (*page 255*)

1. Who is the *I* of the poem?

2. What things has he seen and heard and done, and how have these affected him?

3. Discuss the implications, both religious and philosophical, of the second stanza from the end. In what way are these lines a kind of explanation of the whole poem?

4. What does the poet achieve by beginning and ending his poem with the same somber and somehow prophetic lines?

Khayyám: *from* THE RUBÁIYÁT OF OMAR KHAYYÁM (*page 257*)

1. The Roman poet Horace gave the advice "Carpe diem," which means "Seize [or pluck] the present." Read aloud quatrains from *The Rubáiyát* in which you find the same idea expressed. You might enjoy comparing these quatrains with Robert Herrick's brief lyric, "To the Virgins to Make Much of Time."

2. What evidence do you find that for many years Omar Khayyám had sought and failed to find serious answers to the problems of life? What effect did this failure have on his view of life?

3. *Fatalism* is a concept which sees human beings as puppets driven and controlled by inexorable fate. Point out quatrains in *The Rubáiyát* which clearly exhibit this belief.

4. Discuss the importance of imagery and symbolism in the total effect created by the poem.

Matran: CHILDHOOD IN ZAHLA (*page 262*)

1. In what ways does this poem suggest childhood everywhere? Are there any details that suggest a particular place or culture?
2. How would you characterize the childhood described in the poem?

Nu'ayma: O BROTHER (*page 263*)

1. Each of the first three stanzas is built upon a contrast. What do these contrasts have in common? How do the last two stanzas differ from the first three?
2. Comment on lines 25–27. Do you accept the point of view expressed here? Do you agree or disagree with the solution to the problem expressed in the last three lines?
3. How do you interpret the term *brother* in this poem?

Rumi:

Like all Islamic mystics, Rumi believed that God is present in all things, that everything is a manifestation of Him, that man can become one with God not through reason but through love and purification, and that life is continued when the soul ascends and reaches the "universal spirit" (God) and is absorbed into it.

A good way to begin the study of Rumi's work might be to read Wordsworth's "Ode on Intimations of Immortality" in which the child "trailing clouds of glory" still retains memory of the heaven from which it has come. Wordsworth, too, sees the presence of God in all things.

Remembered Music (*page 265*)

1. What is the "remembered music" of the title?
2. What is the role of this music in communication between God and man?

The Truth Within Us (*page 266*)

1. What idea is developed in the first stanza? What is meant by: "The signs . . . I behold within;/Without is naught but symbols of the Signs"?
2. If the *orchard* (line 1) is an outward manifestation of God, what then is the *Orchard* (line 12)? What is Rumi saying about the nature of the Perfect Man?

The Evil in Ourselves (*page 266*)

1. Why does the Lion jump into the well?
2. What does this fable have to say about man?

The Soul of Goodness in Things Evil (*page 267*)

1. What argument does Rumi present in this brief poem?
2. Relate the line "No fancy in the world is all untrue" to the title.

The Progress of Man (*page 268*)

1. Trace the stages of the development of the soul as Rumi outlines them here.
2. What attitude toward death might grow from this belief in the development of the soul? What attitude toward life does the poem express?

Al-Zahawi: TO MY WIFE (*page 269*)

1. This poem and General Su Wu's "To His Wife" (page 20) were written about two thousand years apart. What is similar about the situation that gives rise to each poem? What other similarities do you find? What differences do you note?

Japanese Literature

Tanka (*page 270*)

1. Pick any one of the *tanka* printed in the text. Expand it, substitute explicit statement for subtlety, fill in any details necessary for complete understanding. Now, what have you lost?

2. To make these poems readable in English, Rexroth has abandoned the strict form of the Japanese originals. By what means has he retained the feeling of suggestiveness that supposedly typifies the original *tanka*?

3. Discuss the contribution of the simple vocabulary (as well as the absence of difficult concepts and classical allusions) to the appeal of these poems.

Naga Uta by Hitómaro (*page 275*)

1. Discuss the implications of the word *But* (line 6) in "The Bay of Tsunu." What change in tone takes place with the introduction of this one word?

2. Compare the *tanka* "In the empty mountains" by Hitómaro with this poem. What similarities do you find? What differences?

3. The death of a loved one is often a cue for sentimentality, but we could not justifiably accuse Hitómaro of falling into this trap in "When she was still alive." What saves the poem from becoming sentimental? What keeps it pure, honest?

4. Note the imagery in these poems. What does it contribute to the total effect?

Haiku (*page 278*)

1. In the Japanese, the intensity and suggestiveness of *haiku* is derived partly from the strict organization of the content, partly from the way in which the content is expressed. Unable to impose the Japanese structure upon the English language, and feeling that some rigidity was necessary, Henderson has substituted assonance and rhyme for the syllable pattern. Try rewriting a few of the *haiku*, eliminating the sound patterns. Do you find that Henderson's tighter structure adds to or detracts from meaning?

2. Skim through these *haiku*, noting the recurring themes. Based on these themes, how would you explain the universal popularity this poetic form enjoys?

3. Can you think of any reasons why American and English poets have attempted little original poetry in the *haiku* form?

4. Critics and translators disagree on whether *tanka* or *haiku* is better—more aesthetically satisfying—poetry. Which do you find more pleasing, and why?

The Nō Play (*page 283*)

Seami(?): THE DAMASK DRUM (*page 284*)

1. Analyze the differences between the technique of the *Nō* play and the usual Western drama by examining (*a*) the presentation of the necessary background (exposition) at the beginning of the play, (*b*) the nature and the role of the chorus, (*c*) the use of the supernatural (the ghost of the gardener).

2. Clearly much of the pleasure deriving from the Nō drama comes from the language. In one passage, the Chorus concludes:

> I thought to beat the sorrow from my heart,
> Wake music in a damask drum; an echo of love
> From the voiceless fabric of pride!

Discuss the metaphors in this passage and relate them to the meaning of the play.

3. What is the function of the last speech delivered by the Chorus?

Mishima: THE DAMASK DRUM (page 290)

1. Compare the setting of Mishima's "Damask Drum" with the setting of Seami's. Compare the number and kinds of characters in the two plays.

2. Compare the two plays in their portrayal of the motivation behind getting the old man to beat the damask drum.

3. The Mishima play presents a variety of views on the nature of love. Explore the meaning of Iwakichi's definition of love as "something that shines on the one you love from the mirror of your own ugliness"; of Kaneko's "Love is the architecture of the emotion of disbelief in genuine articles."

4. At the end of Mishima's play, why can't Hanako Tsukioka hear the drum which Iwakichi (and apparently the audience) hears?

Akutagawa: HELL SCREEN (page 307)

1. Define the point of view Akutagawa uses in "Hell Screen." Why does the speaker say at the end of section 6, "I may have told the wrong end of the story first"? Has he made a mistake in telling his story in this way?

2. Explain the role of the monkey who is called Yoshihide after the artist.

3. Why are the stories of the two apprentices to Yoshihide included (the one in chains, almost bitten by a snake, the other almost sacrificed to the horned owl)?

4. Near the end of the story, in section 19, when Yoshihide's daughter is burning to death in the carriage, both the artist and his lord react in unusual ways to the event. Explain their reactions.

5. A difficult but rewarding study is a comparison of this work with Thomas Mann's novella, *Tonio Kroger*. Both Mann and Akutagawa say essentially the same thing: that the creator, haunted by an awful compulsion for artistic perfection, becomes an inhuman observer unable to relate to a world of people. Compare and contrast the very different characters, situations, devices by which these two writers reach their conclusion.

Anonymous: THE BAMBOO CUTTER AND THE MOON CHILD (page 328)

1. Discuss the different ways the five suitors go about performing their assigned tasks. Why do you think so much space in the story is devoted to the behavior of the suitors and their fates? Why is it necessary to the tale that not a single suitor honorably completes his task?

2. Enjoyment of fantasy depends upon a willing suspension of disbelief on the part of the reader. We are willing to let the storyteller have his say so long as he does not betray the world he has himself created. Why is "In ancient times . . ." a good way to begin a fantasy? Discuss the nature of the fantastic and the supernatural in the story, determining whether the storyteller has remained within the bounds of fantasy appropriate to his world. What other tales do you know that include the discovery of a mysterious child or center on impossible tasks assigned a suitor? Discuss similarities and differences.

3. How, according to the story, did Mount Fujiyama get its name?

Anonymous: HOICHI THE EARLESS (*page 340*)

1. How do the supernatural elements in this Japanese story resemble or differ from supernatural stories of other cultures with which you are familiar?
2. What is the function of the first paragraph of the tale?
3. Both "Hōichi the Earless" and "The Bamboo Cutter and the Moon Child" contain elements of the supernatural. The latter may be considered a fairy tale. Would you classify "Hōichi the Earless" as a fairy tale? What important differences do you find between the two stories?

Ibusé: THE CHARCOAL BUS (*page 347*)

In many ways, "The Charcoal Bus" seems to be an allegory of modern Japan during and after World War II. The exchange of the conductor for the driver, described at the beginning of the story, suggests the change in Japanese leadership after the defeat of the Japanese in the war.

1. What does the young married couple represent?
2. Who might the old farm couple who help push for awhile when the bus stalls in front of their house be?
3. How about the bus—why *charcoal?*

Kikuchi: THE MADMAN ON THE ROOF (*page 354*)

1. Compare and contrast the attitude of the parents and of the brother to Yoshitaro's madness.
2. In his long speech in defense of his brother, Suejiro says: "But wouldn't it be foolish to become normal merely to suffer?" What would you reply to such a statement?
3. What is the purpose of the closing episode, in which the two brothers observe the sunset, while the parents and others leave?

Shiga: SEIBEI'S GOURDS (*page 363*)

1. Early in the story, Seibei mistakes the bald head of an old man for a gourd, and laughs at his mistake. Explore the relationship of this episode to the rest of the story.
2. What first attracts Seibei's attention to the gourd that precipitates the wrath of the schoolmaster? What is the effect on Seibei when his father destroys all his gourds?
3. Shiga relays his message (or theme) with concise and piercing irony by relating the history (the two sales) of the confiscated gourd at the end of the story. Discuss.
4. What would be the effect on the story of removing the first and last paragraphs?

Tanizaki: THE THIEF (*page 367*)

In many ways "The Thief" is a *tour de force* in manipulation of the point of view. . . .

1. Discuss the point of view as a means of building suspense and creating surprise.
2. What is revealed about the character and personality of the narrator, other than that he is a compulsive thief?
3. Contrary to the thief's prediction, Higuchi becomes a success in life while Hirata disappears from view. What are the implications of this concluding detail?

Tayama: ONE SOLDIER (*page 376*)

1. Why is the story entitled "One Soldier"? What is the effect of such limited scope?

2. Traditionally wars have been associated with honor, bravery, glory. How are these aspects treated in the story?

3. The story sticks strictly to the point of view of the one soldier, but it opens out beyond his immediate experiences. Explain this structure.

4. Analyze the last two paragraphs, with particular emphasis on the effect of the details selected for presentation.

BIOGRAPHIES OF AUTHORS

Abul-'Ala al-Ma'arri (973–1057)

Syrian-born al-Ma'arri was four when he was stricken with smallpox, a disease that left him sightless for the remainder of his life. The handicap did not prevent him from becoming one of the greatest poets of Islam, but it did much to embitter him toward life. His works, though bold and unconventional (he never, for example, used his poetry as a vehicle for praising powerful leaders as did many of his contemporaries), won him the respect of the people; and he achieved a prominent position during his lifetime. Today his grave is a national monument, each year visited by thousands of tourists. His works include *Al Fusual Wa'-l-Ghayat*, written in imitation of Koranic style, and *The Epistle of Pardon*, which is not unlike Dante's *Divine Comedy*.

Yamabe no Akahito (d. 736)

Akahito was a personal attendant of the Emperor Shōmu and accompanied him on his travels through the country. In a period that is acclaimed as the golden age of Japanese poetry, he is considered almost the equal of Hitomaro.

Akutagawa Ryūnosuké (1892–1927)

Sometimes called the Poe of Japan, Akutagawa has been one of the most popular Japanese writers in the West. Although he worked as a teacher and as a newspaperman, he spent most of his life writing. He resurrected old legends but invested them with a psychological dimension. He was a perfectionist in style and experimented repeatedly with the short story, his most congenial form. Two of his short stories, "Rashomon," a tale of thievery and death, and "In a Grove," which relates a single event from several points of view, were combined to make the highly acclaimed Japanese film *Rashomon*, a probe into the nature of perception and reality.

Aharon Amir (1923–   )

Writer, poet, editor, and translator, Amir was born in Palestine. After graduating in Oriental Studies at the University of Jerusalem, he became editor of *Keshet*, a literary quarterly. His novel *Les Soldats du Matin*, which was written in French, was published in 1961. During the Israeli-Arab war of 1948 he served in the Israeli army.

Mulk Raj Anand (1905–   )

Mulk Raj Anand, writer, teacher, and editor, describes himself as a radical and a humanist. He recently completed *Morning Face*, a two-volume autobiographical novel. A professor of art and literature, he also edits an important Indian art magazine.

David Avidan (1934–   )

The first published collection of poems by the Israeli poet, Avidan, caused a violent reaction in readers and critics who value conventions in poetry. His work, ego-centered and reflecting the age in which he lives and writes, has about it an austerity and toughness that echoes Hemingway. As one critic put it, his poems are a "gamble for all or for nothing."

Matsuo Bashō (1644–1694)

Bashō, the greatest of all writers of *haiku*, was born into a family of samurai—men of the warrior class—at a time of great peace and stability in Japan. At about eight, he was taken into the service of a nobleman where he served as a page to the noble's son. His young master taught Bashō much and by the time he was nine he had written his first verses. Though he wrote most of his life, he did not reach the peak of his ability until the last ten years of his life. Though some of Bashō's poems are infused with a religious mysticism (possibly influenced by Zen Buddhism, a religion he embraced late in life), most are simple descriptions of real scenes and real events, with just enough detail to communicate an emotion to the reader.

Avraham Ben-Itzhak (1883–1950)

Ben-Itzhak was born in Galicia, then part of Austria, and studied at the Universities of Vienna and Berlin. In 1913 he migrated to Palestine and became a high-school teacher. Besides writing poetry he has translated Hebrew literature into German.

Ory Bernstein (1936–   )

Born in Tel Aviv and educated at the University of Jerusalem, Bernstein belongs to the Sabra (Israeli born) crop of poets, who began to emerge after the Israeli War of Independence of 1948. He has served as an officer in the Israeli army.

Hayyim Nahman Bialik (1873–1934)

Born in 1873 in a small Russian village, the young Bialik was given an orthodox Hebrew education but indulged himself in the works of contemporary Jewish writers. When he was twenty, he moved to Odessa, then an important center of Jewish culture. With the Communist Revolution he traveled to Berlin and finally to Tel Aviv, where he lived until his death. His work reflects the poverty of his early life and the effects of adversity upon his people in a verse that echoes the structures of Biblical poetry. Bialik also wrote legends, essays, and short stories, and translated, among other things, Cervantes' *Don Quixote*.

Taniguchi Buson (1715–1783)

Buson, considered second only to Bashō as a writer of *haiku*, is equally famous as a painter, and many of his poems are in themselves lovely pictures. His subject matter displays a wide variety of interests and a great appreciation of the ever-changing world. Of all the great *haiku* writers, Buson is considered the best craftsman.

Chauras (11th–12th centuries)

Little is known of the poet who wrote "Black Marigolds," and the few facts we have are disputed. He is called both Chauras and Bilhana, and is identified as a Kashmiri poet. In addition to the *Chaurapanchasika*, which is sometimes called "Black Marigolds" and sometimes "Fifty Stanzas of the Thief," he is the author of *Vikramānkadeva-Charita*, an epic telling of the military prowess of King Vikramaditya, a powerful ruler of the late 11th and early 12th centuries.

Dhumketu (1892–   )

Dhumketu, psuedonym of Gaurishanker Goverdhanram Joshi, is one of the veterans of modern Indian literature. He has published more than forty-five works, including among them novels, travel books, satires, plays, life sketches, short stories, and an autobiography.

Fu Hsüan (d. 287 A.D.)

Fu Hsüan, an early Chinese poet, began life as a poor orphan but achieved fame and wealth, largely through his literary talents. Although he was known to have been a prolific writer, only sixty-three of his poems have survived.

Maxim Ghilan (1931–   )

Ghilan was born in Lille, France, and migrated to Palestine in 1944. As a youth he joined the Haganah, a clandestine organization for Jewish self-defense. In addition to being a poet, he is an essayist, short-story writer, and translator.

Hafiz (1320–1391)

Hafiz (the name means "one who knows the Koran by heart") was born Sham ud-din Mohammed in the Persian city of Shiraz, where he spent most of his life. His poetry tells of love and wine, God and the hereafter, the instability of all things human, constancy and friendship, generosity and adherence to high ideals. Some have ranked him with Shakespeare and Dante as one of the greatest poets the world has ever known.

Tawfiq al-Hakim (1902–   )

This Egyptian-born playwright and novelist is considered the uncontested master of modern Arabic drama. His trilogy, *Everything in One*, is a vast work dealing with life in modern Egypt.

Han-shan (7th or 8th century)

Han-shan was supposedly a poor and eccentric scholar living in retirement at a place called Cold Mountain in the T'ien-t'ai Highlands. Apart from what can be gleaned from the poems themselves, the only information about him is contained in the preface to the poems written by Lu Ch'iu-yin, a government official. It is possible that the complete legend is nothing more than a literary fiction.

Kakinomoto no Hitómaro (c. 680-c. 710)

Hitómaro is believed to have been born and reared in Nara, the first permanent capital of Japan. He entered the Imperial court as a minor official, and the court activities are celebrated in some of his poetry. His skillful use of *tanka* and *naga uta* (two major Japanese poetic forms) made him one of Japan's greatest poets. He is revered for the humanity and deep concern for his fellowmen reflected in his works.

Lady Horikawa (12th century)
Not much is known about Lady Horikawa's life except she was Maid of Honor to the Empress Dowager Taiken of Japan.

Ibusé Masuji (1898–)
Born in Hiroshima prefecture, Ibusé Masuji went to Tokyo University to study art and French literature. He soon gave up his studies to become a writer. He has written a number of novels, some historical, others thoroughly contemporary. The latter tend to be nonrealistic, sometimes whimsical, and often symbolic or allegorical.

Issa (1762–1826)
Among the general Japanese reading public, Issa is perhaps the best-loved of the *haiku* poets. In his work he lays bare emotions, the pains of unhappy life, religious doubts. He identified himself with almost all his subjects, often adding the words "—and Issa too" to his *haiga* (drawings accompanying a written *haiku*).

Al-Jahiz (? –869)
Al-Jahiz of Basra was a brilliant man, but so ugly that a member of the nobility decided against giving him a job as a tutor once he saw him. His works are numerous: he wrote on rhetoric, animals, etiquette, beauties, misers. *The Book of Animals*, from which "Flies and Mosquitoes" is taken, is not a treatise on zoology but a collection of answers to questions on specific animals.

Jibran Khalil Jibran (1883–1931)
During his youth this Syrian-born poet and painter migrated to the United States where he is best-known as the author of *The Prophet*, a book of romantic and idealistic essays on many subjects.

Yehudah Karni (1884–1948)
Yehudah Karni was born in Russia and, like many other Russian Jews, migrated to Palestine to escape the virulent anti-Semitism prevalent in Czarist Russia. He wrote many poems on the theme of nature and life in Palestine, the latter emphasizing the turbulence that existed prior to the foundation of the republic of Israel. In 1944 he was awarded the Bialik Prize for poetry for his work titled *Jerusalem*.

Ka-Tzetnik 135633 (? –)
Ka-Tzetnik, which is translated as "an inmate of a concentration or extermination camp," is the pseudonym of Yehiel De-Nur. The author of *The Clock Overhead* was an inmate of the concentration camp at Auschwitz in Poland during World War II. De-Nur and his wife Nina, who is his translator, live in Tel-Aviv.

Omar Khayyám (d. 1123)
The Islamic poet best known to the West is probably Omar Khayyám, author of the *Rubáiyát*. Besides being a poet, Khayyám was a philosopher, mathematician, astronomer, and physician. Highly respected, he was a friend of important government officials and scholars. The philosophy presented in the *Rubáiyát* is the result of his spiritual torment as he searched for truth, his concern about the enigmas of existence, his revolt against the hypocrisy and fanaticism of the dogmatically religious. Though he enjoyed life, he was not, as many Westerners believe, a drunkard and a sensualist.

Kikuchi Kan (1888–1948)

One of the most popular Japanese writers, Kikuchi Kan attended schools in Tokyo and Kyoto, and was a friend (from schooldays) of Akutagawa Ryūnosuké. He was a prolific writer who made a great deal of money with his magazine serials and his plays. But his most enduring writing is the work he produced before 1920. "The Madman on the Roof" was published in 1916.

Lao Shê (1899–1966)

Lao Shê, born Shu Shê-yü in Peiping, has written many novels and short stories noted for their humor and their author's masterful sense of dialect. He spent some time out of China lecturing at the London School of Oriental Studies, but he has since returned to his native land.

Li Po (c.710–c.762)

Li Po had a reputation for improvising verses any place, any time, and especially when he had had his fill of wine. For some twenty years he wandered about from place to place, staying with friends and relatives, taking odd jobs, or living as a recluse. For a short period he served in the court, where he became a favorite of the Emperor. But because of enemies or irresponsibility—or perhaps for both reasons—he was dismissed from the Emperor's service and again became a wanderer. In the Western world, Li Po is considered one of the greatest Chinese poets of all time.

Lusin (1881–1936)

Chou Shu-jen (whose pen name was Lusin) spent his childhood in desperate poverty and his adult life attempting to right at least some of the wrongs in the China of his time. In his writing he savagely attacked the victimizers of the underprivileged classes as well as those poverty-stricken people who clung to the very customs that kept them down. Though he attempted to stay out of politics, politicians kept claiming him for their side, and when the battles began between the Kuomintang party and the Communists he wrote less and less. Shortly before he died, he said: "I feel I shall perhaps have nothing to say from now onwards. When the terror dies away, I do not know what will come: it may not be anything good." He died as he had begun; in extreme poverty, while trying to unite his people against the Japanese.

Mao Tun (1896–   )

Shen Yen-ping wrote under many pseudonyms, the best known being Mao Tun. In stories such as "Spring Silkworms," he describes with a wealth of authentic detail the Chinese peasantry. Deftly and artistically, with great art and tremendous power, he portrays the sufferings of his country and its people.

Khalil Matran (1872–1949)

Born in Lebanon, Matran later took up residence in Egypt. Apart from his own poetry he earned fame for his several translations of Shakespeare into Arabic.

Aharon Megged (1920–   )

Megged brings to his writing an interesting and varied background. Polish-born, he emigrated to Palestine with his family when he was six; he helped to set up a fishing community (kibbutz) on the Mediterranean; he worked at a variety of jobs; he spent two years in the United States as a cultural representative; and he now edits a weekly literary magazine. His work, which includes short stories, novels, and plays, is usually humorous, sometimes satiric, but gently so.

Yukio Mishima (1925–1970)

One of the most popular Japanese writers outside Japan, Yukio Mishima was born in Tokyo and studied law at Tokyo University. But even before he took his law degree, he began to write and publish fiction. His first collection of stories appeared in 1944; several of his novels have become popular in English translation. His work reveals an interest in the sordid underside of human character and a fascination with deviant psychological behavior. Mishima also wrote a number of plays, including several Nō dramas. He based his Nō plays on earlier traditional versions, but he modernized settings and characters, and introduced modern psychological insights.

Ariwara no Narihira (9th century)

Narihira is the legendary great lover of Japanese literature, and many Nō plays have been written around his exploits. His major work, *The Tales of Isa*, is a collection of poems prefaced with headnotes that explain the settings and the moods of the characters, thus making them more comprehensible to the reader.

Mikha'il Nu'ayma (1889–   )

Lebanese-born Nu'ayma was one of many Islamic writers to leave his homeland for the United States shortly after the turn of the century. In addition to being a poet, he is a fine literary critic.

Dan Paggis (1930–   )

Unlike many of his contemporaries, this young Israeli writer shows little influence by writers of other countries in his work. One of his favorite devices is to work with Biblical themes, giving them a new twist and a new meaning for today's world.

Po Chü-i (772–846)

This poet's clear style, his avoidance of allusions and ambiguities, earned him during his lifetime a unique popularity among his contemporaries of all classes. As a young man, he entered the Chinese government service and his career followed the familiar pattern of promotions, setbacks, and final success.

Rumi (1207–1273)

Jala-uddin, called "Rumi" because he came from the Roman sector of Turkey, founded the little-understood religious sect or mystical school called Maulana. The Maulana believe that God is manifested in everything, that love, tolerance, and resignation are the way to union with God. Its members, commonly called whirling dervishes, attempt to gain Oneness with God through a dance which starts at a slow cadence and becomes a whirling frenzy. Rumi's most famous work is *Mathnawi*, one of Persia's great mystical works. Its style is simple, sincere, beautifully poetic.

Seami (1363–1443)

Seami (also spelled Zeami) Motokiyo was, in a sense, the Shakespeare of Japan. He began acting at the age of seven, attracted the favors of the shōgun (at that time the actual ruler of Japan), and launched a career that was to lead to the writing of some 240 plays. Together with his father, he shaped the Nō drama out of popular theatrical traditions of the time, and it has endured to this day as the oldest living drama in the world.

Achintya Kumar Sen Gupta (1903–   )

Sen Gupta has felt the influences of both Western realism and Indian romanticism and in his work he has experimented with both traditions. Besides short stories, he writes novels and poetry.

Shin Shalom (1905–   )

Polish-born and German-educated, Shalom Shapira, who writes under the pseudonym Shin Shalom, moved to Palestine as a young man. Much of his poetry is lyrical; some deals with national and cosmic themes; most contains elements of mysticism. Besides writing, Shalom works as editor of a literary magazine.

Shiga Naoya (1883–1971)

Although Shiga's life has been long, his body of work is not large, primarily because he is a meticulous stylist who takes great labors on each work he publishes. Critics generally consider his greatest novel to be *A Dark Night's Journey*, written in two parts during the period 1921–1937; it is a work of deep pessimism and gloom. The subtlety and stylistic brilliance of Shiga's work render it extremely difficult to translate. For this reason, his reputation outside Japan lags behind his reputation at home.

Masaoka Shiki (1867–1902)

Shiki, born during a time of great change in Japan, became the leader of a literary revolution that attacked the established order, particularly the rules that for generations had greatly influenced poetic composition. He stressed naturalness in writing, advised his followers to write to please themselves, suggested that each writer know all kinds of *haiku*, but develop a style of his own.

Yaakov Shteinberg (1887–1947)

Poet, dramatist, and short story writer, Shteinberg was born in Russia and migrated to Palestine in 1914. Much of his early work depicts Jewish life in the Ukraine and is written in a skeptical tone. His later work appears to have been influenced by a belief that there exists an unbreakable spiritual bond between Russian Jews and their former country.

Bhatta Somadeva (12th century)

It is said that Somadeva wrote the more than three hundred tales that make up his *Kathasarit Sagara* to amuse an old woman, the grandmother of the king of Kashmir. Out of either excessive humility or its opposite, Somadeva claimed that the stories were told to him by Siva, the Hindu god of destruction and restoration and of the fine arts. His tales, many of them surprisingly modern in tone and structure, borrow extensively from earlier Sanskrit collections; but in all cases he has given the old something new, thus making each tale uniquely his own. The *Kathasarit Sagara* appeared in both poetic and prose versions.

Su Tung-p'o (1036–1101)

Su Tung-p'o, a Chinese poet whose real name was Su Shih, was a man of many interests and many talents. In political life, whether serving the emperor at the court or in the provinces, he worked for the betterment of the people—fighting for famine relief, for prison reform, for flood control. He was a painter as well as a writer. In the latter field he excelled in serious historical essays and in whimsical prose and poetry.

General Su Wu (c. 100 B.C.)

Su Wu, a general in the Chinese army, wrote poetry—as did many of his countrymen—much as we might keep a diary. Legend has it that the Emperor Wu Ti of the Han Dynasty sent Su Wu to negotiate with enemy troops. In the course of an enforced stay in the Mongolian desert, Su Wu somehow managed to fix a message to the leg of a wild goose before its southward migration. The goose was shot by the Emperor who then took steps to secure Su Wu's release.

Sir Rabindranath Tagore (1861–1941)

Tagore, who received the Nobel prize for literature in 1913, did much to institute social and educational reforms in his native India. Born in Calcutta of a distinguished family, he was educated in Europe. He returned to India to establish a university at Bengal. In 1915 the English knighted him, but four years later he resigned the honor in protest against British treatment of the Indians. Tagore was a painter and musician as well as the author of prose and poetry. He was at his best when writing of nature and of childhood. Much of his prose and poetry has an aura of mysticism.

Junichiro Tanizaki (1886–1965)

One of the most "Japanese" of modern Japanese novelists, Junichiro Tanizaki was an admirer of such Western writers as Edgar Allan Poe and Oscar Wilde, and his first work showed their influence. After the catastrophic earthquake that hit Tokyo in 1923, Tanizaki left his native city for Kyoto, the ancient capital of Japan. This move turned out to be more than geographical; Tanizaki's fiction seemed also to move out from under the shadow of Western fiction and back into traditional Japan. His most popular novel is *The Makioka Sisters* (1946–1948), a long work portraying with precision the affairs of a family and the life of an era. Tanizaki's work is marked by an eye for the minor but telling detail and for a sometimes bizarre psychological probing.

Tayama Katai (1871–1930)

Without formal university training, Tayama early became interested in books and read widely in Japanese and Western literature. He wrote a number of novels which failed, but finally hit his stride after the Russo-Japanese War of 1904–1905, in which he served as a newspaper correspondent. Out of these experiences, he wrote his greatest fiction in the naturalistic tradition popular at the time, with emphasis on frankness and sordid detail. "One Soldier," published in 1908, is typical of his best work. It is remarkable for its anti-war attitude at a time of Japanese expansionism.

Ki no Tsurayuki (882–946)

Tsurayuki held several high offices in the Imperial court. Besides being a poet and prose writer, he was one of Japan's most skilled calligraphers. In 905 he was the principal editor of the first publication of an Imperial anthology, and author of the preface.

Tuan-mu Hung-liang (c. 1900–   )

Manchurian-born Tuan-mu Hung-liang was a leader in the futile resistance movement against the Japanese invasion of his country in the early 1930's. His wife, who helped in the resistance, was killed by the Japanese in Hong Kong. Tuan-mu Hung-liang's fiction is a sometimes tender, sometimes violent celebration of his land and its sorrows.

Tu Fu (712–770)

While many Westerners consider Li Po supreme among Chinese poets, the Chinese accord that honor to Li Po's friend and sometime drinking companion, Tu Fu. Tu Fu's poetry often finds him complaining of heavy taxes, military conscription, and the price of food. To read his complete work is to read an honest but lyrical portrayal of the China of his time.

Wang Chien (c. 830 A.D.)

A brilliant scholar, Wang Chien rose to become a governor of a district of China. His official career, however, was abruptly cut short when he offended one of the Imperial clansmen. Thereafter he devoted his time to writing verse.

U Win Pe (1922–   )

U Win Pe is a poet, short-story writer, economist, and translator. A graduate of Harvard, he has worked in the Ministry of Planning of the Union of Government of Burma.

Otomo no Yakamochi (718–785)

Son of a famous Japanese poet, Yakamochi's works comprise over five hundred poems. His official career was chequered; he became Vice-Minister for War, then was relegated to a governorship. After his death he was deprived of all honors because of a crime committed by a member of his family.

Yüan Chi (210–263)

Yüan Chi lived during a time of division and turmoil in China and his poetry is essentially that of a recluse. His work reveals a profound melancholy and a taste for the macabre, often startling image.

Jamil Sidqi al-Zahawi (1863–1936)

Al-Zahawi was born in Iraq. A radical reformer in politics and verse, he was an ardent nationalist and vigorously opposed the Europeanization of his country.

PRONUNCIATION KEY

The pronunciation of each word is shown after the word, in this way: **ab bre vi ate** (ə brē′vē āt). The letters and signs used are pronounced as in the words below. The mark ′ is placed after a syllable with primary or strong accent, as in the example above. The mark ′ after a syllable shows a secondary or lighter accent, as in **ab bre vi a tion** (ə brē′vē ā′shən).

Some words, taken from foreign languages, are spoken with sounds that otherwise do not occur in English. Symbols for these sounds are given at the end of the table as "Foreign Sounds."

a	hat, cap	o	hot, rock	ə represents:	
ā	age, face	ō	open, go	a in about	
ä	father, far	ô	order, all	e in taken	
		oi	oil, voice	i in April	
b	bad, rob	ou	house, out	o in lemon	
ch	child, much			u in circus	
d	did, red				
		p	paper, cup		
e	let, best	r	run, try		
ē	equal, see	s	say, yes	**foreign sounds**	
ėr	term, learn	sh	she, rush		
		t	tell, it	Y as in French *du*. Pronounce ē with the lips rounded as for English ü in **rule**.	
		th	thin, both		
f	fat, if	ŦH	then, smooth		
g	go, bag				
h	he, how			œ as in French *peu*. Pronounce ā with the lips rounded as for ō.	
		u	cup, butter		
i	it, pin	u̇	full, put		
ī	ice, five	ü	rule, move		
				N as in French *bon*. The N is not pronounced, but shows that the vowel before it is nasal.	
j	jam, enjoy				
k	kind, seek	v	very, save		
l	land, coal	w	will, woman		
m	me, am	y	young, yet		
n	no, in	z	zero, breeze	H as in German *ach*. Pronounce k without closing the breath passage.	
ng	long, bring	zh	measure, seizure		

The pronunciation key is from the *Thorndike-Barnhart High School Dictionary,* copyright 1968 by Scott, Foresman and Company.

ABUL-'ALA AL-MA'ARRI, 408; selection, 239

Adventures of Gilgamesh, The, 111

AKAHITO (YAMABE) NO, 408; selection, 271

AKUTAGAWA, RYŪNOSUKÉ, 408; selection, 307

AMIR, AHARON, 408; selection, 138

ANAND, MULK RAJ, 409; selection, 181

Apprentice Priestling, The, 282

Ars Po, 146

Asian Languages, 389

Avenue in Ellul, 142

AVIDAN, DAVID, 409; selection, 139

Bamboo Cutter and the Moon Child, The, 328

Bamboo Trick, The, 207

BASHŌ (MATSUO), 409; selections, 278, 279

BEN-ITZHAK, AVRAHAM, 409; selections, 141, 142

BERNSTEIN, ORY, 409; selection, 143

BIALIK, HAYYIM NAHMAN, 409; selections, 144, 145

Bible (The King James Version), selections from, 125 ff.

Birds Have Thoughts, 143

Bitter Love, A, 23

Black Marigolds, selection from, 194

Blessing, 141

Blind Girl, The, 174

Book of Animals, The, selection from, 253

BUSON (TANIGUCHI), 409; selections, 280

Cat, The, 173

Charcoal Bus, The, 347

CHAURAS, 410; selection, 194

Childhood in Zahla, 262

Chu-ch'ēn Village, 34

CHUNG, LING; selection, 12

CIV, 275

Cleaving, The, 237

Clock Overhead, The, selection from, 147

Clouds, 278

Cold Mountain Poems of Han-shan, The, 39

Confidence Men, The, 213

Conscience, 281

Contentment in Poverty, 281

CV, 277

Damask Drum, The (Mishima), 290

Damask Drum, The (Seami), 284

Dance of the Torches, The, 171

DHUMKETU, 410; selection, 201

Divan, The, selections from, 241 ff.

Drawing of a Horse by General Ts'ao at Secretary Wêi Fêng's House, A, 30

Ecclesiastes 3, 136

Epilogue to Robinson Crusoe, 170

Evening in Jerusalem, 157

Evil in Ourselves, The, 266

Flies and Mosquitoes, 253

FU HSÜAN, 410; selection, 18

GHILAN, MAXIM, 410; selection, 146

Golden Bells, 33

Gold Watch, The, 181

Great Buddha at Nara, The, 281

HAFIZ, 410; selection, 241

HAKIM, TAWFIQ AL-, 410; selection, 245

HAN-SHAN, 410; selection, 39

Hearing That His Friend Was Coming Back From the War, 37

Hearty Welcome, A, 28

Hell Screen, 307

HITÓMARO (KAKINOMOTO) NO, 410; selections, 272, 275, 277

Hōichi the Earless, 340

HORIKAWA, LADY, 411; selection, 273

Humanized World, A: An Appreciation of Chinese Lyrics, 12

IBUSÉ, MASUJI, 411; selection, 347

In a Wide Wasteland, 279

In the Moonlight, 282

ISSA, 411; selections, 281

Jade Mountain, The, selections from, 23 ff.

JAHIZ, AL-, 411; selection, 253

JIBRAN, JIBRAN KHALIL, 411; selection, 255

KARNI, YEHUDAH, 411; selection, 157

KA-TZETNIK 135633, 411; selection, 147

KHAYYÁM, OMAR, 411; selection, 257

KIKUCHI, KAN, 412; selection, 354

Koran, The, selections from, 236 ff.

Lady Who Was a Beggar, The, 50
LAO SHÊ, 412; selection, 65
Last Train, The, 65
Letter, The, 201
Lightning at Night, 279
LI PO, 412; selections, 23, 24, 25
LUSIN, 412; selection, 77
LVI, 273
LXXXIX, 274
LXXXV, 274

Madman on the Roof, The, 354
Mahabharata, selection from, 189
MAO TUN, 412; selection, 90
MATRAN, KHALIL, 412; selection, 262
Meditations, The, selections from, 239 ff.
MEGGED, AHARON, 412; selection, 158
MISHIMA, YUKIO, 413; selection, 290
My Lord, the Baby, 218

Name, The, 158
NARIHIRA (ARIWARA) NO, 413; selection, 273
New and the Old, The, 282
Night Abroad, A, 27
Night in the Watch-Tower, 29
Nothingness, 138
NU'AYMA, MIKHA'IL, 413; selection, 263

O Brother, 263
One Soldier, 376
On Hearing Chün the Buddhist Monk from Shu Play His Lute, 24
On Meeting Li Kuêi-nien down the River, 26
On My Return, 145
On the Birth of His Son, 38
On the Gate-Tower at Yo-Chou, 27
Overthrowing, The, 236

PAGGIS, DAN, 413; selection, 170
Parting at a Wine-Shop in Nan-king, 25
Persistence, 278
Philosophers, The, 36
Plucking the Rushes, 22
PO CHÜ-I, 413; selections, 33, 34, 36
Poor Man's Son, The, 279
Preliminary Challenge, 139
Prelude to Glory, 224
Progress of Man, The, 268
Psalm 8, 132
Psalm 19, 133

Psalm 23, 133
Psalm 45, 134
Psalm 95, 135
Psalm 98, 135

Regret, 21
Red Cockatoo, The, 36
Remembered Music, 265
Remembering Golden Bells, 33
Remembering My Brothers on a Moonlight Night, 26
River of Madness, The, 245
Rubáiyát of Omar Khayyám, The, selection from, 257
RUMI, 413; selections, 265, 266, 267, 268

Savitrí's Love, 189
SEAMI, 413; selection, 284
Seibei's Gourds, 363
SEN GUPTA, ACHINTYA KUMAR, 414; selection, 207
SHALOM, SHIN, 414; selections, 171, 173
SHIGA, NAOYA, 414; selection, 363
SHIKI (MASAOKA), 414; selections, 282
SHTEINBERG, YAAKOV, 414; selection, 174
Sigh from a Staircase of Jade, A, 23
SOMADEVA, BHATTA, 414; selection, 213
Song of Ch'ang-kan, A, 24
Song of Man, 255
Song of War-Chariots, A, 31
Sorrows of the Lake of Egrets, The, 103
Soul of Goodness in Things Evil, The, 267
Sound, The, 280
South of the Great Sea, 19
Spring Breeze, 280
Spring Silkworms, 90
Story of Samson (Judges 13–16), 125
Summer Garments, 280
Summer Is Dying, 144
Summer Voices, 279
Sun Path, The, 279
SU TUNG-P'O, 414; selection, 38
SU WU, GENERAL, 415; selection, 20
Symphony in White, 280

TAGORE, SIR RABINDRANATH, 415; selection, 218
TANIZAKI, JUNICHIRO, 415; selection, 367
TAYAMA, KATAI, 415; selection, 376

Thief, The, 367
To His Wife, 20
To My Retired Friend Wêi, 28
To My Wife, 269
Treasure Trove, 282
Truth Within Us, The, 266
TSURAYUKI (KI) NO, 415; selection, 274
TUAN-MU HUNG-LIANG, 415; selection, 103
TU FU, 416; selections, 26, 27, 28, 29, 30, 31

Unity, The, 238

V, 271

WANG CHIEN, 416; selection, 37
Widow, The, 77

WIN PE, U, 416; selection, 224
Wish, A, 281
Woman (Anonymous), 17
Woman (Fu Hsüan), 18

XVII, 272
XXI, 272
XXII, 272
XXIII, 272
XXX, 273

YAKAMOCHI (OTOMO) NO, 416; selection, 274
YÜAN CHI, 416; selection, 21

ZAHAWI, JAMIL SIDQI AL-, 416; selection, 269

INDEX OF TRANSLATORS

ANDREWS, C. F., 218

BELL, GERTRUDE LOWTHIAN, 241
BIRCH, CYRIL, 50
BIRMAN, ABRAHAM, 138, 139, 143, 157, 171, 173
BYNNER, WITTER, 23, 24, 25, 26, 27, 28, 29, 30, 31

DE-NUR, NINA, 147
DHUMKETU, 201
DUTT, ROMESH, 189

FERRIS, ANTHONY RIZEALLAH, 255
FITZGERALD, EDWARD, 257

GASTER, THEODOR H., 111
GHILAN, MAXIM, 146
GILES, H. A., 17
GIVTON, MINNA, 158

HARRIS, F. B., 328
HEARN, LAFCADIO, 340
HENDERSON, HAROLD G., 278, 279, 280, 281, 282
HIBBETT, HOWARD, 367
HUGHES, GLENN, 354

IWASAKI, YOZAN T., 354

JACOBS, ARTHUR, 141, 142

KEENE, DONALD, 290

KIANG KANG-HU, 23, 24, 25, 26, 27, 28, 29, 30, 31

LEVIANT, CURT, 174

MATHERS, E. POWYS, 194
MORRIS, IVAN, 347, 363

NICHOLSON, REYNOLD A., 239, 253, 265, 266, 267, 268
NORMAN, W. H. H., 307

PAYNE, ROBERT, 65, 103
PICKTHALL, MOHAMMED MARMADUKE, 236

REXROTH, KENNETH, 271, 272, 273, 274, 275, 277

SARGENT, G. W., 376
SEN GUPTA, ACHINTYA KUMAR, 207
SILK, DENNIS, 170
SNOWMAN, L. V., 144, 145
SNYDER, GARY, 39–49

WALEY, ARTHUR, 18, 19, 20, 21, 22, 33, 34, 36, 37, 38, 284
WANG, CHI-CHEN, 77, 90
WILSON, H. H., 213

YUAN CHIA-HUA, 65, 103

ZELDIS, CHAYYIM, 147